# How to Prepare for SAT II:

# Writing

GEORGE EHRENHAFT

Chairman of the English Department
Mamaroneck High School, Mamaroneck, NY

*Tim Lee*

BARRON'S

*Dedicated with admiration and respect to the Mamaroneck High School English Department*

## About the Author

George Ehrenhaft, a graduate of Columbia College and Ohio State, has taught students for over two decades. He is the author of *Writing a Successful College Application Essay*. Mr. Ehrenhaft resides in Katonah, N.Y.

*All inquiries should be addressed to:*
Barron's Educational Series, Inc.
250 Wireless Boulevard
Hauppauge, New York 11788

Library of Congress Catalog Card No. 93-39649

International Standard Book No. 0-8120-1477-4

**Library of Congress Cataloging-in-Publication Data**

Ehrenhaft, George.
　How to prepare for SAT II : writing / George Ehrenhaft.
　　p. cm.
　Includes index.
　ISBN 0-8120-1477-4 :
　1. English language—Composition and exercises—
Examinations, questions, etc.—Study guides. 2. College
entrance achievement tests—United States. I. Barron's
Educational Series, Inc. II. Title. III. Title: SAT II :
Writing Test.
LB1631.5.E47　　1994
808.042′076—dc20　　　　　　　　93-39649
　　　　　　　　　　　　　　　　　　CIP

PRINTED IN THE UNITED STATES OF AMERICA
567　10

# CONTENTS

## PART IV   THE ESSAY QUESTION

## PART V   TESTS FOR PRACTICE

# PREFACE

The College Entrance Examination Board, known familiarly as the College Board, was founded in 1901. During the Board's first decades, college applicants were given all-essay tests in a variety of specific subjects. In 1926 verbal and mathematical multiple-choice questions replaced the essays and ever since have dominated college entrance tests. In 1974 the Test of Standard Written English (TSWE) came into being. For the first time, writing skills were considered important enough to become the subject matter of a separate exam. The TSWE, however, consisted of only short-answer questions and failed to satisfy critics who thought that in order to measure students' writing ability, a real essay, an actual sample of a student's written work, must be included on a test. Three years later, in 1977, the English Composition Test (ECT) with essay was born, and a technique for standardizing the evaluation of essays was developed. From then on, everyone who took the December "English Achievements," as the test has commonly been called, was required to write an essay.

Now, as the College Board approaches its one hundredth birthday, another revision of college admissions tests has taken place. The SAT II: Writing Test has replaced both the TSWE and the ECT. Beginning in May 1994, everyone who takes the SAT II: Writing Test must not only answer multiple-choice questions about writing but must also write an essay. According to the College Board, a new writing test was needed to ensure that students in the 1990s and beyond will be better prepared for college. The new test also reflects changes taking place in America's schools and more accurately measures what students are learning about writing in classrooms nationwide.

This book, as its title suggests, is a study guide to the SAT II: Writing Test. As a test preparation guide, it describes and explains the test and tells students what they need to know. It offers plenty of test-taking advice and gives students countless opportunities to practice, practice, practice—which, in the end, may determine whether their test scores will help them push open the gates to their college of choice.

Whether this book becomes a steady companion for months prior to the test, or whether students merely browse through its pages the night before, using it is likely to improve performance. Barron's test preparation books have a long history of helping students achieve better scores on crucial examinations like the SAT II: Writing Test. Like all Barron's books, this one has been meticulously researched and developed to provide students with accurate and up-to-date review material. As the nation's leading publisher of study aids, Barron's feels an extra responsibility to the millions of students who depend on Barron's books. Therefore, as they turn the pages of this book, students can feel confident that they've come to the right place.

# PART I

# INTRODUCING SAT II: WRITING

Purpose of the Test

Overview and Content

Taking the Test

After the Test

# PURPOSE OF THE TEST

The SAT II: Writing is meant to test your knowledge of writing. By earning a high score on this exam, you will demonstrate that you can

1. identify and correct mistakes in English expression,
2. revise the writing of others, and
3. plan and write an essay in a relatively short time.

A college may want to know these facts about you because success in many college courses relates directly or indirectly to writing skills. Good grades are often based not only on what you know about the content of History 101 or Introduction to Psychology, but also on how effectively you can show your professor what you know, which, much of the time, is done by writing essays.

In addition, because colleges prefer academically able students, admissions officials review test scores while screening applications. Test results on standardized tests like the SAT II enable them to compare students from different secondary schools and diverse backgrounds. Also, many colleges use the scores to place incoming students in freshman classes and to provide guidance and advisory services.

More specifically, the SAT II: Writing Test shows how thoroughly you've mastered the skills practiced by most accomplished writers of expository prose, the kind generally used for essays, reports, term papers, and other nonfiction writing. One group of questions tests your ability to recognize errors in standard English usage and grammar. Another set of questions asks you to choose the most effectively worded sentence from a group of five alternatives. Since writers often need to edit and revise their work, a third segment of the test asks you questions about how to improve the text of an essay. Finally, you'll have to write your own essay on an assigned topic.

Altogether, then, the test reveals some of what you have learned about the art of writing, particularly the art of writing essays.

# OVERVIEW AND CONTENT

The test consists of 60 multiple-choice questions to be answered in 40 minutes and an essay to be written in 20 minutes.

---

### STRUCTURE OF THE TEST
### Time allowed: One hour

---

60 Multiple-choice questions: 40 minutes
   30 Usage questions
   18 Sentence-correction questions
   12 Revision-in-context questions
A written essay assignment: 20 minutes

---

Theoretically, a writing test that combines short-answer questions with an essay question will produce a clear, accurate profile of a student's writing skill. A short-answer test limits students' chances to demonstrate their proficiency in writing. An all-essay test, on the other hand, might hurt the chances of students who misinterpret the assignment or who know nothing about the topic they are asked to write on. Low test scores in such cases would have more to do with test-taking skills than with the ability to write. The design of the new SAT II: Writing Test, however, fairly reflects current trends in the writing instruction and allows students to demonstrate what they have learned.

## What the Multiple-Choice Questions Show

Although the questions come in three formats, they all ask you to do generally the same thing: find the writing flaw in a sentence or passage, and either identify it or choose a better version from among five alternatives. In theory, when you can recognize problems in others' writing, you are less likely to make the same mistakes in your own. If the theory always held true, of course, editors and English teachers, or anyone else who spends lots of time hunting others' writing errors, would be the world's best writers, an assertion that is far from the truth. Nevertheless, recognizing errors and weaknesses in writing is what you will be obliged to do on the short-answer portion of the test.

## USAGE QUESTIONS

These questions ask you to recognize errors in grammar and standard English usage. There is no need to name or label the errors. You only have to find them. Nowhere on the test, in fact, must you identify errors by name. Your performance may improve if you can tell a pronoun from a preposition, but you are not tested on that sort of information. Once you've located the error, if there is one (some of the items will contain no error), that's it. Just go on to the next question.

## ❑ Sample Questions

---

*INSTRUCTIONS*: The underlined and lettered parts of each sentence below may contain an error in grammar, usage, word choice (diction), or expression (idiom). Read each sentence carefully, and identify the item that contains the error. Indicate your choice by filling in the corresponding space on your answer sheet. Only the underlined parts contain errors. Assume that the rest of each sentence is correct. No sentence contains more than one error. If a sentence contains no error, the correct choice is always (E) (No error).

---

1. The task of filling out several college appli-
                   (A)
cations are time-consuming and exhausting.
     (B)       (C)             (D)
No error.
  (E)

Ⓐ Ⓑ Ⓒ Ⓓ Ⓔ

*EXPLANATION*: The subject of the sample sentence is *task*, a singular noun. The verb *are* is plural. Because the subject and verb don't agree, one of them must be wrong. Since the subject is not underlined, you must assume it is correct. Therefore, the answer is (B). All the other underlined words are written in standard English.

To answer this question correctly, you must know the rule that subjects and verbs must agree in number. That is, you can't use a singular subject and a plural verb, and vice-versa. Even if you can't state the rule, you may arrive at the right answer because the verb *are* sounds strange or out of place in the sentence.

**2.** Colleges <u>favor</u> applicants with high grades,
       (A)
<u>varied</u> interests and activities, and
  (B)
<u>they should earn</u>  <u>a good</u> score on the SAT II:
    (C)         (D)
Writing Test. <u>No error</u>.
        (E)

Ⓐ Ⓑ Ⓒ Ⓓ Ⓔ

*EXPLANATION:* As you read the sample sentence, your attention was probably drawn to (C), where there are at least two problems. The first is the word *they*, a pronoun that must refer to a specific noun. It's hard to tell whether *they* refers to colleges or to applicants because the reference is ambiguous.

A more critical problem, however, is faulty parallelism. The writer offers a series of characteristics that help students get into college: (1) high grades, (2) varied interests and activities, (3) . . . wait—the writer has shifted away from the pattern set by (1) and (2). Instead of using phrases consisting of an adjective and a noun, the writer changes to an altogether different format. Standard English requires that items listed in a series be expressed in parallel form. To be consistent with the items that came before, (C) should read simply *a good score on the SAT II: Writing Test.* Therefore, (C) is the correct answer.

**3.** <u>Yesterday</u> the dean announced the time of the
    (A)
SAT II and <u>sends</u> all students a letter <u>that</u>
        (B)             (C)
wished <u>them</u> good luck. <u>No error</u>.
    (D)         (E)

Ⓐ Ⓑ Ⓒ Ⓓ Ⓔ

*EXPLANATION:* The events described in the sample sentence took place in the past—yesterday, in fact. The verb *sends* is in the present tense. Since the writer is describing past action, the verb should be in the past tense (*sent*). Therefore, (B) is the choice that

contains an error. Besides, it is wrong to shift from one tense to another in mid-sentence.

In colloquial speech, the present tense is sometimes used to talk about the past, as in: "So, yesterday they *board* the plane and *settle* into their seats, when all of a sudden the flight attendant *announces* . . . ," but it is rarely used in standard written English.

## SENTENCE-CORRECTION QUESTIONS

These questions ask you to recognize errors in a sentence and then tell which of five alternatives is the correct or better version of the sentence. The errors may be grammatical, as in the usage questions, or they may be errors in expression or style. Your sense of what sounds best is being tested here. Again, no labeling of errors is required, and some items will contain no error.

## ❑ Sample Questions

> *INSTRUCTIONS:* The underlined sections of the sentences below may contain errors in standard English, including awkward or ambiguous expression, poor word choice (diction), incorrect sentence structure, or faulty grammar, usage, and punctuation. In some items, the entire sentence may be underlined. Read each sentence carefully and identify which of the five alternative versions most effectively and correctly expresses the meaning of the original. Indicate your choice by filling in the corresponding space on your answer sheet. Choice (A) always repeats the original. Choose (A) if none of the other choices improves the original sentence.

**1.** Many students insist that the schoolwork in junior year is far harder <u>than senior year</u>.

(A) than senior year
(B) than the schoolwork in senior year
(C) than senior year's schoolwork
(D) in comparison to senior year
(E) compared to schoolwork in senior year

Ⓐ Ⓑ Ⓒ Ⓓ Ⓔ

*EXPLANATION:* The original sentence compares *schoolwork* and *senior year*, a comparison that is illogical. Since the writer clearly intended to compare schoolwork in junior year and schoolwork in senior year, (A) can't be right.

Choice (B) makes the comparison clear. Expressing the comparison with phrases in parallel form (i.e., *schoolwork in junior year* and *schoolwork in senior year*) conveys the meaning that the writer intended. Therefore, (B) is the correct answer.

Choice (C) is wrong. Although grammatically correct, it is stylistically weak because the phrase *schoolwork in junior year* is not parallel to *senior year's schoolwork*.

Choice (D) is wrong because the phrase contains an awkwardly worded and unnecessary comparison. The word *harder* has already set up the comparison. It is redundant to make another by using the phrase *in comparison*.

(E) is wrong for the same reason as (D).

To answer this question you need to know that comparisons should be stated in parallel grammatical form. Or your awareness of what sounds right may lead you to the correct answer.

**2.** Studying and taking practice tests helps students raise their SAT II scores.

(A) Studying and taking practice tests
(B) Studying and practicing tests
(C) Studying, along with taking practice tests,
(D) By study and practicing tests
(E) Due to studying and practicing tests

Ⓐ Ⓑ Ⓒ Ⓓ Ⓔ

*EXPLANATION:* The sample sentence has a compound subject (*studying and taking*), made up of two different and distinct activities. The correct verb would be *help*, but you can't change *helps* to *help* because *helps* is not underlined. Instead, you must search the choices for a singular subject, one that goes with the singular verb *helps*. Only (C) contains a singular subject (*Studying*). Therefore, (C) is the correct answer.

To answer this question, you need to know that verbs must agree with their subjects, and that inserting phrases beginning with such words as *along with*,

*in addition to*, and *with* has no influence on the number (singular or plural) of the verb. On the other hand, your sense of what sounds correct may also lead you to the answer.

**3.** The SAT II: Writing Test has the effect <u>to make</u> teachers and students think more about the need to write effectively.

(A) to make
(B) to force
(C) in making
(D) of making
(E) by making

Ⓐ Ⓑ Ⓒ Ⓓ Ⓔ

*EXPLANATION:* In the sample sentence, the verb *make* is used in its infinitive form, *to make*. English grammar books will tell you that infinitives are most often used as nouns, as in "*To take* this test is fun," but also as adjectives, "You have the skill *to improve*," and as adverbs, "Study *to do* better." Knowing the grammatical uses of infinitives, however, isn't likely to lead you to the correct answer. Rather, in this and other sentence-correction questions, you have to depend on your sense of language and your ear to find the right answer. The sample sentence just doesn't feel right or sound natural. Nor do any of the other choices except (D), which expresses the idea of the sentence in regular English idiom.

## REVISION-IN-CONTEXT QUESTIONS

These questions ask you to recognize errors and weaknesses in the complete text of two students' essays. You may be asked about each essay in its entirety, about parts of them, or about individual sentences and phrases in each. Some questions may pertain to grammar and usage, some to expression and style. Most, however, will ask you to find flaws in organization, faulty emphasis on certain ideas, illogical development, and disjointed thinking—any defect, in fact, that characterizes imperfect writing.

## ❑ Sample Questions

> *INSTRUCTIONS:* The passages below are the unedited drafts of two students' essays. Some of each essay needs to be rewritten to make the meaning clearer and more precise. Read the essays carefully.
>
> Each essay is followed by questions about changes that might improve all or part of its organization, development, sentence structure, use of language, appropriateness to the audience, or use of standard written English. Choose the answer that most clearly and effectively expresses the student's intended meaning. Indicate your choice by filling in the corresponding space on the answer sheet.

### *Sample Essay for Revision-in-Context Questions*

[1] As people grow older, quite obviously, the earth does too. [2] And with the process of the earth aging, we must learn to recycle. [3] The idea of using things over and over again to conserve our supply of natural resources is a beautiful one. [4] Those who don't see how easy it is to recycle should be criticized greatly.

[5] As we become more aware of the earth's problems, we all say "Oh, I'd like to help." [6] However, so few really do get involved. [7] Recycling is a simple, yet effective place to start. [8] Taking aluminum cans to the supermarket to be recycled is an ingenious idea. [9] It attracts those who want the money (5 cents a can), and it is also a convenient place to go to. [10] In addition, in almost every town, there is a Recycling Center. [11] I know that there are separate bins for paper, bottles, cans, etc. [12] This is a convenient service to those who recycle. [13] It is so easy to drive a few blocks to a center to drop off what needs to be recycled. [14] This is just another simple example of how easy it really is to recycle and to get involved. [15] Those who don't see its simplicity should be criticized for not doing their part to help make the world a better place.

[16] When I go to other people's houses and see aluminum cans in the garbage, I can honestly say I get enraged. [17] Often I say, "Why don't you just recycle those cans instead of throwing them out?" [18] What makes me even more angry is when they say "We have no time to recycle them." [19] Those people, I feel, should be criticized for not recycling in the past and should be taught a lesson about our earth and how recycling can conserve it.

**1.** Which of the following most effectively expresses the underlined portion of sentence 2 below?

*And with the process of the earth aging, we must learn to recycle.*

(A) with the aging process of the earth
(B) the process of the earth's aging
(C) as the earth ages
(D) with the aging earth's process
(E) as the process of the earth's aging continues

*EXPLANATION:* This question asks you to find an alternative to a rather awkward group of words, composed of two phrases, *with the process* and *of the earth aging*. The second is graceless and ungrammatical. It should have read *of the earth's aging*, because in standard usage, nouns and pronouns modifying gerunds are usually written as possessives. Knowing what it should have been, however, is not much help in answering the question. You still must select from the five alternatives the one best way to express the essay writer's idea. In the context of the whole sentence, two of the choices (B) and (D) make no sense at all. (A) also borders on incomprehensibility. Left with (C) and (E), the better choice is (C) because it is more concise and it expresses exactly what the writer intended.

**2.** Considering the essay as a whole, which of the following best explains the main purpose of the second paragraph?

(A) To explain the historical background of the topic
(B) To provide a smooth transition between the first and third paragraphs
(C) To define terms introduced in the first paragraph
(D) To give an example of an idea presented in the first paragraph
(E) To present a different point of view on the issue being discussed

*EXPLANATION:* To answer this question you need to have read the whole essay. You also need to know the way individual paragraphs function in an essay— any essay. (More on that in Part III of this book.) Here, all five choices describe legitimate uses of a paragraph, but they don't all apply to this particular essay. Choices (A), (C), and (E) can be quickly discarded. Choice (B) is a possibility because in a unified essay every paragraph (except the first and last) in some sense serves as a bridge between paragraphs. Because the second paragraph is the longest in the essay, however, its main function is probably more than transitional. In fact, it develops by example an idea originating in the first paragraph—how easy it is to recycle. Therefore, (D) is the best choice.

**3.** Which of the sentences below most effectively combines sentences 10, 11, and 12?

    (A) Recycling centers offer recyclers conven-ience by providing separate bins for pa-per, bottles, and cans and by being lo-cated in almost every town.

    (B) Recycling centers, located in almost every town, serve recyclers by providing con-venient bins to separate paper, bottles, and cans.

    (C) Almost every town has a recycling center with separate bins for paper, bottles, and cans, and this is a convenient serv-ice for people who want to recycle.

    (D) People who want to recycle will find recy-cling centers in almost every town, pro-viding a convenient separation of paper, bottles, and cans into bins.

    (E) For the convenience of recyclers, separate bins for paper, bottles and cans are pro-vided by almost every town's recycling center

Ⓐ Ⓑ Ⓒ Ⓓ Ⓔ

*EXPLANATION:* In a series of short sentences, every idea carries equal weight. By combining short sen-tences, writers may emphasize the important ideas and subordinate the others. To answer this question, then, you have to decide which idea expressed by the three sentences ought to be emphasized. Since two of sentences (11 and 12) refer to the convenient ar-rangement of recycling centers, that's the point to stress. In the context of the whole essay, the other sentence (10), which pertains to the location of recy-cling centers, contains less vital information. Usu-ally, the main point of a sentence is contained in the main, or independent, clause, and secondary ideas are found in subordinate, or dependent, clauses.

With that principle in mind, read each of the choices. (A) and (C) give equal weight to the location and convenience of recycling centers. (D) stresses the location rather than the convenience. (E) subordinates properly but changes the meaning. Therefore, (B) is the correct answer. In (B), information about the loca-tion of recycling centers is contained in a subordinate clause included parenthetically inside the main clause. (See Part III of this book, for a more detailed discus-sion of these matters.)

## THE ESSAY QUESTION

## Why Include an Essay on the Test?

Quite simply, to see how well you write. Your an-swers to a few dozen multiple-choice questions about writing reveal your ability to recognize good, error-free prose. To an extent they also indicate your test-taking skills. But to truly demonstrate how well you write under pressure, you must write. The essay, therefore, provides colleges with helpful information about how well you can (1) think, (2) organize ideas, (3) express yourself, and (4) use English.

    1. You demonstrate your ability to *think* by show-ing that you understand the assigned topic, that you have something to say about the topic, and that you can come up with a few ideas or spe-cific examples to support or illustrate your point of view.

    2. Your ability to *organize* is shown by arranging ideas according to a purposeful plan. Good writers almost always use a plan instead of re-lying on the order in which ideas just happened to pop into their heads.

    3. You show how well you *express yourself* by clearly conveying what is in your mind to a reader. Having good ideas is not enough. Ef-fectively communicating your ideas to some-one else indicates that you really know what you're talking about.

4. You show your *mastery of English* by using the conventions of standard written English—that is, by writing correctly.

Overall, the essay question is meant to show how well you'll be able to produce the kind of writing required in many college courses, writing that explains or defends an opinion, persuades readers to accept your point of view, describes a plan or process, or provides information in support of a thesis or idea. Most likely, you've written these kinds of essays during high school, although rarely in 20 minutes, the time allowed on the SAT II: Writing Test.

Here is a set of typical instructions for every SAT II essay question:

---

*INSTRUCTIONS:* Plan and write an essay in response to the assigned topic. During the 20 minutes allowed, you should develop your thoughts clearly and effectively. A plain, natural style is probably best. Try to include specific evidence or examples to support of your views.

The number of words is up to you, but quantity is far less important than quality. In general, however, a single paragraph may not give you the chance to develop your ideas sufficiently. You must limit your essay to the answer sheet. Please be advised, therefore, to write on every line, keep narrow margins, and write compactly enough to fit your essay in the space provided. Try to write as legibly as you can.

BE SURE TO WRITE ONLY ON THE ASSIGNED TOPIC. AN ESSAY WRITTEN ON ANOTHER TOPIC WILL RECEIVE NO CREDIT.

---

The wording on the actual SAT II will be different from these directions, but the message never varies.

## What Will You Write About?

No one can predict exactly. Most likely, you'll be given a rather general statement or quotation on a broad subject such as human behavior or society's values and morals. Then you'll be asked to agree or disagree with the statement and to support your position with evidence drawn from history, contemporary life, literature, or from your personal observation and experience. The question is not meant to trick or to stump you. The topic won't be controversial. It won't

anger or excite you. Nor will it be beyond the understanding of any reasonably literate high school student. The assignment will be to write an essay on the topic—not a story, not a poem, not a letter, not a TV sketch—only an essay.

Your essay need not follow a prescribed format, but you may get the best results with a straightforward, no-nonsense essay consisting of some sort of introduction, a body of material that supports your opinion, and an appropriate conclusion. Variations are possible, but you probably won't have time to be too inventive. What you say is completely up to you. There is no right or wrong answer. The only requirement is that you write on the given topic. You'll be heavily penalized for an essay that strays from the topic, regardless of how beautifully it is written.

## ❑ Sample Essay Topics

A new topic is assigned each time the SAT II: Writing Test is administered. You do not have a choice of topics. Although the topics are unpredictable, they never fail to be presented in one of three ways: (1) Quotation, (2) Fill in the blank, or (3) Response to a statement, situation, or issue.

1. *Quotation:*

---

There's an old proverb that says, "Spare the rod and spoil the child." To put it another way, fear of punishment keeps people in line. In contrast, some people maintain that holding out a promise of reward is a more effective way to control human behavior. Where do you stand on this issue? In your essay support your point of view with examples drawn from your studies, from reading, or from personal observation and experience.

---

2. *Fill in the blank:*

---

The world is an imperfect place, and one could throw the stone of criticism in many different directions. One direction in which I would throw a stone is _____ .

Complete the above statement by naming a school, local, national, or world condition that, in your opinion, deserves to be criticized. In an essay, explain why.

---

3. *Response to a statement, situation or issue:*

> "The American Dream" is an often-used phrase in our culture. The meaning of the phrase has kept changing, however, as our society has changed. The earliest settlers dreamed of religious, political, and personal freedom. Millions of immigrants dreamed of economic opportunity. Native Americans, perhaps, dreamed of being left alone on their land, and African-Americans of full and equal participation in society.
>
> Write an essay in which you discuss "The American Dream" of the 1990s. Don't comment on your personal dream (college, a good job, marriage, etc.), but rather on what you see as a collective American dream, based on your observation, study, or reading.

Clearly, there cannot be a right or wrong response to such questions. In your essay, you must merely take a position and try to explain it as thoroughly as you can. Part IV of this book offers numerous practical suggestions for approaches to essay questions like these.

## How Long Does It Have to Be?

There's no required length. In fact, the College Board's readers are instructed to ignore the length of essays. Yet it's not likely that a reader will award a high score to a half-finished paragraph or to a series of meager or empty paragraphs. Effective development of the main idea matters most, not the number of words. Even an incomplete essay can earn the highest rating if it is well-developed up to the point where it stops.

## How Will the Essay Be Graded?

Your essay will be evaluated by two readers, each a high school or college teacher who has been in-structed to read it *holistically*. That is, they've been told to spend no more than two or three minutes reading it and then to assign a grade from 1 (worst) to 6 (best) based on their general impression of the writing. They won't mark you down a certain number of points for spelling errors or reduce your score for each grammatical mistake. Rather, your essay will be evaluated by its cumulative effect. In creating an effect, though, everything in the essay counts, from punctuation and word choice to organization and logic.

Handwriting is not supposed to count, but frankly, it's hard to imagine that readers, in spite of themselves, won't be slightly put off by handwriting that is difficult to decipher. Nevertheless, readers try to be fair, to reward students for what they have done well, not to dwell on mistakes and weaknesses. When rating an essay, readers compare it to the other essays written on the same topic at the same time. Your essay, therefore, won't be competing against some ideal essay written by a professional writer. "The scale is hooked up to the papers we receive, not some heavenly scale," says the College Board's chief reader. A score of 4, 5, or 6 on an essay indicates an above-average performance for the particular SAT II in writing that you took. A score of 1, 2, or 3 means a below-average performance. To further prevent reader bias of any kind, your name, sex, school, and other identifying information won't appear on your essay paper. Instead, you will be presented as a supermarket bar code, and your essay will stand or fall completely on its own. Although the holistic evaluation of essays is far from an exact science, experienced readers of the same paper rarely differ by more than one grade. When a difference of more than two grades occurs, a third reader makes the final assessment.

The two grades assigned to the essay are totaled to determine your score on this section of the SAT II. The score will be reported to you and to the colleges of your choice as the sum of the two evaluations (from 2 to 12).

# SAT II Sample Essays (with a comment to each writer)

The following six samples are actual essays written by high school seniors in a testing situation. Composed in 20 minutes, the essays have been typed exactly as written.

The students were given the following topic:

> There's an old proverb that says, "There's no great loss without some gain." Another way to put it is, "Every cloud has a silver lining." Do you agree or disagree with this view? Support your position with illustrations from your observation, studies, reading, or personal experience.

### Claire W's Essay

"That which does not kill you gives you strength." This proverb was obviously written by a wise man. The proverb is undoubtedly true, but it raises a question that needs to be answered: Is it true in every situation? A bad experience may leave a person stronger, but whether the positive results have a greater effect than the negative ones more than likely depends on the situation. Therefore, the proverb is correct but does not account for the fact that one may gain from a loss, but at the same time be damaged in some irreparable way.

A perfect example of an unpleasant but strengthening experience is junior year in high school. Some argue that, although it seemed unfair and cruel to be placed under the stress of so much work as well as so much responsibility, they later realize that, thanks to the experience, they now know how to be organized and efficient. One can certainly understand this logic. In addition to efficiency, kids emerging from junior year have an incredible ability to keep their lives in perspective, a value many adults lack.

Yet, despite the constructive results, one can't help wondering whether the pain of being a junior was worthwhile. During junior year, conscientious students learned how to be workaholics, hell-bent on succeeding and ready to discard many of their other beliefs and morals in order to achieve success. Some students grow so nervous about taking exams and how exams will affect acceptance into a university that they resort to cheating. Then there are the kids who give up extracurricular activities as well as jobs because they have too heavy a schedule in addition to school. So even though people learn to be efficient and think objectively about how they are conducting their lives, one must wonder if this is worth the price they pay.

Although it is certainly true that every great loss may have some gain, gain is not always more constructive than the loss is devastating and debilitating. People can be made strong by bad experiences, but there is always the danger that they can also be permanently weakened.

**Comment to Claire:** *By substituting a proverb of your own choice at the beginning, you give your essay a unique twist. Although not perfect, your essay is very well-organized. There is a logical progression of thought from beginning to end. The parts are tied together with transitions. You stick to the subject and support the main idea sufficiently and appropriately. The essay also demonstrates your ability to vary your sentences and use appropriate language. Your approach to the topic, while not unique, is certainly not mundane. Overall, the essay is interesting and creates the impression that you have a solid command of essay-writing skills. You have earned a "6," the highest rating. Congratulations!*

### Brad Z's Essay

The statement that every cloud has a silver lining is one that holds true to me in a recent situation in my life. Just three years ago, I was faced with the realization that we were moving away from my laid-back, sunsoaked, California lifestyle, into the hair-pulling, pressure-cooking, bagel-eating atmosphere of New York.

The first thoughts that crossed my unexperienced mind were those of confusion and despair. How could I move to a place where the streets are lined with thieves and not sand, where the air smells of factory smoke and not of fresh sea air, and where I, most importantly, had no friends. The dark shadow of depression sunk in slowly as the reality of moving became clearer and clearer to me.

Sitting in my hammock, deep in my fertile back yard, I began to think of the pros of living on the east coast. I would be meeting new people, become aware of new culture, and gaining experiences that most people don't have a chance at. Gradually, in this case the silver lining enveloped the once menacing cloud and now, as I sit here in New York, with time comfortable behind me, I look up at the silver cloud and smile.

*Comment to Brad: Your essay is an appealing and unified account of a personal experience that illustrates why you believe in the wisdom of the old proverb. You have used colorful and fresh language, which works both for and against you. The language provides interest but also creates the impression that you use words more for show than for substance, as though you didn't have that much to say. Your essay could have earned the highest rating if it had contained fewer awkward sentences, especially toward the end. Your essay is rated "5."*

### Cindy R's Essay

There's an old proverb which says, "There's no great loss without some gain." This statement says basically that even disaster sometimes holds promise for gain. Although the proverb may be valid on rare occasions, I can't agree with it. How can anything be favorable about the loss of a good thing?

In the novel, *The Great Gatsby* by Fitzgerald, for example, nothing good came out of the loss of Gatsby's life. Likewise, in the novel *The Grapes of Wrath* by Steinbeck, the Joad family consistantly faced disaster and loss, and in the end they were worse off than before.

On the other hand I admit that history shows that loss is accompanied by gain. For example in World War II many lives were lost but understandings of both peace and principle were learned. Then again in the Vietnam War, many lives were lost, but in the states people learned they had a voice in the government and protested against the war.

If disaster occurs and people can learn from their mistakes, then the gain is evident. But to always say that "Every loss has some gain" is looking unrealistically at life.

*Comment to Cindy: You've stated your position on the proverb very clearly. You have also cited several examples that support your point of view. Because the examples remain undeveloped, however, the second and third paragraphs sound more like a list than like a discussion. Nevertheless, transitions throughout the essay give the piece a sense of unity. The essay shows that you have a reasonable grasp of basic writing skills. The overall presentation warrants a score of ''4.''*

### Steve R's Essay

The person who said, "Every cloud has a silver lining," which consequently is a very popular saying, must have been a truly naive. It may be valid in some experiences to declare such a thing, but what really well-defined values or results have evolved from the "storm clouds" of war, violence, and poverty?

Wars have ensued since even further in the past than historians have recorded, and at the present war is still an existing threat to the societies of our world. What, therefore, is so advantageous about such inhumane violence? All that we have been offered from war is constantly new technological methods by which to kill your fellow man/woman.

Poverty and hunger, too, are issues faced throughout the world. There are countless programs and movements to counteract these problems, but their effectiveness is relatively minimal. And besides, what is so enlightening about poverty? Does your knowledge of the truth that people are starving and moneyless make ourselves and our world a better place?

I could go on and on about the uncountable dilemmas we face as inhabitants of this world, but that would seem rather redundant. There are some problems which have been worked at successfully for a long time. However, I am expecting the day when those "clouds" which linger above our world will suddenly yield dismal rain.

*Comment to Steve: Your essay is thoughtful but not very effectively written. Although well-organized, many of the ideas are stated awkwardly and imprecisely. You've made a real effort to develop your ideas, especially in the second and third paragraphs, but the point of the last paragraph is obscure. You vary your sentence structure to create interest, but the imprecise use of words detracts from the overall effectiveness of the essay. The essay is rated ''3.''*

### Christina B's essay

The statement, "Every cloud has a silver lining" is something everyone has heard one time or another. The truth in it depends on the type of person you are. To some people it holds very true. These people are optimists, and "Every cloud has a silver lining," is their battle cry. Optimists can find something good about the most dire situations. They will never concede that there is not something good about every one, person, place, or thing.

For some this statement is among the most hysterical they've ever heard. They are pessimists, and as the cliche goes they see the glasses half empty instead of half full. Pessimists don't believe much, and usally can find something wrong with everything.

I personally don't believe this statement because I have been in many situations from which no good has come out of. I guess I'm a pessimist.

**Comment to Christina:** *Your essay is organized logically, but it focuses on the definition of optimist and pessimist, not on your view on the validity of the proverb. You have avoided taking a stance on the issue until the end and provide no support for coming down on the side of pessimism. You've made a couple of interesting word choices and written a unified piece, but the writing is commonplace and fairly dull. A number of writing errors weaken the overall effect of the essay. Your essay is rated ''2.''*

 ### Sandy T's Essay

In my life there have been great losses. There have been deaths of close friends and other disapointments. However, I never realized that with all these disapointments also came personal victories and even very good times.

In 6th grade my best friend was a guy named Mark. We did everything together. We played sports, looked at girls and went to school where we were in the same class. I will never forget how many fun things we did together. By the end of the 6th grade, though, he told me the terrible news, his father got a job in Singapore and they were moving this summer. We spent as much time together but finally he had to move. We stayed in contact for a couple of months or even years but then the writing stopped and never heard of him again. I lost a great friend. It was sad time from my childhood.

**Comment to Sandy:** *Part way through the essay you lost sight of the essay's purpose. The connection between the beginning and the end of the essay is obscure. The writing contains several flaws in both sentence structure and standard English usage. Overall, it demonstrates poor essay-writing skills and a lack of competence. This essay is rated ''1.'' Sorry!*

# TAKING THE TEST

## Preparation

Multiple-choice questions, which make up two thirds of the SAT II: Writing Test, are intended to measure what you've learned about using the written language. The remaining one third, the essay, is a writing aptitude test. But the news is good even for struggling writers: Studying for this test can improve—correction: *will* improve—performance.

Actually, your preparation for the SAT II: Writing Test probably began when you learned to read and write. Although the stories and compositions you wrote while growing up may have contributed to your present writing ability, experts will say it was reading that really made the biggest difference. Reading helped you develop a sensitivity to words and how they create meaning. It increased your awareness of the world, gave you information, and added to the fund of experience and knowledge that you draw upon as you write. It also built up your vocabulary and developed the sense of the rhythm and sound of language that now enables you to distinguish between what is written well and what is written poorly.

If you are planning to take the SAT II: Writing Test in the near future, you can't expect to read your way to a high score. The next best thing, though, is to study the contents of this book. Take all suggestions seriously, write plenty of 20-minute essays on the sample topics, do the practice multiple-choice tests, check your answers, read the answer explanations, and learn from those you missed. Also, study the principles of grammar and English usage. (For the test you don't need to know that many, but they are important. Without realizing it, you probably know and use most of them, anyway.) Above all, become test-smart. That is, know how questions are constructed and what you are being tested on. Know exactly what you must do to answer the questions in each section of the test. Know how to analyze questions and eliminate incorrect choices. Know when to guess at an answer and when to move on to the next question. In short, know the format of the test and learn the tactics that have helped countless students do their best on this kind of college-entrance test. This book is designed to help you do just that.

## Choosing a Test Date

SAT IIs are given five times a year—November, December, January, May, and June. Since the SAT II is principally an achievement test, the longer you wait, the more you are likely to know. Therefore, unless you are taking it just for the experience, as some students take PSATs, you should probably delay taking it until you actually need it for applying to college. Many students take the exam for practice at the end of their junior year in high school and then take it again at some point in senior year. Juniors planning to submit an early-decision application to college may need to take the May or June test. In any case, the descriptive publications sent out by colleges to prospective applicants will include information about when the college expects you to take this test. Some colleges don't require SAT II: Writing. Still, you may improve your chances of gaining admission if your transcript contains a decent test score, particularly if your high school grades don't tell the real story of your ability as a writer.

If you have a choice, the best time to take SAT IIs in science, history, math, or foreign languages is when the material is fresh in your mind, usually right after you've finished a course in that subject. The SAT II: Writing Test is different, however, because most secondary schools don't offer courses devoted exclusively to the study of English grammar, standard usage, or 20-minute essay writing. Therefore, take the exam when you feel best prepared, perhaps after intensive work in school, after attending test-preparation classes, or after mastering the contents of this book.

## Registering for the SAT II: Writing

The exact dates, costs, and sites are listed in the College Board publication, *Registration Bulletin for SAT I: Reasoning Tests and SAT II: Subject Tests,* probably available in your school's guidance or administrative office. Or you can contact:

> College Board ATP
> PO Box 6200
> Princeton, NJ 08541–6200
> Telephone: 609/771–7600
> 510/653–1564
> (Bay Area, CA)

You'll be sent a booklet containing registration forms, instructions for signing up for the exam, and useful information about test scores, such as how to arrange to have scores reported to colleges, how to cancel, verify, or challenge a score, etc.

Ask also for *Taking SAT II: Subject Tests*, a publication containing additional information about the Writing Test.

## Using This Book to Prepare

This book will help you do your best on the SAT II: Writing Test. It leads you step by step through a program of study and review of what you need to know. Ideally, you ought to have weeks or months to prepare. The more time the better, but even if your test date is just around the corner, the book contains enough descriptive material, practical test-taking hints, and sample questions to make it worth your while to spend at least a few hours perusing it. In fact, except for retaking all your high school English courses over again, working through the pages of this book might be the best thing you can do to prepare.

Each section of the book has a particular function and purpose:

Part I—To introduce you to the SAT II: Writing Test and to get you started.

Part II—To assess your present level of writing ability.

Part III—To prepare you to answer the three types of multiple-choice questions on the SAT II: Writing.

Part IV—To prepare you to write the essay.

Part V—To systematically check your growth and progress using practice examinations to be taken under simulated test conditions.

For the most thorough preparation, start at the beginning of the book and work your way through to the end. If time is short between now and your test date, focus on the parts of the book that deal with the writing skills you are most concerned about. For example, if you need to brush up on English usage and grammar, concentrate on Part III. If essay writing concerns you most, turn to Part IV. Wherever you begin, though, be sure to study the question formats. Parts I, III, and IV contain plenty of useful information about each type of question used on the exam.

To use the book most fruitfully, choose the features that apply to you:

| If you want . . . | then . . . |
| --- | --- |
| A profile of what you know about English grammar and usage | Start with the multiple choice questions in the Self-Assessment in Part II. Record the results on the Performance Evaluation Chart at the end of the test. At a glance, you'll see what you know and what you need to study. |
| An assessment of your essay writing | Choose a practice essay question from Part IV. Compare your essay to the sample essays, each graded on a 1 to 6 scale. |
| Descriptions of each type of question on the exam | Read Part I for an overview. Then turn to Parts III and IV for more detailed analyses and explanations. |
| Instructions on how to write an essay in 20 minutes | Turn to the review of essay-writing principles in Part IV. Learn how to use the time most effectively. |
| A review of the English grammar and usage needed for this test | See the Usage section of Part III. Use it for study and for a handy reference while working on sample questions. |
| Model exams to be taken under simulated test conditions | Take the exams in Part V. Allow an hour for each one. As you answer the questions, apply the tactics you learned in this book. |

## Smart Test-Taking Techniques

For years some teachers and SAT tutoring services have asserted that, by analyzing previous exams and memorizing giveaway clues in the wording of questions, it's possible to outsmart the test. If the claim were true, the College Board, in order to be fair to all students, would undoubtedly scramble and rephrase the questions on all its subsequent exams. Since no test is perfect, gimmicks may sometimes help to crack open the test, but nothing can substitute for knowing your stuff and learning a few time-tested methods of taking standardized tests.

You wouldn't be reading this if you had not already had some success as a student. Therefore, you are probably a practiced test taker and know a thing or two about what works best for you. No matter how skillful you are, though, you can't be sure that additional techniques won't make you an even better test taker.

In the following profile of smart test takers, maybe you'll discover a pointer or two that you've overlooked before. Check your own test-taking skills against this generalized portrait. Not all successful test takers use the same set of skills, but they do share some common traits.

---

### Smart Test Takers

Smart test takers get to the testing site early, feeling relaxed but alert after a good night's rest. They are familiar with the format of the test and with the directions for each type of question. They have learned how to pace themselves, they've reviewed the material, and they've taken several practice exams.

When they arrive at the site, they have their admission papers in order, including their photo IDs. They carry two sharpened pencils (in case one breaks) with erasers and two pens (in case one runs dry) in their pocket or purse. They choose a well-lighted seat in the testing room, usually away from the door, away from traffic areas, away from the proctor's desk, and away from flaky friends who may tap their pencils, snort, or breathe heavily during the test. They recognize the need to concentrate. They put other matters out of their minds. They are emotionally at peace. The night before, they've tried not to quarrel with their brothers or fight with their girlfriends. The

---

ability to focus on the test means a lot. They have one-track minds heading in one direction only—to answer every question carefully and correctly. They exude confidence because they know just what to expect on the test.

When the signal comes to begin work, they open their test booklets and go straight to work. They skip over the instructions because they already know precisely what to do. They move deliberately ahead, ever watchful for an occasional booby trap or hidden hazard. They believe that SAT II test writers are not devious types, but are basically good-hearted people whose job is testing, not trapping.

When smart test takers are not sure of an answer, they know when to guess and when to give up. When in doubt, they mark the question to remind themselves to review it later. They periodically check their answer sheets to make sure that their answers match the correct questions, especially after they've skipped a question.

After answering the last question, they go back and redo the marked questions. If time remains, they review all their answers, fully using every minute allowed for the test. They avoid doodling on their answer sheet, and before they turn it in, they erase any stray marks so that the scoring machine won't try to read anything but the answers.

---

## Answering Usage Questions

Each question is presented to you as a unique problem, unrelated to other questions on the test. To start, read the whole sentence to yourself, listening with your mind's ear to what it sounds like. If something sounds odd, like an off-key note in a piece of music, you may well have landed on the correct answer. Focus your attention on awkward-sounding words and phrases. Using your knowledge of English usage and grammar, try to explain why your ear may have detected an error. For example, a mismatch between the subject of a sentence and its verb, or a sudden switch from present to past tense may have alerted you to the presence of an error. If you detect no error, of course, (E) must be your answer, but if you find that (E) is your answer more than 20 percent of the time (six out of thirty questions), you may be missing some errors.

Pay particular attention to underlined verbs. Verbs seem to create the most problems in English because so many things can go wrong with them. Their tenses are prone to be shifty, they disagree with subjects, they change in number, and they sometimes suffer from irregularity. Knowing how troublesome verbs can be, SAT II test writers consistently ask many questions that involve verb usage. You'll find plenty of detailed information about verbs and their errant ways in Part III of this book.

## Answering Sentence-Correction Questions

Begin by carefully reading the whole sentence. Repeat: the *whole* sentence, and not just the underlined words, which may be perfectly correct by themselves. If they contain an error, it will not be apparent until you've read the rest of the sentence. For example, here are the underlined words from a sentence-correction question:

> One cannot work at a leisurely pace on the SAT II,

Perfect. Not an error in sight. Now read the whole sentence:

> One cannot work at a leisurely pace on the SAT II, or you won't finish answering the questions.

Notice that the writer has shifted from the pronoun *one* in the first part of the sentence to the pronoun *you* in the rest, a mistake detected only by a reading of the entire sentence. If anything strikes you as odd, or you instantly spot a mistake, then reread the whole sentence systematically, substituting, in turn, choices (B), (C), (D), and (E) in place of the underlined words. Don't waste time rereading the sentence with choice (A), which is the same as the original. Start with (B). Because your job is to find the *best* answer, not just the one that is grammatically correct, you must read all the choices before deciding on the answer. In many questions every choice may be equally correct, but the one that is "more equal" than the others will be the right answer.

If the given sentence sounds right to you, it may contain no error, and the correct answer will be (A). In previous SAT II-type tests, (A) has rarely been the correct answer more than about 10 percent of the

time. If, when taking practice tests, your (A)s exceed this number, you may not be discriminating enough in your search for errors. But this is not a hard and fast rule. Every test is different.

In sentence-correction questions, errors with verbs are common, as are problems with comparisons, pronoun reference, and use of standard English idiom, but these are only a few of the errors you might be asked to find. For more detailed information about how to recognize sentence errors, turn to Part III of this book.

## Answering Revision-in-Context Questions

Opinions differ on the best approach to answering revision-in-context questions. Some experts advise you to read each essay first and then read the questions. Others say just the opposite: read the questions before tackling each essay. Which technique should you employ? The only answer is the one that works best for you. Try both methods while doing practice exercises in this book. Only then will you know which approach to use on the test.

### If You Read the Essay First

There's more to reading an essay than meets the eye. In fact, you have at least three options to try. Give each one an honest chance to work.

*Option A.* Read the essay carefully from start to finish. Don't try to remember every detail. Nor should you immediately start to pick out writing flaws, for you might easily get bogged down in problems that are irrelevant to the questions. As you read, keep asking yourself, "What is the main point of this essay? What is it really about?" Knowing the main idea facilitates answering organization questions as well as questions about the function of a particular paragraph. Identifying the writer's intent could also help with sentence-combining questions because you'll recognize which ideas ought to be emphasized.

*Option B.* Skim the essay for its general idea. Read faster than you normally would, using just enough care to get an impression of what the author is saying. Once you've caught its drift, go right to the questions. As you begin to anwer the questions, you'll have to reread the essay. The second reading will reinforce your understanding and perhaps enable you to answer some of the questions more astutely.

*Option C.* Skim the essay to get its general meaning; then go back and read it more thoroughly. Two readings, one fast and one slow, will give you a surer grasp of the essay than if you read it only once. Then proceed to the questions, feeling secure that you can concentrate on finding the right answers rather than worrying about what the essay says.

### If You Read the Questions First

Reading the questions before the essay gives you perspective on the task that lies ahead. How many questions deal with the whole piece, how many with individual parts? Are there any sentence-correction questions that could be answered even without reading the essay? If you know that several of the questions pertain to, say, the second paragraph, you'll know where to focus your reading. Be aware that reading the questions first by no means exempts you from reading the entire essay. It's crucial to know what it says, no matter when you read it.

## Order of Questions

ᵀ⁻ each set of usage questions and sentence-correction ͍estions, items are arranged by level of difficulty, with the easiest first and the hardest last. Students sometimes assume that when they come to a question they can't answer that all the remaining questions will be too hard for them. That could be a costly mistake. Not everyone will necessarily find question 9 harder than 8, or 14 harder than 13. For this reason, if you come to a question that stumps you, don't even think of giving up. Because your mind works differently from everybody else's, you may often find later questions easier to answer than earlier ones. If you come to a question that stumps you, don't agonize over it. Just go on to the next one. Go back later if time permits. Go as far as you have time for. The last question may be about something you know, even if you missed several of the previous ones.

Revision-in-context questions are not arranged in order of difficulty. Because they follow the progress of the passage, it makes sense to answer them in the order they are presented to you. But don't be a slave to the order. If sentence-correction questions are your forte, get them out of the way before concentrating on the others. It may also be useful to answer all the specific questions before dealing with questions about the relationship between paragraphs or ques-

tions about passage as a whole. As before, if you can't answer a question, don't stop. In the revision-in-context section especially, the last question is likely to be as easy as the first.

## What About Guessing?

Guess only when you can eliminate one or more of the five choices. Here's why:

Multiple-choice questions are worth one point each. Every correct answer will add a point to your raw score (the total number of correct responses). For every wrong answer, however, your raw score will be lowered by one quarter point. An item left blank will neither add to nor take away from your score. Subtracting credit for wrong answers is meant to discourage blind guessing. So if you haven't a clue about how to answer a question, leave it blank. But if you can confidently eliminate one of the five choices, it probably pays to guess. The odds are four to one that you'll be right. Not terrific odds, but suppose that on four of the sixty questions, you can eliminate one wrong answer, and you guess four times. If you guess right just once you will have earned a point and lost three quarters of a point, a net gain of one quarter. If you leave all four blank, you will gain nothing. Yes, it is a gamble because you could make four incorrect guesses, but the chances of losing every time are only one in four. And you could get lucky and hit two, three, or even four correct answers.

When a question gives you trouble, and you can't decide among, say, three choices, common wisdom says that you should go with your first impulse. You may be right. Testing experts and psychologists agree that there's a better than average chance of success if you trust your intuition. However, there are no guarantees, and because the mind works in so many strange ways, relying on your initial choice may not work for you.

Another piece of folk wisdom about guessing is that if one answer is longer than the others, that may be your best choice. That is not information you should depend on, however. In fact, since economy of expression is a virtue in writing, the shorter choice may more often be the best answer.

## Writing the Essay

Writing an essay in 20 minutes is a real challenge. Even the College Board acknowledges that such an abbreviated span of time may not be enough to fully measure a student's writing ability. But at the moment that's all you've got, and no one taking the test will have a second more than you do to complete the assignment.

Normally, most essay writers proceed through a series of steps, which may include thinking about the essay, jotting down ideas, taking notes, doing research, outlining ideas, and more. During the actual composing of the essay, some writers often work very slowly, agonizing over every word and sentence, rewriting often, and then rewriting what they've rewritten. Even some journalists, accustomed to working under the pressure of deadlines, would be hard-pressed to produce a good essay in 20 minutes.

Unfortunately, though, you have no choice. You have to condense into a few minutes all the steps that another writer, enjoying the luxury of time, might stretch into hours or even into days. You've probably had the experience before. An essay exam in social studies, for instance, tested not only what you knew but how quickly you could spill what you knew onto the page.

Unlike an exam in a specific course, the SAT II essay has no content to study ahead of time. It emphasizes what you can do instead of what you know. The three best ways to prepare for writing the essay are to practice, practice, and practice. Choose any of the sample essay topics found in Part IV or V of this book. Follow the SAT II guidelines for the essay question. Write an essay each day for several days in succession, or until you get the feel of 20 minutes' writing time. How much time do you spend thinking about the topic and jotting down notes? How long do you spend actually composing words on your paper? How many minutes do you reserve for editing and proofreading? Practice and adjust all the steps until you get the timing right. Pace yourself. Take a watch to the test in case there's no clock at the test site. But even more important than a watch is your grasp of time, acquired through practice.

### Getting the Most Out of 20 Minutes

No one can tell you exactly how much time to spend on each step. What works for someone else may not work for you. Some students pour their thoughts onto the page. Others perfect each sentence before starting the next one. You have to find and practice your own best method. Adapt the following schedule to suit your own writing method:

Prewriting: 3–5 minutes
  (Reading and analyzing the topic, deciding what to say, making a list of ideas, and arranging the ideas in order)
Composing: 10–15 minutes
  (Setting words on paper, developing ideas fully, choosing effective words, determining paragraphs, unifying the essay with transitions)
Revising, editing, and proofreading: 3–5 minutes
  (Rearranging ideas, altering sentence structure, reviewing word choices, checking for errors in grammar and mechanics, including proper spelling, punctuation, and capitalization.)

Notice that no time has been set aside for choosing an essay title. No title is necessary. Nor has time been set aside for neatly recopying your first draft. Since scrap paper is not permitted and you're allowed but one answer sheet for your essay, you won't be penalized for crossing out or imperfect handwriting, as long as the essay is readable.

Considering the limits of time and paper, don't expect to write a long essay. An essay of more than 300 words is almost unheard of. Essays of about 200 words are closer to the mark. Sometimes an even shorter piece will do, but not much shorter because it may seem superficial, as though you didn't know how to develop your ideas. Quantity is less crucial than clarity and effectiveness of expression.

A short essay must be well-focused. For most topics, it's better to write a well-defined, detailed essay on a limited subject than to generalize broadly about a lot of subjects. The sharper your focus, the better.

### How the Test Is Scored

Your essay is evaluated by two readers, as explained earlier. The multiple-choice questions are machine-scored. (Because the scanning machine can't distinguish between an answer and a stray pencil mark on the page, keep your answer sheet immaculate.) The entire test is scored on a scale of 200 to 800. The essay will count for one third of the total score. In addition to the total, you will receive subscores for both the essay and the short answer sections of the test. Along with your scores, the College Board will send you a booklet entitled *Using Your College Planning Report* that contains a substantial amount of interpretive information to help you understand what your score means.

# AFTER THE TEST

On your SAT II registration form, you are asked to list the colleges to which you'd like the results mailed. Not every college requires this test. If you send your score to colleges that didn't ask for it, there's no telling how your score will be treated. Most likely, it will work neither for nor against you. At colleges that have expressly asked you to take the SAT II: Writing Test, though, results are likely to be scrutinized and to become one of the criteria on which an admissions decision is based. It's not likely to make or break you, though. It's only one more piece of information in your total application package. It would be rare for your performance on a writing test to count more heavily than your grades in school, extracurricular activities, SAT scores, and any unusual or highly developed talents you may have. Whether it counts more or less than recommendations, your application essays, other SAT II test results, or the impression you left on an interviewer depends largely on the college's needs and admissions policies, as well as on the pool of applicants currently seeking admission. Your proposed major may also be considered. A dismal score on a writing test and your intent to study journalism may raise some eyebrows in the college admissions office. One thing is certain, however: A high score on any SAT II will never hurt your chances of getting into your college of choice. In fact, good scores on SAT IIs may offset mediocre grades or some other blemish in your academic record.

To insure that colleges see only your very best scores on the SAT II, you may wish to take advantage of the Score Choice option offered by the College Board. With this option, you merely tell the College Board to hold your test results until you've had a chance to review them. Afterwards, you instruct the College Board either to forward the scores to the colleges you've designated or to withhold the scores. If you decide that the score is too low and that you can do better by retaking the test, then the results on the first test will never be known to anyone except you and your high school. At the time you register for the test, you will be asked to complete an Authorization to Release Scores, a form on which to indicate whether you wish to exercise the Score Choice option. If you expect to take the SAT II only once, there would be no point in holding back the test results, but if you plan to take the test over, you would probably be served best by waiting until you see how you did. Whether to choose the option is a decision you should probably make with the help of your college advisor.

Another option available to students taking the SAT II: Writing Test is the Writing Sample Copy Service, which provides you with an actual copy of the essay you wrote on the test. Only you may ask to receive a copy of your essay. Counselors, advisors, and teachers will not see the essay unless you decide to share it with them. It makes good sense to exercise this option, particularly if you plan to take the test again. By reviewing this sample of your writing with the help of an English teacher or other trusted reader, you can analyze its strengths and weaknesses and quite likely improve your score the next time.

Although SAT II scores are used for admissions decisions, they serve in other ways, too. Colleges frequently consult the scores when placing freshmen in courses. For example, an applicant who has a fine record but who wrote a poor essay may be accepted on the condition that he or she takes a noncredit remedial writing course during the summer or during the first semester of freshman year. Similarly, an outstanding performance on the writing test could lead to an exemption from the customary freshman composition course. On campus, representatives from the college newspaper, literary publications, or yearbook sometimes court freshmen who have submitted high scores.

All that is in the future. More immediately, it's time to get ready to take this exam, one more of the myriad things to attend to during your last years in high school. It's not unusual to feel stressed, perhaps even overwhelmed, by the challenges of applying to college, keeping up your grades, and maintaining some sort of balance in life between work and play. Perhaps it's comforting to know that millions of students before you have met the challenges successfully. You can, too, particularly if you don't allow the experience to get you down. Grit your teeth if you must; be cheerful if you can. Now turn to the next page and go to work on the Self-Assessment in Part II. And good luck!

# PART II

# SELF-ASSESSMENT

# INTRODUCTION

This Self-Assessment, as the name suggests, is a test, similar in length and format to the SAT II: Writing, which enables you to assess your strengths and weaknesses as a writer. Administer the test to yourself as though it were the real thing: Set aside an uninterrupted hour. Find a quiet place at a table or desk. Remove all distractions, sharpen your pencil, read the directions, and go to work. Mark your answers on the Answer Sheet on page 27. Allow yourself 40 minutes to complete the multiple-choice questions. Then give yourself 20 minutes to write the essay. You may use both sides of a sheet of lined composition paper, about $8 \frac{1}{2} \times 11$ inches, or use pages 42–43, which approximates the size of an official SAT II essay response sheet. Either way, don't write more than you can fit on two sides of a sheet of paper.

After completing the test, check your answers against the Answer Key on page 44, and fill in each section of the Performance Evaluation Chart on page 44. Your score on each section, in addition to your total score, will give you a profile of what you are good at and what you need to study during the time between now and the SAT II: Writing Test. In addition, the chart will indicate the types of questions you answered most successfully. If you earn a high score on usage questions, for example, but scored low on revision-in-context questions, you'll know exactly what to study in the future.

Also read the answer explanations, paying particular attention to the items you got wrong. Don't ignore the explanations of those you got right, though. You may discover a pointer or two that could be helpful in future writing tests.

Although it is difficult to assess your own essay, you should not shy away from trying. Let the essay cool for a while—maybe even for a day or two—and then insofar as possible, reread it with an open mind and a fresh pair of eyes. Rate your essay using the Self-Scoring Guide on page 51. Try also to find a trusted and informed friend, a teacher, or a parent to read, assess, and discuss your essay with you.

Are you ready to begin? Good luck!

# ANSWER SHEET FOR
# SELF-ASSESSMENT

## Usage

1. Ⓐ Ⓑ Ⓒ Ⓓ Ⓔ
2. Ⓐ Ⓑ Ⓒ Ⓓ Ⓔ
3. Ⓐ Ⓑ Ⓒ Ⓓ Ⓔ
4. Ⓐ Ⓑ Ⓒ Ⓓ Ⓔ
5. Ⓐ Ⓑ Ⓒ Ⓓ Ⓔ
6. Ⓐ Ⓑ Ⓒ Ⓓ Ⓔ
7. Ⓐ Ⓑ Ⓒ Ⓓ Ⓔ
8. Ⓐ Ⓑ Ⓒ Ⓓ Ⓔ
9. Ⓐ Ⓑ Ⓒ Ⓓ Ⓔ
10. Ⓐ Ⓑ Ⓒ Ⓓ Ⓔ
11. Ⓐ Ⓑ Ⓒ Ⓓ Ⓔ
12. Ⓐ Ⓑ Ⓒ Ⓓ Ⓔ
13. Ⓐ Ⓑ Ⓒ Ⓓ Ⓔ
14. Ⓐ Ⓑ Ⓒ Ⓓ Ⓔ
15. Ⓐ Ⓑ Ⓒ Ⓓ Ⓔ
16. Ⓐ Ⓑ Ⓒ Ⓓ Ⓔ
17. Ⓐ Ⓑ Ⓒ Ⓓ Ⓔ
18. Ⓐ Ⓑ Ⓒ Ⓓ Ⓔ
19. Ⓐ Ⓑ Ⓒ Ⓓ Ⓔ
20. Ⓐ Ⓑ Ⓒ Ⓓ Ⓔ
21. Ⓐ Ⓑ Ⓒ Ⓓ Ⓔ
22. Ⓐ Ⓑ Ⓒ Ⓓ Ⓔ
23. Ⓐ Ⓑ Ⓒ Ⓓ Ⓔ
24. Ⓐ Ⓑ Ⓒ Ⓓ Ⓔ
25. Ⓐ Ⓑ Ⓒ Ⓓ Ⓔ
26. Ⓐ Ⓑ Ⓒ Ⓓ Ⓔ
27. Ⓐ Ⓑ Ⓒ Ⓓ Ⓔ
28. Ⓐ Ⓑ Ⓒ Ⓓ Ⓔ
29. Ⓐ Ⓑ Ⓒ Ⓓ Ⓔ
30. Ⓐ Ⓑ Ⓒ Ⓓ Ⓔ

## Sentence Correction

31. Ⓐ Ⓑ Ⓒ Ⓓ Ⓔ
32. Ⓐ Ⓑ Ⓒ Ⓓ Ⓔ
33. Ⓐ Ⓑ Ⓒ Ⓓ Ⓔ
34. Ⓐ Ⓑ Ⓒ Ⓓ Ⓔ
35. Ⓐ Ⓑ Ⓒ Ⓓ Ⓔ
36. Ⓐ Ⓑ Ⓒ Ⓓ Ⓔ
37. Ⓐ Ⓑ Ⓒ Ⓓ Ⓔ
38. Ⓐ Ⓑ Ⓒ Ⓓ Ⓔ
39. Ⓐ Ⓑ Ⓒ Ⓓ Ⓔ
40. Ⓐ Ⓑ Ⓒ Ⓓ Ⓔ
41. Ⓐ Ⓑ Ⓒ Ⓓ Ⓔ
42. Ⓐ Ⓑ Ⓒ Ⓓ Ⓔ
43. Ⓐ Ⓑ Ⓒ Ⓓ Ⓔ
44. Ⓐ Ⓑ Ⓒ Ⓓ Ⓔ
45. Ⓐ Ⓑ Ⓒ Ⓓ Ⓔ
46. Ⓐ Ⓑ Ⓒ Ⓓ Ⓔ
47. Ⓐ Ⓑ Ⓒ Ⓓ Ⓔ
48. Ⓐ Ⓑ Ⓒ Ⓓ Ⓔ

## Revision-In-Context

49. Ⓐ Ⓑ Ⓒ Ⓓ Ⓔ
50. Ⓐ Ⓑ Ⓒ Ⓓ Ⓔ
51. Ⓐ Ⓑ Ⓒ Ⓓ Ⓔ
52. Ⓐ Ⓑ Ⓒ Ⓓ Ⓔ
53. Ⓐ Ⓑ Ⓒ Ⓓ Ⓔ
54. Ⓐ Ⓑ Ⓒ Ⓓ Ⓔ
55. Ⓐ Ⓑ Ⓒ Ⓓ Ⓔ
56. Ⓐ Ⓑ Ⓒ Ⓓ Ⓔ
57. Ⓐ Ⓑ Ⓒ Ⓓ Ⓔ
58. Ⓐ Ⓑ Ⓒ Ⓓ Ⓔ
59. Ⓐ Ⓑ Ⓒ Ⓓ Ⓔ
60. Ⓐ Ⓑ Ⓒ Ⓓ Ⓔ

# SELF-ASSESSMENT TEST

## USAGE

INSTRUCTIONS: The underlined and lettered parts of each sentence below may contain an error in grammar, usage, word choice (diction), or expression (idiom). Read each sentence carefully, and identify which item contains the error. Indicate your choice by filling in the corresponding space on your answer sheet. Only the underlined parts contain errors. Assume that the rest of each sentence is correct. No sentence contains more than one error. Some sentences may contain no error, in which case the correct choice will always be (E) (No error).

SAMPLE QUESTIONS

1. Someone who does not feel love lives
       (A)
   with a void in their life. No error.
    (B)         (C)  (D)     (E)

2. When Tom went to the authorities, he
                            (A)
   winds up being arrested for a crime he
    (B)  (C)
   had not committed. No error.
        (D)          (E)

SAMPLE ANSWERS

1. Ⓐ Ⓑ ● Ⓓ Ⓔ

2. Ⓐ ● Ⓒ Ⓓ Ⓔ

---

1. On the counter, overflowing with whipped
   (A)
   cream, at least a half-cup of chopped walnuts,
                    (B)
   and hot fudge is ice cream sundaes for
                   (C)
   everyone not on a diet. No error.
    (D)                   (E)

2. By the time Nick arrived at the campsite, the

   tents had been set up, the fire had been lit, and
         (A)                      (B)
   there wasn't hardly anything to do except relax
          (C)                        (D)
   and enjoy the mountain air. No error.
                                (E)

3. Someone in the audience asked whether she
                                (A)
   would of been as intimidated had she been
     (B)                        (C)
   better prepared for the magnitude and fury of
     (D)
   the crowd. No error.
              (E)

4. Although I wish it could be otherwise, by this
                    (A)       (B)
   time next week I will have had surgery on my
                    (C)
   knee, which was injured during a hockey game
              (D)
   last winter. No error.
              (E)

5.  While touring in <u>eastern</u> countries of Europe last
                        (A)
    summer, Brian found that the Czechs,

    <u>on the whole</u>, seemed <u>more friendlier</u> to tourists
        (B)                      (C)
    <u>than</u> the Slovaks. <u>No error</u>.
     (D)                      (E)

6.  The study reveals that the <u>average duration</u> of
                                (A)        (B)
    phone calls <u>being</u> made from the phone booths
                  (C)
    in these two railway stations <u>were</u> forty-six
                                    (D)
    seconds. <u>No error</u>.
              (E)

7.  Fundraising for charities <u>such as</u> the Red Cross
                                (A)
    and the United Way has always seemed like a

    noble profession <u>to Charles</u>, and <u>after</u> he
                       (B)              (C)
    graduates from Fordham he hopes to become

    one. <u>No error</u>.
    (D)    (E)

8.  My mother is an extremely <u>light</u> sleeper, and
                                (A)
    <u>no matter</u> how <u>quiet</u> I come into the house at
      (B)             (C)
    night after she <u>has gone</u> to bed, she hears me
                      (D)
    and calls out my name. <u>No error</u>.
                            (E)

9.  Before the game, the stadium was filled with the

    sound of <u>everyones'</u> voices <u>raised</u> in a rousing
              (A)                   (B)
    rendition of "<u>Take Me Out to the Ballgame</u>,"
                          (C)
    after which the <u>President</u> threw out the first ball.
                      (D)
    <u>No error</u>.
      (E)

10. He looked <u>like</u> a walking fashion plate, <u>with</u> his
               (A)                                (B)
    clothes from The Gap and his hair nearly

    <u>shaved</u> off in the style of the <u>1990s</u>. <u>No error</u>.
      (C)                              (D)      (E)

11. Harvey suggested that <u>we</u> order plenty of both
                            (A)
    kinds, <u>since</u> either mushrooms or pepperoni on
            (B)
    pizza <u>is</u> bound to satisfy <u>everybody's</u> tastes.
           (C)                       (D)
    <u>No error</u>.
      (E)

12. John W. Davis is a good trial lawyer who, like

    <u>most</u> wary predators on the prowl, <u>has learned</u>
     (A)                                    (B)
    to capitalize <u>on</u> the mistakes and weaknesses of
                   (C)
    <u>their</u> opponents.  <u>No error</u>.
     (D)                    (E)

13. It's clear that wars have been <u>wedged</u>, <u>that</u>
    (A)                              (B)      (C)
    masterpieces have been painted, and that books

    have been written, <u>all for the</u> same reason.
                         (D)
    <u>No error</u>.
      (E)

14. Excitedly putting on hats, coats, mittens, and

    boots, <u>the blizzard</u> looked to the children in the
            (A)
    room like the snowstorm of <u>their</u> young lives,
                                 (B)
    the one <u>against which</u> all the snows of the
              (C)
    future <u>would be measured</u>. <u>No error</u>.
            (D)                    (E)

15. Unsure whether the adoption agency would
                                          (A)
    choose them, the young couple sought help

    from the court, which held that their home
     (B)                              (C)
    would be better than the others for the infant.
                      (D)
    No error.
      (E)

16. The theory, in fact, means that parents'
                   (A)              (B)
    influence being exerted on their children

    affect not only one generation but three or even
    (C)
    as many as four. No error.
       (D)         (E)

17. Having learned that Norway had resumed
        (A)                       (B)
    whale hunting, environmental and animal-rights

    groups began threatening boycotting Norwegian
                              (C)
    products, including salmon and skis. No error.
              (D)                         (E)

18. Martha believed that, if she would have played
                                 (A)
    better during the latter part of the season, her
    (B)             (C)
    team might have been invited to the regional
         (D)
    tournament. No error
               (E)

19. Sandra, confident in her creative ability,
                      (A)
    has enrolled in the School of Design to study
      (B)                                (C)
    painting, graphics, drawing, art history, and

    Architecture 101. No error.
        (D)          (E)

20. If we were to take him for face value and not try
       (A)               (B)
    to analyze, to dissect, and to explain possible

    ulterior motives, then I, for one, would agree
                            (C)      (D)
    that he is telling the truth. No error.
                                  (E)

21. According to the theory of synergy, two people
      (A)
    working together develop more brainpower and
      (B)          (C)
    creativity than the sum of them operating apart.
                              (D)

    No error.
      (E)

22. The report stated that most teenagers prefer a
                     (A)
    small breakfast more than a modest lunch,
                     (B)
    largely because they have less time in the
    (C)                      (D)
    morning than during the middle of the day.

    No error.
      (E)

23. Neil, the lead guitarist with Wretched
                    (A)
    Dream, has been praised as the player with a
           (B)
    more sophisticated sense of musicianship than
    (C)
    any other member of the group. No error.
        (D)                        (E)

24. Various circumstances outside the home, such

    as, for example, the type of a neighborhood in
                      (A)
    which one grows up, have a profound effect
                        (B)           (C)
    on one's personality and psyche. No error.
       (D)                           (E)

25. I don't doubt that, were I to choose the most
                      (A)      (B)
    influential teacher I have had during

    high school, it would have to be her. No error.
    (C)                           (D)      (E)

26. When Nathan arrived home, his feet were

    swollen beyond belief  because he was
             (A)                      (B)
    standing on the sidewalk the entire day
                                (C)
    protesting the city's new housing policy.
    (D)
    No error.
    (E)

27. Nicole discovered almost too late that the
                                      (A)
    solution to the perpetual problem with her

    dance instructor had been facing her
                      (B)
    right before her eyes the whole time. No error.
    (C)                    (D)          (E)

28.  Tonight's disappearance of three villagers
     (A)
    had been such a striking occurrence, that many
    (B)              (C)
    questions are bound to be asked. No error.
                  (D)              (E)

29. Social scientists are searching for specific data
                      (A)
    from which to draw a definitive, nationwide
    (B)
    profile of the connection between poverty with
                    (C)                      (D)
    the dropout rate from urban high schools.

    No error.
    (E)

30. In the beginning, the collect calls, all of them
                                      (A)
    made after midnight, had little to do with them
                                          (B)
    realizing that Jenny was having trouble with her
                        (C)
    roommate and with her studies. No error.
                (D)              (E)

**DON'T STOP.  PLEASE CONTINUE WITH THE NEXT QUESTIONS.**

## SENTENCE CORRECTION

INSTRUCTIONS: The underlined sections of the sentences below may contain errors in standard English, including awkward or ambiguous expression, poor word choice (diction), incorrect sentence structure, or faulty grammar, usage, and punctuation. In some items, the entire sentence may be underlined. Read each sentence carefully and identify which of the five alternative versions most effectively and correctly expresses the meaning of the original. Indicate your choice by filling in the corresponding space on your answer sheet. Choice (A) always repeats the original. Choose (A) if none of the other choices improves the original sentence.

SAMPLE QUESTION

The campers slept more poorer the first night than the second.

(A) more poorer
(B) less poorer
(C) poorest
(D) more poorly
(E) more poorest

SAMPLE ANSWER

Ⓐ Ⓑ Ⓒ ● Ⓔ

31. Anthony brang three college acceptance letters to his counselor with a smile of triumph on his face.

(A) Anthony brang three college acceptance letters to his counselor with a smile of triumph on his face.
(B) Anthony brought three college acceptance letters to his counselor with a smile of triumph on his face.
(C) Anthony, with a smile of triumph on his face, brang three college acceptance letters to his counselor.
(D) Smiling triumphantly, Anthony brought three college acceptance letters to his counselor.
(E) Wearing a smile of triumph on his face, three college acceptance letters were brought by Anthony to his counselor.

32. Susan was not aware, of course, that someone has stole her examination and that she will have to take it again next week.

(A) Susan was not aware, of course, that someone has stole her examination
(B) Susan wasn't aware, of course, that someone has stolen her examination

(C) Susan isn't aware, of course, that someone had stole her examination
(D) Of course, Susan does not know that her examination has been stolen
(E) Of course, the knowledge that her examination has been stolen is not known by Susan

33. Both novels deal with immigrants from Africa who, overcoming obstacles, advance themself in America in spite of society's unjust treatment towards black people.

(A) obstacles, advance themself in America in spite of society's unjust treatment towards black people
(B) obstacles, advance themselves in America in spite of society's unjust treatment towards black people
(C) obstacles—for example, the unjust treatment of blacks in American society—nevertheless succeed
(D) obstacles—namely, the unjust treatment in society towards black people—nevertheless advance themselves in America
(E) obstacles, being black, are treated unjustly by Americans, but succeed nevertheless

34. The book's descriptions of the country and the town, along with its recent release as a movie, <u>explains its sudden increase in sales</u> in bookstores nationwide.

   (A) explains its sudden increase in sales
   (B) explains it's sudden increase in sales
   (C) explain its sudden increase in sales
   (D) is why the book is suddenly selling well
   (E) are explanations as to why sales have suddenly increased

35. The atmosphere in the classroom was changed when the snow started to fall <u>outside, and the teacher could not get them to pay attention to the lesson after that</u>.

   (A) outside, and the teacher could not get them to pay attention to the lesson after that
   (B) outside, and the teacher could not get the children to pay attention to the lesson after that
   (C) outside, in spite of the teacher's efforts, the children wouldn't pay attention to the lesson after that
   (D) outside, causing them to lose attention to the lesson, despite the teacher's effort
   (E) outside, the teacher was unable bring the class's attention back to the lesson after that

36. To improve school spirit, to improve student and teacher morale, and above all, <u>turning the school into a place of learning are</u> the difficult and often frustrating jobs of a high school principal.

   (A) turning the school into a place of learning are
   (B) turning the school into a place of learning is
   (C) the effort to turn the school into a place of learning is
   (D) to turn the school into a place of learning is
   (E) to turn the school into a place of learning are

37. When you hear thunder and see flashes of lightning in the distance on a hot summer afternoon, <u>a person should not plan to go swimming even if they are perspiring</u>.

   (A) a person should not plan to go swimming even if they are perspiring
   (B) people should not plan on going swimming even if they are perspiring
   (C) people should avoid swimming even if perspiring
   (D) swimming should be avoided even when perspiring
   (E) avoid swimming, even if you are perspiring

38. Health care has become a dominant issue in modern <u>society almost everyone</u> knows about the problem and is concerned.

   (A) society almost everyone
   (B) society; that is evidenced by the fact that almost everyone
   (C) society, and that almost everyone
   (D) society; in fact, almost everyone
   (E) society, which almost everyone

39. Without a compass, Columbus could not have sailed to America, Ponce de Leon could not have searched for the Fountain of Youth, <u>nor would Magellan's circumnavigation of the globe have occurred, either</u>.

   (A) nor would Magellan's circumnavigation of the globe have occurred, either
   (B) and Magellan's circimnavigation of the globe would not have taken place
   (C) and Magellan wouldn't circumnavigate the globe
   (D) and Magellan could not have done a circumnavigation of the globe
   (E) and Magellan could not have circumnavigated the globe

40. The letter was intended for <u>Betsy and him, but the actual recipients of the bad news were Peter and I</u>.

   (A) Betsy and him, but the actual recipients of the bad news were Peter and I
   (B) Betsy and I, but the actual recipients of the bad news were Peter and I

(C) Betsy and him, but Peter and me actually received the bad news

(D) Betsy and he, but the actual recipients of the bad news turned out to be Peter and me

(E) Betsy and I, but the bad news was actually received by Peter and I

41. Does anyone seriously doubt any more that democracy is <u>as good, if not better, than</u> communism.

    (A) as good, if not better, than

    (B) as good or as better than

    (C) as good as, if not better than,

    (D) better than, if not as good as

    (E) as good as, if not more better than

42. The suspense lurking beneath the surface of his short <u>stories, as well as in his novels, make Hawthorne one of the more, if not the most, enduring writers</u> of nineteenth century American fiction.

    (A) stories, as well as in his novels, make Hawthorne one of the more, if not the most, enduring writers

    (B) stories and novels makes Hawthorne one of the more, if not the most, enduring writers

    (C) stories and novels make Hawthorne one of the more or most enduring writers

    (D) stories, as well as that in his novels, makes Hawthorne the most enduring, if not moreso, writers

    (E) stories, in addition to novels, make Hawthorne a more enduring, if not the most enduring, writer

43. <u>Wandering through the little town that he had once called home, everything</u> was different: the barbershop was now a hardware store, the deli had been replaced by a laundromat, and his family's home had been turned into a condominium.

    (A) Wandering through the little town that he had once called home, everything

    (B) He wandered through the little town that he had once called home, everything

    (C) As he, wandering through the little town that he had once called home, saw that everything

    (D) Wandering through his ex-hometown, everything

    (E) Wandering through the little town that he had once called home, he saw that everything

44. Convinced that few of his townspeople knew the condition of the drinking water, <u>pamphlets were printed by Strauss to explain the dangers and urging people to boil their water</u>.

    (A) pamphlets were printed by Strauss to explain the dangers and urging people to boil their water

    (B) pamphlets were printed by Strauss to explain the dangers and to urge people to boil their water

    (C) the dangers were explained in pamphlets printed by Strauss, who urged people to boil their water

    (D) Strauss printed pamphlets to explain the dangers, urging people to boil their water

    (E) Strauss printed pamphlets that explained the dangers and urged people to boil their water

45. According to many students and teachers, *Romeo and Juliet* <u>is equally as good as *Macbeth*, although neither of them are as good as *Hamlet*</u>.

    (A) is equally as good as *Macbeth*, although neither of them are as good as *Hamlet*

    (B) is equally good of *Macbeth*, although neither of them are as good as *Hamlet*

    (C) is the equal of *Macbeth*, although neither is as good as *Hamlet*

    (D) equals *Macbeth*, although neither of them equal *Hamlet*

    (E) and *Macbeth*, although neither of them are as good as *Hamlet*, are equal

46. <u>In the aftermath of the Depression, artists in the United States sought to capture images of a simpler country</u>, a land whose essence could be found in its rural, agrarian, or pioneer roots.

    (A) In the aftermath of the Depression, artists in the United States sought to capture images of a simpler country

(B) In the Depression's aftermath, the United States sought the capture of images by artists of a simple country

(C) After the end of the Depression was over, artists in the United States sought to capture images of a simpler country

(D) After the Depression, images of a simpler country were sought to be captured by artists

(E) Images of America, a simpler country, tried to be captured by artists after the Depression

47. Since Lisa did not intend to go to college after graduation, <u>she took little interest in her high-school work and, to the surprise of no one, did poorly</u>.

(A) she took little interest in her high-school work and, to the surprise of no one, did poorly

(B) this caused her to take little interest in her high-school work, and, to the surprise of no one, she did poor

(C) and not to anyone's surprise did poorly with little interest in her high-school work

(D) she did poor in her high-school work, to the surprise of no one

(E) and her performance in high-school was poor, surprising no one

48. Today's newspaper says that mathematics in Japan is far more popular among high school students <u>than students in America</u>.

(A) than students in America

(B) than among students in America

(C) than it is among students in America

(D) than mathematics is among students in America

(E) than between American and Japanese students

**DON'T STOP.  PLEASE CONTINUE WITH THE NEXT QUESTIONS.**

## REVISION-IN-CONTEXT

<u>INSTRUCTIONS</u>: The passages below are the unedited draft of two students' essays. Some of each essay needs to be rewritten to make the meaning clearer and more precise. Read the essays carefully.

Each essay is followed by six questions about changes that might improve all or part of its organization, development, sentence structure, use of language, appropriateness to the audience, or its use of standard written English. Choose the answer that most clearly and effectively expresses the student's intended meaning. Indicate your choice by filling in the corresponding space on the answer sheet.

### ESSAY A

*[1] There are many reasons making it cruel to keep animals penned up in zoos for the sole purpose of letting families gawk at caged creatures. [2] There has to be a better reason to imprison animals than merely to allow visitors to drop a quarter into a food dispenser so that one can feed the monkeys or the elephant. [3] One might argue that it is educational. [4] If someone is so dumb that they don't know what a zebra looks like, they should pull out an encyclopedia and look it up. [5] Humans have no right to pull animals from their natural environment and to seal their fate forever behind a set of cold metal bars. [6] Animals need to run free and live, but by putting them in zoos we are disrupting and disturbing nature.*

*[7] Then there is the issue of sanitary conditions for animals at the zoo. [8] When the animals have been at the zoo for a while they adopt a particular lifestyle. [9] They lounge around all day, and they're fed at a particular time. [10] They get used to that. [11] That means that they would never again be able to be placed back in their natural environment. [12] They would never survive. [13] And if they reproduce while in captivity, the offspring are born into an artificial lifestyle. [14] After a few generations the animals become totally different from their wild and free ancestors, and visitors to the zoo see animals hardly resembling the ones living in their natural habitat.*

*[15] The vicious cycle should be stopped before it is too late. [16] The whole idea of a zoo is cruel. [17] If zoos are not cruel and if, as some people say, they serve a useful purpose, then why not put* homo sapiens *on display, too?*

49. Which is the most effective revision of the underlined segment of sentence 1 below?

    *There are many reasons making it cruel to keep animals penned up in zoos for the sole purpose of letting families gawk at caged creatures.*

    (A) Many reasons exist for the cruelty of keeping animals penned up in zoos
    (B) It is a cruel practice to keep animals penned up in zoos
    (C) The reasons are numerous to object to the cruelty experienced by animals locked in cages
    (D) There are several reasons for it being cruel toward animals to lock them up in zoos
    (E) Locking up animals in zoos a cruel practice especially

50. Which revision of the underlined segment of sentence 2 below is best?

    *There has to be a better reason to imprison animals than merely to allow visitors to drop a quarter into a food dispenser so that one can feed the monkeys or the elephant.*

    (A) so that the feeding of monkeys and the elephants can take place
    (B) for the feeding of the monkeys and the elephant to occur
    (C) in order to buy the monkeys or the elephant food
    (D) so they're buying feed for the monkeys or the elephant
    (E) to buy a handful of feed for the monkeys or the elephant

51. Taking sentence 3 into account, which of the following is the most effective revision of sentence 4?

    (A) Reading about animals in the encyclopedia rather than studying them first hand.
    (B) In an encyclopedia you can gain more information about zebras and other animals.
    (C) Viewing the animal in a zoo is clearly more informative than looking at a picture in a book.
    (D) Doesn't everyone know what a zebra looks like, even little children?
    (E) But if someone is so dumb that they don't know what a zebra looks like, they should look it up in an encyclopedia.

52. Which of the following reasons most accurately describes the author's intention in the selection of words used in the underlined segment of sentence 5 below?

    *Humans have no right to pull animals from their natural environment and to seal their fate forever behind a set of cold metal bars.*

    (A) to inform the reader that animals in the zoo live in cages
    (B) to propose a solution to the plight of animals in the zoo
    (C) to arouse in the reader an emotional response to the problem
    (D) to appeal to the reader to weigh both sides of the issue
    (E) to convince the reader that animals don't enjoy being in the zoo

53. Which of the following revisions of sentence 7 is the best topic sentence for paragraph 2?

    (A) Life in captivity causes animals to change.
    (B) No one favors zoos that deliberately try to change the lifestyle of animals in captivity.
    (C) Living conditions for animals in the zoo are ordinarily harsh and cruel.
    (D) Living in the zoo, conditions for animals affect them permanently.
    (E) Life in the zoo for animals is not a bowl of cherries.

54. Which revision most effectively combines sentences 10, 11, and 12?

    (A) Because they would never be able to survive again back in their natural environment, they grow used to being fed.
    (B) Having grown used to regular feedings, the animals would be unable to survive back in their native environment.
    (C) Growing accustomed to that, placing them back in their native habitat and being unable to survive on their own.
    (D) They, having gotten used to being fed regularly, in their natural environment would never survive.
    (E) Being unable to survive back in their natural environment, the animals have grown accustomed to regular feedings.

## ESSAY B

*[1] In the twentieth century, women have held a major part in influencing social change and social status. [2] In such developing countries as Saudi Arabia, restrictions on women are gradually being lifted, and they have gained the right to be in public without your head covered.*

*[3] In the area of social status, women have fought for better treatment and more respect. [4] An example of this is the fight for women in the workplace. [5] Not long ago most women stayed at home and took care of their families, while their husbands worked at white collar and blue collar jobs. [6] But now many women work as doctors, lawyers, and other established positions. [7] Women are finally out in the work force competing with men for the same jobs.*

*[8] In the area of politics and government, many women have attained high positions. [9] Hillary Rodham Clinton became a role model for many young women in this country. [10] Two women are now members of the U.S. Supreme Court. [11] Several women also are governors, senators and representatives. [12] There will never again be an all-male cabinet. [13] Ever since women's suffrage, women have won the rights reserved for men. [14] The result was that women now have a voice in the actions of our country.*

*[15] In the areas of health, medicine, sciences and the military, women have also come into their own. [16] Although the world still has a long way to*

*go before women achieve total equality with men, the twentieth century may long be remembered as the time when the first steps were taken.*

55. Considering the essay as a whole, which revision of sentence 1 would serve best as the essay's opening sentence?

(A) The social status of women has undergone a major change during the twentieth century.

(B) Twentieth century women will have a major influence in changing their social status.

(C) As a major influence in the twentieth century, women have had their social status changed.

(D) Under the influence of twentieth century women, their status has changed.

(E) Being influenced by social change in the twentieth century, the status of women has changed.

56. Which is the most effective revision of the underlined segment of sentence 2 below?

*In such developing countries as Saudi Arabia, restrictions on women are gradually being lifted, <u>and they have gained the right to be in public without your head covered</u>.*

(A) for example, women are gaining rights like the one to be in public bareheaded

(B) which means that they have gained the right to be in public with their heads uncovered

(C) and they have the right, for example, for you to go bareheaded in public

(D) and women now have gained the right to be bareheaded in public

(E) to the extent that women can exercise the right of going into public with their head uncovered

57. Which is the best revision of the underlined segment of sentence 6 below?

*But now many women work as doctors, as lawyers, and <u>other established positions</u>.*

(A) in other professions

(B) as other professionals

(C) other established jobs

(D) other professional positions

(E) as other professional capacities

58. Which revision of sentence 8 provides the best transition between the second and the third paragraphs?

(A) The competition has extended into politics and government, where many women have replaced men in high positions.

(B) Irregardless, in the field of politics and government many women have attained high positions.

(C) High positions in government and politics have been attained by women.

(D) Among the jobs that women have attained are in politics and government.

(E) The world of politics and government has changed because women have attained high positions.

59. Sentence 8 is the topic sentence of the third paragraph. Which of the following is the best revision of sentence 9?

(A) The wife of the President, Hillary Rodham Clinton, made herself a role model for many young American women.

(B) In the 1992 national election, Hillary Rodham Clinton helped her husband win the Presidency of the United States.

(C) After seven years as Prime Minister of England, Margaret Thatcher was finally defeated by a male, John Major.

(D) While she was the leader of India, Indira Ghandi was assassinated.

(E) In recent years both Margaret Thatcher of England and Indira Ghandi of India, for example, served as leaders of their countries.

60. Which sentence in the third paragraph should be revised or deleted because it contributes least to the development of the main idea of the paragraph?

(A) Sentence 10

(B) Sentence 11

(C) Sentence 12

(D) Sentence 13

(E) Sentence 14

**PLEASE STOP WORK. USE WHATEVER TIME IS LEFT BEFORE THE 40-MINUTE TEST PERIOD EXPIRES TO CHECK YOUR ANSWERS.**

# ESSAY

**Time allowed: 20 minutes**

INSTRUCTIONS:  Plan and write an essay in response to the assigned topic. During the 20 minutes allowed, you should develop your thoughts clearly and effectively. A plain, natural style is probably best. Try to include specific evidence or examples to support your views.

The number of words is up to you, but quantity is far less important than quality. In general, however, a single paragraph may not give you the chance to develop your ideas sufficiently. You must limit your essay to the answer sheet. Please be advised, therefore, to write on every line and write compactly enough to fit your essay in the space allowed. Try to write as legibly as you can.

BE SURE TO WRITE ONLY ON THE ASSIGNED TOPIC. AN ESSAY WRITTEN ON ANOTHER TOPIC WILL RECEIVE NO CREDIT.

---

In an address to Congress in 1941, President Franklin D. Roosevelt, describing his vision for the world's future, said, ". . . we look forward to a world founded upon four essential human freedoms. The first is freedom of speech and expression . . . The second is freedom of every person to worship God in his own way. . . .The third is freedom from want . . .The fourth is freedom from fear."

If you had the chance to add a fifth freedom to this list, what would it be? Feel free to invent a new freedom or to choose one that already exists in the Bill of Rights or elsewhere. Please explain the reasons for your choice.

This space reserved for your personal bar code

**SAT II: WRITING**
**ESSAY**
**Time allowed: 20 minutes**

FOR OFFICE USE

Topic: **FREEDOM**

First reader _____

Second reader _____

Third reader (if needed) _____

The space below is for your essay. Please restrict your writing to the designated area.

Please continue your essay on the next page if you need more room.

# ANSWERS

(See next page for answer explanations)

| | | | | | |
|---|---|---|---|---|---|
| 1. C | 11. E | 21. D | 31. D | 41. C | 51. C |
| 2. C | 12. D | 22. B | 32. D | 42. B | 52. C |
| 3. B | 13. B | 23. E | 33. C | 43. E | 53. A |
| 4. E | 14. A | 24. A | 34. C | 44. E | 54. B |
| 5. C | 15. E | 25. D | 35. B | 45. C | 55. A |
| 6. D | 16. C | 26. B | 36. E | 46. A | 56. D |
| 7. D | 17. C | 27. C | 37. E | 47. A | 57. B |
| 8. C | 18. A | 28. B | 38. D | 48. D | 58. A |
| 9. A | 19. D | 29. D | 39. E | 49. B | 59. E |
| 10. E | 20. B | 30. B | 40. A | 50. E | 60. E |

# PERFORMANCE EVALUATION CHART

## I. Self-rating Chart

Usage, Questions 1–30 ............ Number correct _____
Sentence Correction, Questions 31–48 ............ Number correct _____
Revision-in-Context, Questions 49–60 ............ Number correct _____

Subtotal _____

*Penalty.* Subtract 1/4 point (.25) for each incorrect answer. _____
(No penalty for unanswered questions)

TOTAL SCORE _____

## II. Key to Self-rating

| | Usage | Sentence Correction | Revision-in-Context | Total |
|---|---|---|---|---|
| Excellent | 27–30 | 17–18 | 11–12 | 55–60 |
| Very good | 23–26 | 14–16 | 9–10 | 46–54 |
| Good | 19–22 | 11–13 | 7–8 | 37–45 |
| Fair | 15–18 | 9–10 | 5–6 | 29–36 |
| Poor | 10–14 | 6–8 | 3–4 | 19–28 |
| Very poor | 0–9 | 0–5 | 0–2 | 0–18 |

## ANSWERS EXPLAINED

(Page numbers refer to relevant material for study or review.)

*Usage*

1. **C** Error in subject-verb agreement. The plural noun *sundaes* requires a plural verb. Use *are* instead of is. (page 57)

2. **C** Double negative. Both *wasn't* and *hardly* are negative words. Use *was  hardly*. (page 99)

3. **B** Diction error. The correct verb is *would have been*. (page 72)

4. **E** No error.

5. **C** Error in comparative degree. Don't use *more* with an adjective or adverb in the comparative degree. Use *friendly* instead of *friendlier*, or delete *more*. (page 68).

6. **D** Error in subject-verb agreement. The singular noun *duration* requires a singular verb. Use *was* in place of *were*. (page 57)

7. **D** Ambiguous pronoun reference. The pronoun *one* refers to no specific antecedent. (page 85)

8. **C** Diction error. An adjective may not modify an active verb. Use *quietly* instead of *quiet*. (page 72)

9. **A** Error in possessives. Because *everyone* is singular, the apostrophe should precede the -*s*. Use *everyone's*. (page 107)

10. **E** No error.

11. **E** No error.

12. **D** Error in pronoun-antecedent agreement. The antecedent John W. Davis requires a singular pronoun. Use *his* instead of *their*. (page 82)

13. **B** Diction error. The correct word is *waged*. (page 72)

14. **A** Dangling modifier. The introductory phrase that begins *Excitedly putting on . . .* should modify *children*, not *blizzard*. (page 98)

15. **E** No error.

16. **C** Error in subject-verb agreement. The singular noun *influence* requires a singular verb. Use *affects* instead of *affect*. (page 57)

17. **C** Verb form error. Use the infinitive *to boycott* in place of *boycotting*. (page 62). To avoid a double com-parison, use *to* in place of *more than*. (page 62)

18. **A** Verb tense error. Use *had* (past perfect) in place of *would have* in clauses beginning with if. (page 64)

19. **D** Faulty parallelism. *Architecture 101*, a course name, is not in the same grammatical form as the other elements in the series. (page 70)

20. **B** Error in idiom. In standard English usage, the expression is *at face value*. Use the preposition *at* in place of *for*. (page 91)

21. **D** Incorrect pronoun. Use a possessive pronoun before a gerund. Use *their* in place of *them*. (page 94)

22. **B** Faulty comparison. Both the word *prefer* and the phrase *more than* suggest the same idea. (page 68)

23. **E** No error.

24. **A** Error in idiom. In standard usage the phrase is *type of neighborhood*. Delete *a*. (page 91)

25. **D** Pronoun choice. Pronouns in the predicate that follow a *being* verb are predicate nominatives, which must be in the nominative case. Use *she* in place of *her*. (page 94)

26. **B** Verb tense error. The past perfect tense should be used to express action completed prior to some other past event or action. Use *had been* instead of *was*. (page 64)

27. **C** Diction error. The phrases *facing her* and *right before her eyes* are redundant. Delete one of them. (page 72)

28. **B** Verb tense error. The past perfect tense should not be used to make a statement about something that exists at the present time. Use *is*, *was*, or *has been*. (page 64)

29. **D** Error in idiom. The preposition *between* introduces a phrase that requires *and*. Use *and* instead of *with*. (page 91)

30. **B**    Incorrect pronoun. Use a possessive pronoun before a gerund (*realizing*). Use *their* instead of *them*. (page 94)

### Sentence Correction

(Although some choices contain multiple errors, only one or two major errors are explained for each incorrect choice. Page numbers refer to material for further study)

31. **D**    Choice A contains the nonstandard usage *brang* instead of *brought*. Also the phrase *with a smile of triumph* modifies *counselor* instead of *Anthony*.
Choice B eliminates the misused verb, but not the misplaced modifier.
Choice C uses *brang* instead of *brought*.
Choice D is the best answer.
Choice E contains a dangling participle; the phrase that begins *Wearing a smile* should modify *Anthony* instead of *letters*. Also, it is wordy, for where else but on his face, would Anthony wear a smile?
(See *Faulty verb forms*, page 123, and *Misplaced modifiers*, page 118.)

32. **D**    Choice A contains verbs that switch from the past tense to present perfect; also *has stole* is a nonstandard form of the verb *to steal*.
Choice B is a variation of A, although *has stolen* is standard usage.
Choice C contains verbs that switch from the present to the past perfect.
Choice D is the best answer.
Choice E is an awkwardly worded passive construction.
(See *Shifts in verb tense*, page 119, and *Faulty verb forms*, page 123.)

33. **C**    Choice A contains the nonstandard usage *themself* instead of *themselves*, and the nonstandard phrase *treatment towards black people* instead of *treatment of black people*.
Choice B properly uses *themselves* but fails to correct the faulty idiom.
Choice C is the best answer.
Choice D is wordy and clumsy.
Choice E contains a misplaced modifier. The phrase *being black* modifies *obstacles* instead of *immigrants*.
(See *Awkwardness*, page 127, and *Misplaced modifiers*, page 118.)

34. **C**    Choice A contains a singular verb, *explains*, that fails to agree with the plural subject, *descriptions*.
Choice B is the same as A, and also errs in its use of the contraction *it's*.
Choice C is the best answer.
Choice D uses a singular verb.
Choice E is long-winded and awkwardly expressed.
(See *Subject-verb agreement*, page 122.)

35. **B**    Choice A contains the pronoun *them*, which does not to refer to any specific noun or other pronoun.
Choice B eliminates the reference problem by replacing the pronoun with the noun *children*. It is the best answer.
Choice C contains a comma splice.
Choice D is a variation of A.
Choice E contains a comma splice.
(See *Pronoun problems*, page 124, and *Comma splice*, page 114.)

36. **E**  Choice A violates the parallelism of the series of phrases.
Choice B is the same as A and also introduces the singular verb *is*, which does not agree with the compound subject.
Choice C is a variation of A.
Choice D is parallel but uses a singular verb.
Choice E is the best answer.
(See *Faulty parallelism*, page 116, and *Subject-verb agreement*, page 122.)

37. **E**  Choice A shifts the pronoun from second person to third person and incorrectly links a plural pronoun, *they*, with a singular antecedent, *person*.
Choice B shifts the second person pronoun to third person.
Choice C is a variation of B.
Choice D shifts the grammatical subject from *you* to *swimming*.
Choice E is the best answer.
(See *Shift in pronoun person*, page 120, and *Sentence shifts*, page 119.)

38. **D**  Choice A is a run-on sentence.
Choice B is properly punctuated but excessively wordy; also, in standard usage *evidence* is a noun, not a verb.
Choice C contains faulty subordination.
Choice D is the best answer.
Choice E contains mismatched sentence parts; the clause that begins *which almost* has no grammatical relationship with the earlier part of the sentence.
(See *Run-on sentences*, page 113, and *Mismatched sentence parts*, page 114.)

39. **E**  Choice A is not parallel to the other phrases in the series.
Choices B and C also lack parallelism.
Choices D and E are parallel, but E is a better choice because it is more closely parallel and is less wordy.
(See *Faulty parallelism*, page 116.)

40. **A**  Choice A is the best answer.
Choice B improperly uses the nominative case pronoun *I* as the object of the preposition *for*.
Choice C improperly uses *me* in place of *I*.
Choice D improperly uses *he* instead of *him*.
Choice E improperly uses *I* instead of *me*.
(See *Pronoun problems*, page 124.)

41. **C**  Choice A lacks the standard *as . . . as* construction needed to complete a comparison.
Choice B is is awkwardly worded.
Choice C accurately completes the comparison. It is the best answer.
Choice D is meaningless.
Choice E contains *more better*, an error in comparative degree.
(See *Faulty comparisons*, page 123.)

42. **B**  Choice A uses a plural verb, *make*, with a singular subject, *suspense*.
Choice B is the best answer.
Choice C is a variation of A and makes a clumsily worded comparison.
Choice D is wordy and contains a clumsily worded comparison.
Choice E is the same as choice A and also is long-winded.
(See *Subject-verb agreement*, page 122, and *Faulty comparisons*, page 123.)

43. **E**  Choice A contains a dangling participle; the phrase that begins *Wandering through* should modify *he* instead of *everything*.
Choice B contains a comma splice.
Choice C awkwardly separates the subject and verb.
Choice D is a variation of A.
Choice E gives the initial participial phrase a pronoun *he* to modify. E is the best answer.
(See *Misplaced modifiers*, page 118.)

44. **E**  Choice A contains a dangling modifier;  the phrase that begins *Convinced that* should modify *Strauss* instead of *pamphlets*. Also, its two verb phrases are not in parallel form.
Choices B and C leave the modifier dangling.
Choice D uses *urging*, the progressive form of the verb, instead of *to urge,* the infinitive.
Choice E is the best answer.
(See *Misplaced modifiers*, page 118, and *Faulty parallelism*, page 116.)

45. **C**  Choice A contains the redundant phrase *equally as good as*. It also uses the plural verb *are* with the singular subject neither.
Choice B contains nonstandard idiom *equally good of*  and a verb *are* that fails to agree with its  subject, *neither*.
Choice C is the best answer.
Choice D uses a plural verb *equal* with a singular subject *neither*.
Choice E contains a plural verb and singular subject and unnecessarily separates the main verb from the sentence subject.
(See *Subject-verb agreement*, page 122, and *Faulty comparisons*, page 123.)

46. **A**  Choice A is correct.
Choice B is expressed in a clumsy manner and makes little sense.
Choice C is wordy and contains a redundancy: *After the end* and *was over*.
Choice D is passive and does not fit the wording of the clause that follows.
Choice E distorts the meaning and lacks a grammatical relationship to the rest of the sentence.
(See *Awkwardness*, page 127, and *Mixed constructions*, page 121.)

47. **A**  Choice A is the best answer.
Choice B is set off by a comma splice; it also contains an adjective *poor* where an adverb is needed.
Choice C contains a mixed sentence construction.
Choice D contains an adjective *poor* instead of an adverb to modify the verb *did*.
Choice E contains faulty coordination that turns the sentence into a fragment.
(See *Mismatched sentence parts*, page 114; *Incomplete sentences*, page 112; *and Choosing between adjectives and adverbs*, page 80.)

48. **D**  Choices A and B compare mathematics and students, an illogical comparison.
Choice C asserts that Japanese students like Japanese math more than American students like Japanese math—certainly not the intent of the sentence.
Choice D states the comparison correctly. It is the best answer.
Choice E makes no sense.
(See *Faulty comparisons*, page 123.)

## Revision-in-Context

49. **B**  Choice A is awkwardly constructed.  The phrase *for the cruelty of keeping animals* is cumbersome. Moreover, the sentence suggests that cruelty to animals can be justified—the opposite of what the writer intended to say.

Choice B states the idea clearly and economically. It is the best answer.

Choice C is wordy and awkwardly expressed.

Choice D is wordy and awkwardly expressed.

Choice E, which lacks a main verb, is a sentence fragment.

50. **E**  Choice A is awkwardly constructed and illogical.   It suggests that animals are fed because a machine dispenses food.

Choice B says that animals are fed because a machine dispenses food—an illogical statement.  Also, the phrase *to occur* is not needed.

Choice C is awkwardly worded. The noun *food* should be closer to the verb *buy*.

Choice D contains a faulty pronoun reference. The pronoun *they* has no specific referent.

Choice E accurately and concisely expresss the intended idea. It is the best answer.

51. **C**  Choice A is a sentence fragment. It lacks a main verb.

Choice B contradicts the idea that zoos can be educational.

Choice C accurately develops the idea introduced in sentence 3 that zoos can be educational. It is the best answer.

Choice D is irrelevant to the idea in sentence 3.

Choice E is written with a hostile and inappropriate tone.

52. **C**  Choice A is not the best answer because most readers probably know that zoos house animals in cages. Moreover, highly charged language is not ordinarily used merely to pass along information.

Choice B is unrelated to the words in question.

Choice C is the best answer. The choice of words is meant to shock and disturb the reader.

Choice D suggests that the author is trying to be objective, but the words in question are hardly objective.

Choice E describes the purpose of the entire essay but not the particular words in question.

53. **A**  Choice A introduces the main idea of the paragraph. It is the best answer.

Choice B raises an issue not mentioned in the remainder of the paragraph. Therefore, it is not a good topic sentence for the paragraph.

Choice C contains an idea not discussed in the paragraph. The paragraph focuses on how animals behave in captivity, not on living conditions at the zoo.

Choice D contains a dangling modifier. The phrase *Living in the zoo* should modify *animals* instead of *conditions*.

Choice E contains a frivolous cliché that is not consistent with the tone of the essay.

54. **B**  Choice A is grammatically correct, but it reverses the cause-effect relationship stated by the original sentences.

Choice B accurately and economically conveys the ideas of the original sentences. It is the best answer.

Choice C is a sentence fragment. It lacks a main verb. The *-ing* forms of verbs (e.g., *growing, placing, being*) may not be used as the main verb without a helping verb, as in *was growing, is placing,* and so on.

Choice D is grammatically correct but stylistically awkward mainly because the subject *They* is too far removed from the verb *would . . . survive*.

Choice E is virtually meaningless because the cause-effect relationship has been reversed.

55. **A**  Choice A accurately describes the content of the essay. The original introductory sentence is misleading. The essay is about changes in the status of women, not about the role women played in causing the changes. It is the best answer.

Choice B is a variation of the original introductory sentence but the use of the future verb tense fails to convey the actual content of the essay.

Choice C is a confusing sentence consisting of two illogically unrelated clauses.

Choice D fails to convey the contents of the essay. It also contains the pronoun *their*, which does not have a clear antecedent.

Choice E is virtually meaningless. It also contains a dangling participle. The phrase that begins *Being influenced* . . . should modify *women*, not *status*.

56. **D**  Choice A inserts a comma splice between *lifted* and *for example*. Two independent clauses should be separated by a period or semicolon.

Choice B contains the pronoun *they*, which lacks a specific referent.

Choice C improperly shifts pronouns from third person to second person.

Choice D is effectively expressed. It is the best answer.

Choice E is cumbersome and awkwardly worded. The phrase *the right of going into public* contains an idiom error. The correct phrase is *right to go into public*.

57. **B**  Choice A contains faulty diction. Doctors and lawyers are not professions; they are professionals working in the fields of medicine and law.

Choice B properly revises the phrase in question. It is the best answer.

Choice C contains faulty parallelism. Words in a series should be grammatical equivalents. *Doctors* and *lawyers* are people, not *jobs*.

Choice D, like choice C, contains faulty paralellism. *Doctors* and *lawyers* are people, not *positions*.

Choice E contains faulty idiom. The standard usage is *"in" other professional capacities*.

58. **A**  Choice A provides a smooth transition by alluding to the discussion of competition in the second paragraph and introducing the main topic of the third. A is the best answer.

Choice B uses a nonstandard transitional word *irregardless,* which in the context makes no sense.

Choice C contains no specifically transitional material.

Choice D would be a decent transition were it not for its mixed construction. The first half of the sentence doesn't fit grammatically with the second half.

Choice E introduces a new idea that is unrelated to the content of the third paragraph.

59. **E**  Choice A is illogical; becoming a role model is not an example of attaining a high position in politics and government.

Choice B is not a good example of an attaining a high position in politics.

Choice C is irrelevant. Margaret Thatcher's defeat is not an example of an achievement in politics and government.

Choice D is slightly off the mark. The sentence emphasizes Indira Ghandi's assassination instead of her leadership.

Choice E gives two good examples of women who have attained a high position in politics and government. It is the best answer.

60. **E**  All the sentences except sentence 14 support the idea stated in the topic sentence, that women have made gains in politics and government. Therefore, choice E is the best answer.

### *Essay*

To evaluate your essay, use the Self-Scoring Guide on the next page. You may wish to tear out the Guide for easy reference. For a review of principles of good writing, please turn to Part IV of this book.

# SELF-SCORING GUIDE FOR THE SAT II ESSAY

## SELF ASSESSMENT

**Using this guide.** Rate yourself in each of the six categories on the left. Circle the item that most accurately describes your performance. Enter the numbers on the rating guide below. Then calculate the average of the six ratings to determine your total score. On the SAT II itself, two readers will rate your essay on a scale of 6 (high) to 1 (low). The score will be reported to you as the sum of the two ratings, from 12 (best) to 2 (worst).

Note that on the SAT II, essays are judged in relation to other essays written on the same topic. Therefore, this Self-Scoring Guide may not yield a totally accurate prediction of the score you can expect to earn on the actual exam. Because it is difficult to achieve objectivity when assessing your own writing, you may improve the validity of your score by having a trusted friend or teacher read your essay and rate it using this scoring guide.

*Remove scoring guide by cutting on dotted*

| | 6 | 5 | 4 | 3 | 2 | 1 |
|---|---|---|---|---|---|---|
| **PURPOSE OF THE ESSAY** | Very clear and insightful; fresh and engaging | Quite clear and insightful; interesting | Fairly clear and with some insight; marginally interesting | Somewhat clear but some confusion, too; fairly dull | Largely unclear and confusing | Extremely confusing |
| **ORGANIZATION AND DEVELOPMENT** | Meticulously organized and thoroughly developed; coherent and unified | Well organized and sufficiently developed; basically coherent and unified | Reasonably organized and developed; mostly coherent and unified | Somewhat organized and developed; some incoherence and lack of unity | Little organization and meager development; mostly incoherent and void of unity | No apparent organization or development; incoherent and lacking unity |
| **USE OF SENTENCES** | Effectively varied and engaging; essentially error-free | Varied and interesting; one or two minor errors | Adequately varied and interesting; some errors | Somewhat varied and marginally interesting; one or more major errors | Little variation and basically dull; some major errors | Uniformly repetitious and dull; numerous major errors |
| **CHOICE OF WORDS** | Interesting, sensitive, and effective; basically error-free | Generally interesting, clear and effective; one or two inaccuracies | Occasionally interesting and effective; one or two errors in diction or idiom | Somewhat dull and ordinary; some errors in diction or idiom | Mostly dull and conventional; several errors | Dull, immature; numerous errors in diction and idiom |
| **GRAMMAR AND USAGE** | Error-free | Occasional minor errors | Several minor errors | Some major errors | Frequent major errors | Severely flawed |
| **OVERALL IMPRESSION** | Demonstrates excellent skills and writing competence | Demonstrates good skills and competence | Demonstrates adequate skills and competence | Suggests fair skills and competence | Demonstrates poor skills and competence | Demonstrates lack of skill and competence |

For rating yourself

**Rating Guide**
Each category is rated 1 (low) to 6 (high)

Purpose of the Essay              _____
Organization and Development      _____
Use of Sentences                  _____
Choice of Words                   _____
Grammar and Usage                 _____
Overall Impression                _____
TOTAL                             _____
    Divide total by 6 to get final score: [    ]

For a second opinion

**Rating Guide**
Each category is rated 1 (low) to 6 (high)

Purpose of the Essay              _____
Organization and Development      _____
Use of Sentences                  _____
Choice of Words                   _____
Grammar and Usage                 _____
Overall Impression                _____
TOTAL                             _____
    Divide total by 6 to get final score: [    ]

PART

# MULTIPLE-CHOICE QUESTIONS

Overview

Usage Questions

Sentence-Correction Questions

Revision-in-Context Questions

Answers to Practice Exercises

# OVERVIEW

Two thirds of the SAT II: Writing consists of multiple-choice questions, which come in three formats:

- 30 Usage Questions, which ask you to locate errors in grammar and usage.
- 18 Sentence-Correction Questions, which ask you to correct writing errors.
- 12 Revision-in-Context Questions, which ask you to identify and revise weaknesses in the early drafts of two different essays.

This part explains what you need to know in order to answer the three types of questions. It also offers numerous practice exercises for sharpening usage skills. A foundation in grammar is helpful but not essential. The very fact that you are preparing to take the SAT II suggests that you know more grammar than you may think. Perhaps the terminology of grammar is a muddle in your mind, but if you speak and write skillfully enough to be understood by others, you must have mastered at least the greater part of English grammar and usage.

## The Difference Between "Usage" and "Grammar"

Although the words are often used interchangeably, *standard usage* describes the actual language spoken and written by educated people who, in a very general way, occupy positions of leadership and influence in society. *Grammar*, on the other hand, is a set of rules that describe or define the way sentences are constructed. Language authorities often disagree over which expressions and idioms should be acceptable in standard English. On the SAT II, though, you won't be invited to join the debate. The exam will present problems in grammar and usage that have definite, unambiguous solutions.

Readers of this part who have recently studied grammar will find themselves on familiar terrain. Others, who have long been away from verbs and clauses, will find grammatical concepts reviewed and illustrated. Those who never studied grammar at all needn't despair. Although some of the material may seem slightly daunting at first glance, anyone who can read these words can learn the grammatical concepts tested on the SAT II.

If you feel uninformed about grammar, do something about it. Study! Study deliberately but slowly, learning a little bit at a time. Like any complex system of rules, grammar takes time to master. Perseverance helps, but avoid getting bogged down trying to memorize every detail. Rather, save your energy for the exercises and the model tests. You might borrow a complete guide to grammar from your school or library and spend many profitable hours browsing and reading. If time is short between now and the test, read and absorb as much of this part as you can. Learn the suggested strategies for answering the questions, do the exercises, and take the practice tests in the back of the book. At the very least, become familiar with the format of the questions.

# USAGE QUESTIONS

On this section of the test you will be given thirty sentences, most of which contain an error in grammar and usage. Your job is to identify which underlined portion of each sentence contains the error. Some sentences will have no error.

SAMPLE USAGE QUESTION

<u>After reading</u> the two stories, the class <u>decided</u>
   (A)                                 (B)
<u>that the second one</u> was the <u>best</u>. <u>No error.</u>
     (C)                  (D)    (E)

Ⓐ Ⓑ Ⓒ Ⓓ Ⓔ

The sentence contains an error in comparison. English usage dictates that, when two things are compared, the *comparative* degree *(better, smoother, more able)* is to be used; the *superlative* degree *(best, smoothest, most able)* is reserved for comparing more than two things. Therefore, the correct answer is (D).

Knowing the rules for comparatives and superlatives could have led you to the answer. But even if you never heard the rule, you might still have been drawn to choice (D) by your innate sense of the way English sounds. In other words, your language "ear" told you something was amiss. A sensitive ear will serve you well not just in the usage section, but in all sections of the SAT II.

Although the SAT II is the latest of the writing tests administered by the College Board, usage questions have long been standard fare on college admissions exams, including the predecessors of the SAT II—the Test of Standard Written English (TSWE) and the English Composition Test (ECT). Each time these exams were administered, students were given sentences containing errors to be identified. On every test the sentences were different, but the kinds of errors remained fairly constant. Some errors showed up on every test, some occasionally, some rarely, and some never.

The following chart, compiled from a survey of previous usage tests, summarizes in general terms the frequency with which students were asked to identify certain kinds of errors.

*Level 5* <u>A near certainty</u>. Errors of these kinds have shown up consistently in the past, often three or more times on the same test.
          Agreement of subject and verb
          Verb forms
          Verb tense
          Use of comparisons
          Diction (word choice)

*Level 4* <u>Highly probable</u>. These errors have appeared regularly, with one or two instances on each test.
          Agreement of pronoun and antecedent
          Pronoun reference
          Parallel construction
          English idiom

*Level 3* <u>Likely</u>. Sentences with these errors have appeared on most tests.
          Pronoun choice
          Double negatives

*Level 2* <u>Possible</u>. Items containing errors of these kinds have shown up occasionally.
          Punctuation (run-on sentences and comma splices)
          Possessives

*Level 1* <u>Conceivable</u>. Sentences with these errors are not likely to show up but can't be ruled out.
          Spelling
          Capitalization

Although past practices are likely to continue, the make-up of future SAT II exams can't be predicted with certainty. Therefore, if you are aiming for a high score on the SAT II, don't depend exclusively on what the chart shows. Use it as a guide but not as the ultimate secret for success on the exam. To be sitting pretty on test day, study and master this part, and devote quality time to the usage problems most likely to appear on the exam. Study also the material pertaining to questions you missed on the Diagnostic Test in Part II of this book and on Practice Tests A–E in Part V. If you complete the exercises and tests without making errors, pat yourself on the back, toss this book away and take a walk. Or better yet, help a friend who is still sweating over the ins and outs of English usage.

---

**Level 5 usage problems**

Sentences containing these kinds of errors have shown up consistently in the past, often three or more times on the same test.

Agreement of subject and verb, below
Verb forms, page 62
Verb tense, page 64
Use of comparisons, page 68
Diction (word choice), page 72

---

## AGREEMENT OF SUBJECT AND VERB

The subject of a sentence and its verb must make a match, like a nut and a bolt. A mismatch in **number** occurs when a writer tries to use a singular subject with a plural verb, or vice versa. That's why *the books was* and *the book were* are nonstandard usages. A mismatch in **person** is less often a problem because it applies only when the verb is a form of *to be*. It occurs when the subject is a pronoun and the writer uses a verb of a different person, as in *he are, you is, they am.*

Few native English speakers have a problem making a proper match when the subject immediately precedes the verb. But many agreement errors occur when a clause or phrase intervenes between the subject and verb, causing the writer instinctively to match the verb with the closest noun or pronoun.

*Delivery* (singular subject) of today's newspapers and magazines *have been* (plural verb) delayed.

The prepositional phrase *of today's newspapers and magazines* blurs the relationship between subject and verb. The plural noun *magazines* misleads the writer into using a plural verb. With singular subject and verb properly matched, the sentence reads:

*Delivery* of today's newspapers and magazines *has been* delayed.

Or with matched plural subject and verb:

*Deliveries* of today's newspapers and magazines *have been* delayed.

A similar problem occurs when the verb precedes the subject.

Here *comes* (singular verb) my *brother and sister* (plural subject).

When subject and verb are matched:

Here *come* (plural verb) my *brother and sister* (plural subject).

A third problem in agreement occurs when the writer is not sure whether the subject noun is singular or plural.

*Neither* (singular subject) of the children *have* (plural verb) enough money for lunch.

*Neither* (singular subject) of the children *has* (singular verb) enough money for lunch.

In order to locate errors in subject-verb agreement on the SAT II, it helps to become familiar with the language constructions most apt to cause problems:

## 1. Intervening Words Between Subject and Verb

a. Verbs must agree with the subject noun or pronoun, not with words mistakenly thought to be the subject.

Her *understanding* of the arrangements *is* that the bride will carry red roses.

The *problems* created by the budget deficit *are* incomprehensible by the average citizen.

The 1996 Olympic *Games*, regardless of the opposition, *are scheduled* to be in Atlanta.

The *decision*, which has been under discussion all day, *is* expected soon.

✩ b. Verbs must agree with the subject and are not influenced by intervening phrases beginning with *in addition to, along with, as well as,* or other similar phrases.

*One* of his paintings, in addition to several photographs, *is* on display in the library.

Her *parents*, as well as Helen, *make* the decision.

## 2. Subjects Composed of More Than One Noun or Pronoun

a. Nouns, both singular and plural, when joined by *and*, are called compound subjects and need plural verbs.

The *picture and text go* inside this box.

The *graphics and the photos are surrounded* by a thick double line.

Several locust *trees and* a green *mailbox stand* outside the house.

b. Compound subjects thought of as a unit need singular verbs.

*Green eggs and ham is* Reggie's favorite breakfast.

Their *pride and joy*, Samantha, *was born* on Christmas Day.

c. Singular nouns joined by *or* or *nor* need singular verbs.

A *Coke* or a *Pepsi is* what I thirst for.

*Neither my history teacher nor my economics teacher plans* to discuss the crisis.

d. When a subject consists of a singular noun and a plural noun joined by *or* or *nor*, the number of the verb is determined by the noun closer to the verb.

*Either a pineapple or some oranges are* on the table.

*Neither the linemen nor the quarterback was* aware of the tricky play.

e. When a subject contains a pronoun that differs in person from a noun or another pronoun, the verb must agree with the closer subject word.

Neither Meredith nor *you are* expected to finish the job.

Either he or *I am* planning to work late on Saturday.

f. When the subject is singular and the predicate noun is plural, or vice versa, the number of the verb is determined by the subject.

The *bulk* of Wilkinson's work *is* two novels and a collection of travelogues.

Two *novels and a travelogue are* the bulk of Wilkinson's work.

## 3. Subject Words That May Be Singular or Plural

Collective nouns sound singular but may be plural, depending on how they are used. *A family*, for example, is singular. But if you are thinking of all the separate individuals, *family* takes a plural verb.

The *family* (members) *are* arriving for the wedding at different times.

Other collective nouns include *group, crowd, team, jury, soybeans, audience, herd, public, dozen, class, band, flock, majority, committee, heap* and *lot*. Other words and expressions governed by the same rule are units of time, money, weight, measurement, and all fractions.

The *jury is* going to decide today.

The *jury are* returning to their homes tomorrow.

The *majority favors* a formal senior prom.

The *majority have* their tickets for the boatride.

## 4. Subject Words That Are Singular but Sound Plural

The names of books, countries, organizations, certain diseases, course titles, and other singular nouns may sound like plurals, because they end in s, but they usually require a singular verb.

*Killings is* a fascinating book by Calvin Trillin.

*The United States is* the only country not to ratify the treaty.

*The Daughters of the American Revolution is* sponsoring an essay contest.

*Measles is* going around the school.

*Computer Sciences is* the fastest-growing under-graduate major in the university.

## 5. Subjects Consisting of Indefinite Pronouns

Subjects consisting of indefinite pronouns like *everyone*, *both* and *any* pose a special problem. Some indefinite pronouns must be matched with singular verbs, some with plural verbs, and some with one or the other, depending on the sense of the sentence. There's no getting around the fact that you need to know which number applies to which pronoun, although an ear attuned to the sound of English will be a big help.

a.  These words, although they sound plural, get singular verbs: *each, either, neither,* the "ones" *(anyone, no one, everyone, someone)* and the "bodies" *(anybody, everybody, nobody, somebody).*

> *Each* herb in the garden *is* different.
> *Each* man and woman in the room *gets* only one vote.
> *Either* lake in those mountains *is* good for swimming.
> *Neither* of these parks *belongs* to the homeless people.
> *Everyone* who works hard *is* definitely going to earn an "A."

b.  These words get plural verbs: *both, many, few, several.*

> In spite of rumors to the contrary, *both are* on the verge of bankruptcy.
> *Several* in the band *are* not going of the trip to Boston.

c.  These words get singular verbs in some instances and plural verbs in others: *any, none, some, all, most.* Notice that all these pronouns imply a quantity or an amount: (*all* the people, *some* men, *most* women). If the amount is deemed a unit, consider the words to be singular, but if the amount consists of individual units, think of the words as plural.

> *Any* of the bracelets in the collection *is* suitable.
> (The collection of bracelets is considered to be a unit.)

> *Any* of the guides *are* able to answer your question. (Each guide is considered to be an individual.)
> *None* of the sparkplugs *is* defective.
> *None* of the people *are* going to remain behind.
> *All* of the spaghetti *is* gone.
> *All* of the students *are* writing their term papers this weekend.

## 6. When Subjects Follow Verbs

When the subject of the sentence follows the verb, the verb takes its number from the subject, as usual.

> Behind the building *was* an *alley.*
> Behind the building *were* an *alley and a vacant lot.*
> There *is* only one *can* of peas left.
> Here *are* the *book and the pen* I promised to lend you.

### Finding the Subject of the Sentence

Mistakes in subject-verb agreement frequently occur when the writer or speaker loses track of the subject of the sentence, but once the subject is nailed down, everything else, including the verb, usually falls into place. Every sentence has a stated subject except those that give a command or make a request, in which case the subject is understood to be *you.*

> *(You)* Get over to the gym on the double!
> *(You)* Please lend me your English homework.

### The "bare bones" approach.

To find the subject of long sentences, reduce the sentence to its "bare bones." That is, strip away everything but its subject (a noun or pronoun) and its verb. Easier said than done, true, but not formidable if you remember that you'll never find the subject in (1) a prepositional phrase, (2) a dependent clause, or (3) a phrase that interrupts the flow of the sentence.

1. Look first for **prepositional phrases**, which are composed of a preposition and the name of someone or something: *up the wall, over the counter,* and *around the town.* Cross out all the prepositional phrases in these examples:

> In the middle of the night, Penny studied.
> Most of the sentences are in the book.

One of Frank's friends is in need of help.

Once you've done that, you're left with only the bare bones—the subject and verb of each sentence:

| Complete Sentence | Bare Bones |
| --- | --- |
| In the middle of the night, Penny studied. | Penny studied |
| Most of the sentences are in the book. | Most are |
| One of Frank's friends is in need of help. | One is |

2.  Look for **dependent clauses**, those portions of a sentence that contain a noun and a verb but are not complete sentences because they often begin with words and phrases such as *although, as, as though, because, before, even though, if, in spite of, regardless of, since, so that, unless, which, whenever, whether, while,* and *whose.*

Cross out the dependent clauses in these examples: (*Hint*: A comma frequently separates the dependent clause from the main clause.)

After Laurie finished the exam, she celebrated.

When you've done a few sentences, it becomes easy.

Andy helps out whenever he has the time.

Once you've eliminated all dependent clauses, you're left with the main clause, which contains the bare bones of the sentence:

| Complete Sentence | Bare Bones |
| --- | --- |
| After Laurie finished the exam, she cheered. | she cheered |
| When you've done a few sentences, it becomes easy. | it becomes easy |
| Andy helps out whenever he has the time. | Andy helps out |

If you hadn't crossed out the dependent clauses, you may have searched for the subject and verb of the sentence in the wrong place.

3.  Look for **interrupters**, portions of the sentence that impede the smooth flow of the main idea. They come in many forms, from one word (*however, nevertheless*) to dozens. Usually they are set off by commas.

Cross out those portions of each sentence that interrupt the flow of the main idea:

Susan, an optimist from the day she was born, worried.

Examples, if nothing else, help.

Willie, who got a ticket for doing 60 in a 30 MPH zone, paid the fine.

After you've crossed out the words that interrupt the main thought, only the bare bones remain:

| Complete Sentence | Bare Bones |
| --- | --- |
| Susan, an optimist from the day she was born, worried. | Susan worried |
| Examples, if nothing else, help. | Examples help |
| Willie, who got a ticket for doing 60 in a 30 MPH zone, paid the fine. | Willie paid the fine |

If you hadn't crossed out the interrupting words, you might not have identified the subject and verb.

The bare bones of a sentence are sometimes obscured by any number of assorted phrases and clauses. But if you carefully peel away those sentence parts that cannot contain the subject and verb, you're likely to find just what you're looking for. Here is an example of how to dissect a sentence:

Whenever you succeed in making a subject and a verb agree, not always an easy task for a writer, especially in a long and complicated sentence, the writing sounds literate.

First, locate and underline all the nouns and pronouns.

Whenever <u>you</u> succeed in making a <u>subject</u> and a <u>verb</u> agree, not always an easy <u>task</u> for a <u>writer</u>, especially in a long and complicated <u>sentence</u>, the <u>writing</u> sounds literate.

One of the underlined words must be the subject, but which one? The first three underlined words, *you, subject,* and *verb,* are in a dependent clause starting with *whenever,* so they are disqualified. The next nouns, *task* and *writer,* are in a phrase that interrupts the flow of the sentence. Reject them. The next one, *sentence,* is in a prepositional phrase. Count it out, too. You're left with one noun, *writing,* which is the subject of the sentence. Since the only verb that goes with the subject is *sounds,* you've found the bare bones of the sentence, *writing sounds literate.* The subject agrees with the verb, as it should.

PRACTICE EXERCISE IN SUBJECT-VERB AGREEMENT

In some of the following sentences the subject does not agree with the verb. Using the "bare bones" approach, locate the subject and the verb in each sentence, and write them correctly in the space provided. Some sentences may be correct.

1. Tucker's talent in chess and weight lifting, one of our school's most popular sports, prove his mental and physical strength. *proves*

   _____

2. The book that told stories of thirteen young men who died fighting forest fires were gripping to read. *was*

   _____

3. At the end of the season, the team, regardless of whether they win the championship, are splitting up. *is*

   _____

4. Either Don or you *are* is going to lead the class discussion on Tuesday.

   _____

5. Jane and Mark, who began their yard cleanup business last spring, have decided to hire two new helpers.

   _____

6. There are many levels on which a reader can identify and connect with this book

   _____

7. Admission proceeds from the concert *are* is going toward rebuilding the gazebo, which was burned down by vandals during the summer.

   _____

8. Tomorrow, a rescue team *is* are expected to arrive at the site of the crash.

   _____

9. Before they were laid off by the company, neither the assistant managers nor Mr. McCallum were told that their jobs were in danger. *was*

   _____

10. Either the Democrats or the Republicans *are* is going to win the election.

    _____

11. For further information on the new train schedule, contact the stationmaster.

    _____

12. Politics *has* have always been one of Dave's passions.

    _____

13. Charles Darwin, along with his contemporary Abraham Lincoln, *is* are among the most impressive figures in nineteenth century history.

    _____

14. Kate Green, one of the hottest jazz pianists in town and known for something called "three-dimensional playing," and her accompanist, Lenny, *are* is planning a tour of the Midwest during September.

    _____

15. Nancy, along with her friend Sluggo, appears to be coming down the escalator.

    _____

16. The fact that most citizens seem to think that Congress is terrible but that their *its* own representatives are good makes the outcome of the elections predictable.

    _____

17. Here's *are* the two statutes to which the the defense lawyer referred during the hearing.

    _____

18. Either Dan or his partners in the group *are* is going to show up at the gig on Saturday night.

    _____

19. The paved parts of Todd Road, which runs four miles east from here, is *are* only about three hundred yards long.

    _____

20. Gerry's teacher, as well as the program coordinator and the dean, are going to make the decision.

   _____

21. No one in the drum corps, in spite of how they all feel about the issue, want to participate in the rally.

   _____

22. Happy memories of the days on the river, not loyalty to the school, is what brought the crew back for a reunion.

   _____

23. A shipment of twenty tons of rice and eight tons of beans were loaded onto the freighter.

   _____

24. About a million and a half dollars has been spent on repairing the road to Chatham.

   _____

25. The recession that we are experiencing at present, despite contrary indications, are going to end by next summer.

   _____

*Answers on page 154.*

## VERB FORMS

Of all the parts of speech in the English language, verbs are the most apt to be used incorrectly, a fact that explains why sentences containing verb errors regularly appear on standard English usage tests. The root of many errors lies in verb forms. Most verbs have three principal forms: (1) present, (2) past and (3) past participle.

## 1. Present

I *shout*, you *scream*, they *stampede*; Jack *shouts*, it *screams*, and so on. Using the present form of verbs is easy, as is forming the **present participle** of a verb, formed by adding *-ing* to the present form.

| Present | Present Participle |
|---------|--------------------|
| *scream* | *(is) screaming* |
| *shout* | *(is) shouting* |
| *stampede* | *(is) stampeding* |

## 2. Past

I *shouted*, you *screamed*, they *stampeded*; Jack *shouted*, it *shouted*, and so on.

The past is formed by adding *-d* or *-ed* to the present form of **regular** verbs. Many verbs are **irregular**, however. Their past is formed in other various ways: *sleep–slept, ride–rode, swim–swam, is–was, are–were, go–went, catch–caught,* and so on. Because irregular verbs follow no consistent pattern, they must be memorized. Native speakers of English learn most irregular verb forms as they learn to talk, although some verbs like *lie–lay* (to recline) and *lie–laid* (to place) remain a lifelong mystery for many people.

## 3. Past Participle

I *have shouted*, you *have shouted*, they *have shouted*; Jack *has shouted*, it *has shouted*, and so on.

The past participle form of regular verbs presents no problem. Just add *have* or *has* to the past form of the verb. (The same applies when *had* is added.) When verbs are irregular, though, past participle forms follow no consistent pattern: *choose–have chosen, came–have come, swam–have swum, rose–have risen,* and many others.

For your reference, here is a list of the principal parts of the many frequently used irregular verbs:

| **LIST OF IRREGULAR VERBS** | | |
|---------|------|---------------------------|
| **Present** | **Past** | **Past participle** (Add *have, has,* or *had*) |
| awake | awoke | awakened |
| bear | bore | borne |
| beat | beat | beaten |
| begin | began | begun |
| bid (to command) | bade | bidden |
| bite | bit | bitten |
| break | broke | broken |
| bring | brought | brought |
| burn | burnt *or* burned | burnt *or* burned |
| burst | burst | burst |
| catch | caught | caught |

## LIST OF IRREGULAR VERBS

| Present | Past | Past participle (Add *have, has,* or *had*) |
|---|---|---|
| choose | chose | chosen |
| come | came | come |
| dive | dived *or* dove | dived |
| dream | dreamt *or* dreamed | dreamt *or* dreamed |
| drink | drank | drunk |
| drown | drowned | drowned |
| dwell | dwelt *or* dwelled | dwelt *or* dwelled |
| fight | fought | fought |
| flee | fled | fled |
| fling | flung | flung |
| freeze | froze | frozen |
| get | got | got *or* gotten |
| hang (a thing) | hung | hung |
| hang (a person) | hanged | hanged |
| lay | laid | laid |
| lead | led | led |
| lend | lent | lent |
| lie (to recline) | lay | lain |
| lie (to tell an untruth) | lied | lied |
| put | put | put |
| ring | rang | rung |
| rise | rose | risen |
| set | set | set |
| shine (intransitive) | shone | shone |
| shrink | shrank *or* shrunk | shrunk *or* shrunken |
| shut | shut | shut |
| sing | sang | sung |
| sink | sank | sunk |
| sit | sat | sat |
| slay | slew | slain |
| speak | spoke | spoken |
| spit | spit *or* spat | spit *or* spat |
| spring | sprang | sprung |
| sting | stung | stung |
| strive | strove *or* strived | striven *or* strived |
| swear | swore | sworn |
| swim | swam | swum |
| swing | swung | swung |
| tear | tore | torn |
| tread | trod | trod *or* trodden |
| wake | woke *or* waked | waked *or* woken |
| wear | wore | worn |
| write | wrote | written |

Usage questions on the SAT II ignore regular verbs, which are too easy for students on their way to college. Rather, they tests your knowledge of irregular verb forms, most of which you probably know without thinking.

The pilot was pleased when the flight attendant *brang* her a cup of coffee.

Because the past tense of *bring* is *brought*, the sentence contains a usage error.

Dave lit the fire after the sun *had rose*.

Because the past participle of *rise* is *risen*, the sentence contains a usage error.

PRACTICE EXERCISE IN VERB FORMS
Write the correct verb form in each of the following sentences. If in doubt, check the List of Irregular Verbs above.

1. eat  They haven't ___eaten___ out in months.

2. caught  The umpire said that Reggie had ___caught___ the ball before it touched the ground.

3. swim  They ___swam___ across the bay in less than an hour.

4. drink  All the soda had been ___drunk___ by the end of the dance.

5. go  Charlotte had already ___gone___ home by the time Peter arrived.

6. lay (to place)  After the burial, his widow ___laid___ a wreath on the gravesite.

7. shine  The sun ___shone___ all day.

8. shrink  When he put on the sweatshirt, he noticed that it had ___shrunk___.

9. sing  The four of them have already ___sung___ two songs.

10. slay  In the story the king was relieved when Theseus ___slain___ the Minotaur.

11. steal  They concluded that the computer had been ___stolen___ over the weekend.

12. strive  All summer the crew ___strived___ to finish the job in time.

13. wake  The sound of the smoke alarm had ___woken___ the whole family.

14. wear  By Sunday the visitor had ___worn___ out his welcome.

15. break  Dawn had just ___broken___, and the floor was cold under my feet.

16. dive  No sooner had the submarine ___dived___ than the destroyer appeared on the horizon.

17. creep  Last night the cat burglars ___creeped___ up the fire escape.

18. fling  After flunking the test, he ___flung___ his book out the window.

19. swear    Although they *swore* to
secrecy, someone leaked the
news to the press.
20. lead    John Wesley Powell *led*
his expedition down the Green
River in 1869.

*Answers on page 154.*

## The Subjunctive Mood

Technically, the subjunctive is not a separate verb form, but because verbs change when sentences are cast in the subjunctive mood, you should know the uses of the subjunctive.

The subjunctive expresses a condition contrary to fact and usually appears in clauses with *if*, *as if*, or *as though*. In almost every instance, the verb *was* is changed to *were*.

If I *were* (not *was*) rich, I'd buy myself a sailboat. (The sentence is contrary to fact because I am not rich.)

Hal ate the ice cream as though he *were* (not *was)* not on a diet. (This sentence is contrary to fact because Hal is on a diet.)

The subjunctive is also used to convey a sense of doubt.

If only the bus *were* (not *was*) to arrive on time, we might see the launch. (This sentence implies that the bus may not arrive on time.)

Finally, the subjunctive is used to make a recommendation, a request or a demand.

The speaker moved that the motion *be* (not *should be*) tabled.

The lawyer insisted that her client *be* (not *should be*) released on bail.

## VERB TENSE

Verbs describe action (or the lack of it), and by their tense, convey the relative time when an action occurred. Changing the tense of verbs involves changing verb endings and adding words and phrases— *has, have, will, should have, will have*—called *helping* or *auxiliary* verbs. Altogether, the English language offers a speaker or writer six different tenses with which to indicate the relative time that an action took place:

PRESENT:    I *eat* spaghetti every day.
PAST:    She *ate* spaghetti every day.
FUTURE:    Phil *will eat* spaghetti every day.
PRESENT PERFECT:    Monica *has eaten* spaghetti every day.
PAST PERFECT:    Rose *had eaten* spaghetti every day.
FUTURE PERFECT:    They all *will have eaten* spaghetti every day.

All the tenses also have a *progressive* form, created by adding *-ing*, so that you can say things like:

They *are swimming*. (present progressive)
She *was swimming*. (past progressive)
The dog *will be swimming*. (future progressive)
I *have been swimming*. (present perfect)
Charles *had been swimming*. (past perfect)
They *will have been swimming*. (future perfect)

Each of the tenses permits you to indicate time sequence very precisely. Someone not attuned to the different meaning that each tense conveys may say something like this:

When her little brother Johnny was born, Sarah was toilet trained for six months.

Perhaps the meaning of the sentence is clear enough, but if precision is important, the sentence should read:

When her little brother Johnny was born, Sarah *had been* toilet trained for six months.

The revised version, using the past perfect verb *had been*, indicates that the action (Sarah's toilet training) had taken place prior to Johnny's birth. The original sentence actually says that Johnny's birth and Sarah's toilet training took place at the same time—a physical impossibility, since potty training usually takes weeks or even months.

Notice also the difference in meaning between these two sentences:

There was a condo where the the park *was*.
There was a condo where the park *had been*.

Again, the meaning of the first sentence may be clear, but it says that the condo and the park were in the same place at the same time. The revised version more accurately conveys the meaning: The condo replaced the park.

These are subtle differences. Perhaps that's the reason why sentences containing verb tense errors are ordinarily included on usage tests like the SAT II. Such items help to separate students who use English precisely from those who don't.

Notice the distinctions in meaning in the following pairs of sentences:

1. a. Benny was in the army for two years. (Benny is no longer in the army.)

   b. Benny has been in the army for two years years. (Benny is still in the army.)

2. a. Dinner had been on the table for two hours. (Dinner is no longer on the table.)

   b. Dinner has been on the table for two hours. (Dinner is still on the table.)

3. a. A monument will be erected at the site of the battle when the general returns. (After the general gets back the monument will be built.)

   b. A monument will have been erected at the site of the battle when the general returns. (A monument will already have been built by the time the general gets back.)

4. a. She has had no luck in finding her daughter. (She is still trying to find her daughter.)

   b. She had no luck in finding her daughter. (In the past her search was futile, but whether she's still looking is uncertain.)

5. a. Jenny had driven a delivery truck on weekends. (Jenny used to drive a truck.)

   b. Jenny has been driving a delivery truck on weekends. (Jenny still drives a truck.)

On the SAT II you won't be asked to make such obvious distinctions in meaning. Rather, you will be asked to identify sentences, each containing more than one verb, in which the tense of the verbs is inconsistent. That is, the verb tense shifts improperly.

A.   SHIFT:   Because the day *was* (past tense) windy, many leaves *fall* (present tense) to the ground.

    CONSISTENT:   Because the day *was* (past tense) windy, many leaves *fell* (past tense) to the ground.

B.   SHIFT:   In *Night*, Elie Weisel *writes* (present) about the Holocaust and *described* (past) his experience in the death camps.

    CONSISTENT:   In *Night*, Elie Weisel *writes* (present) about the Holocaust and *describes* (present) his experience in the death camps.

Consistency doesn't mean that every verb in a sentence must be in the same tense. Far from it. Verb tenses merely indicate the relative time when events occurred.

C.   SHIFT:   Susie *had gone* (past perfect) to the movies and then *realize* (present) that she *forgot* (past) her wallet at home.

    CONSISTENT:   Susie *went* (past) to the movies and then *realized* (past) that she *had forgotten* (past perfect) her wallet at home.
    or Susie *had gone* (past perfect) to the movies and then *realized* (past) that she *had forgotten* (past perfect) her wallet at home.

Sentence C contains two different tenses because separate actions occurred at different times. Susie forgot her wallet *before* she left home. She realized only later that the wallet was missing. The changes in verb tense are proper because they indicate which action occurred first, which second, and so forth.

Knowing the differences in meaning conveyed by each tense will help you find verb tense errors on the SAT II. Sentences entirely in the simple present, past, or future tense offer no difficulties, but when sentences also contain perfect forms of a verb, you'll need to watch for inconsistencies.

1. Verbs in the *present tense* refer to actions currently in progress; verbs in the present perfect refer to actions occurring at no particular time in the past, actions which may or may not still be in progress.

Adam *has been* (present perfect) captain of the wrestling team for two years.

Affirmative action *has caused* (present perfect) controversy in college admissions offices.

All the bushes *have been transplanted* (present perfect).

2. Verbs in the *past tense* refer to actions completed in the past; verbs in the past perfect refer to actions completed prior to some specific time or moment in the past. The past perfect is needed to indicate which action occured first.

> When Oscar *called* (past), Dorothy *had* already *gone* (past perfect).
>
> Lenny *had killed* (past perfect) the rabbit before George *arrived* (past).

3. Verbs in the *future tense* refer to actions that will occur in the future; verbs in the future perfect tense refer to actions that will be completed at some time in the future but prior to some other future action or event.

> That precinct *will support* (future) the Democratic candidate.
>
> By the time Ellie gets to San Francisco, Dave *will have been gone* (future perfect) for two weeks.

Familiarity with the following conventions governing verb tenses will also help you identify usage errors on the SAT II:

1. A statement that is true is expressed in present tense regardless of the tense of other verbs in the sentence.

> Christmas *is* (present) on December 25.
>
> Sheila *had been taught* (past perfect) that triangles *contain* (present) 180 degrees.

2. In a complex sentence, the verb tense of the dependent clause must be in sequence with the tense of the main verb.

> They *had gone* (past perfect) out for six months before they *told* (past) their parents. (Because their going out preceded telling their parents, the past perfect tense—not the past tense—is needed to show the sequence of events.)
>
> Your teacher *believes* (present) that you *will do* (future) well on the SAT II.
>
> Henry *predicted* (past) that Jenny *will be* accepted by (future) Boston University.

3. In an *if* clause, don't use *would have* to express the earlier of two actions. Instead, use the past perfect.

> No: If Linda *would have driven* more slowly, she would have made the curve easily.

Yes: If Linda *had driven* (past perfect) more slowly, she would have made the curve easily.

No: The ceremony would have been better, if Kirk *would have been* the speaker.

Yes: The ceremony would have been better, if Kirk *had been* (past perfect) the speaker.

4. The tense of infinitives (verbs preceded by *to*, as in *to eat, to snow, to have eaten, to have snowed,* etc.) must be governed by the tense of the main verb and by the meaning of the sentence.

> Ellen *was* (main verb in past tense) happy *to accept* (present infinitive) the invitation. (The present infinitive is used because Ellen accepted the invitation after she felt happy about receiving it.)
>
> She *had hoped* (main verb in past perfect tense) *to attend* (present infinitive) the wedding with Barrett. (Again, the present infinitive is used because it refers to a time after the action described in the main verb.)

When the infinitive refers to a time before the action described in the main verb, the perfect infinitive form must be used.

> Ellen *is* (main verb) happy *to have accepted* (perfect infinitive form) the invitation.
>
> She *knows* (main verb) that not *to have been invited* (perfect infinitive form) is insulting.

5. Participles must be adjusted according to the tense of the main verb. (Many participles end in *-ing*.) When the participle describes an action occurring before the action of the main verb, add *having* and then adjust the participle.

ORIGINAL: *Working* (participle) hard on the essay, Joan hated to reduce the number of words. (Because Joan worked on the essay before cutting it, the participle needs to be changed.)

REVISION: *Having worked* hard on the essay, Joan hated to reduce the number of words.

ORIGINAL: *Walking* (participle) in the woods, Jan spotted a deer. (Because Jan was walking in the woods at the same time as she saw a deer, no change is needed.)

PRACTICE EXERCISE IN VERB TENSE

Most of these sentences contain an error in verb tense. Cross out the incorrect verb and write the correct one in the spaces provided. Some sentences contain no error.

1. They biked to the top of the mountain and then ~~come~~ back down in time to eat lunch.

   _Came_

2. The garage mechanic ~~thinks~~ that Mrs. Murphy ~~has brought~~ her car in last night.

   _thought    brought_

3. For anyone with enough brains to think about it, now ~~was~~ the time to work out the solution.

   _is_

4. Don told the class repeatedly that Kiev ~~was~~ the capital of Ukraine.

5. If the wagon train ~~would~~ have reached Salt Creek in time, the massacre would have been prevented.

   _had_

6. The aircraft controller expects to ~~have spotted~~ the plane on radar by noon.

   _spot_

7. The family already finished dinner when the doorbell rang.

   _had_

8. First he built a fire, then dragged a log over to use as a seat, and finally collected enough wood to burn all night.

9. Mindy broke the doll her aunt ~~gave~~ her for her last birthday.

   _had given_

10. Talking with Horatio, Hamlet began to suspect foul play in the kingdom.

11. When they drove to Vermont, they ~~had~~ stopped for lunch at Burger King.

12. The trooper ~~pulls~~ him over and gave him a speeding ticket.

   _pulled_

13. ~~Working~~ all year to improve her writing style, Debbie got a story published in the paper.

   _Having_

14. Matilda took an SAT course for six months before she learned how to solve that kind of problem.

   _had_

15. That night at the show we met many people we ~~saw~~ that afternoon.

   _had seen_

16. If I ~~was to have~~ a dream like that, I think I'd die!

   _were_

17. Reading _War and Peace_, I know that Pierre falls in love with Natasha.

   _Having read_

18. When the drought hit eastern Africa, the Somalis began to suffer.

19. ~~Thinking~~ long and hard about what to do, Ted decided to apply to the Naval Academy.

   _Having thought_

20. Greta does so well in her practice runs that she ~~had decided~~ to train for the New York Marathon.

   _has decided_

*Answers on page 154.*

## USE OF COMPARISONS

Because you are taking the time to read these words, you probably agree that it makes more sense to prepare for the SAT II than to take the test without preparation. Students who study for the test are far more likely to earn high score than students who don't. Most educators agree that a long-term study plan will pay off more handsomely than a cramming session the week before. But even a study blitz the night before is better than nothing.

Stop! Have you noticed something unusual about the opening paragraph of this section? Every sentence makes a comparison. The first three sentences use a common word order pattern for comparisons: *more . . . than.* The last sentence uses *better . . . than.* If you failed to notice that the first paragraph contains four comparisons, it's only because comparisons are common in writing and speaking. We make them all the time. All our stated preferences and choices are based on comparisons:

A is a better answer than B.

I'd rather have chicken than hamburger today, so I'll take some Kentucky Fried.

He thinks that the United States is a kinder, gentler nation than it was in the '60s.

Cancun is the best place to go for spring break.

Some sentences on the SAT II may test your understanding of the rules governing the use of comparisons. In addition to knowing about comparative degrees, you need know that standard English usage requires comparisons (1) to be complete, (2) to be stated in parallel form, and (3) to compare two things that may logically be compared. The SAT II is likely to give you sentences that ignore one or more of these requirements.

## 1. Comparative Degrees

Most comparisons are made by using different forms of adjectives or adverbs. The degree of comparison is indicated by the ending (usually *-er* and *-est*) or by the use of *more or most* (or *less* and *least*). The English language offers three degrees of comparison: *positive, comparative,* and *superlative.*

| Positive | Comparative | Superlative |
| --- | --- | --- |
| tall | taller | tallest |
| dark | darker | darkest |
| handsome | handsomer *or* more handsome | handsomest *or* most handsome |
| cool | cooler | coolest |
| graceful | more graceful | most graceful |
| able | abler *or* more able | ablest *or* most able |
| prepared | less prepared | least prepared |
| happily | more happily | most happily |
| soon | sooner | soonest |

The list shows that adjectives in the comparative degree are formed with the ending *-er* or by placing *more* (or *less*) in front of the positive form. Similarly, adjectives in the superlative degree are formed with the ending *-es* or by putting *most* or *least* in front of the positive form.

As always, however, some words deviate from the pattern:

| Positive | Comparative | Superlative |
| --- | --- | --- |
| good | better | best |
| well | better | best |
| bad | worse | worst |
| little | less | least |
| much | more | most |
| many | more | most |

In order to recognize errors in comparative degree on the SAT II, acquaint yourself with the pertinent guidelines:

a. To form the comparative and superlative degrees of one-syllable words, add *-er* or *-est* to the positive form (*brave, braver, bravest; late, later, latest*).

b. To form the comparative and superlative degrees of most two-syllable words, use *more* or *most*, or *less* or *least*, (*more famous, most nauseous, less skilful, least jagged*). Some two-syllable words follow the guidelines for words of one syllable (*pretty, prettier, prettiest*), although you wouldn't err by applying the rule for two-syllable words (*more pretty, most pretty*).

c. To form the comparative and superlative degree of three-syllable words and of all words ending in *-ly* , use *more* and *most*, or *less* and *least* (*beautiful, more beautiful, most beautiful; gladly, more gladly, most gladly*).

d.  Use the comparative degree to compare two things.

> This test was *harder* than that one. (Two tests are being compared)
>
> My *younger* sister takes dancing lessons. (The speaker has two sisters)

e.  Use the superlative degree to compare three or more things.

> This is the *hardest* test we've had all year. (They've had at least three tests)
>
> My *youngest* sister takes dancing lessons. (The speaker has at least three sisters)

f.  Never create a double comparison by putting words like *more*, *most*, *less*, and *least* in the same phrase with words in the comparative or superlative degrees. For example, avoid *more friendlier, less prouder, most sweetest, least safest*. Such usages are both ungrammatical and redundant. Instead, use adjectives and adverbs in the positive degree: *more friendly, less proud, more sweet, least safe*.

PRACTICE EXERCISE IN COMPARATIVE DEGREE
Find the errors in comparative degree in the following sentences. Write the correct usage in the spaces provided. Some sentences are correct.

1.  Ross is a lot more rich [richer] than his brother

_____

2.  Although both Stephen King and Tom Clancy write thrilling books, King is the best story teller. [better]

_____

3.  Because there were two topics to write on, Bill chose the easiest one. [easier]

_____

4.  This is by far the greater [greater] dinner than I have ever eaten.

_____

5.  Sarah is about the forgetfulest person I've ever met. [most forgetful]

_____

6.  *Hamlet* is performed the most often of any of Shakespeare's plays.

_____

7.  Jim couldn't tell who is most stubborn—his sister or his brother.

_____

8.  Both situations were terrible, but Ron first tried to fix the worst of the two.

_____

9.  The climbers would be smart to take the less harder route up to the summit.

_____

10.  After weighing the three fish he caught, Phil decided to throw the lightest one back.

_____

11.  Lynne's victory was more sweeter because her opponent had beaten her last year.

_____

12.  Bill's idea was profounder than Al's.

_____

13.  Both I-95 and the parkway will take you to New Haven, but the latter is the fastest route.

_____

14.  Because more policemen have been assigned to the beat, the people feel securer.

_____

15.  That was the most unkindest remark I ever heard.

_____

16.  Trust became a bigger issue than either taxes or crime in the election campaign.

_____

17.  It was obvious to everyone that Frankie's team was more superior to Johnny's.

_____

18. Because she felt unsure about her performance, the result was all the more nicer.

_____

19. Which is longest—the Mississippi River or the Colorado?

_____

20. In the autumn Vermont has the prettier colors than most other states.

_____

*Answers on page 154.*

## 2. Incomplete Comparisons

In everyday speech people give emphasis to their opinions by saying things like ''We had the best time,'' and ''That was the worst!'' Technically, these are incomplete comparisons and in standard English would probably have to be finished in some way.

> **We had the best time in Chicago** (compared to the time we had in New York and in Philadelphia.)
>
> **That was the worst accident** (compared to the others that have occurred at the same intersection.)

An incomplete comparison made colloquially may suffer no loss of meaning, but standard written usage calls for unmistakable clarity.

a. *Incomplete comparisons that cause ambiguity:* On the SAT II you may find sentences that lack all the words needed to make a comparison clear.

> INCOMPLETE: **Mark visited his aged aunt longer than Cathy.** (This could mean either that Mark spent a longer time with his aunt than Cathy did, or that Mark spent more time with his aunt than he spent with Cathy. To eliminate the ambiguity, simply complete the comparison.)
>
> COMPLETE: **Mark visited his aged aunt longer than Cathy did.**
>
> **Mark visited his aged aunt longer than he visited Cathy.**

Additional words are also needed to complete this comparison:

> INCOMPLETE: **Boys like marshmallows more than girls.** (This may mean that boys prefer marshmallows to girls—an unlikely proposition—

or that boys like marshmallows more than girls do.)

> COMPLETE: **Boys like marshmallows more than girls do.**

b. *Comparisons using ''as''*: A comparison using *as* usually requires a repetition of the word: *as* good *as* gold, *as* fast *as* a plane flies, *as* high a price *as* I've ever seen, and so on. In colloquial speech, however, the second *as* is often omitted.

> INCOMPLETE: **On the exam Nicole expects to do *as* well if not better than the first time.**
>
> COMPLETE: **On the exam Nicole expects to do *as* well *as*, if not better, than the first time.**

Stylistically, the complete version may sound somewhat stiff, but it follows standard usage, which is what the SAT II is all about.

c. *Comparing one thing to a group of which it is a part:* Standard usage calls for the use of *other* or *else* when making comparisons like these:

> INCOMPLETE: **Lieutenant Henry was braver than any pilot in the squadron.** (This suggests that Henry was not a member of the squadron. If he belonged to the squadron, however, add *other* to complete the comparison.)
>
> COMPLETE: **Lieutenant Henry was braver than any *other* pilot in the squadron.**
>
> INCOMPLETE: **Diana talks more nonsense than anyone in the class.** (This suggests that Diana is not a member of the class. If she is in the class, however, add *else* for complete accuracy.)
>
> COMPLETE: **Diana talks more nonsense than anyone *else* in the class.**

## 3. Parallelism in Comparisons

Use the same grammatical forms when comparing parallel ideas. Compare an idea expressed in a phrase, for example, with another idea also expressed in a phrase. Ideas in clauses should be compared to other ideas in clauses, and so forth.

> NOT PARALLEL: *To go skateboarding* **is no longer as popular as** *rollerblading*.

In this sentence, the popularity of skateboarding is compared to the popularity of rollerblading. The phrase *to go skateboarding* is a verbal. But *roller-blading* is a noun. Because two different grammatical forms are used, the comparison is not parallel.

> PARALLEL: *To go skateboarding* is no longer as popular as *to go rollerblading*. (The comparison, made with verbs, is in parallel form.)

> or PARALLEL: *Skateboarding* is no longer as popular as *rollerblading*. (The comparison, made with nouns, is in parallel form.)

> NOT PARALLEL: As a poet, Ogden Nash was admired more for his *humor* than for *what his poems had to say*. (*Humor* is a noun, *what his poems had to say* is a clause.)

> PARALLEL: As a poet, Ogden Nash was admired more for his *humor* than for his *ideas*.

## 4. Illogical Comparisons

Logic breaks down when two or more unlike things are compared.

> ILLOGICAL: Boston's *harbor* is reported to be more polluted than any *city* in the country. (This sentence is meant to compare pollution in the Boston harbor with pollution in the harbors of other cities, but it fails to achieve its goal. Instead, it illogically compares Boston's harbor with a city.)

> LOGICAL: Boston's *harbor* is reported to be more polluted than *the harbor of any other city* in the country.

> ILLOGICAL: Unlike most *cars* on the street, *Ellie* has her Toyota washed almost every week. (The sentence is intended to compare Ellie's car with the other cars on the street. But it manages only to compare Ellie to the other cars, an illogical comparison.)

> LOGICAL: Ellie's *Toyota*, unlike *most cars* on the street, is washed almost every week.

> ILLOGICAL: The accountant found that *business* was bad during the third quarter, just like *Tony*. (Instead of comparing the accountant's findings to Tony's findings, this sentence claims that both Tony and business were bad.)

> LOGICAL: Like *Tony*, the *accountant* found that business was bad during the third quarter.

PRACTICE EXERCISE IN COMPARISONS

Find the errors in comparison in the following sentences. Write a correct version of the sentence in the space provided. Some sentences may be correct.

1. Jane is more efficient than any member of the committee.

   _____

   _____

   _____

2. Adam looks more like his father than his brother. does

   _____

   _____

   _____

3. When I went to see *Streetcar*, I disliked Stanley as much as Mitch. did

   _____

   _____

   _____

4. Phil works faster than George on most jobs.

   _____

   _____

   _____

5. Oscar was as tired as if not more tired than Pete.

   _____

   _____

6. To do the research for my paper, I had to read do more reading more than telephoning.

   _____

   _____

   _____

7. Although she's younger, Lillian looks as old as if not older than Dorothy.

   _____

   _____

   _____

8. They talked more about Chekhov's stories than about his plays.

   _____

   _____

   _____

9. Allyn's canoe was destroyed in the rapids, just like his partner. was

_____

_____

_____

10. I read Fitzgerald's *The Great Gatsby*, an author I have come to love more than any other.

I love

_____

_____

_____

11. I am more interested in hiking than Peter.

_____

_____

_____

12. Biology is more popular than any science.

_____

_____

_____

13. It's been said that walking is better for you than to jog the same distance.

_____

_____

_____

14. The students respect Mr. Phillip's teaching style more than Mr. Green.

_____

_____

_____

15. His ears were bigger than Ross Perot.

_____

_____

_____

16. It took him longer to reach Trenton than Camden.

_____

_____

_____

17. Which is cheaper—flying to Washington or to take the train?

_____

_____

_____

18. The lawyer insisted that her job took more hours than a teacher.

_____

_____

_____

19. Wearing baseball caps is more popular now than Walkmans.

_____

_____

_____

20. Cindy has applied to as many colleges if not more than Joanne.

_____

_____

_____

*Answers on page 154.*

## DICTION

Diction simply means word choice. Faulty diction generally occurs when (1) a word is used that means something other than what is intended (e.g., *eminent* instead of *imminent, or sensory* in place of *sensual*, (2) an inappropriate word is used (e.g., a colloquial expression like *freaked out* or *you guys* in a formal context), or (3) a grammatically incorrect word is used (e.g., *good* instead of *well* after a certain verb, or *where* instead of *when*, as in "the time *where* he took the train").

The usage section of the SAT II tests your ability to recognize all three kinds of diction errors, but the vast majority will probably be the third kind, for which, among other things, you need to know particularly when to use an adjective and when to use an adverb.

# 1. Confused Words

The potential for writers to use one word when they mean another has no bounds. Some words are outright malapropisms—"the *crutch* of the problem" instead of "the *crux* of the problem"—words confused because they sound somewhat alike. But on the SAT II you're far more likely to be asked to distinguish between words with subtle shades of meaning and words that are frequently misused.

> A crowd of angry students *aggregated* outside the principal's office.

The meaning of this sentence is clear enough. The writer certainly intended to say that students congregated, or gathered together, outside the principal's office. Although the word *aggregated* means "collected," or "gathered together," in standard usage it ordinarily refers to inanimate material. Concrete, for instance, is an aggregate of sand, cement, and gravel. Therefore, using *aggregated* to refer to a group of people is an example of faulty diction.

> Except for Andy, the class was *disinterested* in listening to chamber music.

Again the meaning of the sentence is apparent. The word *disinterested* is used as a synonym for *uninterested*. In standard usage, however, *disinterested* really means "impartial or unbiased." A disinterested baseball fan, for example, might be fascinated by what happens at the ballpark, but doesn't care which team wins the game. Because *disinterested* has come to mean *uninterested* in colloquial usage, the two words are on the verge of being accepted as synonyms. In standard usage, however, *disinterested* may not be a substitute for *uninterested*.

Because the number of confused words stretches far and wide into the English language, it would be impracticable to list all of them here. Many obvious and frequently misused words appear on the list in Part IV, pages 203–206. Beyond those, you'll need to depend on your vocabulary and your sensitivity to the meanings of words to identify nonstandard usages on the SAT II. The following sentences illustrate the kinds of distinctions that you should be prepared to make:

### allusion/illusion/delusion

> The author of the story made an *allusion* to the three witches in *Macbeth*.

(allusion = a reference to)

> The colored lights created the *illusion* that the gym was a beautiful dance hall.

(illusion = an unreal or misleading image)

> Convinced that he was a reincarnation of the King of Spain, Tom lived in a *delusion*.

(delusion = false belief)

### alternate/alternative

> Because the road was under construction, they took an *alternate* route to Cairo.

(alternate = a substitute)

> Hitchhiking into town was an *alternative* that Harry hadn't considered.

(alternative = choice between two or more things or courses of action)

### appraise/apprise

> To accurately *appraise* the value of a house takes time and knowledge of the market.

(appraise = set a value on)

> When the ferry gets in, please *apprise* me of its new schedule.

(apprise = to advise, to inform)

### eminent/imminent

> Several *eminent* people marched in the parade.

(eminent = well-known, important)

> The darkening sky suggested that a thunderstorm was *imminent*.

(imminent = on the verge of happening)

### famous/infamous

> After he left prison, he became a *famous* surgeon.

(famous = well-known)

> He masterminded the *infamous* jewel heist at the Waldorf.

(infamous = well-known but for a negative reason; notorious)

### nauseated/nauseous

> After the bumpy ride, Susan felt *nauseated*.
>
> (nauseated = sick)
>
> The spoiled meat left a *nauseous* odor in the refrigerator.
>
> (nauseous = sickening, disgusting)

### regardless/irregardless

> They will go to work *regardless* (not *irregardless*) of the strike.
>
> (regardless = in spite of; irregardless = nonstandard synonym for regardless)

### sensory/sensuous/sensual

> Walking through that rose garden was a *sensory* delight.
>
> (sensory = pertaining to one or more of the five senses)
>
> A vase with a *sensuous* shape stood on the windowsill.
>
> (sensuous = gratifying to the senses)
>
> It was clearly a mistake to print that *sensual* advertisement in *My Weekly Reader*.
>
> (sensual = pertaining to the pleasures of the senses, especially fleshly pleasures)

### torturous/tortuous

> Running a mile was a *torturous* experience for Millie.
>
> (torturous = agonizing, painful)
>
> Meredith and Ellen followed a *tortuous* trail to the summit.
>
> (tortuous = winding, full of curves)

## 2. Inappropriate Word Choice

Standard usage usually dictates that sentences be consistent in their style and tone. Serious, formal writing demands formal diction, just as colloquial writing calls for more informal, everyday diction. The lines between colloquial and standard and between informal and formal usage are blurry and constantly in flux. On the SAT II you won't encounter words that provoke debate among linguists and grammarians. The problems you'll face will be clear and universally acknowledged violations of standard practice. For example, you may find a sentence in which a word or expression is out of place.

> Immediately before the swearing-in ceremony, the President and President-elect hung out with the Chief Justice on the inaugural platform.

High officials may *meet, talk, confer, joke,* and *laugh* together, but they don't *hang out*.

Although you should be aware of various forms of nonstandard diction, such as slang and the trendy words and expressions of everyday, informal speech— *bummer, cool, stoned, dissed,* and so on— you're not likely to be faced with such obvious violations of standard usage on the exam. Rather, you'll be given words and phrases that are used widely in colloquial, everyday speech and writing but have not earned a place in the formal speech and writing of most literate people.

> His thermometer is different than mine. Use *different from* rather than *different than*.
>
> Try and come to the rally. Use *try to* instead of *try and*.
>
> A lot of the buildings are run-down. Use *many* instead of *a lot*.
>
> Where is the pen *at*? Don't use *at* after *where*.

You may also find common words and phrases that are considered too colloquial (*O.K., guy, a lot*), redundant (*new beginning, repeat again, meet together*), illogical (*most unique, free gift*), and just plain improper (*anywheres, hisself*) to be considered standard usage.

## List of Diction Errors

No list of diction errors can ever be complete because any time someone speaks or writes, a new error may be born. The items on this list, however, are worth studying because they represent the usage mistakes that you're apt to encounter on the SAT II. In addition, they may heighten your awareness of faulty diction in the language you read and hear every day. Finally, knowing some usages to avoid may help you to improve your own writing.

### a lot/lots of

> COLLOQUIAL: Debbie likes her job *a lot*.
>
> STANDARD: Debbie likes her job *very much*.
>
> COLLOQUIAL: *Lots of* children watch cartoons on Saturday mornings.
>
> STANDARD: *Many* children watch cartoons on Saturday mornings.

## around/about

COLLOQUIAL:   The mail usually comes *around* noon.

(Avoid using *around* to designate time, distance, or any other quantity, as in *around five hours, around three miles, around a hundred books*, and so on. Rather, use *about*.)

STANDARD:   The mail usually comes at *about* noon.

## at

NONSTANDARD:   Where is the dictionary *at*? (Don't use *at* after *where*.)

STANDARD:   Where is the dictionary?

## badly

COLLOQUIAL:   The twins *badly* want tickets to the Grateful Dead concert.

(Use *badly* to mean *poorly*, or *of low quality*, not as a substitute for *very much*.)

STANDARD:   The twins *desperately* want tickets to the Grateful Dead concert.

## because (used after reason)

NONSTANDARD:   The *reason* for her back pain *is because* she has poor posture.

(Use *that* instead of *because*.)

STANDARD:   The *reason* for her back pain *is that* she has poor posture.

## being as/being that

NONSTANDARD:   *Being that* hurricanes are common, no one builds houses close to the water.

(*Being that* and *being as* should not be used in place of *because*.)

STANDARD:   *Because* hurricanes are common, no one builds houses close to the water.

## both alike

REDUNDANT:   The two brothers are *both alike* in appearance.

(Because *alike* implies a comparison, *both alike* is redundant.)

STANDARD:   The two brothers are *alike* in appearance.

## bring/take

NONSTANDARD:   On your way to town, *bring* this package to the post office.

(*Bring* and *take* may not be used interchangeably. When movement is away from the speaker, use *take*; when movement is toward the speaker, use *bring*.)

STANDARD:   On your way to town, *take* this package to the post office, and please *bring* me a receipt.

## bunch

COLLOQUIAL:   A *bunch* of girls drove off in a light blue mini-van.

(Use *bunch* for objects bound or growing together, like flowers and grapes, not for people.)

STANDARD:   A *group* of girls drove off in a light blue mini-van.

## cute, clever

COLLOQUIAL:   Mr. Martin proposed a *cute* idea for a Halloween celebration.

(*Cute* refers only to the look of things, like clothes and kittens; it is not a synonymn for *clever* or *ingenious*.)

STANDARD:   Mr. Martin proposed a *clever* idea for a Halloween celebration.

## different than/different from

COLLOQUIAL:   Rich people are *different than* you and me.

STANDARD:   Rich people are *different from* you and me.

## each other/one another

COLLOQUIAL:   At midnight, all the people on the bus wished *each other* a Happy New Year.

(*Each other* refers to two; *one another* refers to more than two.)

STANDARD:   At midnight, all the people on the bus wished *one another* a Happy New Year.

## else

REDUNDANT:   Don't sit under the apple tree with anyone *else* but me.

(In the phrases *anyone else* and *no one else*, *else* is unnecessary.)

STANDARD: Don't sit under the apple tree with *anyone* but me.

**flunk**

COLLOQUIAL: Did Marian *flunk* the quiz as badly as I did?

STANDARD: Did Marian *fail* the quiz as badly as I did?

**former/latter**

NONSTANDARD: After visiting Colby, Bates, and Bowdoin, Joey chose the *latter*.

(Both *latter* and *former* refer to two.)

STANDARD: After visiting Colby, Bates, and Bowdoin, Joey chose Bowdoin.

After visiting Bates and Bowdoin, Joey chose the *latter*.

After visiting Bowdoin and Colby, Joey chose the *former*.

**free gift**

REDUNDANT: Upon opening a bank account, customers will receive a *free gift*.

(Gifts, by definition, are free; otherwise they wouldn't be gifts.)

STANDARD: Upon opening a bank account, customers will receive a *gift*.

**funny**

COLLOQUIAL: Paul noticed a *funny* smell in the garage.

(*Funny* means humorous, not *strange* or *odd*.)

STANDARD: Paul noticed a *strange* smell in the garage.

**goes/went**

COLLOQUIAL: Then he *goes*, "Get out of the house, Helen!" Then she *went*, "Not until I've done the dishes."

(The verbs *to go* and *to say* in all their forms are not interchangeable in standard English.)

STANDARD: Then he *said*, "Get out of the house, Helen!"

Then she *said*, "No, not until I've done the dishes."

**graduate**

COLLOQUIAL: It took Vinny five years to *graduate* high school.

STANDARD: It took Vinny five years to *graduate from* high school.

**guy**

COLLOQUIAL: A *guy* on the train was singing at the top of his lungs.

STANDARD: A *man* (*person, passenger, commuter*) was singing at the top of his lungs.

**hisself/themself**

NONSTANDARD: At ten months, he could walk by *hisself*.

STANDARD: At ten months, he could walk by *himself*.

NONSTANDARD: Bodybuilders like to look at *themself* in the mirror.

STANDARD: Bodybuilders like to look at *themselves* in the mirror.

**in/into**

NONSTANDARD: Hal went *in* the store to buy a soda.

(Avoid using *in* when you mean *into*. *In* means "within," while *into* refers to the motion of going from outside to inside. For example, after you go *into* the kitchen, you are *in* the kitchen.)

STANDARD: Hal went *into* the store to buy a soda.

**is when/is where**

COLLOQUIAL: Snorkeling *is when* you swim under water with a mask and air tube.

(Don't use *is where* or *is when* in writing a definition.)

STANDARD: Snorkeling *is* swimming under water with a mask and air tube.

COLLOQUIAL: A fault in tennis *is where* the serve misses the box.

STANDARD: A fault in tennis *occurs when* the serve misses the box.

**kind of/ sort of**

COLLOQUIAL: Doug was *kind of* upset when he heard the news.

(Avoid using *kind of* and *sort of* when you mean *very, rather*, or *somewhat*.)

STANDARD: Doug was *somewhat* upset when he heard the news.

COLLOQUIAL: I heard a *sort of* loud crash in the backyard.

STANDARD:  I heard a *very* loud crash in the backyard.

## like/as

NONSTANDARD:  Adam plans to write a letter of complaint, just *like* Sandra does.

(In standard English, *like* is not an acceptable substitute for *as*, *as if*, or *as though*.)

STANDARD:  Adam plans to write a letter of complaint, just *as* Sandra does.

NONSTANDARD:  The cat meowed *like* it wanted to come in.

STANDARD:  The cat meowed *as though* it wanted to come in.

## like/maybe

COLLOQUIAL:  There were *like* twenty cars in the parking lot.

The suspect was *maybe* twenty years old.

(Avoid using *like* and *maybe* in making estimates. Use *approximately*, *perhaps,* or *about*.)

STANDARD:  There were *approximately* twenty cars in the parking lot.

The suspect was *about* twenty years old.

## mean

COLLOQUIAL:  Jill has never been *mean* to her little brother, although he's a brat.

STANDARD:  Jill has never been *cruel* to her little brother, although he's a brat.

## more preferable

REDUNDANT:  The city is a *more preferable* place to live.

(Because preferable already implies a comparison, *more preferable* is redundant.)

STANDARD:  The city is a *preferable* place to live.

## natural instinct

REDUNDANT:  All living creatures possess a *natural instinct* for survival.

(By definition, instincts are natural; therefore, *natural* is unnecessary. Also, because dead creatures don't have the survival instinct, *living creatures* is redundant, too.)

STANDARD:  All *creatures* possess an *instinct* for survival.

## out loud

COLLOQUIAL:  Norma heard her name called *out loud* in the middle of the church service.

STANDARD:  Norma heard her name called *aloud* in the middle of the church service.

## on account of

COLLOQUIAL:  *On account of* the snow, hardly anyone came to the meeting.

STANDARD:  *Because* of the snow, hardly anyone came to the meeting.

## plan ahead for the future

REDUNDANT:  The guidance department helps students *plan ahead for the future*.

(Since one cannot plan backwards, *ahead* is unnecessary.)

STANDARD:  The guidance department helps students *plan* for the future.

## plenty

COLLOQUIAL:  It must have been *plenty* cold because the pipes froze last night.

(In standard usage, *plenty* is not a synonym for *very*.)

STANDARD:  It must have been *very* cold because the pipes froze last night.

## reason is because . . .

COLLOQUIAL:  The *reason* for the delay *is because* of mechanical trouble.

STANDARD:  The *reason* for the delay is mechanical trouble. (See **because**.)

## right

COLLOQUIAL:  Just before the holidays, the stores are *right* crowded.

(In standard usage, *right* is not a synonym for *very*.)

STANDARD:  Just before the holidays, the stores are *very* crowded.

## so

COLLOQUIAL:  Nikita thought that Maria was hungry, *so* he brought her a donut.

(While not incorrect, the use of *so* as a synonym for *therefore* is extremely informal and borders on colloquial usage. Because inserting *therefore* in place of *so* will make the sentence a run-on, the sentence must be recast.)

STANDARD:  *Because* he thought that she was hungry, Nikita brought Maria a donut.

COLLOQUIAL:  The third problem is *so* hard.

(In standard usage, *so* should not be used as a synonym for *very*.)

STANDARD:  The third problem is *very* hard.

## spoken dialogue

REDUNDANT:  Neil Simon's plays are crammed with witty *spoken dialogue*.

(*Dialogue*, by definition, is *spoken*.)

STANDARD:  Neil Simon's plays are crammed with witty *dialogue*.

## try and/try to

COLLOQUIAL:  Please *try and* fix the leak in the faucet.

STANDARD:  Please *try to* fix the leak in the faucet.

## unique

ILLOGICAL:  This is the *most unique* painting in the museum.

(*Unique* literally means "one of a kind;" therefore *most unique*, a phrase that makes a comparison, is illogical.)

STANDARD:  This is the *most unusual* painting in the museum.

ILLOGICAL:  He has a *rather unique* job, painting the numbers on city buses.

(Because *unique* means "one of a kind," *rather unique* is illogical.)

STANDARD:  He has a *unique* job, painting the numbers on city buses.

## unexpected surprise

REDUNDANT:  Martha found an *unexpected surprise* on the doorstep.

(A *surprise*, by definition, must be *unexpected*.)

STANDARD:  Martha found a *surprise* on the doorstep.

## used to

NONSTANDARD:  Brian *use to* arrive late to class almost every day.

(The phrase *use to* is never correct. Use *used to*.)

STANDARD:  Brian *used to* arrive late to class almost every day.

## usual habit

REDUNDANT:  George's *usual habit* was to jog three miles daily.

(A *habit*, by definition, is something that is *usual*.)

STANDARD:  George's *habit* was to jog three miles daily.

## where/that

NONSTANDARD:  Duke noticed *where* the room needed a paint job.

(Avoid *where* as a substitute for *that*.)

STANDARD:  Duke noticed *that* the room needed a paint job.

## when/where

COLLOQUIAL:  An overture is *when* a short piece of music precedes an opera or show.

(Avoid using *when* and *where* in writing definitions.)

STANDARD:  An overture *is* a short piece of music that precedes an opera or show.

COLLOQUIAL:  The blitz was *where* the Germans bombed London during WW II.

STANDARD:  The blitz *was* the German bombing of London during WW II.

PRACTICE EXERCISE IN DICTION

Find nonstandard, colloquial, and redundant usages in the following sentences. Write the standard words or phrases in the spaces provided. Some sentences may be correct; some may contain more than one error.

1. A bunch of hay dropped off the truck on its way to Dover.

_____

2. Bruno flunked his driving test three times before he secured a license.

_____

3. Mrs. Grant felt plenty scared to go into that cave because of the snake.

_____

4. This plate is an exactly identical replica of those that Willie stored in the attic.

_____

5. At the reunion, a dozen people sat in a circle and told stories about each other.

_____

6. Susan left Washington at about noon and expects to arrive home around six.

_____

7. After Lee fell off the diving board, he goes, ''I'm not hurt. Believe me, I'm all right.

_____

8. That's just the sort of belt I'm looking for.

_____

9. The scratching on the door clearly indicated that the cat wanted in.

_____

10. As the recipient of the award, Jack graduated high school with strong emotional feelings about his teachers.

_____

11. No mail will be delivered on Friday on account of the holiday.

_____

12. After George stood up in the rowboat, Harry pushed him in the lake.

_____

13. Seeking revenge, George later pushed Harry off of the dock.

_____

14. That empty lot is where my grandmother's house use to be.

_____

15. A transliteration is when the text is translated word for word, irregardless of how it sounds.

_____

16. When the true facts come out, the case will be settled in an instant.

_____

17. Given the choice of Monday, Wednesday and Friday for her talk, Gwen chose the latter.

_____

18. All the mistakes in Brian's essay, make it seem as though he never learned the art of proof-reading.

_____

19. Because John plans to bring the newspaper home, you needn't bother.

_____

20. At the end of the evening there was no one else but me in the room.

_____

21. The coach waited on Calvin for half an hour before he told the bus driver to leave.

_____

22. Please be sure and clean up the mess you left after lunch.

_____

23. The reason she declined the invitation is because her mother was worried.

_____

24. Those uniforms are different than those worn last year.

_____

25. Up until her sixteenth birthday, Jen had never gone to the movies alone.

_____

*Answers on page 155.*

## 3. Choosing Between Adjectives and Adverbs

A common error in diction occurs when an adjective is used where an adverb is required. The reverse— using an adverb where an adjective belongs—also occurs, but less frequently. Either way, however, your preparation for the SAT II should include practice in putting adjectives and adverbs in their proper place.

To begin, try to identify errors in these three sentences:

(a) Children who are addicted to television often behave violent in the classroom.

(b) The sun blazed down steady from morning until night.

(c) I feel badly that Randy performed bad on the test.

If you recognized the error in each sentence, you're on the right track, and if you corrected the errors, you should have no trouble with similar items on the exam. Further, if you knew exactly why *violent* should be *violently* in sentence (a), why *steady* should be *steadily* in (b), and why *bad* and *badly* should exchange places in (c), you probably have a firm grasp of adjective and adverb usage. But if you didn't notice the errors, or if only your ear for language told you that something was amiss, the following discussion will be useful.

Many adverbs end in *-ly* (*violently, steadily, badly*), but so, unfortunately, do many adjectives (*friendly, lovely, elderly*). Also, several words are sometimes adjectives and sometimes adverbs, depending on how they are used in a sentence.

| Word | Used as Adverb | Used as Adjective |
|------|----------------|-------------------|
| fast | She runs *fast*. | She lives in the *fast* track. |
| straight | Go *straight* for a change. | Draw a *straight* line |
| late | They arrived *late*. | It's too *late* to go. |
| hard | She works *hard*. | Have some *hard* candy. |
| low | The branch hung *low*. | I hear a *low* hum in the engine. |
| slow | Go *slow* on that road. | He took a *slow* boat to China. |
| loud | Don't talk so *loud*. | A *loud* bang echoed in the room. |

While preparing for the SAT II, don't try to memorize which words are adverbs and which are adjectives. Instead, study the principles that govern their use.

### Adjectives

Adjectives are words that describe, or modify, nouns and pronouns.

*Good* is an adjective. Like any adjective it can be used to describe a noun, as in *good* apple, *good* book and *good* night. That's easy.

*Good*, along with some other adjectives, sometimes causes trouble when used after a verb. *Good* should not be used after most verbs, so avoid *talks good, drives good, writes good,* and so on.

*Good*, as well as other adjectives, however, may be used after some verbs (called *linking verbs*), *such as look, smell, taste, feel, appear, stay, seem, remain, grow, become*, and all forms of *to be*. Therefore, it's perfectly correct to say *sounds good, feels good*, and *is good*. (Notice that many, but not all, linking verbs refer to the senses.)

Sometimes linking verbs are used as active verbs. *Look*, for example, is a linking verb when referring to someone's health or to the appearance of things, as in *The day looks good for flying*. But it is an active verb when it refers to the act of looking, as in *Margie looked sadly at her sick dog*. If you're not sure whether a verb is used as a linking verb or as an active verb, substitute a form of the verb *to be* in its place. If the sentence retains its basic meaning, the verb may well be a linking verb. For example:

The juice *tastes* good. The juice *is* good.

She will *stay* asleep for a hundred years.

She will *be* asleep for a hundred years.

(Replacing the verb in question with a form of *to be* pretty well maintains the meaning of the sentence. Therefore, *tastes* and *stay* must be linking verbs and may be followed by any adjective you choose: *sour, sweet, tart, spoiled; happy, satisfied, cool, depressed*, and so on.)

### Adverbs

Adverbs, often identified by their *-ly* endings, usually describe, or modify, a verb, an adjective, or another adverb. Much of the time they supply answers to such questions as How? When? How much?

Where? In what sequence? To what extent? In what manner?

> How does Roger run? Roger runs *well.* (The adverb *well* modifies the verb *runs.*)
>
> How did the grass look? The grass looked *mostly* brown. (The adverb *mostly* modifies the adjective *brown.*)
>
> When should Mattie go to school? Mattie should go to school *now.* (The adverb *now* modifies the verb *go.*)
>
> How much did it rain last night? It rained *enough* to flood the cellar. (The adverb *enough* modifies the verb *rained.*)
>
> Where did Carole sit? Carole sat *down.* (The adverb *down* modifies the verb *sat.*)
>
> In what manner did Carole sit down? Carole sat down *quickly.* (The adverb *quickly* modifies the verb *sat.*)

On the SAT II, when you need to choose between an adjective or an adverb, follow this procedure: Find the verb and determine whether it is a linking verb. If it is, use the adjective. If it isn't, use the adverb. (More often than not, the verb is likely to be one of those which acts sometimes as an active verb.) Also, if the word modifies an adjective or another adverb, remember to use the adverb. If it modifies a noun or pronoun, use the adjective.

*Linking Verbs vs. Active Verbs.* Most mistakes involving adjective/adverb usage occur when no distinction is made between the linking verbs and active verbs being modified. The following review will help you to tell one from the other.

a. Use adverbs to modify active verbs

> The kite spun *crazily* in the air. (*Crazily* is an adverb; it explains how the kite spun; therefore, *crazily* modifies, or clarifies, the active verb *spun.*)

When the verb is clearly active, it may be followed only by an adverb, never by an adjective.

| NONSTANDARD: | Roger runs *good.* |
| STANDARD: | Roger runs *well.* |
| NONSTANDARD: | Margie looked *sad* at her sick dog. |
| STANDARD: | Margie looked *sadly* at her sick dog. |
| NONSTANDARD: | The police responded *quick* to the call. |
| STANDARD: | The police responded *quickly* to the call. |

b. Use adjectives to modify linking verbs

> Minestrone soup tastes *good.* (*Good* is an adjective; it describes the soup. You can tell that *tastes* is a linking verb because you can replace it with *is,* a form of *to be,* without appreciably changing the meaning of the sentence.)

If *tastes* were an active verb, the adverb *well* would be needed. To say that soup *tastes well* is nonsense, however. After all, soup gets tasted by people; it doesn't itself have the capacity to taste anything.

| NONSTANDARD: | Laurie felt *anxiously* prior to the interview. |
| STANDARD: | Laurie felt *anxious* prior to the interview. |
| NONSTANDARD: | Milk will stay *freshly* in the refrigerator. |
| STANDARD: | Milk will stay *fresh* in the refrigerator. |
| NONSTANDARD: | Rover smelled *badly* after swimming in the swamp. |
| STANDARD: | Rover smelled *bad* after swimming in the swamp. |

PRACTICE EXERCISE IN ADJECTIVE/ADVERB USE
Check each of these sentences for faulty use of adjectives and adverbs. Write the correct word in the spaces provided. Some sentences are correct.

1. The nurse felt bitterly that she had contracted AIDS from a patient.

   _____

2. There is simply no justification for the judge's ruling.

   _____

3. Meredith's bike is old, but it rides smoothly

   _____

4. The soprano sang the aria beautiful, in spite of her head cold.

   _____

5. The black Mercedes drove slow up the gravel driveway.

   _____

6. Castro looked down cynical on the people as-sembled in the plaza.

_____

7. Agnes played the part of the mother superficially.

_____

8. No other basketball team blends as smooth as the Lakers.

_____

9. Mark always feels good after a long run and a hot shower.

_____

10. Be sure the door is shut secure because it often swings open by itself.

_____

11. He walked down the hall completely oblivi-ously to the trail of papers he left behind.

_____

12. Tim and Maria spoke frankly about their prob-lem.

_____

13. The coach talked slow about the team's decline during the second half.

_____

14. The audience remained calmly, even when the hall began to fill rapidly with smoke.

_____

15. No problem; I can do both jobs easy.

_____

16. When the phone rang, he picked it up, optimisti-cally that it was Sheila calling.

_____

17. When they carried Terry off the the field, every-one thought he was hurt bad.

_____

18. John never feels shyly about reading his poems in public.

_____

19. Amy spoke sincere when she promised to repay the money.

_____

20. Jill looked mischievous at Jack as they secretly walked up the hill.

_____

*Answers on page 155.*

---

**Level 4 usage problems**

Errors of these kinds have appeared regularly, with one or two instances on each test.

Agreement of pronoun and antecedent, below
Pronoun reference, page 85
Parallel construction, page 89
English idiom, page 91

---

## AGREEMENT OF PRONOUN AND ANTECEDENT

Pronouns are convenient words that help to stream-line the language. As stand-ins for nouns, pronouns allow us to speak and write without repeating the same nouns over and over.

WITHOUT PRONOUNS: Amy saw that Amy's family's garbage was piling up. Amy decided to burn Amy's family's garbage in a steel drum behind Amy's family's house.

WITH PRONOUNS: Amy saw that *her* family's garbage was piling up. *She* decided to burn *it* in a steel drum behind *her* house.

Indefinite pronouns (*anyone, everybody*) some-times don't need antecedents, but others, often called personal pronouns, do. Antecedents are the word or words that would have to be repeated if the pronoun did not exist. In the example shown, the pronouns *her* and *she* refer to Amy. *Amy* is the antecedent of the pronouns *her* and *she*. The pronoun *it* refers to garbage. *Garbage* is the antecedent of the pronoun *it*.

On the SAT II, you may be asked to identify errors that occur when pronouns and antecedents fail to agree with each other in number, gender, and person.

## 1. Agreement in Number

If the antecedent is singular, the pronoun must be singular. If the antecedent is plural, the pronoun must be plural. Problems with this simple rule occur when antecedents are words like *everyone, anybody,* and *each*, words that sound plural but in standard usage are considered singular. In informal speech, on the other hand, this distinction is observed mostly by those for whom standard usage is habitual. Because you are being tested on your knowledge of standard English on the SAT II, you could do yourself a favor by making a deliberate effort to abide by the rules of standard English in your own conversation, regardless of how unnatural it may sound at first.

> INFORMAL:  Despite the evidence, *everybody* (singular) is sticking to *their* (plural) own side of the story.

> STANDARD:  Despite the evidence, *everybody* (singular) is sticking to *his* (singular) own side of the story.

> INFORMAL:  *Nobody* (singular) on the team thinks that *they* (plural) caused the defeat.

> STANDARD:  *Nobody* (singular) on the team thinks that *she* (singular) caused the defeat.

Errors often occur in sentences in which the following words and phrases serve as antecedents to pronouns: *each, either, neither,* the "ones" (*anyone, no one, everyone, someone*) and the "bodies" (*anybody, everybody, nobody, somebody*), and *a person*. With a few exceptions, these are singular words should be followed by singular pronouns.

> *Each* of the boys is too busy to think about writing *his* practice essay.

> *Neither* girl wants to be the first to deliver *her* speech.

> *Everybody* in the class is looking for *his* folder.

In general, the rules governing agreement in number between pronouns and antecedents resemble the rules for agreement between subject and verb, explained on pages 57–60.

a.  Singular antecedents joined by *or* or *nor* require singular pronouns.

> *John or Fred* will wave *his* arms to signal the start of the show.

> Neither *Ellie nor Sera* wanted to attend *her* graduation ceremony. (If the antecedents are of mixed sex—e.g., *Ellie or Fred* —the phrase *his* or *her* could be used, although good writers shun the phrase, preferring to alter the structure of the sentence in order to avoid using it.)

b.  Singular antecedents joined by *and* require plural pronouns.

> *Maryanne and her boyfriend* took *their* seats in the balcony.

c.  Plural antecedents joined by *and*, *or*, or *nor* require plural pronouns.

> The *cows and the horses* were put back in *their* stalls.

## 2. Agreement in Gender

If the antecedent is masculine, the pronoun must be masculine. If the antecedent is feminine, the pronoun must be feminine. And if the antecedent is neuter, the pronoun must also be neuter.

> MASCULINE:  *Mr. Griffen* found *his* car missing from the parking lot.

> FEMININE:  *Mrs. Arnold* donated *her* late husband's clothes to the poor.

> UNCERTAIN:  A *student* came to the office to report that *he* could not open *his* locker.

> *Everyone* in the room felt confident that *he* could easily pass the quiz.

> MIXED:  *Neither* John nor Mary brought *his* folder to the meeting.

> NEUTER:  The *school* is proud of *its* reading scores.

Notice that the masculine pronouns *he, him*, and *his* are used when the gender of the antecedent is either uncertain or mixed. Although masculine pronouns have long been preferred, the custom is slowly dying. In an era when sexual equivalence is a fact of life, the SAT II is not likely to compel you to accede to the preference for masculine pronouns, but you should know the custom anyway, and follow it if asked.

While the antecedent in the mixed sentence above agrees with the pronoun *him* in number (both are singular), it does not agree in gender. If such a construction were to appear on the SAT II (an unlikely prospect), consider it correct, however odd or sexist it may sound. Ideally, the writer should have recast the sentence:  John and Mary did not bring their folders to the meeting.

## 3. Agreement in Person; Shift in Pronoun Person

Pronouns are categorized by *person*:

First person pronouns: *I, we, me, us, my, mine, our, ours*

Second person pronouns: *you, your, yours*

Third person pronouns: *she, he, it, one, they, him, her, them, his, her, hers, its, their, theirs, ours*

Pronouns must be in the same person as their antecedents. Agreement in person is rarely a problem except when a switch from one person to another occurs in midsentence. Consistency is the key.

INCONSISTENT:    When *I* (first person) walk *my* (first person) dog in that neighborhood, *you* (second person) must follow a very strict leash law.

CONSISTENT:    When *you* (second person) walk *your* (second person) dog in that neighborhood, *you* (second person) must follow a very strict leash law.

The revised sentence could also have been rewritten in first person: When *I* walk *my* dog . . . *I* must follow . . . .

The need to be consistent applies also to the use of *indefinite* pronouns, that is pronouns of indeterminate specificity, such as *all, any, anyone, each, none, nothing, one, several, many,* and others. Indefinite pronouns are usually considered to be in the third person.

*Few* (third person) have ever served *their* (third person) country with the fervor of Lieutenant Green.

*Somebody* (third person) had *his* (third person) knapsack stolen last week.

INCONSISTENT:    *One* can't pass by the site of the group home without feeling that *you* did the right thing.

CONSISTENT:    *One* can't pass by the site of the group home without feeling that *he* did the right thing.

The revised sentence could also have been written in second person:

*You* can't pass . . . etc.

Or, if one had wished to be very formal, the *one . . . one* sequence might have been used:

*One* can't pass by the site of the group home without feeling that *one* did the right thing.

Again, on the SAT II, look for consistency between pronouns and antecedents.

PRACTICE IN EXERCISE IN PRONOUN AGREEMENT
Some of these sentences contain errors in agreement between pronoun and antecedent or shifts in pronoun person. Make corrections in the space provided. Some sentences are correct.

1.  The coach said that everyone on the football team will be required to get their physicals by the start of Tuesday's practice.

_____

2.  When a person is laid off a job, you collect unemployment.

_____

3.  During the debate, each of the candidates for President—Bush, Clinton, and Perot—made their followers proud.

_____

4.  Somebody on the girls' volleyball team left their jacket in the locker room.

_____

5. If you are prepared to deliver the speech to the class, one [your] can expect to take your turn on Monday.

_____

6. All of his relatives have their own condos.

_____

7. Not one of us likes to have their [his] leg pulled.

_____

8. The trees were wearing its [their] fall colors.

_____

9. I have a good time at parties because you [I] get so much to eat.

_____

10. Neither Mary nor Joanne has told their [her] mother the truth.

_____

11. If you want to get better at the piano, one [you] really needs to practice.

_____

12. All those who want to go on the trip must bring your [their] money tomorrow.

_____

13. The library is again displaying their [its] collection of rare books.

_____

14. In that class, our teacher held conferences with us once a week.

_____

15. I find that I have to play every day in order to keep yourself [myself] in shape.

_____

*Answers on page 155.*

## PRONOUN REFERENCE

Pronouns sometimes lead unwary writers into problems of clarity. Sentences in which a pronoun fails to refer directly to an antecedent, often called a *faulty reference*, may cause confusion and may, in fact, convey a meaning that contradicts what the writer actually intended. Faults usually occur when the reference is either (1) ambiguous, or (2) implied.

### 1. Ambiguous References

Some references are ambiguous because the pronoun could refer to one or more antecedents.

> The teacher told the student that it was *her* responsiblity to hand out the books.

Who is responsible? The teacher or the student? Because the pronoun *her* may refer to either the teacher or the student, the sentence needs to be rewritten:

> The teacher told the student that one of her responsibilities as teacher was to hand out books.

A sentence containing two or more pronouns with ambiguous references can be particularly troublesome and unclear:

> Mike became a good friend of Mark's after *he* helped *him* repair *his* car.

Whose car needed fixing? Who helped whom? To answer these questions, the sentence needs to be rewritten:

> Mike and Mark became good friends after Mark helped Mike repair *his* car.

This version is better, but it's still uncertain who owned the car. One way to set the meaning straight is to use more than one sentence:

> When Mark's car needed repairs, Mike helped him do the job. After that, Mike and Mark became good friends.

One common way to revise a sentence containing an ambiguous pronoun reference is to replace the pronoun with a noun. If that proves to be stylistically awkward, the sentence may need a thorough overhaul. In the usage section of the SAT II, however, all you need to do is recognize the problem.

> AMBIGUOUS:   Arnie showed his brother Ken a copy of a photo *he* had taken.

(Who took the picture?)

> CLEAR:   Arnie showed a copy of a photo he had taken to his brother Ken.

> AMBIGUOUS:   When Dave phoned his father, *he* wasn't feeling well.

(Who felt ill?)

> CLEAR:   Dave felt ill when he phoned his father.

> AMBIGUOUS:   Marie told her mother that *she* was working too hard.

(Who was working too hard?)

> CLEAR:   Marie said to her mother, "I'm working too hard."

On the SAT II, be vigilant any time you come across a pronoun. Check carefully to see that it refers directly and clearly to a specific noun or another pronoun. If it doesn't, you may have located a pronoun reference error.

## 2. Implied Reference

An implied reference occurs when the idea to which the pronoun refers is not actually stated. Rather, it is suggested by the sentence or inferred by the reader. Errors of this kind frequently involve the pronouns *it, they,* and *you* and the relative pronouns *which, that,* and *this.*

In everyday speech, pronouns are used freely, despite imprecise references:

> On the news last night, *they* said that unemployment is down again.

Both the speaker and the listener know that *they* refers to the newscaster. The message is clear. In standard English, though, a pronoun needs a more definite antecedent or the pronoun needs to be replaced with a noun:

> On the news last night, *Peter Jennings* said that unemployment is down again.

Pronouns are often mistakenly used to refer to a possessive.

> In Ken Kesey's novel *One Flew Over the Cuckoo's Nest, he* describes life in a mental ward.

The pronoun *he* obviously refers to Kesey, but the word Kesey does not appear in the sentence, and Kesey's, a possessive noun, is not an viable substitute. Therefore, the sentence must be rewritten.

> In the novel *One Flew Over the Cuckoo's Nest,* the author, Ken Kesey, describes life in a mental ward.

Here are more sentences that illustrate the use of pronouns without definite antecedents:

> INDEFINITE:   In my school, *you* may leave the building when you are not in class.

> STANDARD:   In my school, students may leave the building when they are not in class.

> INDEFINITE:   The skinheads' behavior is unlawful, since *they* beat up foreigners almost at will.

> STANDARD:   Skinheads behave unlawfully, since they beat up foreigners almost at will.

> INDEFINITE:   During the intermission, *they* sold cookies and soft drinks.

> STANDARD:   During the intermission, the club members sold cookies and soft drinks.

In standard usage, the pronoun *it* may sometimes be used without a definite antecedent. It is perfectly acceptable, for instance, to use *it* as it appears at the beginning of the sentence you are now reading. It also may be employed in such expressions as *it's going to snow, it says here, it seems that, it is morning,* and others. On the SAT II, however, you should be as wary of *it* as you are of all other pronouns.

> IMPLIED:   On the front page, *it* says that a UFO was sighted in Ohio.

(What is *it*? No doubt the front page, but a proper antecedent may not be part of a prepositional phrase.)

> CLEAR:   The front page of the newspaper says that a UFO was sighted in Ohio.

> IMPLIED:   Pugachev was a Robin Hood figure who stole from the rich and gave *it* to the poor.

(Certainly *it* refers to money, jewelry, and other booty, but the antecedent is not stated.)

CLEAR:  Pugachev was a Robin Hood figure who stole money from the rich and gave *it* to the poor.

IMPLIED:  A good listener needs to be patient, and Frank does not have *it.*

(*It* probably means ''patience,'' but the word is only implied; the verbal, *to be patient*, may not serve as an antecedent.)

CLEAR:  A good listener needs patience, a quality that Frank lacks.

A problem with the relative pronouns *which, that*, and *this* arises when writers try to establish a tie between the pronoun and several items in a series

At Thanksgiving our family eats a big turkey dinner, then views a tape of last year's celebration, and finally, sings songs around the piano, *which* makes Thanksgiving my favorite holiday. (One might wonder precisely what makes the holiday special. Is it the turkey? The video? The singing? The writer is probably implying that the spirit of family togetherness makes Thanksgiving his favorite holiday, but family unity is never stated. Therefore, the pronoun *which* lacks a specific antecedent.)

In like manner, watch for relative pronouns that are improperly used to refer to rather general or ambiguous ideas instead of to specific nouns and pronouns.

Homeless people accuse the mayor of indifference to their plight, *which* has been disproved. (What has been disproved? That an accusation was leveled at the mayor? That the mayor is indifferent? The intended meaning is unclear because *which* has no distinct antecedent.)

A good doctor must be considerate and supportive, but *that* is not Jones's forte. (The antecedent of *that* is only implied. A more specific antecedent would make the sentence clearer.)

IMPLIED:  Some students prefer Hemingway to *The Hobbit, which* makes for more interesting class discussions.

CLEAR:  Some students' preference for Hemingway over *The Hobbit* makes for more interesting class discussions.

IMPLIED:  The girls arrived unprepared for a long hike, *which* Ted thought was unacceptable.

CLEAR:  Ted thought it was unacceptable for the girls to arrive unprepared for a long hike.

IMPLIED:  He didn't mean to be disrespectful, but *this* did not improve the situation.

CLEAR:  Although his disrespect was unintentional, the situation did not improve.

Occasionally, a pronoun refers to an antecedent too far removed in the sentence to make the relationship clear, and at other times a pronoun may appear to refer to the wrong antecedent.

MISPLACED:  Harry wore his new hat to the park, *which* is blue and has a big white "C" on the front.

CLEAR:  Harry came to the park wearing his new blue hat with a big white "C" on the front.

MISPLACED:  When I wanted to put the blanket away in the closet, *its* door was stuck.

CLEAR:  When I wanted to put the blanket away, I found the closet door stuck.

Because sentences containing misplaced pronouns are so obviously faulty, it is improbable that you'll find any on the SAT II, but you never can be certain.

PRACTICE EXERCISE IN PRONOUN REFERENCE
Some of the sentences that follow contain faulty pronoun references. Write the offending pronoun in the space provided. Some sentences are correct.

1. Mrs. Parker loves to knit and spends most of her time doing it.

_____

2. I answered the test questions, collected my pencils and pens, and handed them in.

_____

3. Peg told Harvey that she wanted only a short wedding trip to Bermuda, which lies at the root of their problem.

   _____

4. In San Francisco they have many wonderful restaurants.

   _____

5. If the chairs are arranged in a circle, it will be more effective.

   _____

6. His father let him know that he had only an hour to get to the airport.

   _____

7. In the paper it says who won the swim meet.

   _____

8. During Bush's admininstration, he sent troops to fight in the Persian Gulf.

   _____

9. In some states you can get a driver's license at age 15.

   _____

10. Henry, an ambulance driver, disapproves of war, but drives it to the front lines.

    _____

11. In Fitzgerald's *The Great Gatsby*, he writes about the American Dream.

    _____

12. When teenagers loiter outside the theater on Friday night, they give you a hard time.

    _____

13. In the early '80s, they hadn't even heard of AIDS.

    _____

14. Its economy is in disarray, but Russia will weather the crisis.

    _____

15. His father had taught him how to survive in the woods, which saved his life.

    _____

16. She's written a great deal of fiction, but she has never shown them to anyone.

    _____

17. Karen smokes a pack a day, drives like a maniac, and never does her schoolwork, which makes her father very angry.

    _____

18. The Cossacks' attitude toward women is hostile, since they believe that women are like their personal slaves.

    _____

19. Sharon loves to ski and believes it to be the king of all sports.

    _____

20. After the interview, Mike told Tom that he thought Dartmouth was a good place to spend four years.

    _____

21. Frankie has been interested in playing major league baseball, and he aspires to be one someday.

    _____

22. If they won't sell anymore tickets, it means that they are sold out.

    _____

23. Sara is studying social work in college and would like to become one when she graduates next year.

    _____

24. During a summer in Newport, Rob spent every day on the water, which is at the root of his interest in going to Annapolis.

25. If someone buys an old used car, he had better be prepared to pay for repairs.

*Answers on page 155.*

## PARALLEL CONSTRUCTION

Imagine driving along a road when all of a sudden the parallel lines between the lanes start to spread, then converge, overlap and turn into zigs and zags. Confusing, right? And dangerous, too. While it's not quite as perilous for phrases and clauses to lack parallelism, like the road, a sentence containing unbalanced ideas may be in need of repair. Orderly construction in a sentence keeps the arrangement of parallel ideas set side by side in the same grammatical form. For example, a sentence describing the contents of a school locker might read this way:

The locker held a down jacket, sweat pants, three sneakers, two left-handed gloves, an unused lunch, a broken ski pole, a hockey puck, six used tissues, a cheap camera, and a hiking boot.

Every item on this inventory is the name of an object, each expressed in essentially the same grammatical form—a noun preceded by one or two adjectives. No problem. When the owner of the locker wrote a list of favorite pastimes, however, the sentence lost its balance.

The contents of my locker reveal that I like skiing, hiking, to take pictures, and running.

The message is clear, but the phrase ''to take pictures'' is out of sync with the other items on the list. It is not parallel to the *-ing* words on the list. To bring all the items into line, the sentence needs revision.

I like skiing, hiking, taking pictures, and running. (All the items are stated as nouns—more specifically

as gerunds, nouns that sound like verbs because of their *-ing* endings.)

Alternatively, the sentence might have been constructed with verbs in parallel form:

I like to ski, hike, take pictures, and run.

To identify faulty parallelism on the SAT II, you need to know the features of parallel construction:

1. Parallel ideas in a series should be expressed in the same grammatical form. Each idea should be equally important to the meaning and structure of the sentence. Parallel ideas are frequently joined by the conjunctions *and, but, for, or, yet, so* or *nor*.

Her parents objected *to the loud music she played* and *to the late hours she kept.* (The parallel ideas are grammatically identical. Both are prepositional phrases, *to the loud music,* and *to the late hours,* followed by a pronoun, *she,* and past tense of a verb, *played* and *kept.*)

After graduation she promised *to turn the volume down* and *to come home earlier.* (The coordinated ideas consist of infinitive forms of verbs, *to turn, to come,* followed by a noun, *volume* and *home,* and an adverb, *down* and *earlier.*)

2. When used to compare or contrast, parallel ideas should be grammatical equivalents.

*Going out* to eat no longer thrills me as much as *to cook* at home. (The gerund *going out* should not be paired with the infinitive *to cook* )

*Going out* to eat no longer thrills me as much as *cooking* at home.

They are worried more *about public opinion* than for *what the effect of the proposal may be.*

(The prepositional phrase *about public opinion* should not be paired with the clause *what the effect of the proposal may be.*)

They are worried more *about public opinion* than *about the effect of the proposal.*

3. Parallel ideas are often expressed with pairs of words like *either/or, neither/nor, whether/or, both/and,* and *not only/but also.* Such pairs signal the presence of parallel construction in a sentence. Usage errors occur when one or the other of the pair is situated too far from the parallel ideas.

I *either* plan to invite my aunt *or* my uncle to go with me to the movies. (The signal word *either* is too far removed from the parallel phrases, *my aunt* and *my uncle*. Its placement misleads the reader into thinking that the verb *plan* is one of the parallel ideas. The sentence needs to be revised.)

I plan to invite *either* my aunt *or* my uncle to go with me to the movies.

Signal words need to be placed where they clearly distinguish parallel ideas.

> POOR:    Alice *both* started on the basketball and the volleyball teams.
>
> PROPER:  Alice started on *both* the basketball and the volleyball teams.

4.  When articles, prepositions, and conjunctions appear before the first in a series of parallel words, they may have to be repeated before the others in the series as well.

Our mechanic did a better job on my car than his.

(It's unclear whether two mechanics worked on the same car or one mechanic worked on two cars. To clear up the confusion, the preposition *on* should be repeated.)

Our mechanic did a better job *on* my car than *on* his.

Sometimes repeating an article is necessary.

Before accepting the offer, Dick spoke with the president and treasurer of the company. (It's unclear whether Dick spoke with two people or with one person holding two jobs. Repeating *the* clarifies the meaning.)

Before accepting the offer, Dick spoke with *the* president and *the* treasurer of the company.

5.  Parallel ideas should be logical equivalents.

Jim is six-feet tall, kind, and a New Yorker. (Physical features, personality traits, and place of residence are not logically coordinated ideas.)

Jim, a six-foot tall New Yorker, is kind. (Still not terribly logical, this sentence at least emphasizes only one of Jim's qualities—his kindness.)

On Wednesday, Marge not only ate a peanut butter sandwich but got married.

(This sentence is grammatically perfect, but unless its purpose is to get a laugh, it flies in the face of logic.)

Rumors to the contrary, peanut butter sandwiches and marriage are not equivalents.)

Before getting married on Wednesday, Marge ate a peanut butter sandwich.

*or* On Wednesday, after eating a peanut butter sandwich, Marge got married.  (Subordinating one of the ideas restores the logic, however bizarre.)

PRACTICE EXERCISE IN PARALLEL CONSTRUCTION
Look for flaws in parallel construction in the sentences below. Write a corrected version of the offending word or phrase in the space provided. Some sentences may be correct.

1.  Mrs. Taylor is interesting, humorous, and inspires her classes to do better.
    _inspirational_____

2.  The announcer not only was accused of being a bigot but too stupid to continue working at the station. _of being_
    _____

3.  Since Jenny started taking AP Math, she has worked harder and fewer parties.
    _gone to_____

4.  Her job consisted mostly of writing and typing letters, reports and various types of telephone calls. _preparing_  _answering_  _a_
    _____

5.  Mike likes to go to bed early and getting up _to get_ early to do his work.
    _____

6.  My cat Sylvia was short-haired, affectionate, intelligent, and disappeared for days at a time.
    _____had a habit of disappearing_

7.  Maddie hasn't yet decided whether to be an art historian or commercial art. _a_  _artist_
    _____

8.  The audience at the graduation ceremony ~~both~~ felt _both_ pride and satisfaction when the announcement was made.
    _____

9. The policeman walked into the courtyard, got caught in a crossfire, and was shot in the chest.

_____

10. Either way, Nat expects to move to the country because he loves nature and live simply because he doesn't have much money. *plans to*

_____

11. The kids had not only scattered their books all over the bus but also the sidewalk. *all over*

_____

12. His ideal house would be in a good location, with land around it, and with a view. *have* *have a...*

_____

13. Joan's pencil was broken, yellow, and came from this box. *pencil*

_____

14. His training in design would help him to know how to furnish the house simply and decorating would be simple, too. *house simply*

_____

15. The landlady told him that he could not have a hotplate in his room and showers after 11:00 o'clock. *neither* *not take*

_____

16. On the other hand, hearing no car horns and buses and to be miles from friends may cause him to be bored and restless. *being*

_____

17. Either the mouse will find a quick way into the attic or will gnaw at the siding for days. *either*

_____

18. City living is exciting, convenient, and provides plenty of entertainment. *entertaining*

_____

19. Maybe after he wins the lottery, he'll have an apartment in town, a house in the country, and find a job in the suburbs.

_____

20. I feel that Adam has the ability to win his match, he'll defeat Tommy in the sectionals, and he'll emerge eventually as the best wrestler in the state.

_____

*Answers on page 156.*

## ENGLISH IDIOM

Idiom, like diction, discussed earlier (pages 72–78), is related to word choice. An idiom is a group of words or an expression peculiar to the language that cannot be explained logically or grammatically. It exists as a custom of usage known to all who use the standard tongue. Most native speakers of the language have learned idioms as naturally as they learned to walk.

The hikers decided to walk *to* the mountain.
The hikers arrived *at* the mountain.
The hikers camped *on* the mountain.

Any native speaker of English knows the differences in meaning conveyed by the prepositional phrases *to the mountain, at the mountain*, and *on the mountain*. For someone just learning to speak English, however, "arrive *to* the mountain" would make perfect sense. After all, since one goes *to* the store, *to* the subway and *to* the beach, why not arrive *to* the mountain as well? The answer is plain: it's not idiomatic English.

Actually, the English language is filled with words, expressions, and phrases that defy rational explanation but are still considered standard usage. We say "three-*foot* ruler" when we mean "three-*feet*." A building "burns *down*," a piece of paper "burns *up*," and stew in a pot just "burns." Both *flammable* and *inflammable* mean the same thing—easily set on fire. Why these and many other such quirks exist is anyone's guess. We accept them without question because they are simply part of our language.

On the SAT II you may find sentences containing faulty idiom. To identify errors in idiom you must follow your instincts and your ear for the language. There are no specific guidelines to help you untangle problems in idiom. An awkward sounding word or phrase may be the most telling clue to the presence of faulty idiom.

> The First Amendment is invoked *in those times* when journalists are asked to disclose their sources. (The phrase *in those times* is awkward. Replace *in* with at, which often refers to time—*at* four o'clock, *at* the turn of the century—or, better, delete the phrase altogether.)

> The First Amendment is invoked when journalists are asked to disclose their sources. (This revised sentence is not only more graceful but more economical than the original.)

> A knight was faithful to his king, to his church, and to his lady, and he would gladly die in the name of them. (The phrase *in the name of them* is grammatical but awkward.)

> A knight was faithful to his king, to his church, and to his lady, and he would gladly die in their name.

Each error in English idiom is unique. Although many errors involve the faulty use of prepositions, you may just as easily find liberties taken with verbs, adverbs or any other part of speech. Faulty idiom may distort a common English expression or be a colloquial usage that a writer has tried to pass off as standard.

| | |
|---|---|
| FAULTY: | My parents are not exactly strict *in* when I should be home on Saturday night. (Faulty use of preposition) |
| STANDARD: | My parents are not exactly strict *about* when I should be home on Saturday night. |
| FAULTY: | *In appreciation about* her service to the shelter, she was given the Volunteer-of-the-Month Award. (Incorrect use of idiomatic phrase) |
| STANDARD: | *In appreciation of* her service to the shelter, she was given the Volunteer-of-the-Month Award. |
| FAULTY: | There was no opposition *in regards* to the showing of the "R" rated film. (Incorrect use of idiomatic phrase) |
| STANDARD: | There was no opposition *with regard* to the showing of the "R" rated film. |

| | |
|---|---|
| FAULTY: | Phil and George are ready for *working* at a moment's notice. (Faulty use of verb) |
| STANDARD: | Phil and George are ready *to work* at a moment's notice. |
| FAULTY: | The story is *filled up* with allusions to Norse mythology. (Unnecessary preposition added to verb) |
| STANDARD: | The story is *filled* with allusions to Norse mythology. |
| COLLOQUIAL: | Susan can't help *but think* that she lost her purse at the bus station. (Grammatically correct, but nonstandard. On the SAT II, therefore, this would be an example of faulty idiom.) |
| STANDARD: | Susan can't help *thinking* that she lost her purse at the bus station. |
| COLLOQUIAL: | When last seen, the man carried *a kind of a* knapsack. (Colloquially acceptable, but a nonstandard usage.) |
| STANDARD: | When last seen, the man carried *a kind of* knapsack. |

PRACTICE EXERCISE IN ENGLISH IDIOM

Identify the errors in English idiom in the following sentences. Write revised versions in the spaces provided. Some sentences may contain no error.

1. It was an honor to die at battle for their religion.

   _____

   _____

   _____

2. After the ceremony, the newlyweds ascended up the stairs.

   _____

   _____

   _____

3. I hope that the admissions office will comply to my request for an extension.

   _____

   _____

   _____

4. Unless the call comes soon, we will lose out on a lucrative business venture.

_____

_____

_____

5. When she returned, it felt as though she'd never been away.

_____

_____

_____

6. Please type up your paper and submit it tomorrow.

_____

_____

_____

7. For the first time, Rita felt independent from her 9 to 5 schedule.

_____

_____

_____

8. The posse went in pursuit after the horse thieves.

_____

_____

_____

9. As a child he had a great interest for dinosaurs and other prehistoric creatures.

_____

_____

_____

10. The two teachers walked down the corridor arguing against each other about the plan.

_____

_____

_____

11. When they looked closely at the wreck, they couldn't help to see that the car was traveling too fast.

_____

_____

_____

12. Mary doubts if she'll continue to run the carnival next year.

_____

_____

_____

13. The fugitive was capable to do anything to avoid capture.

_____

_____

_____

14. Among other things, the Bill of Rights guarantees freedom from religion and the press.

_____

_____

_____

15. He was the type of a student who said little in class but wrote long papers.

_____

_____

_____

16. No new plans were developed in respect to the environment.

_____

_____

_____

17. The two agencies must cooperate in cases where interstate commerce is concerned.

_____

_____

_____

18. Columbus sailed west in search for a way to the Indies.

_____

_____

_____

19. The soldier could not endure that kind of a pain without passing out.

_____

_____

_____

20. The children are waiting on the bus to arrive.

_____

_____

_____

*Answers on page 156.*

---

**Level 3 usage problems**

Sentences containing these errors have appeared on most previous tests.

Pronoun choice, below.
Modifiers, page 97
Double negatives, page 99

---

## PRONOUN CHOICE

Eleven common English pronouns—*I, me, he, she, him, her, they, them, we, us* and *you*—cause more confusion than almost any other words in the language. Most of the time you can probably depend on your ear to tell you what's right and what's wrong. For example, you'd never say, "Let I off!" to the bus driver. But sometimes you can't rely on the sound of a sentence. Then it helps to know that those eleven troublesome pronouns fall into two groups:

| Group 1 | Group 2 |
|---------|---------|
| I | me |
| he | him |
| she | her |
| they | them |
| we | us |
| you | you |

In grammatical terms, the pronouns in the first group are in the *nominative case;* pronouns in the second group are in the *objective case.*

Remember that you mustn't mix pronouns from different cases in the same phrase. You may not, for example, use such pairs as *she and them* or *they and us.*

Any time you need a pair of pronouns and you know that one of them is correct, you can easily pick the other from the same group. If you don't know either pronoun, though, substitute *I* or *me* for one of

the pronouns. If *I* seems to fit, you're in Group 1; if *me* fits better, use Group 2.

Elvis asked that (*he, him* ) and (*she, her*) practice handstands.

Insert *me* in place of one of the pronouns. That will give you:

Elvis asked that *me* practice handstands.

Since nobody would say that seriously, *I* must be the word that fits:

Elvis asked that *I* practice handstands.

So the pronouns you need come from Group 1, and the correct version of the original sentence would be:

Elvis asked that *he* and *she* practice handstands.

Now, if you can observe a few more rules, you should be well-equipped to handle most of the pronoun errors that may appear in the standard usage section of the SAT II.

1. Use Group 1 (nominative case) pronouns in the subject of sentences and in the predicate nominative—i.e., words in the predicate that identify, define, or mean the same as the subject.

Then *he* and *I* went home. (*he and I* = subject)

When *we* went out for pizza, *he* and *she* fought over the check. (*he and she* = subject)

The person in the photo is *I*. (*person* = subject; *I* = predicate nominative—i.e., pronoun with same meaning as subject)

The instructors in the course were *he* and Donald. (*instructors* = subject; *he* = predicate nominative)

2. Use Group 2 (objective case) pronouns when the pronoun shows up in a phrase with a preposition, as in:

BETWEEN *you* and *me*, TO Sherry and *her*, AMONG *us* women, AT *us*, FROM *her* and *him*, WITH *me* and *you*.

3. Use group 2 pronouns when the pronoun refers to the person to whom something is being done.

Terry invited *him* to to the prom.

The waiter gave *her* and *me* orange soda.

4. To find the correct pronoun in a comparison, as in "Jackie runs faster than (*her, she*)," first complete

the comparison with the verb that would follow naturally. That will tell you which pronoun to use.

Jackie runs faster than *she* runs.
My brother has bigger feet than *I* do.

Because you would never say "Jackie runs faster than *her* runs" nor "My brother has bigger feet than *me* do," the correct pronouns are *she* and *I*:

Jackie runs faster than *she*.
My brother has bigger feet than *I*.

Apply the same principle to comparisons using *as*.

Carol is as tough as *he* is.
She is twice as fast as *they* are.
The department could use a stronger leader such as *she* is.
A woman such as *I* am could solve the problem.

5. When a pronoun is side by side with a noun (*we* boys, *us* women), eliminate the noun to determine which pronoun to use.

(*We, Us*) seniors decided to take a day off from school in late May. (By dropping the noun *seniors*, you can easily tell which pronoun is correct. Since no one would say "*Us* decided to take," *we* is clearly the correct choice.)

This award was presented to (*we, us*) students by the teachers. (Drop the noun *students*, and the proper choice of pronoun becomes clear.)

This award was presented to *us* by the teachers.

6. Use possessive pronouns (*my, our, your, his, her, their*) before a *gerund*, a noun that looks like a verb because of its *-ing* ending.

*Her* asking the question shows that she is alert. (*Asking* is a gerund.)

Mother was upset about *your* opening the presents too soon. (*Opening* is a gerund.)

*Their* coming home late upset the evening's plans. (*Coming* is a gerund.)

Not every word with an *-ing* ending is a gerund. Sometimes it's a participle that modifies the pronoun. Such cases usually call for pronouns from the objective case.

I hope you don't mind *my* intruding on your conversation. (Here *intruding* is a gerund.)

I hope you don't mind *me* intruding on your conversation. (Here *intruding* is a participle.)

Whether an *-ing* word is a gerund or a participle often depends on emphasis. If the emphasis is on the action, the word is a gerund, which requires a possessive pronoun. If the emphasis lies on the pronoun more than on the action, the word is a participle, which requires an objective pronoun. If this confuses you, take heart. It's reasonably safe to say that on the SAT II you won't be tested on any principle as ambiguous as this one. Nevertheless, the rule is worth knowing.

PRACTICE EXERCISE IN PRONOUN CHOICE
Find the pronoun errors in the following sentences. Write the correct pronoun in the space provided. Some sentences contain no errors.

1. The biggest difference between her and I is our view on abortion.    *me*

   _____

2. My aunt sent Sam and I a calendar for the new year.    *me*

   _____

3. We're going to ask Gretchen and he to go to the movies on Saturday.    *him*

   _____

4. Remember, this secret is strictly between you and I.    *me*

   _____

5. Us women take sexual harassment very seriously.    *We*

   _____

6. Are you expecting Jonathan and he to call tonight.    *him*

   _____

7. You apparently misunderstood that message that Joe and him left behind.
*he*

_____

8. Him and I plan to drive to Danbury tonight.
*He*

_____

9. Them singing at the top of their lungs disturbed the quiet neighborhood.
*Their*

_____

10. Marie is going to treat Holly and me to lunch on Friday.

_____

11. Tim is more interested in applying to Colgate than her.
*she does*

_____

12. Did you stay as long as them at the dance?
*they did*

_____

13. The group asked us guys to pitch in on the drive for canned goods.

_____

14. The last match of the season was a tie between the Tigers and they.
*them*

_____

15. The last time I saw him, he was as tall as me, if not taller.
*I am*

_____

16. The proceeds, we think, should be given equally to my sister and I.
*me*

_____

17. You questioning their authority really upset them.
*Your* *on*

_____

18. How could anyone enjoy them arguing the whole time?
*their*

_____

19. The job could never have been done without him and I.
*me*

_____

20. They know it was him who took the keys.
*he*

_____

21. The office hadn't been told of them coming to pick up the keys.
*their*

_____

22. Trudy said that she hasn't seen Sally or him all day.

_____

23. They refused to let us boys into the building after dark.

_____

24. Did you hear about him falling and breaking his foot?
*his*

_____

25. Him and me alternated driving the car, despite his refusing to renew his license.
*He* *I*

_____

26. Nina was obviously feeling better than her after the accident.
*she*

_____

27. Six of them visited Roger and I after the ceremony.
*me*

_____

28. Since I had a test, I told them that Mark and him could have the tickets.
*he*

_____

29. I never spoke with them, neither she nor her sister.
*her*

_____

30. The superintendent promised to hold the apartment for we girls.

_____

*Answers on page 156.*

## Who and Whom

The rules for personal pronoun usage apply also to *who* and to *whom*.

1. Use *who* (or *whoever*) for all subjects.

Everyone *who* wants pizza, step forward, please. (The pronoun *who* is the subject of the verb *wants*.)

2. Use *whom* (or *whomever*) when it is an object of the preposition.

Reed was a man in *whom* many people placed their trust. (The pronoun *whom* comes after the preposition *in*.)

3. Use *whom* when it refers to the person to whom something is being done.

The new secretary, *whom* we hired today, looks like competent person. (The pronoun *whom* is the object of the verb *hired*. Consequently, *whom* and not *who*, is the correct choice.)

4. *Who* and *whom* are also used to ask questions. As interrogative pronouns, they follow the same rules as personal pronouns.

Who left his socks in the kitchen?

(The pronoun *who* is needed because it is the subject of the verb *left*.)

To *whom* was the letter addressed?

(The pronoun *whom* is needed because it is the object of the preposition *to*.)

Whom do you trust?

(The pronoun *whom* is needed because it is the object of the verb *do trust*.)

A good way to tell which interrogative pronoun to use is to substitute *he* for *who* and *him* for *whom*. If the substitution works, you will have chosen the correct pronoun.

(*Who, Whom*) left his socks in the kitchen? (*He* left his socks in the kitchen. Since *he* fits and *him* does not, the correct pronoun is *who*.)

To (*who, whom*) was the letter addressed? (It was addressed to *him*. Since *him* fits and *he* doesn't, the correct pronoun is *whom*.)

(Who, Whom) do you trust? (We trust *him*. Since *him* fits and *he* doesn't, the correct pronoun is *whom*.)

## MODIFIERS

Words, phrases, and clauses are often used to modify, that is, to tell something about or to limit a particular word or statement.

Harold closed the *red* door. (The adjective *red* tells something about the noun *door*. Therefore, *red* "modifies" *door*.)

At the store, Maude bought a new thermometer *that was guaranteed to be accurate*. (The clause *that was guaranteed to be accurate* modifies the noun *thermometer* because it tells something about the thermometer.)

## Misplaced Modifiers

Modifiers must be placed so that they modify the right words and no others.

Martin *only* loves Sharon. (Here *only* modifies *loves,* and if Martin feels nothing but love for Sharon—no admiration, awe, respect, or any other emotion—then the modifier is aptly situated. If, however, the sentence is intended to state that Martin has but one love, Sharon, then *only* is misplaced. Properly placed, *only* should come either before or after *Sharon*.)

Martin loves *only* Sharon.

*or*

Martin loves Sharon *only*.

Nicky decided *when she had finished the job* to quit. (In this sentence, the clause *when she had finished* is the modifier. But it's hard to tell whether it modifies *decided or quit*. If it modifies *decided*, Nicky made her decision to quit after she had completed the work. If it modifies *quit*, Nicky probably made her decision to quit at some point before she finished the work. )

When she had finished the job, Nicky decided to quit.

Nicky decided to quit when she finished the job. (Now the meaning of both sentences is unambiguous.)

Sentences on the SAT II sometimes contain misplaced modifiers that cloud the meaning. To avoid ambiguity, modifiers should be as close as possible to the words they modify.

MISPLACED:  Philip donated his old car to a charity *that no longer ran well.* (The modifier *that no longer ran well* is too far from *car*, the word it modifies.)

CLEAR:  Philip donated his old car *that no longer ran well* to a charity.

MISPLACED:  The bowling alley lends out shoes to its customers *of all sizes.* (The modifier *of all sizes* should be closer to *shoes*, the word it modifies.)

CLEAR:  The bowling alley lends out shoes *of all sizes* to its customers.

MISPLACED:  A bone was given to the dog *we didn't want.*

CLEAR:  A bone *we didn't want* was given to the dog.

## Dangling Modifiers

A more common modification error on the SAT II is the sentence in which the modifier has no word to modify. This error is called a *dangling modifier* or *dangling participle.*

*Climbing the ladder,* Pete's head knocked over the paint can.

*Planning to stay indoors,* my jacket was flung into the closet.

*While picnicking in the park,* ants got into the corn chips.

The ludicrous meaning of these sentences may not strike you immediately, but look again, and you'll see a bizarre world in which heads climb ladders, jackets make plans, and ants go on picnics. In each sentence the modifiers are participles, often identifiable by *-ing* endings. But the participles lack something to modify. To correct the error, add at least one noun or pronoun to be modified, or rewrite the whole sentence using an adverbial clause.

*Climbing the ladder,* Pete knocked over the paint can with his head. (Adding the noun *Pete* clears up the dangling participle.)

*Because I planned to stay indoors,* my jacket was flung into the closet. (To make the meaning clear, the participle has been replaced by a clause.)

*While Jenny and Dave picnicked in the park,* ants invaded the corn chips. (The clause *While Jenny and . . . .* solves the problem.)

DANGLING:  *At the age of ten,* my family emigrated from Poland.

CLEAR:  *When I was ten,* my family emigrated from Poland.

DANGLING:  *While talking on the phone,* the stew burned in the pot.

CLEAR:  *While I talked on the phone,* the stew burned in the pot.

DANGLING:  *Still sound asleep at noon,* my mother thought I might be sick.

CLEAR:  My mother thought I might be sick *because I was still sound asleep at noon.*

Some dangling participles have become acceptable in a few common usages:

*Generally speaking,* no one has the right to interfere in the case.

*To make the meaning clear,* the participle should be replaced.

No one quibbles about such idiomatic usages, though, and you're not likely to be asked about them on the SAT II.

PRACTICE EXERCISE IN MISPLACED AND DANGLING MODIFIERS

Rewrite any of the sentences below that contain a misplaced or dangling modifier. Some sentences may be corrected by shifting the placement of one or more words. Others may need substantial revision, and still others may be correct.

1.  While watching the game on TV, lunch was served by Norm and Matt.

    _____

    _____

    _____

2.  After finishing the math homework, that pizza tasted great.

    _____

    _____

    _____

3. While Ellen was cleaning her room, the bike was stolen.

_____

_____

_____

4. Bob left the hamburger on the table that had been overcooked.

_____

_____

_____

5. After a quick breakfast, the schoolbus picked me up.

_____

_____

_____

6. Being conceited and snobby, I cringe whenever I see Suzanne heading my way.

_____

_____

_____

7. Totaled beyond repair, Archie knew that he'd have to buy a new car.

_____

_____

_____

8. Stopping to rest after the hike, a grizzly bear stood in front of me.

_____

_____

_____

9. The story has finally been told after 150 years of the Donner Party.

_____

_____

_____

10. Carlos, after arriving from Honduras, described his ordeal in my class.

_____

_____

_____

11. A report was submitted about the bank robbery by the police.

_____

_____

_____

12. Driving down the mountain road, a rock hit my windshield and smashed it.

_____

_____

_____

13. Although almost a thousand years old, the painting looks almost new.

_____

_____

_____

14. Canceling the meeting was the right thing to do under the circumstances.

_____

_____

_____

15. Used all night long to illuminate the steps, I needed new batteries for the flashlight.

_____

_____

_____

*Answers on page 156.*

## DOUBLE NEGATIVES

In some languages, two negatives in the same sentence are thought to be a means for emphasizing a point. In English, however, two negatives usually mean nothing more than an error in standard usage.

They *didn't* do *nothing* wrong.

*Didn't* is a negative term; so is *nothing*. One or the other, but not both, is sufficient to make the point:

They did *nothing* wrong.

*or* They *didn't* do anything wrong.

In some constructions, especially when *not* modifies an adjective with a negative prefix like *un-*, *in-*, and *im-*, a double negative is acceptable because the paired words actually make a positive statement:

It was *not uncommon* for Lola to sleep late on weekend mornings. (Lola usually slept late on Saturday and Sunday mornings.)

For the bus to arrive on time is *not impossible.* (It is possible for the bus to arrive on time.)

The schedule was *not* at all *incomplete.* (The schedule was complete.)

On the SAT II, however, you will be expected to recognize double negatives that are improperly constructed. Look for two variations of the word *no* (*no, not, nothing, nobody, never*), including contractions like *don't, can't, won't, hasn't, shouldn't,* and so forth, in the same sentence.

It *doesn't* make *no* difference to him where his daughter goes to college.

For at least a century there *haven't* been *nothing* but rabbits in these hills.

Be particularly vigilant for words like *hardly* and *scarcely*. They, too, should be considered negative words.

You *can't hardly* tell one bird from another without a guidebook.

*Can't* is negative; so is *hardly*. Use one or the other, but not both, to make the point:

You can *hardly* tell one bird from another without a guidebook.

*or* You *can't* tell one bird from another without a guidebook.

Watch out, too, for negative words followed by *but* and *only*, which are also regarded as negative. Therefore, expressions like *can't help but* and *haven't only* violate the rule against using double negatives.

DOUBLE NEGATIVE: Ann *can't help but* tell everyone what to do.

STANDARD: Ann *can't help* telling everyone what to do.

DOUBLE NEGATIVE: They *hadn't but* scheduled a few days to complete the job.

STANDARD: They *had* scheduled *but* a few days to complete the job.

PRACTICE EXERCISE IN DOUBLE NEGATIVES
Correct the double negatives in the following sentences by writing the correct version in the spaces provided. Some sentences may contain no error.

1. They can't hardly afford to pay the rent, much less take a vacation.

2. The museum didn't have no paintings by Picasso.

3. I haven't heard of no reason to reject the offer.

4. Such an experience as he went through is not unheard of.

5. Pierre hadn't but one last wish to make before he died.

6. For a farmer there are neither easy answers nor practical solutions.

7. We didn't have no cause to stop at Reggie's place on the way over.

_____

_____

_____

8. In the vial there wasn't scarcely a drop of poison left for Juliet.

_____

_____

_____

9. She hasn't but a few weeks left before quitting her job.

_____

_____

_____

10. The family hasn't never taken a vacation together before now.

_____

_____

_____

*Answers on page 157.*

---

**Level 2 usage problems**

Usage errors of these kinds have shown up occasionally on previous tests.

Punctuation, below.
Sentence fragments, run-ons and comma splices, page 104

---

## PUNCTUATION

Proper punctuation is worth something. For example, notice the difference between $500.00 and $50,000. Commas, periods, apostrophes, quotation marks, and exclamation points are cheap, but they are priceless when it comes to accurate English usage. It's reasonable to say that most literate people know the cus-

tomary marks of punctuation. But you can't assume that they know how to use them. The comma is especially abused. As often as a comma appears where it has no business, it is left out of places where it ought to be. That the abuse of commas is rampant may be partly explained by the flexibility of rules governing their use, many of which may be bent for the sake of clarity. (A writer may choose to insert a comma, for example, between the next-to-last item in a series and the word *and*, as in "sugar, spice, and everything nice." Then again, the writer may leave it out, provided its exclusion doesn't gum up the intended meaning.) When an SAT II sentence violates a law of punctuation, a misused comma or semicolon will almost certainly be responsible. The other marks of punctuation are generally ignored by English usage tests.

### Commas

Approximately half a dozen rules govern comma usage:

1. Commas are often used to signal pauses between the clauses of a complex sentence.

While Marnie rowed the boat started to sink.
(This sentence contains two clauses, one subordinate to the other. To avoid confusion, a comma is needed to separate the clauses.)
While Marnie rowed, the boat started to sink.

Not every complex sentence requires a comma, however. Short clauses, say, up to five or six words, often don't need commas. Nor do sentences in which the adverbial clause follows the main clause.

The boat started to sink while Marnie rowed.

2. Commas are used to set off nonessential words that interrupt the flow of a sentence.

Allyn, *however,* was left off the list. Janet, *on the other hand,* was included. (The interrupting word *however* and the phrase *on the other hand* are bracketed by commas. You can tell whether such words are nonessential interrupters simply by eliminating them. If the sentence preserves its basic meaning without them, they are probably nonessential interrupters.)

In grammatical terms, nonessential information is called *nonrestrictive*; essential information is called *restrictive.* Use commas for nonrestrictive material; don't use commas for restrictive material.

> All students who need to see the admissions rep from Tufts may leave the room at 10:00. (The information contained in the clause *who need to see the admissions rep from Tufts* is probably essential to the meaning of the sentence. If the information were nonessential, its elimination would not substantially alter the basic meaning of the sentence.)

> All students may leave the room at 10:00. (Because the sentence now means something quite different from the original, the clause is essential and, therefore, requires no commas.)

More often than not, the context and intention of a sentence determine whether the interrupting words are essential or nonessential.

> ESSENTIAL:  Janet took her car to the mechanic who knows everything about Volvos. (The clause *who knows everything about Volvos* is not set off by a comma. Assume, therefore, that Janet had a choice of mechanics and picked the one who is a Volvo expert.)

> NONESSENTIAL:  Janet took her car to the mechanic, who knows everything about Volvos. (In this sentence the clause *who knows everything about Volvos* is set off by a comma. Assume, therefore, that the information in the clause is not essential to establishing the mechanic's identity. Rather, it is extra information, incidental to the point of the sentence.)

> ESSENTIAL:  The members of the band who went on the trip had a great time. (Not every band member went on the trip, but those who went had a ball.)

> NONESSENTIAL:  The members of the band, who went on the trip, had a great time. (In this sentence, the whole band enjoyed the trip.)

> ESSENTIAL:  The man who robbed the convenience store was arrested.

> NONESSENTIAL:  The man, who robbed the convenience store, was arrested.

On the SAT II you'll never be obligated to determine whether material should be essential or nonessential. Whatever material appears in a sentence will clearly be one or the other.

3.  Use a comma to separate two independendent clauses joined by the conjunctions *and, but, for, or, nor, yet,* or *so.*

> The competition is the stiffest in many years, *but* it won't keep Lauren from winning the race.

> It was an emergency, *so* I came without my shoes.

> Philip had better call my mother to tell her I'll be late, *or* I'll be in big trouble.

> Don't bother the dog, *and* she won't bite you. (If both clauses are very short, a comma may be optional, as in "I am sorry and Susan is sorry, too.")

Do not use—repeat: **do not use** a comma to connect two independent clauses that are **not** joined by a conjunction (*and, but, for, or, nor,* or *so*). Were you to do so, you would have created a *comma splice,* a first cousin to a *run-on* sentence, discussed in the next section.

It is also improper to use a semicolon in place of a comma, except in a series in which the items themselves contain commas.

> On his college tour Mike visited Portland, Maine; Cambridge, Massachusetts; Hartford, Connecticut; and Albany, New York. (Without semicolons to separate items in the series, a reader might think that Mike had gone to eight places instead of only four.)

4.  Use commas in a series.

> My friend's car needs new tires, a battery, a tailpipe, and a tune-up.

> A well-dressed, dapper gentleman stepped out of the taxicab.

> History, English, math, and science are my easiest courses.

You may skip the comma before the last item in the series if the meaning is clear without it.

5.  Use commas to set off appositives. An appositive is a noun or phrase that identifies another noun in the same sentence.

> Hal Rogers, *my neighbor,* went to Ireland last summer. (The phrase *my neighbor* is an appositive. It is in apposition to *Hal Rogers,* the subject of the sentence.)

> Calculus, *the hardest math course offered in this school,* enrolled sixty students for next year. (The phrase *the hardest math course offered in this school* is set off by commas because it is in apposition to *Calculus,* the subject of the sentence.)

When an appositive contains information that is essential to the meaning of the sentence, no commas are required.

> My brother *Peter* is in law school. (No commas set off the appositive *Peter*. You may assume, therefore, that the speaker has more than one brother. By omitting the commas you know that it's brother Peter—not brother Claude—who goes to law school. If commas have been included, you may assume that Peter is the speaker's only brother and that his name is nonessential information.)

6. Commas are used to separate parts of addresses, dates, and geographical names, and are also used in dialogue. Even though there is virtually no chance that the SAT II will give you a question involving these uses of a comma, you should know them, anyway.

> The postcard said, "As of September 30, 1994, Mary Harding, currently of 11 Denby Lane, Shaftsbury, Vermont, will be living at 2002 Commonwealth Avenue, Boston, Massachusetts."
>
> "How nice," said Sylvia. "Mary will now be just five minutes away."
>
> "Well," replied Gerard," I think it's more like ten."

## PRACTICE EXERCISE IN PUNCTUATION

In the sentences below insert commas where they are needed, remove them where they are not. Also, beware of errors in the use of semicolons. Some sentences may contain no error.

1. While Bill was riding his bike got a flat tire.

2. The mailman did not leave the package for Jeff was not at home.

3. After doing her homework Millie as you might expect talked on the phone for an hour.

4. His work criticized many commonly held beliefs however and it was strictly censored.

5. The car, which ran into mine, was a Buick.

6. Dad went to the airport to pick up Dave and Ellie went to the train station to meet Debbie.

7. The people who live by the water must be prepared for occasional flooding.

8. The boat was seventy-five feet long eighteen feet wide and it had a mast about eighty feet high.

9. To anyone interested in flying planes hold endless fascination.

10. Jeff and Steve left alone for the weekend invited all their friends to a party.

11. I need street maps of Boston; and Portland, Maine.

12. Some of theories dealt with the political social and religious ideas of the time.

13. Students, who want to try out for the chorus, have been asked to report to room 330.

14. Doug for example is both a scholar and an athlete.

15. Monica refused to go, unless Phil went with her.

16. The author Peter Jenkins walked five thousand miles across the United States.

17. After all she did for him what she could.

18. Starting in Minnesota the Mississippi runs all the way to the Gulf of Mexico.

19. Harold Watkins who comes from Chicago won a full tuition scholarship to Columbia.

20. Although the characters in the book are stereotypes they were interesting to read about.

21. Yo-Yo Ma the famous cellist will perform a recital on Saturday night.

22. This test covers Spanish literature culture and history; and it lasts for three hours.

23. Michelle is pretty tall and dark but her older sister Norma is pretty short and light.

24. Sean the twin brother of Ian was struck by a car while crossing the street.

25. Irving the window washer dropped by last evening.

*Answers on page 157.*

## SENTENCE FRAGMENTS, RUN-ONS, AND COMMA SPLICES

Sentence errors frequently occur in the Sentence-Correction questions of the SAT II, but occasionally a fragment, run-on, or comma splice finds its way into a question in the Usage section.

## Sentence Fragments

As its name suggests, a sentence fragment is an incomplete sentence. It may look complete, but it isn't. It is often a phrase or a clause that starts with a capital letter and ends with a period. It may contain a noun that appears to be the grammatical subject, as well as a verb that looks as though it describes action or a state of being, but as a unit of language it is still not a complete sentence.

Search for the telltale signs that often indicate the possible presence of a sentence fragment. Look for clauses that begin with subordinating conjunctions and phrases that begin with participles, prepositions, and appositives.

1. Fragments often begin with a subordinating conjunction, a word like *although, because, before, even though, while, unless, if, when, while,* or one of many others. Such a word signals the presence of a dependent clause. By itself, a dependent clause is a fragment. Paired with an independent clause, it becomes part of a complete sentence. In other words, it "depends" on another clause for completeness.

**Because the Supreme Court begins to hear cases on the first Monday in October.** (This is a dependent clause beginning with the subordinating conjunction *because*. It is a sentence fragment because it is not paired with an independent clause.)

**Because the Supreme Court begins to hear cases on the first Monday in October, the building will be closed at the end of the summer.** (Now the dependent clause is part of a complete sentence.)

**While the crowd cheered wildly for the home team.** (This is a dependent clause beginning with the subordinating conjunction *while.*)

**The visitors ran away with the game while the crowd cheered wildly for the home team.** (The addition of an independent clause completes the sentence.)

2. Fragments sometimes begin with participles.

**Having no place to go but into the railroad station.** (This fragment begins with a participial phrase. To complete the thought, add a comma and an independent clause.)

**Having no place to go but into the railroad station, the homeless man lay down on the park bench.**

3. Fragments sometimes begin with prepositional phrases.

**On the terrace near the flagpole.** (To complete the thought, add a verb and the grammatical subject of the sentence.)

**On the terrace near the flagpole stood Molly and Tom, waiting to have their picture taken.**

4. Fragments sometimes are made up of nouns in apposition.

**The ingredients for making the lasagna—pasta, tomato sauce, ground meat and spices.** (The series of ingredients is in apposition to the noun *ingredients*. To complete the sentence add a verb and a predicate.)

**The ingredients for making the lasagna—pasta, tomato sauce, ground meat and spices—stood on the kitchen counter.**

## Run-on Sentences and Comma Splices

Unlike sentence fragments, run-on sentences express complete thoughts, but they do so by improperly joining two independent sentences into one. Compound sentences, which are also made up of two or more complete sentences, use conjunctions like *and, but, for, so, yet, or* and *nor* to show where one sentence ends and another begins. Run-ons contain no markers at all to show the juncture between sentences.

**The rain flooded our cellar there were three inches of water to pump out.** (This run-on consists of two sentences. The first: The rain flooded our cellar. The second: There were three inches of water to pump out. Properly punctuated with a period and a capital letter, there would be no mistaking where the break between sentences occurs.)

When a run-on is joined by a comma instead of the proper punctuation, the error is known as a *comma splice*. That is, a comma has been improperly used to join, or to splice, two independent sentences. Comma splices are variations of run-on sentences and occur with greater frequency than run-ons without punctuation.

> Tracy worked hard on the project, she should have earned a higher grade. (This sentence contains a comma splice. Replace the comma with a period and start a new sentence with *She*.)

> Tracy worked hard on the project. She should have earned a higher grade.

## Semicolon

A semicolon may be substituted for a period when two sentences are so closely related that to pause between them would unnecessarily break the continuity of thought between them.

> Melissa adores Cheerios; she eats them every morning.
> The book had been left out in the rain; it was ruined.

Remember, however, that a semicolon is not a substitute for a comma except when used to separate items in a series when one or more of the items contains a comma.

> Last summer he read *Alas, Babylon; Look Homeward, Angel;* and *Ah, Wilderness!*
> In the basket were two bunches of grapes, one green and one red; red apples; and a yellow squash.

Although rare, a semicolon can also be used to separate coordinate clauses in a compound sentence joined by *and, but, for, or, so* or *nor* when one or both of the clauses contains commas.

> She was accepted at Berkeley, Wisconsin, and Michigan; and Northwestern put her on the waiting list.

PRACTICE EXERCISE IN SENTENCE FRAGMENTS, RUN-ONS, AND COMMA SPLICES

Some of the following are sentence fragments; others are run-ons, and still others contain comma splices. In the spaces provided, write whatever is needed to make them complete and proper sentences. Consider using semicolons and conjunctions where appropriate. Some items may be correct.

1. James finished writing the paper at 2:00 am then he went to bed and slept through the class.

   _____

   _____

   _____

2. Open the door for the cat she's been out all night.

   _____

   _____

   _____

3. Although she knows that she's stressed out about the SAT II.

   _____

   _____

   _____

4. Having no more to do with the adminsitration, despite 20 years of loyal service and several prestigious awards for his research.

   _____

   _____

   _____

5. In fact, I noticed his piercing laugh above the noise of the crowd.

   _____

   _____

   _____

6. Which the other members of the class were unable to find in the library.

   _____

   _____

   _____

7. Rose is a good friend, when she makes a promise she keeps it.

   _____

   _____

   _____

8. Though shoveling all the snow from the walk and the driveway took two hours.

_____

_____

9. When she laughs, I laugh when I laugh, she laughs.

_____

_____

10. After the rain, the smell in the garden, as fresh as dew.

_____

_____

11. My grandmother is 83 years old therefore she walks very slowly.

_____

_____

12. Mark and Cathy went to San Diego for Christmas, they came back for New Year's, however.

_____

_____

13. Tony is the only freshman on the team yet he was chosen as the most valuable player.

_____

_____

14. Ross edited the magazine for decades he was followed by Shawn.

_____

_____

15. In spite of her bossy nature, her ego, and her mean streak, her students love her as a teacher.

_____

_____

16. First try to do this exercise without looking in the book, if you can't do it, refer to page 56.

_____

_____

17. A good idea, don't you think, to talk over the problem with his mother, father, and guidance counselor.

_____

_____

18. At the end of the course there is a test, it consists of three essays.

_____

_____

19. Huge redwood trees that had been alive for nearly 2,000 years.

_____

_____

20. She asked the teacher for an extension on the assignment, the teacher agreed.

_____

_____

*Answers on page 157.*

### Level 1 usage problems

Sentences with these errors are not likely to show up on the test, but they cannot be ruled out.

Possessives, below
Capitalization, page 108

## POSSESSIVES

Knowing how to indicate possession is little more than knowing where to put apostrophes. Except in contractions, where one or more letters or digits have been omitted—as in *can't, would've, '90s,* and *where's*—apostrophes always indicate possession.

1. An apostrophe is used in possessive nouns. When the noun ends in any letter but *s,* put the apostrophe at the end of the word and add *s,* as in *Alice's restaurant, women's rights,* and *Sam's moustache.*

2. When the noun (singular or plural) ends in *s,* put the apostrophe after the *s,* as in *leaves' color, classes' attitude, the Smiths' house, horses' stable* and *oceans' currents.* When a singular noun ends in *-s* or *-ss (scissors, Silas, glass, boss),* add the apostrophe to indicate possession, but then add another *s* only if you pronounce it .

> The *boss's* (pronounced *boss-es* ) desk is clean. (Add *s* following the apostrophe.)
> The *glass's* (pronounced *glass-es* ) color is red. (Add *s* following the apostrophe.)
> The *scissors'* (pronounced *scissors* ) handle is green. (Do not add *s* after the apostrophe.)
> The *Jones'* house is all lit up. (No *s* is added unless you say *Jones-es*.)

On the SAT II usage section an error in possessives may occasionally make an appearance. More likely, though, your understanding of possessives will be checked by the sentence correction portion of the exam.

PRACTICE EXERCIS___
In the spaces pro___
form of the italic___
rect.

1. *Pauls* rea___

   _____

2. The future of *Americas* for___ ___
   debated.

   _____

3. *Teams* from all over the country gathered in Washington.

   _____

4. Louise isn't at all interested in joining the *womens* basketball team.

   _____

5. The *girls* locker room is down here, but the *boys* is on the other side.

   _____

6. We are invited to the *Andersons* house for New *Years* Eve.

   _____

7. All of the *Rosses* are going out to eat.

   _____

8. Have you seen *Morris* pipe, which he left here yesterday?

   _____

9. Both of the *computers* keyboards need to be repaired.

   _____

10. He'll be back in two *months* time.

   _____

*Answers on page 158.*

## CAPITALIZATION

capitalization rarely appear on the SAT II
section. Yet the rules of capitalization are
knowing in case you are tempted during the
to identify as an error a word that you think
should be capitalized, or vice-versa.

In june over two hundred seniors will graduate
from this high school. (You probably know that
*June*—and all the other months—are capitalized, but
what about *high school*? Although the temptation
may be great to capitalize high school, don't do it unless it is the name of a particular high school.)

In June over two hundred seniors will graduate
from Mount Anthony High School.

Here, for ready reference, is a summary of the
capitalization rules of standard English.
Capitals are used as the first letter of:

1. Sentences and partial sentences, direct quotes,
and the first lines of traditional poetry.

Capitalization is a barrel of fun, isn't it? So far,
so good. This book says, "Most capitalization
rules are easy to follow."

2. A sentence following a colon:

The rule is simple: What you see is what you get.

Capitals are also used for:

1. Proper nouns—names of people, places, organizations, businesses, nations, races, religions,
courses, and more: *Nancy, Central Park, the Red
Cross, American Airlines, France, African-American,
Catholics, the Old West, Columbia University, Art History, Mother, Lakeview High School* (But words that
are not actual names are not capitalized, as in *my
mother, our high school, your dad, the track team, a
history course, an art seminar.*)

2. Words derived from proper nouns: *French,
Shakespearean, Democratic, Marxist.*

3. The important words in the titles of books,
movies, plays, paintings: *The Bible, Gone With the
Wind, Death of a Salesman, The Boating Party.*

4. The name of the deity and pronouns for the deity: *God, Lord, the Almighty, Him, His.*

5. Days of the week, months, holidays, and sometimes periods of history: *Monday, October, Inde-*

*pendence Day, Good Friday, 440 A.D., the Renais-
sance.*

6. The seasons of the year, but only when they are
personified: *Old Man Winter;* directions on a compass,
but only when they refer to the place: *the West, the
Northeast.*

7. Abbreviations of proper names: *U.S., AIDS,
NAACP, AF of L.*

8. The abbreviations of academic degrees: *M.A.,
Ph.D., M.B.A.*

9. People's titles when the title precedes the
name: *President Clinton, Pope John, Judge Thomas,
Coach Martin, Father Guido.*

10. People's titles following the name—sometimes, yes, sometimes, no. To show respect, the title
should be capitalized: *Albert Gore, Vice-President of
the United States; Thomas Sobol, Commissioner of
Education of New York State; Tina Brown, Editor-in-
Chief.* If, on the other hand, the title is used more to
identify a person than to reveal stature, capitals are optional: *Norma Adams, superintendent of schools; Sam,
manager of the ABC bowling alley; Joan Clark, direc-
tor of personnel.*

PRACTICE EXERCISE IN CAPITALIZATION
Add capital letters where they are needed in the following sentences.

1. after the pilgrims crossed the ocean, they
landed at plymouth rock

2. the next president of the united states will
probably be a westerner, or he might come from
the south.

3. yellowstone national park is located in the
western part of the state of wyoming.

4. for christmas he got a black and decker orbital
sander from the sears store next to the old bedford courthouse.

5. the author of the brief on capital punishment in
missouri is justice andrew ryan, chief judge of
the court of appeals in the ninth district.

6. on labor day the bennington county fire department plans to hold a turkey shoot on the field at
miller's pond.

7. the medieval period is called the dark ages in michael crawford's textbook.

8. we expect to celebrate new year's eve again this year by renting a movie of an old broadway musical and by settling down in front of the television set with some canada dry ginger ale and a box of oreos.

9. the judge gave district attorney lederman a book entitled *great cases in contract law* and told her to take it with her on her european tour next summer.

10. according to edith nickerson, the principal of parsons high school, parsons attracts students from the whole west coast. at parsons students may major in drawing and painting, design, graphics, or sculpture. ms. nickerson said, "i attended a similar high school in new england just after the second world war."

*Answers on page 158.*

# SENTENCE-CORRECTION QUESTIONS

In this section of the SAT II you are asked to recognize errors in standard English usage as well as errors in style and expression. You are given eighteen different sentences. A part or all of each sentence is underlined. Then you are given a choice of five ways to express the underlined segment. Your task is to choose which of the five is best. Because choice (A) always repeats the underlined section of the original sentence, select (A) only if you think no change is needed. In any case, never choose an alternative that substantially changes the meaning of the original sentence, however perfect its grammar and style.

## SAMPLE SENTENCE-CORRECTION QUESTIONS

*Type 1: Sentences containing errors in standard usage*

Sandra told the interviewer <u>that she couldn't hardly remember a time that</u> she didn't want to be an interior designer.

(A) that she couldn't hardly remember a time that
(B) when she could not remember a time that
(C) that a time could hardly be remembered when
(D) when she could hardly not be remembering a time when
(E) that she could hardly remember a time when

Ⓐ Ⓑ Ⓒ Ⓓ Ⓔ

The underlined section of the sentence contains a double negative—*couldn't hardly*—clearly an error in standard usage. Choice (A) is wrong because it repeats the error of the original. Choice (B) eliminates the double negative but changes the meaning of the sentence. Choice (C) shifts the sentence to passive voice. Choice (D) is virtually incomprehensible. Choice (E) eliminates the error original error and preserves the meaning. Therefore, (E) is the best choice.

Questions of this type are not far different from the usage questions in the previous section of the SAT II. Finding the right answer depends, in part, on your knowledge of standard English. Refer to the material on usage in this book (page 56–109). Several kinds of usage errors, however, are more suited to the format of sentence-correction questions than to the format of the usage questions. These are discussed and illustrated in this section.

*Type 2: Sentences containing errors in style or expression*

<u>Great enjoyment was experienced by me at the wedding of my sister.</u>

(A) Great enjoyment was experienced by me at the wedding of my sister.
(B) The experience of my sister's wedding was great enjoyment.
(C) Being at my sister's wedding was an experience of great enjoyment.
(D) I greatly enjoyed my sister's wedding.
(E) A greatly enjoyable experience for me was the wedding of my sister.

Because the entire sample sentence is underlined, your task is to determine whether any of the alternatives expresses the idea of the sentence more effectively than the original. All of the choices are grammatically correct. Therefore, you are asked to make a judgment about writing style—that is, about which choice is made up of the best words in the best order. In general, the most effective writing is clear, brief, and bold. Therefore, choice (D) is the best answer. For help in making informed decisions about effective style and expression, read "Problems in Style and Expression," pages 126–129.

*Type 3: Sentences containing errors in usage as well as errors in style and expression.*

Cape Canaveral was renamed Cape Kennedy shortly after JFK <u>was assassinated, its original name was given back to it ten years later.</u>

(A) was assassinated, its original name was given back to it ten years later

(B) was assassinated and it got back its original name ten years later

(C) was assassinated; its original name was restored ten years later

(D) was assassinated, it was restored to its original name ten years later

(E) was assassinated; however, the restoration of its name ten years later

Ⓐ Ⓑ Ⓒ Ⓓ Ⓔ

The underlined text of the original sentence has three problems. The first is punctuation. A comma improperly separates two individual sentences. Correct punctuation for two independent sentences is (1) a semicolon, (2) a period and an initial capital letter for the second sentence, or (3) a comma followed by a conjunction (*and, but, or, nor, for, yet* or *so*).

The second problem is wordiness. The underlined text, which contains thirteen words, is less concise than any of the other choices.

And the third problem is awkwardness. The phrase *was given back to it* has a decidedly ungraceful sound.

Which, then, is the best choice?

Choice (A) repeats the original. Reject it.

Choice (B) adds the conjunction *and* but omits the comma needed between two clauses of a compound sentence. In addition, *it got back its original name* is awkward, due in part to the use of *it* and *its* in the same phrase.

Choice (C) solves all the problems. Therefore, (C) is the best answer.

Choice (D) contains a comma splice. Also, like choice (B), it awkwardly repeats the pronoun *it*.

Choice (E) has a sentence fragment to the right of the semicolon. Moreover, it makes no sense.

These explanations of three sample sentences may have taken you a few minutes to read and comprehend. On the SAT II, under the pressure of time, you are expected to do a similar but more rapid analysis of each sentence. While some questions will have definite right and wrong answers, others will require you to exercise judgment. Two or more of the choices may be grammatically correct, but the right answer will be the one that is more gracefully and ef-

fectively worded than the others. Some items will contain multiple errors, others just one. Some assess your knowledge of standard English usage, but others will expect you to know about sentence structure, writing style, and effective expression.

Although sentence-correction questions may contain any of literally hundreds of flaws, most of the errors are likely to relate to the following problems:

---

## Problems in Sentence Structure

Incomplete sentences, page 112
Run-on sentences, page 113
Semicolon errors, page 113
Comma splices, page 114
Mismatched sentence parts, page 114
    Faulty coordination, page 114
    Faulty parallelism, page 116
    Faulty subordination, page 117
Misplaced modifiers, page 118
Sentence shifts, page 119
    Shifts in verb tense, page 119
    Shifts in pronoun person, page 120
    Shifts in grammatical subject, page 120
    Shifts in voice, page 121
    Mixed construction, page 121
Incomplete and illogical comparisons,
    pages 70–71

### Problems in Standard English Usage

Subject-verb agreement, page 122
Faulty verb forms and tenses, page 123
Faulty comparisons, page 123
Pronoun problems, page 124

### Problems in Style and Expression

Wordiness and redundancy, page 126
Awkwardness, page 127
Passive construction, page 128

---

All the problems on the foregoing list are explained and illustrated on the next pages. The errors unique to sentence-correction questions are covered thoroughly, but the discussions of errors in standard English usage are meant only for your review. For the complete story on usage, turn to pages 56–109.

## PROBLEMS IN SENTENCE STRUCTURE

### Incomplete Sentences

Broadly speaking, a sentence is group of words that begins with a capital letter and ends with an end mark of punctuation. It also conveys a more or less complete thought and is grammatically whole, which means that it has a subject and a verb. You can't always depend on this general definition, however, to distinguish a complete sentence from an incomplete, or fragmentary, sentence. A sentence fragment is partial sentence that often looks remarkably like the whole thing.

> The bike that Harry often borrowed.

This fragment seems to have all the characteristics of a sentence: It starts with capital letter and ends with a period; it conveys a complete thought (*Harry often borrowed the bike* is a complete thought), and it appears to contain a subject and a verb. What makes it a fragment, though, is that the subject *bike* and the verb *borrowed* don't fit together. After all, a bike did not—and cannot—do any borrowing—not in the real world, at least. Obviously, Harry did the borrowing, but the noun *Harry* cannot be the subject of this sentence because it appears in a subordinate clause, *that Harry borrowed*. Therefore, *bike* needs a verb of its own.

> The bike that Harry often borrowed was stolen.

With the addition of *was stolen*, the sentence is now complete.

Sentence fragments usually occur when writers fail to distinguish between dependent and independent clauses, when they confuse phrases and clauses, or when they use verbals as verbs. When you suspect that a sentence is incomplete on the SAT II, uncover its bare bones. That is, deconstruct the sentence by eliminating dependent clauses, phrases, and verbals. If what remains is not a complete sentence, you probably have a fragment on your hands. To find the "bare bones" of a sentence, use the procedure explained in "Finding the Subject of the Sentence," on page 59. Study also "Sentence Fragments, Run-ons and Comma Splices" on page 104 and "Complete Sentences" on page 202.

### SAMPLE QUESTIONS ON SENTENCE FRAGMENTS

1. During the night, the  stars that came  out like diamonds on black velvet.

   (A) stars that came
   (B) stars coming
   (C) stars, which are coming
   (D) stars came
   (E) stars, which came

After eliminating the prepositional phrases from this sentence you are left with *the stars that came out*. The noun *stars* is the subject, but *came* may not be the verb because it is part of the dependent clause *that came out*. Once you remove the dependent clause, only *the stars* remains. Choice (A), therefore, is wrong because it is a sentence fragment. Choice (B) is wrong because an *-ing* form of a verb may not be the main verb of a sentence unless it is accompanied by an auxiliary verb, as in *is singing, has been raining, will be arriving, and so on*. Choices (C) and (E) are also wrong because *which*, like *that, introduces a dependent clause. By the process of elimination, then, Choice* (D) is the best answer.

2. A belief among superstitious people that birthmarks are caused by influences on the mother before the child is born.

   (A) A belief among superstitious people that
   (B) Superstitious people believe that
   (C) Superstitious people believing that
   (D) Among superstitious people the belief that
   (E) Among beliefs of superstitious people are that

The original sentence is a fragment. Only choice (B) contains a subject and an acceptable verb. Therefore, (B) is the best answer.

3. This year's senior class being more involved than last year's.

   (A) being more involved than last year's
   (B) it was involved, moreso than last year
   (C) which was more involved than last year's class
   (D) was more involved than last year's
   (E) involved far more than that of last year

The original sentence is a fragment. Choice (D) contains a suitable verb and an idiomatic predicate. Since none of the others solves the problem, choice (D) is the best answer.

## Run-on Sentences

A run-on sentence consists of two independent clauses without a conjunction (*and, but, or, nor, yet* or *so*) or a mark of punctuation to separate them.

> Birthstones are supposed to bring good luck mine has never brought me any. (Here the independent clauses run together because neither a conjunction or any mark of punctuation separates *luck* and *mine*.)

> Birthstones are supposed to bring good luck, *but* mine has never brought me any. (Adding the conjuction *but* solves the problem. Note also that a comma has also been added. A sentence composed of two or more independent clauses joined by a conjunction usually requires a comma.)

> Plants have a daily rhythm they raise their leaves in the daytime and lower them at night. (Here the independent clauses run together because nothing separates *rhythm* and *they*. A mark of punctuation would solve the problem.)

> Plants have a daily rhythm. They raise their leaves in the daytime and lower them at night. (Creating two separate sentences is a good solution.)

> Plants have a daily rhythm; they raise their leaves in the daytime and lower them at night. (Separating the two independent clauses with a semicolon is an acceptable alternative. In effect, the semicolon acts like a period. Note, however, that the initial letter of the second clause is not capitalized.)

### SAMPLE QUESTION ON RUN-ON SENTENCES

The American colonists hated the King's tax on English <u>tea they drank</u> Dutch tea instead.

(A) tea they drank
(B) tea; preferring to drink
(C) tea drinking
(D) tea, so they drank
(E) tea so they drank

To avoid the run-on sentence, a change is needed where the two independent clauses come together—between *tea* and *they*. Choice (A) does not solve the problem. Choice (B) turns the second clause into a phrase, a good solution only if a comma were to replace the semicolon. Choice (C) needs both a comma and a more graceful style. Choices (D) and (E) add the conjunction so, a good solution but only when the conjunction is preceded by a comma. Therefore, (D) is the best answer. (Incidentally, some people argue that *so*, when used as a conjunction, is nonstandard usage. It is widely accepted in informal English, however, and on the SAT II you may safely consider it standard usage.)

## Semicolon Errors

Misuse of a semicolon is a popular error in sentence correction items on the SAT II. Remember that a semicolon is usually a substitute for a period, NOT for a comma. Correctly used, a semicolon must lie between two independent clauses.

> INCORRECT:  On the test Lucy got a 90; which raised her final average in the course.
>
> (The clause *which raised her final average* is not an independent clause.)
>
> CORRECT:  On the test Lucy got a 90, which raised her final average.

Occasionally, however, a semicolon is used to separate items in a series in which the items themselves contain commas. To avoid confusion, the semicolon serves as a comma:

> In my grandmother's kitchen I found a teapot, a set of dishes, and a bowl made of good china; spoons, knives, and forks made of silver; and a salad bowl, cutting board and two trivets made of fine mahoghany.

> Ellie's flight stops at Honolulu, Hawaii; Jakarta, Indonesia; Bangkok, Thailand; and other cities in Asia.

### SAMPLE QUESTION ON MISUSED SEMICOLONS

Mending a fracture takes from four weeks to a <u>year; depending</u> on the size of the bone, the location, and the age of the person.

(A) year; depending
(B) year; thus depending
(C) year depending
(D) year, it depends
(E) year, depending

In this sentence, the semicolon joins an independent clause and a participial phrase. Because this construction calls for a comma, eliminate (A), (B) and (C). Choice (D) is a comma splice (see below). Therefore, choice (E) is the best answer.

## Comma Splice

A variation of the run-on is a comma splice, a construction in which a comma is inserted where either a period or a semicolon ought to be, or where a comma improperly joins a clause to a phrase or to another clause.

> June found the dog lying dead in the ditch, she didn't tell Henry. (Rid this sentence of the comma splice by adding a conjunction.)
>
> June found the dog lying dead in the ditch, *but* she didn't tell Henry.
>
> The defendant was delighted, he had been acquitted. (Remove the comma splice by replacing the comma with a semicolon.)
>
> The defendant was delighted; he had been acquitted.
>
> California, with more people than any other state, it is a popular place to visit. (Remove the comma splice by deleting the pronoun *it*.)
>
> California, with more people than any other state, is a popular place to visit.

SAMPLE QUESTION ON COMMA SPLICES

Maya Angelou is one of America's outstanding writers, she is known for her poetry, her prose, and her frequent appearances on television.

(A) writers, she is known
(B) writers; she is known
(C) writers famous
(D) writers since known
(E) writers being that she known

A comma is used to join two independent clauses. Choice (A) repeats the problem of the original sentence. Choice (B) is correct because it replaces the comma with a semicolon. Choice (C) needs a comma to be correct. Choices (D) and (E) are clumsy and ungrammatical. Therefore, (B) is the best answer.

## Mismatched Sentence Parts

Sentences with mismatched parts need correction. Sentences in which a subject and a verb fail to agree, or one in which the verb tense inexplicably shifts from present to past are examples of constructions with mismatched parts. Changing a word or two will usually correct such errors. Shifts in larger structural elements need more substantial revision, however, as when clauses are mismatched or when a sentence begins in the active voice and ends in the passive. A breakdown in logic or clear thinking may be also responsible for an error, as when a complex sentence has its main idea stated in a subordinate clause. Recognizing such inconsistencies and incongruities is what this section of the SAT II is all about.

The material that follows explains first, the specific kinds of errors to watch for, and second, how to go about making corrections. When hunting for errors, always keep in mind that sentences work best when their components fit harmoniously and grammatically together.

### *Faulty Coordination*

In everyday conversation it's not uncommon for people to use fairly lengthy compound sentences joined by the conjunctions *and* and *so*.

> In school yesterday the lights went out, *and* we were in the dark for about an hour, *and* the electricity was off, *so* we couldn't use the computers, *and* we heard that a car had hit a utility pole, *and* the driver was killed, *and* they let us go home early.

This sentence tells a story without breaking a single rule of usage or grammar. As written, however, the sentence is stylistically flawed. Not only is it monotonous, but each idea appears in an independent clause, suggesting that each idea is equally important. Clauses of equal rank and structure are called *coordinate clauses* and are often joined by conjunctions (*and, but, or, nor, yet,* or *so*) and sometimes by a semicolon with connective words like *however, moreover, nevertheless, otherwise, therefore, consequently*, and others. Faulty coordination occurs (1) when it is illogical or inappropriate to assign equal importance to coordinate clauses or, (2) when the connecting word fails to create a reasonable relationship between the clauses.

> Tom was at summer camp, and his parents finally decided to split up after twenty years of marriage. (The two coordinate clauses state seemingly unrelated information and contain ideas of unequal importance.)

> While Tom was at summer camp, his parents finally decided to split up after twenty years of marriage. (Changing one of the clauses to a dependent clause places emphasis where it probably belongs.)

> The speaker at the assembly gave a stirring talk, and he is married. (The two coordinate clauses state seemingly unrelated information and contain ideas of unequal importance.)

> At the assembly the speaker, who is married, gave a stirring talk. (Subordinating one of the clauses and embedding it the other gives it less prominence.)

> Ms. Sheraton has become the new assistant principal, and she has never taught. (The conjunction *and* fails to convey a meaningful relationship between the two clauses.)

> Ms. Sheraton has become the new assistant principal, although she has never taught. (The substitution of *although* creates a more sensible contrast between the clauses.)

The sentence may be improved still more by reversing the order of the clauses:

> Although she has never taught, Ms. Sheraton has become the new assistant principal.

Faulty coordination in a sentence may frequently be remedied by placing information of less importance into a dependent clause or by using a connective word that more precisely expresses the relationship between two ideas. But when those remedies don't work, breaking the sentence into two or more pieces may be the only way:

> FAULTY:   In school yesterday the lights went out, *and* we were in the dark for about an hour, *and* the electricity was off, *so* we couldn't use the computers, and we heard that a car had hit a utility pole, *and* the driver was killed, *and* they let us go home early.

> IMPROVED:   In school yesterday we were in the dark for about an hour after the lights went out. Without electricity, we couldn't use the computers, so they let us go home early. We heard later that a car had hit a utility pole *and* that the driver had been killed.

For the sake of unity, it is also better not to shift from one grammatical subject to another between clauses. Maintaining the subject allows readers to pass easily from one clause to the next without realigning their focus. Switching subjects forces readers to stop briefly, refocus, and then continue. Frequent shifts are difficult to grasp and lead to incoherent writing.

> FAULTY:   The plan will be a great success, or great failure will be the result. (*Plan* is the subject of the first clause, *failure* the subject of the second.)

> UNIFIED:   The plan will be a great success, or it will be a great failure. (The subject is maintained between the clauses.)

## SAMPLE QUESTIONS ON FAULTY COORDINATION

1. Elizabeth hopes to attend Ohio Wesleyan, <u>and she has not yet sent in her application.</u>

   (A) and she has not yet sent in her application.
   (B) and she hasn't sent her application in yet.
   (C) but her application hasn't as yet been sent in by her.
   (D) yet the sending of the application has not yet been done.
   (E) although she has not yet sent in her application.

The clauses are related in content, but the conjunction *and* fails to convey their relationship. Therefore, (A) is a poor choice. Choice (B) is almost the same as (A). Choice (C) expresses an apt relationship by using the conjunction *but*, but then it shifts subjects and switches from active to passive construction. Choice (D) shifts subjects and is both wordy and clumsy. Choice (E) conveys the relationship between the clauses and is consistent and direct. All the choices are grammatically correct, but (E) is best.

2. <u>My part-time job in a clothing store will help me as a marketing major, and I am learning the art of salesmanship.</u>

   (A) My part-time job in a clothing store will help me as a marketing major and I am learning the art of salesmanship.

   (B) Learning the art of salesmanship, my part-time job in a clothing store will help me as a marketing major.

   (C) My part time job in a clothing store, where I am learning the art of salesmanship, will help me as a marketing major.

   (D) Helping me as a marketing major is learning the art of salesmaship in my part-time job in a clothing store.

   (E) My part-time job in a clothing store will help me as a marketing major; I am learning the art of salesmanship.

Although the clauses are related, the content of the first clause is probably more important than the content of the second. Choice (A) maintains the equivalence of the two coordinate clauses. Choice (B) properly changes the second clause into a phrase, but the change results in a dangling participle. Choice (C) properly subordinates the second clause and embeds it in the independent clause. Choice (D) turns two clauses into one, but the subject *helping* and the predicate nominative *learning* make an awkwardly worded combination. Choice (E) replaces the conjunction with a semicolon which fails to correct the original error. Therefore, (C) is the best answer.

### *Faulty Parallelism*

In compound sentences that compare or contrast ideas, clauses should be in parallel form. In fact, a series of sentence elements of any kind—phrases, verbs, and even nouns—should be worded in similar grammatical form. When parallelism breaks down readers are thrown off track and may become confused.

Philip pays his taxes and his debts are also paid. (The second clause grates on the reader's sense of balance because its grammatical subject, *debts*, is different from the subject of the first clause, *Philip*. The change in subject also compels a change in verbs from active to passive.)

Philip pays his taxes and he pays his debts. (Now the sentence effectively emphasizes the parallel thoughts.)

Betty was good at oil painting, but I thought her watercolors were not good. (The second clause shifts the reader's focus away from Betty and onto the writer's opinion of Betty's work.)

Betty was good at oil painting but not at watercolor. (By keeping the ideas in parallel form, the focus remains on Betty's skill as an artist.)

Eighteen-year olds are too young to sign contracts, but they may have been driving for years. (The second clause maintains the grammatical subject but it takes an unexpected and perplexing turn. The idea should probably be rephrased.)

Eighteen-year olds may drive but they may not sign contracts.

*or* Eighteen-year olds are permitted to drive but not to sign contracts.

## SAMPLE QUESTIONS ON FAULTY PARALLELISM

1. Plenty of students without financial resources can still go to college because they can borrow money from banks, <u>hold part-time jobs, and scholarships are available</u>.

   (A) hold part-time jobs, and scholarships are available.

   (B) jobs are available, and scholarships are available.

   (C) hold part time jobs, and win scholarships.

   (D) holding part time jobs and winning scholarships.

   (E) holding part time jobs and win scholarships.

The sentence contains three phrases that must be in parallel form. Each phrase must conform to the structure of the first one, *borrow money from banks*. That is, each must start with a verb in the present tense. Only choice (C) follows the pattern; therefore, (C) is the best answer.

2. When buying clothes, smart consumers usually consider how much the item costs, how good it looks, and <u>its durability</u>.

   (A) its durability.

   (B) if it is durable.

   (C) the durability of it.

   (D) the ability of the item to last.

   (E) how well it wears.

The sentence contains three adverbial clauses that must be in parallel form. Two of the three begin with *how*, followed first by an adverb or adjective and then by a verb in the present tense. Only choice (E) follows the pattern; therefore, (E) is the best answer.

3. <u>Growing up in the South</u> and a father who was a career soldier influenced Betsy to apply for an appointment to the U.S. Military Academy at West Point.

   (A) Growing up in the South
   (B) Having grown up in the South
   (C) A Southern heritage
   (D) Being a Southerner
   (E) With a Southern background

The correct answer is the phrase that most closely parallels the subject noun, *father*. Choices (A), (B) and (D) are participial phrases. Choice (E) is a prepositional phrase. Choice (C) is a noun phrase. Therefore, (C) is the best answer.

There's more about faulty parallelism in the usage section of this book. Please refer to "Parallel Construction," pages 89–90.

## *Faulty Subordination*

By means of subordination, writers are able to convey not only the interrelationship of ideas but also the relative importance of one idea to another. Important ideas usually go into the independent clause of a complex sentence, while secondary, or subordinate, ideas are relegated to dependent clauses, phrases, or even to single words. Here, for example, are two statements: Joe rushed to school. He ate a tuna sandwich. The relationship between the two ideas is not altogether transparent, but it can be clarified by subordinating one of the clauses:

While he rushed to school, Joe ate a tuna sandwich. (Subordinating one of the ideas gives the other more prominence.)

The sentence might also have been written:

While he ate a tuna sandwich, Joe rushed to school. (Prominence is given to the main clause, Joe rushed to school.)

The subordinate clause in both these sentences begins with *while*, one of many common subordinating conjunctions. Some others are: *after, although, as if, as though, because, before, if, in order to, since, so that, that, though, unless, until, when, whenever,*

*where, whereas, wherever,* and *whether.* The presence of one of these conjunctions should alert you to the possibility of faulty subordination.

On the SAT II, subordination errors resemble the coordination errors discussed earlier:

1. The relationship between the ideas is neither clear nor logical.

Vanya sought asylum in America, persecuted in her own country. (This sentence reverses the natural order of time. It also puts the effect before the cause.)

Persecuted in her own country, Vanya sought asylum in America. (This sentence states the two ideas in their proper order.)

2. The connecting word, or subordinating conjunction, fails to convey a reasonable or correct relationship between the ideas.

*While* she is fifteen years old, she is afraid of the dark. (The subordinating conjunction obscures both the meaning of the sentence and the relationship between the two statements.)

*Although* she is fifteen years old, she is afraid of the dark. (A new subordinating conjunction clarifies the meaning.)

I saw in the paper *where* the fleet is coming back to Norfolk. (The meaning may be clear, but the word choice is nonstandard.)

I saw in the paper *that* the fleet is coming back to Norfolk.

3. The emphasis is misplaced.

I arrived home from school and I received my acceptance letter from Ohio State. (The conjunction *and* gives equal emphasis to unequal ideas.)

I arrived home from school *when* I received my acceptance letter from Ohio State. (The more important idea is improperly placed in the subordinate clause.)

*When* I arrived home from school, I received my acceptance letter from Ohio State. (Stating the more important idea in the main clause places the emphasis where it belongs.)

In *Macbeth* the king is killed early in the play and he is an effective ruler. (The conjunction *and* gives equivalence to unequal ideas.)

In *Macbeth,* the king, who is killed early in the play, is an effective ruler. (Subordinating one idea and embedding it in the main clause gives emphasis to the other idea.)

In *Macbeth*, the king, who is an effective ruler, is killed early in the play. (Subordinating the other idea and embedding in the main clause changes the emphasis.)

4. The sentence suffers from excessive subordination.

Since she was born on July 4th, her parents named her Liberty, which is a variation of Libby, that happens to be an old family name which belonged to her great aunt who lived in Sparkill, which is a small town near Buffalo. (This sentence is grammatically correct but is weighed down by too many subordinate clauses.)

She was named Liberty because she was born on July 4th. The name is a variation of an old family name, Libby, which belonged to her great aunt from Sparkill, a small town near Buffalo. (The original sentence has been trimmed and divided in two, which vastly improves its style and effectiveness.)

## SAMPLE QUESTIONS ON FAULTY SUBORDINATION

1. Pedro is a new student in the school, and he comes from Portugal.

(A) Pedro is a new student in the school, and he comes from Portugal.
(B) Pedro, being from Portugal, is a new student in the school.
(C) Pedro, a new student in the school, comes from Portugal.
(D) Pedro, a new student in the school and native of Portugal.
(E) Pedro is a new student from Portugal in the school.

The sentence is a grammatically correct compound sentence but could be more effective if one clause were subordinated to the other. Choice (B) subordinates a clause, but the use of *being* oddly suggests that Pedro's presence in the school is related to his nationality. Choice (C) properly subordinates one idea and embeds it in the main clause. Choice (D) is not a complete sentence. Choice (E) alters the meaning of the original sentence. (C) is the best answer.

2. Having slammed her books on the desk, Meg felt angry about failing the test.

(A) Having slammed her books on the desk, Meg felt angry about failing the test.
(B) Having felt angry about failing the test, Meg slams her books on the desk.
(C) Slamming her books on the desk, angry about failing the test.
(D) Angry about failing the test, Meg slammed her books on the desk.
(E) Meg failed the test, therefore, angrily slammed her books on the desk.

The original sentence is ineffective because of an unclear cause-and-effect relationship between the participial phrase and the main clause. The sentence also suggests the following sequence: First, Meg failed the test, then she got angry, and then she slammed her books down. In the sentence, however, this sequence is confused. Choice (B) is better, but the verb tenses are erratic. Choice (C) consists of two phrases and is not a complete sentence. Choice (D) accurately conveys the cause-and- effect relationship and states the ideas in the proper sequence. Choice (E) needs a conjunction to create a grammatical relationship between the sentence parts. (D) is the best answer.

3. When he suddenly started to grin like an imbecile, I was walking with him in the park.

(A) When he suddenly started to grin like an imbecile, I was walking with him in the park.
(B) While I walked with him in the park, he suddenly started to grin like an imbecile.
(C) Suddenly starting to grin like an imbecile, he was walking in the park with me.
(D) He grinned suddenly like an imbecile and walked in the park with me.
(E) Walking in the park with me and suddenly grinning like an imbecile.

The major idea of the original sentence is in the subordinate clause. Choice (B) places the major idea in the main clause. Choice (C) puts the major idea into a phrase. Choice (D) changes the meaning of the original sentence. Choice (E) is a sentence fragment. (B) is the best answer.

## Misplaced Modifiers

For the sake of clarity, place modifying words, phrases, and clauses as close as possible to the sentence element they are meant to modify. Also, be sure to include the word being modified, or you may have a dangling sentence element on your hands.

> The young man in the VW van with the long hair must be on his way to the concert. (The prepositional phrase *with the long hair* is meant to modify *man*. Being misplaced, it modifies *van*.)

> The young man with the long hair in the VW van must be on his way to the concert. (The misplaced phrase has found its proper place.)

> Hurrying to my chemistry lab, the bell rang. (According to this sentence, the bell rang as it was hurrying to class. This construction is a dangling participle because the word being modified has been left out.)

> Hurrying to my chemistry lab, I heard the bell ring. (The grammatical subject *I* is properly modified by the participle *hurrying to class*.)

> To paint well, the easel should be set up in a well-lit room. (According to this construction, easels may paint well by setting themselves up a well-lit room. Since the person who is trying to paint well has been left out, the phrase *to paint well* appears to modify *easel*.)

> To paint well, you should set up the easel in a well-lit room. (The subject *you* is now properly modified by the phrase *to paint well*.)

## SAMPLE QUESTIONS ON MISPLACED AND DANGLING MODIFIERS

1. The award was presented to the actor that was engraved with gold letters.

   (A) The award was presented to the actor that was engraved with gold letters.
   (B) The award that was presented to the actor engraved with gold letters.
   (C) The award was presented to the actor who was engraved with gold letters.
   (D) The award, engraved in gold letters, and presented to the actor.
   (E) The award presented to the actor was engraved in gold letters.

Choice (A) is wrong because the clause *that was engraved in gold letters* modifies actor. Choice (B) contains the same misplaced modifier and is also a sentence fragment. Choice (C) is a variation of (A). Choice (D) is a sentence fragment. Choice (E) has its modifiers in the right place and is the best answer.

For more information on misplaced modifiers, please turn to page 97.

2. Driving to Litchfield, the freezing rain made the road slippery and hazardous.

   (A) Driving to Litchfield
   (B) While we drove to Litchfield
   (C) Enroute to Litchfield
   (D) To drive to Litchfield
   (E) We drove to Litchfield and

Choice (A) is a dangling participle. Choice (B) contains *we*, the proper subject of the action. Choice (C) also contains a dangling element. Choice (D) makes little sense. Choice (E) sets up two vaguely related coordinate clauses. (B) is the best choice.

For a more detailed discussion of dangling modifiers, please turn to page 98.

## Sentence Shifts

A sentence loses its effectiveness when an unexpected grammatical shift occurs from one part to another. Inconsistency may even rob a sentence of its intended meaning. Shifts in verb tense and shifts in pronoun person, among others, are found in the usage section of the SAT II as well as among the sentence-correction questions. Other inconsistencies that may be found in both parts of the exam are shifts in grammatical subject, shifts in voice, and mixed constructions. Still other shifts include those between subject and verb and between pronouns and antecedents. Faulty parallelism is still another kind of grammatical shift. Each of these sentence errors is briefly discussed and illustrated in this section of the book, but for a more thorough explanation, turn to the pages cited.

1. Shifts in verb tense

Before they went out of business, the video store almost gives their tapes away. (The sentence begins in the past tense, then shifts to the present.)

Before they went out of business, the video store almost gave their tapes away. (Now the sentence is cast in the past tense from start to finish.)

Susan agrees that she has been preoccupied lately and said that she was sorry. (This sentence begins in the present tense and ends in the past.)

Susan agrees that she has been preoccupied lately and says that she is sorry. (Now the verb tense is consistently in the present tense.)

## SAMPLE QUESTION ON SHIFT IN VERB TENSE

Jay had been working out in the weight room for several months before the wrestling coach <u>invites him to try out</u> for the team.

(A) invites him to try out
(B) being invited to try out
(C) invited him to try out
(D) had invited him to try
(E) invited him for trying

Choice (A), with a verb present tense, is inconsistent with past perfect tense with which the sentence begins. Choice (B) uses faulty idiom. Choice (C) correctly uses the past tense. Choice (D), with its verb in the past perfect, fails to distinguish the time of the coach's invitation from the time Jay had been working out. Choice (E) uses faulty idiom. (C) is the best choice.

For more discussion of verb tenses, please see page 64.

### 2. Shifts in pronoun person

Graduates of this school need four units of English, and you also need three units of math. (The sentence begins in the third person, then switches to the second person.)

Graduates of this school need four units of English and three units of math. (Third person is maintained.)

If one learns to write a research paper in high school, you can save a lot of time in college. (The sentence begins with the impersonal third person pronoun *one*, then switches to second person, *you*.)

In highly formal writing, use the *one . . . one* sequence:

If *one* learns to write a research paper in high school, *one* can save a great deal of time in college.

In less formal writing, *you* may be used throughout.

If you learn to write a research paper in high school, you can save a lot of time in college.

## SAMPLE QUESTION ON SHIFT IN PRONOUN PERSON

Anyone who is on the cleanup crew, <u>regardless of how old you are</u>, should plan to stay until at least midnight on Friday night.

(A) regardless of how old you are
(B) irregardless of how old one is
(C) regardless of age
(D) irregardless of his age
(E) regardless of how old they are

Choice (A) switches the pronoun from third to second person. Choice (B) maintains the proper person and number but uses the nonstandard *irregardless*. Choice (C) avoids the pronoun problem and is the most economical answer. Choice (D) would be correct except for the nonstandard *irregardless*. Choice (E) uses the plural pronoun *they*, which does not agree with the singular antecedent *anyone*. (C) is the best choice.

For more discussion of pronoun person, please see page 84.

### 3. Shifts in grammatical subject

To fix a flat tire, first jack up the car; then the damaged tire is removed. (The grammatical subject of the first clause is *you [understood]* because it is in the imperative. In the second clause, the grammatical subject shifts to *tire*.)

To fix a flat tire, first jack up the car and then remove the damaged tire. (The grammatical subject, *you [understood]* is maintained.)

## SAMPLE QUESTIONS ON SHIFTS IN GRAMMATICAL SUBJECT

Ask at the front desk when you enter the museum, for, <u>if one gets a pass, they may take photos of any painting they want.</u>

(A) if one gets a pass, they may take photos of any painting they want.
(B) if you get a pass, you may take photos of any painting you want.
(C) with a pass they may take photos of any paintings they want.
(D) photos may be taken of any painting with a pass.

(E) you may take photos of any painting you want, if one has a pass.

The original sentence, as well as choice (A), contains three clauses, each with a different grammatical subject: the first is *you* (understood); the second, *one*; and the third, *they*. Choice (B) casts all three clauses in second person (*you*). Choice (C) shifts the subject from *you* to *they*. Choice (D) maintains the subject but the modifying phrase *with a pass* is misplaced. Choice (E) shifts the subject from *you* to *one*. (B) is the best choice.

### 4. Shifts in voice

After Dan worked all day in the hot sun, a shower was taken to cool off. (The sentence shifts from active to passive voice between the subordinate clause and the main clause.)

After Dan worked all day in the hot sun, he took a shower to cool off. (Now both clauses are in the active voice; in addition, the grammatical subject is sustained between the clauses.)

A good ballgame was seen by Mark and Don when they went to Yankee Stadium. (The sentence shifts from passive to active voice.)

Mark and Don saw a good ballgame when they went to Yankee Stadium. (The entire sentence is constructed in the active voice.)

Active constructions are usually preferable to passive unless the person or thing performing the action is unknown or insignificant, or the the sentence is meant to emphasize that the subject has been acted upon.

| | |
|---|---|
| WEAK PASSIVE: | Leaves are dropped by trees in the fall. |
| ACTIVE: | Trees drop their leaves in the fall. |
| WEAK ACTIVE: | Someone robbed the bank again. |
| PASSIVE: | The bank was robbed again. |

Throughout the sentence-correction section of the SAT II, stay alert for passive constructions. Reject them in favor of active statements unless you see a clear necessity for using them.

### SAMPLE QUESTION ON SHIFT IN VOICE

Because the factory owners and their employees worked together to improve plant efficiency, <u>a big profit was made</u>.

(A) a big profit was made.
(B) the results were making big profits.
(C) the factory owners had made big profits.
(D) making big profits were the result.
(E) resulting in a big profit.

Choice (A) is a passive construction that emphasizes the result rather than who performed the action. Choice (B) is active but ambiguously worded—is *making* part of the verb or is it a gerund? Choice (C) is active but contains an improper shift in verb tense. Choice (D) is passive and contains a singular subject with a plural verb. Choice (E) is an incomplete construction that causes the sentence to be a fragment. (A) is the best choice.

For a detailed explanation of passive and active voice, please turn to page 190.

### 5. Mixed construction

Mixed constructions occur when the beginning of a sentence doesn't fit grammatically or logically with the end. It suggests that part way through the writer forgot how the sentence began. At best, sentences with mixed construction are confusing; at worst, incomprehensible.

Maggie's goal is to become a nurse and is hoping to go to nursing school after graduation. (The grammatical subject *goal* seems to have been forgotten in the second half of the sentence. The verb *is hoping* lacks a reasonable subject.)

Maggie aspires to become a nurse, and she is hoping to go to nursing school after graduation. (By creating a compound sentence with two subjects and two verbs, the problem is solved.)

Maggie, who aspires to become a nurse, hopes to go to nursing school after graduation. (Subordinating one of the clauses may be an even better solution to the problem.)

When Lana came to school with a black eye was a signal that she is an abused child. (The verb *was* needs a subject.)

Lana's coming to school with a black eye was a signal that she is an abused child. (*Coming* is the grammatical subject.)

He asked me what am I doing. (This sentence fuses the constructions needed for both a direct quotation and an indirect quotation. The hybrid turns out to be a mix-up.)

He asked me what I am doing. (This is the proper wording for an indirect quotation.)

He asked me, "What are you doing?" (This is a properly worded direct quotation.)

### SAMPLE QUESTION ON MIXED CONSTRUCTION

The next morning, after Christie's car was found abandoned, <u>there was a nationwide search for the missing author had started</u>.

(A) there was a nationwide search for the missing author had started
(B) there was the beginning of a nationwide search for the missing author
(C) a nationwide search for the missing author had began
(D) there begun a nationwide search for the missing author.
(E) a nationwide search for the missing author began.

Choice (A) contains a subject, *search*, with two verbs of different tenses, *was* and *had started*. Choice (B) eliminates one of the verbs but changes the grammatical subject to *beginning*, a weak alternative. Choices (C) and (D) contain errors in verb form. (E) is the best choice.

## PROBLEMS IN STANDARD ENGLISH USAGE

The rules of standard English that you should know to answer sentence-correction questions are the same as those required for the usage questions. Only the format of the questions is different. Instead of merely recognizing that an error exists, you must also identify the revision that corrects the error. Because the principles of standard usage remain the same, however, studying the usage section of this book will prepare you to handle both types of questions.

Several common usage errors are described and illustrated here. Read the material and try the sample questions. If you miss a question, check the answer explanations, but for a fuller discussion turn to the pages cited.

## Subject-Verb Agreement

Grammatical subjects and verbs must agree in number. That is, a singular subject must have a singular verb, and a plural subject must be accompanied by a

plural verb. The most common errors in agreement arise in the following ways:

1. When intervening words obscure the relationship between subject and verb.
2. When singular subject words sound as though they are plural.
3. When the the same subject word can be either singular or plural, depending on its use.
4. When the subject word is an indefinite pronoun.
5. When the subject comes after the verb.

### SAMPLE QUESTIONS ON SUBJECT-VERB AGREEMENT

1. Some colleges believe that the problem <u>of scholarships and other rewards for good athletes have gotten out of hand</u>.

(A) of scholarships and other rewards for good athletes have gotten out of hand.
(B) of scholarships and other rewards for good athletes has gotten out of hand.
(C) of giving scholarships and granting rewards for good athletes have gotten out of hand.
(D) is out of hand that award good athletes with scholarships and other rewards.
(E) of rewarding good athletes with scholarships are out of hand.

Choice (A) contains a plural verb, *have*, that fails to agree with the singular subject, *problem*. Choice (B) contains a verb that agrees in number with the subject. Choice (C) is a variation of (A). Choice (D) also contains a plural verb, *award*, that does not agree with the subject. Choice (E) contains a plural verb, *are*, that fails to agree with the subject. (B) is the best answer.

2. Behind the house there <u>is just one broken-down shed and one pile of rubble that</u> need to be carted away.

(A) is just one broken-down shed and one pile of rubble
(B) a broken-down shed and a pile of rubble which
(C) stand a broken-down shed and lay a pile of rubble that
(D) are a broken-down shed and a pile of rubble that
(E) you will have found a broken-down shed and a pile of rubble which

Choice (A) has a singular verb, *is*, that fails to agree with the compound subject, *shed and pile*. Choice (B) is a sentence fragment. Choice (C) has two plural verbs—*stand and lay*—with singular subjects. Choice (D) has a plural verb that agrees with plural subjects. Choice (E) changes the meaning of the sentence. (D) is the best answer.

For a detailed discussion of subject-verb agreement, please turn to page 57.

## Faulty Verb Forms and Tenses

Most verbs, when conveying information about the time of a particular event or action follow the pattern of regular verbs. For example, to express the past tense, add *-ed* to the present form of the verb: *walk/walked, cry/cried, type/typed*. To express the future tense, add *will* before the present tense: *will walk, will cry, will type*. A similar pattern is followed for participle forms. Add *have, has* or *had* to the past tense: *have walked, has cried, had typed*.

A problem arises, however, with those verbs—called irregular verbs—that don't follow the pattern. The verb, *to choose*, for example, is *choose* in the present, *chose* in the past, and *chosen* in its participle form. Sentence errors occur when the wrong form is used.

Other errors in verb form occur when writers use an *-ing* form of a verb in place of a more customary form and fail to add a helping verb.

> Julie, at the box office, *selling* movie tickets to the 7:00 o'clock show. (The *-ing* form may not be used as the main verb in a sentence without an helping verb.)
>
> Julie, at the box office, *has been selling* movie tickets to the 7:00 o'clock show. (The addition of the helping verb *has been* corrects the error.)
>
> Julie, at the box office, *sold* movie tickets to the 7:00 o'clock show. (Changing the form of the verb is another solution to the problem.)

### SAMPLE QUESTIONS ON FAULTY VERB FORMS

1. In spite of the cold and the discomfort of making the journey, Max was glad to have underwent the experience of seeing the northern lights.

   (A) to have underwent the experience of seeing
   (B) having underwent the experience of seeing
   (C) to have undergone the experience of seeing
   (D) to see during the experience of
   (E) undergoing the experience of seeing

   Choice (A) uses *have underwent*, a nonstandard form of the verb to *undergo*. Choice (B) changes the form of *have* but retains the nonstandard *underwent*. Choice (C) uses the verb in its proper form. Choice (D) makes little sense. Choice (E) is clumsily worded. (C) is the best answer.

2. Larry King, the talk-show host, skillfully probing his guest's knowledge of the scandal, but showing great tact and uncharacteristic courtesy because he didn't want to jeopardize his opportunity for a news scoop.

   (A) skillfully probing his guest's knowledge of the scandal, but showing
   (B) who skillfully probed his guest's knowledge of the scandal, but showing
   (C) skillfully probed his guest's knowledge of the scandal, showed
   (D) he was skilled in probing his guest's knowledge of the scandal, and showed
   (E) skillfully probing his guest's knowledge of the scandal, showed

   Choice (A) leaves the sentence as a fragment without a main verb. Choice (B) also leaves the sentence bereft of a main verb. Choice (C) lacks a conjunction before the verb *showed*. Choice (D) is a mixed construction. Choice (E) leaves the adverbial clause intact and properly changes the verb to past tense. (E) is the best answer.

   For more detailed information about verb forms, please turn to page 62.

## Faulty Comparisons

A sentence used to make a comparison usually follows a familiar pattern that requires the items being compared to appear in parallel form. All words essential to completing a comparison must be present in order to avoid ungrammatical or illogical comparisons.

### SAMPLE QUESTION ON COMPARISONS

1. In the judgment of some historians, the quality of FDR's presidency is on a par with or better than Wilson but not Lincoln's.

   (A) the quality of FDR's presidency is on a par with or better than Wilson

(B) the quality of FDR's presidency is on a par with or better than Wilson's

(C) the presidency of FDR is on a par or better than Wilson in terms of quality

(D) FDR was good if not a better president than Wilson

(E) FDR was equal or better than Wilson as a president.

Choice (A) compares *quality* and *Wilson*, which are not logically comparable. Choice (B) properly compares the quality of FDR's presidency with the quality of Wilson's presidency. Choice (C) compares *presidency* and *Wilson*, an illogical comparison, and also lacks parallelism. Choice (D) lacks *as*, a word needed to complete the comparison. Choice (E) lacks *to*, a word needed to complete the comparison, and is not parallel to the last clause in the sentence. (B) is the best answer.

2.  David Letterman, the comedian, is funnier and more savage than any comedian on TV.

(A) is funnier and more savage than any comedian on TV.

(B) is the most funniest and the most savage comedian on TV.

(C) is funnier and more savage than any other comedian on TV.

(D) is the funniest and is more savage than any comedian on TV.

(E) is both funnier and more savage than any comedian on TV.

Choice (A) compares Letterman and all comedians on TV, but Letterman cannot be funnier than himself. Choice (B) contains a double comparison, *most funniest*. Choice (C) compares Letterman to other TV comedians. Choice (D) lacks parallelism and is a variation of (A). Choice (E) is also a variation of (A). (C) is the best answer.

For a more detailed discussion of comparisons, please turn to page 68.

## Pronoun Problems

Pronouns must agree in number with their antecedents. Singular pronouns must have singular antecedents. Similarly, plural pronouns must have plural antecedents. Errors occur when antecedents are indefinite, like *everyone, anybody* and *each*, which sound plural but usually are not.

Pronouns must also agree in person throughout a sentence. A sentence cast in second person, for example, should remain so from start to finish.

Pronouns must also refer clearly to an antecedent. Meaning suffers when a pronoun lacks a noun or other pronoun to refer to. Implied references may be equally troublesome because no clear tie exists between the pronoun and the antecedent to which it is meant to refer.

Finally, pronouns must be in the proper case. Nominative case pronouns are reserved for grammatical subjects and predicate nominatives. Objective case pronouns are used everywhere else. Problems arise when writers fail to identify grammatical subjects or when they mix pronouns from different cases in the same phrase.

### SAMPLE QUESTIONS ON PRONOUN PROBLEMS

1.  In most countries around the world, they have laws that allow gay people to serve in the military.

(A) they have laws that allow gay people to serve in the military.

(B) they have laws allowing gay people to serve in the military.

(C) the laws that allow gay people to serve in the military.

(D) their laws allow gay people to serve in the military.

(E) the laws allow gay people to serve in the military.

Choice (A) contains the pronoun *they*, which doesn't refer to any specific noun or pronoun. Choice (B) is the same as (A). Choice (C) is a sentence fragment. Choice (D) is the same as (A) and (B). Choice (E) eliminates the pronoun problem by eliminating the pronoun. (E) is the best answer.

For more discussion of pronoun references please turn to page 85.

2.  The company, which long adhered to a "no-lay-off" policy, began changing their procedures under the pressure of financial losses in the early 1990s.

(A) began changing their procedures under the pressure of financial losses

(B) had begun to change their procedures under the pressure of financial losses

SENTENCE-CORRECTION QUESTIONS 125

(C) began to change its procedures under the pressure of financial losses

(D) under the pressure of financial losses and changing procedures

(E) changing procedures due to the pressure of financial losses beginning

Choice (A) contains a plural pronoun, *they*, which refers to a singular antededent, *company*. Choice (B) is the same as (A). Choice (C) contains the pronoun *its*, which agrees in number with the antecedent, *company*. Choice (D) lacks a verb, causing the item to be a sentence fragment. Choice (E) also lacks a verb, creating a sentence fragment. Choice (C) is the best answer.

For a full discussion of pronoun-antecedent agreement, please turn to page 82.

3.  If you want to travel to third world countries, you should prepare yourself by having all your innoculations brought up to date.

(A) you should prepare yourself by having all your innoculations brought

(B) a person should prepare himself by having all their innoculations brought

(C) persons should prepare themself by having all their innoculations brought

(D) one should prepare himself by having all your innoculations brought

(E) persons should prepare by having all their innoculations brought

Choice (A), cast in the second person (*you*), is consistent with the beginning of the sentence. Choice (B) shifts the sentence from second to third person and also mixes singular and plural pronouns. Choice

(C) shifts the sentence from second to third person and also contains a nonstandard usage, *themself*. Choice (D) shifts the sentence from second to third person and then back to second. Choice (E) shifts the sentence from second to third person. Choice (A) is the best answer.

For more discussion of pronoun person, please turn to page 84.

4.  It was virtually impossible for Fred and I, sitting near the rear of the auditorium, to hear Erica and he on the stage.

(A) Fred and I, sitting near the rear of the auditorium, to hear Erica and he

(B) Fred and me, sitting near the rear of the auditorium, to hear Erica and he

(C) Fred and I, sitting near the rear of the auditorium, to hear Erica and him

(D) Erica and he to be heard by Fred and me, sitting near the rear of the auditorium

(E) Fred and me, sitting near the rear of the auditorium, to hear Erica and him

Choice (A) incorrectly uses the nominative case pronouns *I* and *he* in places where objective case pronouns are needed. Choice (B) incorrectly uses the nominative case pronoun *he* after the infinitive verb *to hear*. Choice (C) incorrectly uses the nominative case pronoun *I* as an object of the preposition *for*. Choice (D) incorrectly uses the nominative case pronoun *he* as an object of the preposition *for*. Choice (E) properly uses objective case pronouns. Choice (E) is the best answer.

For more on pronoun choice, please turn to page 94.

# PROBLEMS IN STYLE AND EXPRESSION

A sentence with perfect structure and impeccable grammar may still be a mess. It may be verbose, poorly phrased, full of cliches, redundant, or clumsy. Your job on the SAT II is to recognize fat, foolish, muddy, and sloppy writing—or, to put it more positively—to choose the sentence that expresses its thoughts most clearly, cogently, and correctly. Twenty-five percent or more of the sentence-correction questions are likely to check your understanding of writing style and effective expression. To answer the questions, you need to apply basic principles of good writing: omit needless words, avoid redundancies, choose words carefully, use the natural order of English idiom, and so forth.

Common errors in style and expression are briefly spelled out below and illustrated with sample questions. Read the material and answer the questions. Turn to Part IV, the essay question section of this book, for more thorough explanations and discussion. In fact, studying Part IV and writing several practice essays could enhance your performance in both the essay and the sentence-correction sections of the SAT II.

## Wordiness

Economy of expression is a virtue. Sentences cluttered with unnecessary words are less effective than tightly written sentences in which every word counts. A well-crafted sentence will be damaged by deleting a word; in contrast, a verbose sentence will be improved.

Your task on the SAT II is to root out superfluous words and phrases. Look for redundancies—words and phrases that needlessly repeat what is already stated or implied. Look also for clauses that might be equally effective as phrases and for phrases that could be reduced to single words.

> During the months of July and August last summer, I had a wonderful summer vacation. (Because July and August are months of the year, and because they fall in the summertime, this sentence has far too many words.)
>
> Last July and August I had a wonderful vacation. (Needless words have been deleted without changing the meaning of the original.)

> As you continue down the road a little further, you will be pleased and delighted with the beautiful and gorgeous views of the scenery that you'll be seeing. (Redundancies abound in this sentence.)
>
> Continuing down the road, you will be delighted with the scenery. (This sentence reduces the initial clause to a phrase and eliminates redundancies, yet the intent and meaning of the original are preserved.)

### SAMPLE QUESTIONS ON WORDINESS

1. Both of my cousins who live in San Francisco speak both Chinese and Russian.

   (A) Both of my cousins who live in San Francisco
   (B) My two cousins in San Francisco
   (C) Both of my two cousins who live in San Francisco
   (D) My two cousins, who lives in San Franciso,
   (E) My two San Francisco cousins of mine

Choice (A) is grammatically correct, although it unnecessarily repeats *both*. Choice (B) reduces the number of words and eliminates the repetition in (A). Choice (C) contains a redundancy, since *both* and *two* mean the same. Choice (D) alters the meaning of the original by placing commas around the subordinate clause. Choice (E) contains a redundancy, *my* and *of mine*. (B) is the best answer.

2. Since there is funds budgeted for biology textbooks, the school will provide new books for all students in the course.

   (A) Since there is funds budgeted for biology textbooks
   (B) Since there are funds budgeted for the purchase of biology textbooks
   (C) A fund for the purchase of biology textbooks has been budgeted, therefore
   (D) Since funds have been budgeted for biology texts, so
   (E) Having budgeted funds for biology texts

Choice (A) contains a plural subject, *funds*, and a singular verb, *is*. Choice (B) properly changes the verb to plural and, therefore, is grammatically correct. Choice (C) contains a comma splice. Choice (D) contains a redundancy: *since* and *so*. Choice (E) has properly reduced the clause to a phrase. Both (B) and (E) are possible answers. Because (E) is less wordy than (B), however, (E) is the better answer.

For a full discussion of economy of expression, please turn to page 193.

# Awkwardness

Awkwardness is a vague term that covers a great many writing weaknesses. Awkwardness sometimes accrues from flawed grammar, such as incorrect pronoun choice or faulty parallelism. At other times, awkward expression originates in flawed sentence structure or misplaced modifiers. Most often, though, it comes about in generally clumsy constructions that have no specific cause except that the words don't fit neatly and smoothly together. Misuse of regular English idiom or poor diction may be responsible. To some extent, you must rely on your ear to detect the sounds of clumsily worded sentences.

## SAMPLE QUESTIONS ON CLUMSY CONSTRUCTION

1. As they entered the cave, Michael found that his eyes did not adjust to the darkness as quickly as Barbara's did, this is being why she found the skull and not he.

   (A) did, this is being why she found the skull and not he.
   (B) did, this is why she, not he, found the skull.
   (C) did; this is why she found the skull and not he.
   (D) did, which being the reason why she found the skull and not him.
   (E) did, being the reason why she found the skull and not him.

   Choice (A) contains *this is being,* an awkward, nonstandard usage. Choice (B) is better but contains a comma splice between *did* and *this.* Choice (C) is standard usage and is properly punctuated. Choice (D) contains *which being,* an awkward, nonstandard usage; it also uses an objective case pronoun *him* instead of *he.* Choice (E) contains *being,* an incomplete construction in the context, and also uses *him* instead of *he.* (C) is the best answer.

2. Vertical take-off and landing aircraft get their fixed-wing capability from high-speed air pumped from slots in the trailing edges of their rotors, in which it increases the airflow over them to create lift.

   (A) rotors, in which it increases the airflow
   (B) rotors, which increases the airflow
   (C) rotors, therefore it increases the airflow
   (D) rotors, the end result being it increases the airflow
   (E) rotors, consequently which increases the airflow

   Choice (A) is awkwardly worded; also, the pronoun *it* does not refer to any specific noun or other pronoun. Choice (B) eliminates the awkwardness and is concise. Choice (C) contains a comma splice. Choice (D) contains the redundancy *end result* and leaves the pronoun *it* without a specific referent. Choice (E) is awkward and ungrammatical. (B) is the best answer.

## SAMPLE QUESTIONS ON IDIOM ERROR

1. Stopping at a dime is what the engineers were after when they designed the brakes for the high-speed train.

   (A) Stopping at a dime is what the engineers were after when
   (B) To stop at a dime is what the engineers were after when
   (C) Stopping at a dime is what the engineers sought as
   (D) Stopping on a dime is what the engineers sought as
   (E) The engineers wanted to stop on a dime while

   Choice (A) uses faulty idiom. In standard usage the expression *"on"* a dime is preferred to *"at"* a dime. Choices (B) and (C) use the same nonstandard idiom. Choice (D) uses correct idiom. Choice (E) uses the correct idiom but says that the engineers, not the train, wanted to stop on a dime. (D) is the best answer.

2. After the two presidents signed the treaty, for all intensive purposes the document had the force of law.

   (A) for all intensive purposes the document
   (B) the document, for all intensive purposes,
   (C) for intents and purposes the document
   (D) for all intents or purposes the document
   (E) for all intents and purposes the document

Choice (A) contains an error in both diction and idiom. The standard idiom is *all intents and purposes*. Choice (B) is a variation of (A). Choice (C) distorts the phrase by omitting *all*. Choice (D) also distorts the idiom by using *or*. Choice (E) contains the proper words of the standard idiom. (E) is the best answer.

For a discussion of English idiom, please turn to page 91. See also the list of common usage errors, page 74.

### SAMPLE QUESTIONS ON FAULTY DICTION

1.  Marissa had disrespected her father by throwing a book at him during their argument over her curfew.

    (A) Marissa had disrespected her father by
    (B) Marissa showed disrespect for her father by
    (C) Marissa was disrespecting her father by
    (D) Marissa's disrespecting her father was shown by
    (E) Having shown disrespect for her father by

Choice (A) uses faulty diction. In standard usage *disrespect* is a noun, not a verb. Choice (B) properly uses *disrespect* as a noun. Choices (C) and (D) are variations of (A). Choice (E) is a sentence fragment. (B) is the best answer.

2.  For modern sailors, ridding their ships of vermin can be as incorrigible as Captain Ahab's quest for the great White Whale.

    (A) can be as incorrigible as Captain Ahab's quest
    (B) can be frustrating as Captain Ahab's quest was
    (C) can be incorrigible as Captain Ahab's quest
    (D) is as able to be a frustration as Captain Ahab's quest was
    (E) can be as frustrating as Captain Ahab's quest

Choice (A) uses faulty diction. The word *incorrigible* does not fit in the context. Words like *frustrating, ill-fated,* or *unsuccessful* would be better. Choice (B) uses acceptable diction but needs another *as* to make the comparison complete. Choice (C) uses faulty diction and lacks a complete comparison. Choice (D) is awkwardly worded. Choice (E) uses proper diction and completes the comparison. (E) is the best answer.

For a discussion of faulty diction and a list of common diction errors, please turn to page 72.

## Passive Construction

Passive construction in a sentence is useful when the performer of an action is either unknown or is not important to meaning.

> PASSIVE: The sun's first rays can be seen at the top of Mt. Katahdin. (Here the sunrise is more important than the people who see it. Therefore, passive construction is preferable to the active.)
>
> ACTIVE: People can see the sun's first rays at the top of Mt. Katahdin.

In general, however, active sentences are more emphatic, more lively, and less wordy than passive. Given the choice between active and passive sentences on the SAT II, go with the active unless you see a very good reason for doing otherwise.

### SAMPLE QUESTIONS ON PASSIVE CONSTRUCTION

1.  The Mideast crisis was discussed and a debate was held by us.

    (A) The Mideast crisis was discussed and a debate was held by us.
    (B) The Mideast crisis was discussed and then we held a debate.
    (C) We discussed and debated the Mideast crisis.
    (D) We discussed the Mideast crisis and then a debate was held.
    (E) We discussed the Mideast crisis and then we held a debate.

Choice (A), constructed in the passive voice, leaves the reader uncertain about who discussed the crisis. Choice (B) begins passive, then shifts to active and leaves the reader uncertain about who discussed the crisis. Choice (C) is active. Choice (D) begins active, then shifts to passive, leaving the reader uncertain about who debated. Choice (E) is active. Both (C) and (E) could be correct answers, but since (C) is more concise, it is the better answer.

2.  <u>Friday's quiz was failed because play rehears-</u>
    <u>als had been held every night that week.</u>

    (A) Friday's quiz was failed because play re-
        hearsals had been held every night that
        week.
    (B) She failed Friday's quiz because she had
        had play rehearsals every night that
        week.
    (C) Friday's quiz was failed because she
        had play rehearsals every night that
        week.
    (D) Having rehearsed for the play every
        night that week, she failed Friday's
        quiz.
    (E) Having had play rehearsals every night
        that week, Friday's quiz was failed.

Choice (A) contains two clauses, each of them passive. No mention is made of who failed the quiz. Choice (B) contains two clauses, each of them active. Choice (C) begins passive and switches to active. Choice (D) contains a participial phrase and an active clause. Choice (E) contains a participial phrase and a passive clause. Both (B) and (D) could be correct answers. Because (D) is more economical and avoids the repetition of *had* and *she,* it is the better answer.

For a complete explanation of passive construction in sentences, please turn to page 190.

# REVISION-IN-CONTEXT QUESTIONS

In this section of the SAT II you must answer questions about how best to revise two different essays. Some questions ask you about deleting or relocating sentences. Others may ask you to determine which is the best revision of a poorly constructed sentence or of a sentence containing nonstandard usage. You may also need to decide on the best way to combine several sentences into one or to identify which rephrasing of a sentence works most effectively as the topic sentence of a paragraph. In effect, you are being asked to participate in revising an early draft of another student's work.

Many revision-in-context questions refer to the same matters found in the usage and sentence-correction sections of the exam, but others pertain to broader concerns: the overall purpose, organization and unity of the entire essay or its parts, for example. Some questions will ask about paragraph development, the interrelationship of two or more sentences, the appropriateness of language, or the quality of the thought that the essay reveals. Whatever the questions, your basic task during this portion of the test is to identify the revisions that make both essays better.

## SAMPLE ESSAY AND QUESTIONS

Each essay is followed by six questions. Before trying to answer the questions, decide which of the following approaches works best for you.

1. *Read the essay carefully from beginning to end.* By having a firm grasp of the essay's meaning you will save time while answering some of the questions. Since you won't have to reread the entire essay, you can devote yourself fully to those portions of the essay singled out by the questions.

2. *Read the essay quickly—faster than you normally would.* A careful reading at this point wastes time and may distract you from your main purpose—to answer the six questions correctly. For the time being, therefore, ignore any errors or weaknesses you may notice. Read the essay carefully enough, though, to gain a sense of what it is all about. Once you've caught its drift, go to the questions, and, as you answer each one, refer to the text as much as necessary.

3. *Skim the essay for its general meaning; then read it again, but more slowly.* After two readings, one quick and one slow, you will know the essay intimately. Then you can concentrate on the questions rather than worry about what the essay says.

Which of the three techniques works best for you can be determined only by experience. As you read this chapter and take the practice tests in Part V, try each method and stick to the one that produces the best results.

Why not start now with this early draft of a student's essay on education in Russia? It is followed by typical revision-in-context questions.

[1] One unavoidable thing that one sees, no matter where you may be in the world, are children. [2] The world's youngsters hold the future of the planet in their hands and must be well-educated. [3] In the United States over 35 million kids attended elementary school in 1992 while there were 29 million Russian children at the same level. [4] Another difference is that American seven-year olds are in second grade and Russian seven-year olds are in first. [5] We can see that because Americans and Russians have different ideas of childhood, their educational systems are different. [6] This applies not just to school, but to outside activities, too.

[7] On the first day of September, seven-year olds in Russia gather around the school with flowers in their hands for their teachers. [8] The uniform of the school is worn by every boy and girl that has been the law ever since

*1936. [9] Everyone, including the parents, then attend a ceremony. [10] School directors, presidents of parents' organizations, and others give speeches, and then the bell is rung to commence classes. [11] School is in session six days a week until May 30th.*

*[12] Russian schools all have the identical philosophy about children. [13] One of their beliefs is that a school knows what is best for youngsters no matter what the parents say. [14] Other aspects of Russian education is that there is a lack of creativity. [15] If you were to walk into a first grade classroom, there wouldn't be any projects or collages on display or hanging on the wall. [16] One reason no one has originality is because teachers do not have many activities and supplies. [17] There are no finger paints, clay, magnetic boards, felt, glue, tape, or other things to expand on a child's creative side. [18] But there may be children's drawings on the classroom walls. [19] They are all identical. [20] On top of this, all the drawings are realistic. [21] Never find pictures of unicorns or two-headed monsters. [22] If someone was to draw a purple sun, he would be scolded by the teacher. [23] There is definitely no creativity or individuality.*

*Type 1.   Questions about standard English usage*

1. Which of the following is the best revision of sentence 14 ?

   (A) Other aspects that mark education in Russia are the lack of creativity.
   (B) Creativity lacking in Russian schools.
   (C) In addition, creativity lacking in schools of Russia
   (D) For example, a lack in creativity is in Russian schools.
   (E) Another aspect of Russian education is its lack of creativity.

This question is strikingly similar to the SAT II's sentence-correction items. Because sentence 14 contains an error in subject-verb agreement, you must find the best error-free alternative. Note that, unlike a sentence-correction question, choice (A) is not a duplicate of the original. Therefore, you may not leave the sentence intact. You must choose a revision, so you must examine all five choices before picking your answer.

Be sure to consider every choice. Although there is only one right answer, more than one of the revisions may be grammatically and technically correct. You must pick the best of the choices, not just any one that happens to be correct. The right answer is always the one that stands out as the very best alternative.

In Choice (A), the plural subject, *aspects,* indicates that the predicate nominative will also be plural. Because *lack of creativity* is singular, this is not a good choice.

Choice (B) is a sentence fragment.

Choice (C) is also a sentence fragment.

Choice (D) contains a transition, *for example,* that lacks a logical relationship with the material that came before. What is *lack of creativity* an example of?

Choice (E) accurately expresses the intended idea.

Choice (E) is the best answer.

2. Which version is the best revision of sentence 1?

   (A) One unavoidable thing that you see, no matter where one is in the world, are children.
   (B) Wherever you go in the world, you see children.
   (C) What you cannot help but see all over the world are children.
   (D) Unavoidably, no matter where you are in the world, are children.
   (E) Wherever you go, unavoidably, are children.

This question, like the previous one, could have been lifted almost verbatim from the sentence-correction portion of the exam. Again, choice (A) is different from the underlined words of the erroneous sentence.

Choice (A) is a mess. It contains a shift in pronoun from second person, *you* to third person, *one.* Its singular subject, *thing,* fails to agree with its plural verb. It is excessively wordy, and its use of the word *unavoidable* is inappropriate. The writer probably intended to say that the world is full of children, but *unavoidable* suggests that children are some sort of an irritant or inconvenience.

Choice (B) eliminates the errors of choice (A) and states the idea concisely and accurately.

Choice (C) contains the nonstandard usage *cannot help but see.* Use *cannot help seeing* instead.

Choices (D) and (E) are awkwardly worded and contain *unavoidably,* a word that conveys a notion of children that the writer could not have intended, as explained in choice (A).

Choice (B) is the best answer.

### Type 2.   Questions about sentence structure

1.   Which revision of sentence 8 is the best?

(A) Wearing the uniform of the school, the law has been in effect for every boy and girl since 1936.

(B) The uniform of the school is worn by every boy and girl, that has been the law ever since 1936.

(C) Starting in 1936, the uniform of the school is worn by every student, which is the law.

(D) Since 1936 the law has required every student to wear a school uniform.

(E) The law, passed in 1936, required that a school uniform must be worn by every boy and girl attending.

Because the sentence-correction part of the exam tests your ability to restructure sentences, you won't find many questions like this one in the revision-in-context section. Nevertheless, it pays to be prepared for even a single question on effective sentence structure.

Choice (A) contains a dangling participle. The phrase that begins *Wearing the uniform* should modify *boy and girl* instead of *law.*

Choice (B) contains a comma splice. A comma may not be used to separate two independent clauses without a conjunction such as *and, but, yet, nor, or,* or *so.*

Choice (C) contains an error in verb tense. The past tense is needed to describe action that took place in the past. Use *was* instead of *is.*

Choice (D) expresses the idea accurately and succinctly.

Choice (E) is grammatically correct but wordy. The use of *required* (past tense) leaves uncertain whether the law is still in effect.

Choice (D) is the best answer.

2.   Which would be the most effective way to combine sentences 18, 19, and 20?

(A) Children's drawings on display are usually realistic and almost all identical.

(B) But there may be drawings on the walls, identical and realistic.

(C) Schoolchildren like to have their drawings displayed on the walls of their class-rooms.

(D) Identical and realistic children's drawings on display on the walls.

(E) But there may be drawings; they are all identical; in addition, they are all realistic.

This sentence-combining question tests your understanding of how best to revise a series of short, choppy sentences.

Choice (A) combines the three sentences concisely and continues to develop an idea introduced earlier in the paragraph by sentences 15–17.

Choice (B) contains misplaced modifiers. The adjectives *identical* and *realistic* modify *walls* instead of *drawings.* In addition, the use of *but,* which suggests that a contrast is about to be made, is misleading.

Choice (C) is a perfectly good sentence but is irrelevant in the context of the essay.

Choice (D) is a sentence fragment. It lacks a main verb.

Choice (E) separates three independent clauses with semicolons. Although grammatically correct, it fails to combine sentences effectively.

Choice (A) is the best answer.

In direct contrast to a sentence-combining question, you may be asked in this section of the test about the best way to revise an excessively lengthy sentence. That is, the essay may contain a long, rambling sentence that, because of cumbersome modifiers and numerous phrases and clauses, needs to be divided into two or more shorter sentences.

### Type 3.   Questions about the effectiveness (organization, development, purpose, thought, and unity) of the whole essay or any of its parts

1.   Which of the following would be the most effective substitute for sentence 1 as both the opening sentence of the essay and the topic sentence of the first paragraph?

(A) What one sees everywhere in the world are children.

(B) Children exist everywhere in the world.

(C) Each country educates its young people in a distinctive way.

(D) The education of young children is the major concern of every country in the whole wide world.

(E) Education is important.

As the initial sentence of the essay, sentence 1 has a tall order: It should introduce the topic, narrow it as much as possible, and draw the reader into the essay. To determine which choice is most successful as an opening sentence, read the whole essay and figure out its main point.

Choice (A) is awkwardly worded because the subject and verb are placed at the end. In addition, it states a self-evident fact that neither introduces the topic of the essay nor engages the reader's interest.

Choice (B) states a self-evident generalization that fails to introduce the topic.

Choice (C) is a broad statement, but it adequately suggests the topic of the essay.

Choice (D) is a verbose variation of choice (C). It also states a dubious idea as a fact: It's doubtful, isn't it, that the education of young children is the *major* concern of *every* country?

Choice (E) is terse but far too general for the main purpose and point of the essay.

None of the choices is excellent. None of them narrows the topic sufficiently for a short essay. Of the five alternatives, however, (C) is the best.

2. Which of the following best describes the purpose of paragraph 2?

(A) To develop the main idea of the essay's first paragraph

(B) To explain an idea introduced in sentence 3

(C) To illustrate sentence 5

(D) To develop sentence 6

(E) To provide background material for the third paragraph

This question is about the relationship between paragraphs, in particular how the second paragraph is related to the others. To answer the question, examine the organization and development of the entire essay. Observe that the first paragraph attempts to introduce the essay's main idea, but extraneous information in almost every sentence is more confusing than enlightening. In the second paragraph the topic of the essay—elementary education in Russia—is made clear. The third paragraph discusses the lack of creativity in Russian classrooms. Having analyzed the essay in this manner, you must now figure out the role of the second paragraph.

Choice (A) is not acceptable because the main idea of the first paragraph is unclear.

Choice (B) is not a good answer because sentence 3 cites statistics which do not pertain to the content of the second paragraph.

Choice (C) accurately describes the function of the second paragraph. Although the main idea of the paragraph is not stated outright, the details imply that the first day at Russian schools is different from opening day in American schools.

Choice (D) is incorrect because the second paragraph does not discuss outside activities.

Choice (E) is not correct because the second and third paragraphs are not closely related.

Choice (C) is the best answer.

3. Considering the sentences that precedes sentence 14, which of the following is the best revision of sentence 14?

(A) Additional aspects of Russian education is that it lacks creativity.

(B) Therefore, children are taught discipline in school rather than at home.

(C) Russian families love their children very much and are glad to send them to school.

(D) Russia, for example, requires children to attend school until they are seventeen.

(E) On the other hand, Russian schools lack many of the luxuries of many American schools.

This question implies that the essay suffers from a lack of coherence. Your task is to choose a revision that strengthens the link between sentence 14 and sentence 13.

Choice (A) is virtually the same as the existing sentence 14. In addition, it contains an error in subject-verb agreement.

Choice (B) develops the idea introduced in sentence 13.

Choice (C) contains material that is irrelevant to sentence 13.

Choice (D) sends the discussion off in a new direction. In addition, the phrase *for example* is misleading. What idea is the example meant to illustrate?

Choice (E) contains new material unrelated to sentence 13.

Choice (B), therefore, is the best answer.

## WHAT YOU NEED TO KNOW TO ANSWER REVISION-IN-CONTEXT QUESTIONS

The revision-in-context section is the most comprehensive part of the exam. Short of having you actually write an essay, it can test almost any aspect of your writing knowledge. A review of the usage and sentence-correction material earlier in Part III will help you to prepare for some of the revision-in-context questions. Pay attention to problems of sentence structure: mismatched sentence parts (page 114), misplaced modifiers (page 118), and sentence shifts (page 119). Take a particularly hard look at the discussions of style and expression, since revision-in-context questions often deal with matters of wordiness and redundancy (page 126), errors in diction and idiom (pages 72 and 91), and passive construction (page 128).

The questions unique to the revision-in-context section deal with the overall effectiveness of an essay—namely, its purpose, organization, development, and logic. You may also be questioned on the structure and function of certain paragraphs as well as the role of individual sentences within paragraphs. To prepare yourself to answer all such questions, study the material and do the practice exercises in the remainder of this part.

## Purpose of the Essay

Once you have read the sample essay, try to articulate its purpose. Then you will be in a position to judge to what extent the purpose has been achieved. A common weakness in early drafts is that they have no apparent purpose. They may circle around a main idea, include irrelevancies, and at times skip from one purpose to another. First drafts oftentimes suffer from aimlessness because writers haven't yet figured out exactly what they want to say, and they hope to discover a purpose as they write. Sometimes they do, sometimes they don't.

Aimlessness is particularly apparent at the beginning of essays. Because they don't know their destination, writers begin with sweeping generalizations about life or the state of mankind. Perhaps you yourself have written all-encompassing openings that resemble one of these:

1. Since humans first walked the earth, they have been curious about the stars.

2. In all of literature there is no character who is as humorous as Tom Jones.

3. Today's rapidly changing society is undergoing an information explosion.

Any of these statements might be used to introduce a book, but short essays like those on the SAT II can rarely accommodate such commodious ideas.

Writers who have planned their essays usually know what they intend to say, have thought about who will read their work, and have made some decisions about the style and tone of their work. If their purpose is strictly to inform, they may adopt an impersonal style, using third person pronouns (similar to the way this paragraph is written). If their purpose is more to entertain, perhaps by telling about an experience, a personal and informal style using first person may be more suitable. On the other hand, if the purpose is to persuade or instruct readers on how to do something, such as how to prepare for the SAT II, the writer may talk directly to the audience, using second person pronouns.

Not all essays follow this pattern, of course, nor should you expect them to. Essay writers often have multiple purposes and complex attitudes toward their subject. The essays to be revised on the SAT II, however, are generally short and simple. Don't look for subtleties, sophisticated techniques, or hidden meanings. Each essay should have a purpose that can be easily and simply articulated. For example:

*The purpose is to inform the reader about how an astronaut is trained.*

*The purpose is to give an informal and entertaining account of the misadventures of a literary character.*

*The purpose is to advise novices about the uses of computers.*

Such statements of purpose will establish the boundaries of the essay. Any material that oversteps the boundaries is fodder for revision-in-context questions.

## Organization of the Essay

Because the essays to be revised on the SAT II are short—from three to five brief paragraphs—their organizational plan should be readily apparent after one or two readings. If you are asked about organization, check the opening paragraph first. Be sure it introduces, limits, and makes clear the purpose of the essay. This can sometimes be done with a single sentence. A good opening will point readers in a particular direction and name the place they're going to. Subsequent paragraphs will set up signposts along the way to remind readers where they have been and where they are headed. If readers lose sight of the direction, the essay's organization may be at fault.

For example, an essay's purpose may be to persuade readers to give up smoking. In outline, such an essay might be organized in this manner:

Introductory paragraph: The ill-effects of smoking
Body of essay {
  Second paragraph: Effects on health
  Third paragraph: High monetary cost of smoking
  Fourth paragraph: Social costs of smoking
}
Concluding paragraph: It's not worth it.

In the outline, antismoking arguments are arranged in a series of paragraphs, each discussing a different aspect of smoking. The organization is logical and clear. Each paragraph contributes a reason for not smoking. If, however, a paragraph were devoted to the history of smoking or to government regulations of the tobacco industry, it would be off the topic and would violate the essay's clear and sensible organization.

An organizational breakdown can occur for any number of reasons, but the main one is that the writer has lost focus of the main idea. As a result, the essay contains distracting or irrelevant material. In an unfocused essay, whole paragraphs may fail to contribute to the development of the essay's thesis, or worse, the essay's conclusion may undermine or contradict its introduction. Also, by devoting excessive attention to one idea, a writer may neglect others. If the essay on the ill effects of smoking, for instance, contained two long paragraphs on smokers' health, the imbalance would alter the essay's main point. In fact, any time the organization changes, the point of the essay also changes. The relationship is that delicate.

In an early draft of an essay, a writer should see to it that a clear basic organization is established. On the SAT II you may be asked to identify or revise sentences that don't fit into the essay's organizational plan. A question may ask you how to revise the sentence, or whether to move or delete it. As you make a decision, define for yourself the point of the essay and how the organization of the essay helps to fulfill it.

## Paragraph Structure, Unity, and Coherence

The revision-in-context section of the SAT II may ask questions about almost any aspect of paragraph writing, from how a paragraph functions in an essay to the use of a transitional word or phrase. It would be useful as you prepare for the exam, therefore, to study the characteristics and uses of paragraphs. No doubt you know many of them already. Paragraphs help you to organize your thoughts, and you probably use them almost without thinking as you shift your attention from one topic to another. Knowing the characteristrics of well-written paragraphs and recognizing paragraphing problems may help you to deal confidently with some of the questions on the exam.

### Structure of Paragraphs

Each paragraph of a well-written essay is, in effect, an essay in miniature. It has a purpose, an organizational plan, and a progression of ideas. You can scrutinize a paragraph in the same manner as you would a complete essay. You can study its structure and development and identify its main idea.

### Topic and Supporting Sentences

Most paragraphs are made up of two kinds of sentences. There is only one of the first kind, the *topic sentence*, which states generally the contents of the paragraph. Of the second kind, the *supporting sentences*, there are likely to be several. They provide the particulars needed to support and develop the topic sentence. Some supporting sentences themselves need support, provided by minor supporting sentences. The paragraph that follows contains examples of each kind of sentence.

*[1] Children with IQs well below average represent an almost insoluble problem for edu-*

*cators. [2] Such children often feel inadequate and rejected by teachers and peers, and feel of little value when they daily fail in a school environment which stresses and rewards academic success. [3] Failure in school is the number one cause of conduct disorders in the school and of juvenile delinquency in general. [4] The best that schools can do for children with low IQs is to teach them how to get by in the world and to teach them a vocation. [5] But vocational training is very limited in many schools. [6] Those that provide such training usually do so only for older adolescents.*

Sentence 1 is the topic sentence of the paragraph. To be convincing, it needs the support of sentences 2–5. Each supporting sentence adds a piece of evidence to prove the point of the paragraph—that children with low IQs create a problem for schools. Sentence 5 is a supporting sentence that requires additional support, provided by sentence 6.

*Location of topic sentences.* A topic sentence can be anywhere in a paragraph, but it usually appears at or close to the start. It isn't always a separate and independent sentence; it may be woven into a supporting sentence as a clause or phrase. (In the paragraph you are now reading, for example, the main idea is stated in the first clause of the initial compound sentence.) Writers vary the location of topic sentences to avoid monotony. They frequently save the topic sentence for the end of the paragraph, letting it stand out boldy as the peak up to which the supporting sentences lead.

In some kinds of writing—especially narrative and descriptive—the topic sentence is often left out altogether. Instead, the paragraph's main idea is implied by the accumulated details and ideas that allow readers to draw their own conclusions. For instance, a writer may set down several observations of a fast food restaurant: the crowd, the noise, the overflowing garbage can, the constant motion, the lines of people, and so on. The description creates an unmistakable impression of a busy place. There's no need for the explicit statement, "It was a busy day at McDonald's." Note the location of the topic sentence in each of the following paragraphs:

*[1] It is pitch dark and very chilly. [2] No one his right mind wants to force open his eyes and leave the cozy warmth of bed and blanket. [3] No one wants to walk in bare feet across the frigid floor to peer out the window to see icy rain slanting down in the early morning gloom. [4] The thought of damp clothes and cold feet keeps you where you are for a few more minutes, at least. [5] **It's hard to get up on a dark winter morning.***

Sentence 5 is the topic sentence. The supporting details in sentences 1–4 lead inevitably to the conclusion that it's hard to get out of bed on a dark winter morning.

*[1] For many years about 50,000 people have been killed annually in automobile accidents on the nation's roads. [2] Seat-belt laws, reduced speed limits, and increased police patrols have had almost no effect on changing the number of fatalities. [3] **The most promising way to bring the figure down, however, is to make cars safer.** [4] Many new cars have airbags on both the passenger and the driver's side. [5] Many also come equipped with antilock brakes. [6] The steel frames of many automobiles have also been strengthened by 50 percent, enabling people to survive crashes that would certainly have killed them before.*

Sentence 3 is the topic sentence. In the paragraph it serves as the pivotal point between the description of the problem (Sentences 1 and 2) and some promising solutions (4, 5, and 6).

The key to unlocking a paragraph's purpose lies in the topic sentence. If a reader fails to catch the main idea, the meaning of the paragraph falls apart. Instead of a coherent unit of meaning, the paragraph may seem to be a scattered collection of independent sentences. The effectiveness of a paragraph, therefore, depends on how tightly the topic sentence is tied to its supporting details. A loose or ambiguous connection weakens the paragraph's effectiveness. On the SAT II you may be asked to improve a paragraph by tightening the link between a topic sentence and the details that support it.

*Transitional and other sentences.* Paragraphs sometimes contain either or both of two other kinds of sentences. One, called the *transitional sentence*, links the thought of a paragraph to that of the previous or subsequent paragraph. It serves as a bridge between two different ideas. In short essays, however, bridges are usually built out of transitional words and phrases, not with full transitional sentences.

The other kind of sentence is one that is rare in a short essay. It announces to the reader, in no uncertain terms, what the writer intends to do:

Having lived with my parents all my life, I have analyzed the circumstances leading to their divorce and explained them below.

This discussion will attempt to sort out the significance of television as a medium for influencing the learning of children from age 3 to 12. Distinctions will be made between early childhood (age 3–7) and middle childhood (8–12).

Such announcements are usually reserved for long expository essays or for subsections of monographs and books. They help to keep readers focused on the purpose of the piece, but they are out of place in short essays.

PRACTICE EXERCISE ON TOPIC SENTENCES

Part A. The following paragraphs have been taken from longer essays. Underline the topic sentence in each. Some paragraphs may have an implied topic sentence.

1. [1] My family has moved so often I sometimes feel like a gypsy. [2] The first time we moved I was only four years old and it didn't bother me. [3] It seemed as though we just got settled, though, when my father announced a new transfer—to California, where I got to start school and where we stayed for three years. [4] But then we heard it was time to move on, and we settled in Minnesota. [5] Just as I was beginning to make friends and get used to the Midwest, the company sent us to Georgia. [6] From there it was two years in England and a year in Washington, D. C. [7] We've been in Massachusetts for almost six months now, and my main problem is answering *that* question, "Where are you from?"

2. [1] Another difficulty is that a person with a police record may have a hard time getting or renewing a driver's license. [2] A conviction for a felony can prevent a person from being able to enter a profession such as medicine, law, or teaching. [3] It can also make it difficult to get a responsible position in business or industry.

[4] Special hearings are required before an ex-convict can hold a government job.

3. [1] Music blasts from twenty boom boxes. [2] Children screech while splashing their friends at the edge of the sea. [3] Teenagers throw frisbees at each other. [4] The waves rush up the sand, gurgle a bit, stop, and retreat. [5] A single-engine plane, trailing a long sign— EAT PIZZA AT SAL'S—flies back and forth. [6] A vendor shouts, "Hey, cold drinks here, getcha cold drinks!" [7] During the summer, the beach is a noisy place.

4. [1] Clothing designers create new styles every year. [2] Therefore, consumers rush out and buy the new styles and cast away last year's designs even before the clothes are worn out. [3] Forgotten styles hang in closets gathering dust. [4] They'll never be worn again. [5] People fall in love with new cars and sell their old models long before they are obsolete. [6] Just for the sake of flashy style and shiny good looks, they scrimp and save their money or go deeply into debt. [7] And for what? [8] Just to look good. [9] All the money goes into the pockets of the manufacturers. [10] If people would get in the habit of buying goods only when they need replacement, waste would become an exception in America instead of a way of life.

5. [1] Perhaps it's true that "all the world's a stage," as Shakespeare said, because I have noticed that I act one way with one group of people and another way with a different group of people. [2] With one person I may act my age or younger. [3] I may act very shy or silly. [4] It's as though I can't control what I'm doing. [5] The circumstances just make me act that way. [6] Then, at another time with different people, I am the life of the party. [7] I won't stop talking, and people think I am four or more years older than I really am. [8] I feel that I can pretend so realistically that I sometimes convince myself that I really am what I'm pretending to be. [9] That's a very scary thought.

6. [1] During these years my family has had about sixty foster children come into our house to

live. [2] We have had children from all backgrounds, races, and religions. [3] Each child brought to our door brings a different tale of misfortune. [4] These stories have gradually grown worse over the years. [5] When we first started, the parents of the child usually wanted him or her but were unprepared or unable, for the time being, to care for their son or daughter. [6] Now, it is not unusual for the mother to be sixteen years old, a drug addict, or a convict. [7] Most of the time the mother is a combination of those. [8] Presently, we have two children living with us. [9] Three of their four parents are in jail, and one of the fathers is unknown. [10] Truly, as time goes on, caring for foster children has become more challenging.

7. [1] True totalitarianism champions the idea that everyone should be subservient to the state. [2] All personal goals and desires should be thrown aside unless they coincide with the common good of society. [3] Freedom for the individual is sacrificed so that the level of freedom for all can be raised. [4] With this philosophy, drastic improvements may be made in a relatively short time. [5] Almost by edict from the head of the society, education and literacy rates can be improved, and unemployment and crime rates may decrease.

8. [1] During adolescence the most obvious change that occurs is physical. [2] Childlike boys and girls suddenly blossom into young men and women. [3] Besides undergoing physical changes, though, this period is usually the time when personal values are explored and molded. [4] Decisions need to be made about what is important and what is not. [5] A struggle takes place within the mind of every adolescent to form a moral and intellectual code that determines the quality of the lives they will have in both the immediate and long-range future.

9. [1] The story by Stephen Crane raises the question whether a soldier who runs away from inevitable death in battle must be considered less of a man than one who stays and dies. [2] To an-

swer the question, one must first define "man." [3] Consider the stereotypical options. [4] There is the Arnold Schwartzenegger type, who, in movies like *The Terminator*, solves all of life's problems by physical strength and advanced weaponry. [5] Then there is the Howard Roark type, a character from *The Fountainhead*, who climbs to the top by using his brilliance and his unyielding integrity. [6] And then there is the Willy Loman type, a man from *Death of a Salesman*, who struggles his whole life pursuing an illusion. [7] At the end he realizes that he has fought a hopeless battle, but at least he has fought.

10. [1] In World War II, the United States dropped two atomic bombs, one on Hiroshima and one on Nagasaki, in order to defeat the Japanese. [2] American history textbooks justify the bombings as something that needed to be done in order to prevent even more deaths during a longer war. [3] Our history books also say that the death toll was about 50,000, while the Japanese claim the bombs took almost twice that many lives. [4] If the United States had lost the war, then the bombings would have been thought to be criminal actions. [5] But since we won, the judgment of history is that the end justifies the means. [6] In fact, throughout history, the war crimes of the victors have repeatedly been justified.

Part B.  Topic sentences have been deleted from each of the following paragraphs. After reading each paragraph, write a suitable topic sentence in the space provided. Omit the topic sentence if none is needed.

1.  _____

_____

_____

My mother's nature is very outgoing, emotional, and impulsive. She enjoys dancing, going to parties, being with lots of people, and spending money very freely. My father, on the other hand, is quiet, reserved, and controlled. He looks at things logically and practically, not giving in to his emotions. He feels more comfortable with only a few, if any, people around and would be content to watch TV or read a book for recreation.

2. _____
_____
_____

This was especially true in track and field. As other countries learned American techniques of training, however, their runners improved. Now athletes from all of the world win as many as or even more medals than track and field stars from the United States.

3. _____
_____
_____

One example of a self-destructive monopoly was the auto industry in the 1950s and '60s. In order to maintain their grip on the domestic market, Chrysler, General Motors, and Ford squelched the competition. Inventions that might have helped them in the long run were ignored. Automobiles were changed very little from year to year. Millions of dollars more were budgeted for advertising than for improving either the cars themselves or the process of manufacturing them.

4. An angry crowd thrust its way into the palace courtyard. Hundreds of people wielding sticks and knives and pastry rollers screamed at the figure who emerged onto the balcony. ''We need bread!'' they shouted, ''we need bread.'' The aristocratic figure above straightened her perfumed hair, wrapped her ermine shawl more tightly around her shoulders, and with a lift of her chin, turned and muttered to one of her ladies in waiting, ''Let them eat cake.''

_____
_____
_____

5. _____
_____
_____

From the first page to the last, I couldn't put it down. The author must have lived with the family in the book because she describes the mem-

bers in lifelike detail. By the end, you know them as though they were your own brothers and sisters. He tells what they ate, how they felt about religion, housing, politics, and even about each other.

6. One day I was smoking in the boys' bathroom when a teacher walked in. He took me down to the principal's office, where I was given a three-day suspension. My parents grounded me for a month, and I didn't get the money my father had promised me to buy my friend's used car.

_____
_____
_____

7. Probably the most important part of this new life is learning to live with your roommates, the people you see most often. Finding the perfect roommate may be impossible.

_____
_____
_____

The person should be a nonsmoker and a quiet person with similar interests to mine. She (it must be a *she*) should be considerate, courteous, generous, thoughtful, studious when I want to be studious, fun-loving when I want to have fun, respectful of privacy and personal property, and, finally, she should have a great sense of humor. In a nutshell, she should be like me.

8. In childhood I did not hestitate to take chances, to jump over the wide cracks in the rocks. Sometimes I made it across with no problems; at other times I was not so lucky. I scraped my knee, bled a little, but came back daring to try again. But now that I am older, I increasingly find myself shying away, afraid to fail, fearful of getting hurt. I live a style of life in which being in control and on top of things is paramount, where being the best and being perfect is what I yearn for. I am afraid to make mistakes, afraid to bleed, and afraid of being powerless. I take fewer chances.

_____
_____
_____

9. _____
   _____
   _____

He knew that he grew irritable more frequently. Why shouldn't he, when the doctors spoke to him as though he were a seven-year old, pronouncing their words deliberately and slowly. They must have thought he was hard of hearing or didn't understand. They constantly forced medicine on him and did everything for him as though he were incapable of helping himself. Sometimes he grew angry about the way people ignored him when he spoke or asked for something. His words were only noise to them. No one listened or carried on a conversation with him any more.

10. They did not have a written language, but by 1000 AD, they had built preplanned apartment houses four and five stories high. The foot-thick walls of oven-baked adobe brick, plastered over smoothly with clay, kept the occupants warm in winter and cool in summer. But by far their greatest architectural achievement was the intricate system of canals and reservoirs that irrigated their fields and brought water for miles across the desert directly into their homes.

   _____

   _____

   _____

*Answers on page 159.*

### Unity and Coherence in Paragraphs

Revision-in-context questions may ask you to identify or revise sentences that weaken paragraph unity or undermine paragraph coherence. When a paragraph deals with more than one main idea, it lacks unity. When sentences fail to connect to each other, the paragraph suffers from lack of coherence.

The following paragraph, for example, lacks unity. It discusses two different ideas, perhaps related in the writer's mind, but probably not in the reader's.

> [1] In the middle of one of our most crowded urban areas—Charlestown, Massachusetts, within sight of downtown Boston—a retired shipyard worker who was born in Ireland lives in a small, peeling frame house on a dead-end street. [2] In his backyard, he grows carrots and snowpeas, zucchini and peppers, and a variety of tomatoes. [3] He says that gardening is his greatest joy in life. [4] As for making money out of the land, it's done by the farmer, the rancher, the miner, the lumberman, the real-estate developer, the builder. [5] Corporations, too, earn money on the land by pumping oil, selling building lots, farming thousands of acres. [6] Banks earn income from the land by lending money to investors, and every village, town, and city in the country fills its coffers with tax money from landowners.

Sentence 4 swings the paragraph in a new direction. To bring it back, the writer should mention the financial rewards of gardening. Revised, sentence 3 might read:

> [3] He says that gardening is not only his greatest joy in life, but also a way to balance his family budget.

On the SAT II you may be asked to decide which of five sentences most effectively bridges the gap between two unrelated ideas and serves to unify the paragraph. In like manner, a question may ask you to replace or revise a sentence that weakens the coherence of a paragraph. In the following paragraph, for example, sentence 4 has no business being there, for it breaks the continuity of thought between sentences 3 and 5.

> [1] Like many other leaders throughout history, George Washington established his authority through the force of his personality. [2] Almost everyone who met him thought that he was charming, dignified, charismatic. [3] Some people of the time referred to him as a "superior being." [4] Yet the Father of Our Country was soundly defeated in 1755, when he first sought elective office. [5] At 6 feet 2 inches in his stockings, he was taller and more impressive than most men of his time. [6] His frame was padded with well-developed muscles, indicating great strength, and his blue-grey penetrating eyes could sparkle with humor at one moment and grow hard and determined at the next. [7] John Adams described him as a "gentleman whose great talents and excellent universal character... would command the respect of all the Colonies."

Coherence could easily be restored by eliminating sentence 4 altogether, but the exam might ask you to determine which of five alternatives is the best revision of the offending sentence. Because the purpose of the paragraph is to show the power of Washington's personality, anything other than a laudatory fact about him weakens the paragraph's coherence. With the irrelevant material deleted, the following sentence is a good replacement for sentence 4:

> *His bearing and presence suggested that he truly deserves to be called the Father of Our Country.*

PRACTICE EXERCISE IN PARAGRAPH UNITY AND COHERENCE
Some of the following paragraphs suffer from either lack of unity, lack of coherence, or both. Identify the problem in each, and write a comment that offers an effective remedy. Some paragraphs may not need revision.

1. [1] *Lord of the Flies* is about a group of English schoolboys stranded on a remote island after an airplane crash. [2] When they arrive, they divide into groups. [3] There are groups at this high school, too. [4] On the island, Piggy is the leader of the group made up of the most intelligent and rational boys. [5] He is a thinker, but he gets killed by another group, the savages, led by Jack. [6] A third group on the island is led by Ralph, who wants law and order and rules. [7] The different groups in the novel are amazingly similar to groups in this school, known as the nerds, the jocks, and the preps.
Comment _____

_____

2. [1] Under the present law, smoking marijuana can have serious consquences for young people. [2] They may find their education interrupted and their future put in doubt by having a police record. [3] An arrest or conviction for a felony can complicate their live and plans. [4] A police record causes embarrassment to a person's family. [5] Parents like to brag about their children's accomplishments. [6] Can you imagine a mother who would be proud of her daughter's experience in the courts and in prison?
Comment _____

_____

3. [1] Today there is general agreement that we are experiencing what is considered an unprecedented change. [2] Established institutions are crumbling. [3] The majority of people no longer live in traditional families that consist of two parents and their children. [4] Old moralities are being brought into question. [5] The United States has an increasingly diverse population. [6] A ghetto child may learn the advantages offered by drugs, crime, gang warfare, and trashing. [7] A child from an upper-class population may learn to question the value of legal justice and egalitarianism. [8] Formerly cohesive groups break up along a series of social and economic lines.
Comment _____

_____

4. [1] Rival political parties make elections meaningful by allowing voters to choose among candidates with contrasting views and interests. [2] Most parties try to unite divided interests within themselves in order to appeal to the greatest number of voters. [3] In the United States and Great Britain, a two-party system has long been effective in uniting various interests. [4] In totalitarian countries, criticism of the party in power may be considered treason. [5] Often, only a single, controlling party is permitted to exist. [6] Elections mean little in such countries, for the people have no real choice among candidates. [7] Nor do they have the freedom to openly criticize their government.
Comment _____

_____

5. [1] Department stores, unless they are like the general stores that still operate in many small towns, usually employ hundreds of people for different jobs. [2] A large number of employees engage in buying, pricing, and selling merchandise. [3] A sales promotion staff promotes sales by advertising and by designing attractive displays of goods to be sold. [4] In recent years, mail-order buying has forced many department stores to go out of business. [5] In addition, the store's comptroller handles financial affairs, such as billing, credit, and payroll. [6] The per-

sonnel department hires employees and deals with employment problems.

Comment _____

_____

6. [1] Scientists consider the porpoise, or bottle-nosed dolphin, one of the most intelligent animals. [2] They can imitate the sounds of human speech, and they communicate with barks, clicks, and whistles. [3] Some rate their intelligence between that of the chimpanzee, long held as the most intelligent nonhuman animal, and the dog. [4] Porpoises can be trained to leap high in the air, jump through hoops, catch a ball, fetch a stick, and even to participate in underwater work by serving as messengers between divers and surface ships.

Comment _____

_____

7. [1] *Robinson Crusoe* is a memorable adventure story about a man marooned on a desert island and was written by the British writer Daniel Defoe. [2] He was born in London in 1660 and started writing only after he went bankrupt in a business career. [3] He wrote about politics, religion, economics, and geography in addition to writing poetry and novels. [4] Today, he is best known for *Robinson Crusoe,* which is but a tiny fraction of his work.

Comment _____

_____

8. [1] Aristotle made valuable contributions to the study of logic. [2] Plato, the teacher of Aristotle and Socrates' star pupil, believed that understanding the nature of perfect forms, such as the circle and the square, leads to understanding ideal forms in all areas of life. [3] Socrates fought the Sophists all his life because he believed in truth, and the Sophists denied the existence of truth. [4] They said that everything was relative, incuding knowledge and morality. [5] The period of ancient philosophy reached its climax in Greece in 600–500 BC.

Comment _____

_____

9. [1] The American pioneers made simple farming implements and household tools. [2] They made pitchforks, for example, by attaching long handles to deer antlers. [3] Brooms were made by fastening together ten or twenty small tree branches. [4] They whittled wooden spoons, bowls and platters, and used gourds and the horns of sheep and other animals for drinking cups. [5] They made graters by punching small holes into a piece of sheet iron. [6] Then they would rub kernels of corn across the jagged surface to make cornmeal.

Comment _____

_____

10. [1] You can't find Potter's Field on a map. [2] It's not a real place. [3] Rather it is the name given to any plot of land reserved for the burial of unidentified and destitute people. [4] The name was first used in the New Testament of the Bible. [5] After Judas betrayed Jesus for thirty pieces of silver, the priests used the money to buy ''the potter's field to bury strangers in.'' [6] Today, in many urban areas, potter's fields have disappeared. [7] Land is too valuable to use for burying the remains of unknown and unclaimed people. [8] For a fraction of the cost, bodies are cremated and ashes thrown into common graves.

Comment _____

_____

*Answers on page 159.*

### Coherence Through Combining Sentences

Paragraph coherence often comes from the repetition of key words or from the use of synonyms and pronouns. These and other transitional words and phrases, such as *also, moreover, in addition, however, but, naturally, of course,* serve as the glue that keeps a paragraph from flying off in different directions. Disjointed paragraphs force readers to slow down, or even stop abruptly at the end of each sentence, pause, and then refocus for the next. Instead of a smooth journey, readers experience mental bumps and jolts. This is never more evident than in a series of short, choppy sentences that would benefit from being combined.

On the SAT II you may be asked to improve a paragraph's coherence by choosing a revision that effectively combines two or three disconnected sentences.

The following paragraph, for instance, consists of several discrete sentences:

> [1] Pompeii was an ancient city. [2] In 79 A.D. the volcano on Mt. Vesuvius erupted. [3] Pompeii was one of the great cities of the Roman Empire. [4] The volcano buried Pompeii under tons of hot, wet ash. [5] The city was near the base of the mountain. [6] In less than a day the city was buried. [7] It just vanished.

No doubt the paragraph is unified in thought—it's all about Pompeii's destruction. But it suffers from incoherence because each detail, no matter how important or how trivial, is stated in a separate sentence. To achieve coherence, the sentences need to be combined:

> [1] The ancient city of Pompeii, one of the great cities of the Roman Empire, lay near the base of Mt. Vesuvius. [2] In 79 A.D. Vesuvius errupted, burying the city under tons of hot, wet ash. [3] In less than a day the great city vanished.

Seven separate sentences have been transformed into three. During the transformation some words were deleted or changed. Key ideas have been emphasized, and other ideas have been put into subordinate sentence elements. Overall, the revised passage exemplifies more skilled, more mature writing.

On the SAT II, the sentences that you will be asked to combine probably won't be a paragraph by themselves. More likely, they will be two or three short sentences within a longer paragraph. When you look at the choices, keep in mind that the most concise or the cleverest revision may not always be the best. Instead, examine the context scrupulously, and select the revision that fits most logically and stylistically into the context of the paragraph.

PRACTICE EXERCISE IN COMBINING SENTENCES
Practice your sentence combining skills. Use the spaces provided to write one or more sentences that combine the ideas of each group. Since any group of sentences can be combined in numerous ways, try to write at least two different versions. When necessary, add, delete, and alter words. Play with alternatives; that's the only way to discover the possibilities and to develop your "sentence sense."

1. She is only thirteen. She is an expert gymnast. She has won recognition.

   _____
   _____
   _____
   _____
   _____

2. An accident occurred. The accident was a hit and run. Broken glass lay on the road.

   _____
   _____
   _____
   _____

3. Aunt Ellen went to the grocery store. She bought tomato juice. The tomato juice was in a glass bottle. The bottle was in a grocery bag. Aunt Ellen dropped the grocery bag. The bottle broke. Aunt Ellen had a mess. The mess was on her hands.

   _____
   _____
   _____
   _____

4. The baseball hit the picture window. The picture window belonged to Mr. Strickman. The glass shattered. The glass shattered in a thousand pieces.

   _____
   _____
   _____
   _____
   _____

5. There was a storm. The snow fell. Snow fell on the roads. It was two feet deep. I could not go

out. I had nothing to do. I watched TV. I worked on a jigsaw puzzle. Time passed slowly.

_____

_____

_____

_____

6. The earth revolves around the sun. It takes about 365 days for a revolution. The earth rotates on its axis. One rotation occurs every 24 hours. The revolution determines the length of the year. The rotation determines the duration of a day.

_____

_____

_____

_____

7. Euripides lived more than 2,000 years ago. He lived in ancient Greece. He wrote plays. The plays were tragedies. The plays are still performed.

_____

_____

_____

_____

_____

8. Music has a unique power. Music often transports people's minds. People dream and think while listening to music. People often feel refreshed after listening to music.

_____

_____

_____

_____

9. Human beings have skulls. Skulls are made up of bones. The skull has twenty-two bones. Eight bones make up the cranium. The cranium pro-

tects the brain. Fourteen bones are used to form the face and jaw.

_____

_____

_____

_____

10. The Hopi Indians value peace and contentment. The word "Hopi" means peaceful and happy. The name reflects the culture. The culture lacks tension. The people lack competitiveness. Material possessions are unimportant. Self-discipline is important. So is restraint. So is concern for the welfare of others. The family is the highest value. The family is the whole Hopi tribe.

_____

_____

_____

_____

_____

*Answers on page 160.*

### Development of Paragraphs

Like an essay, each paragraph should have a recognizable plan. A paragraph may consist of nothing more than a collection of facts that support the topic sentence. Or it may take the form of a brief narrative, its events spelled out in the order they occurred. It may be a comparison and contrast, a definition, an explanation of a process, or a combination of these and other forms.

Depending on the paragraph's purpose, supporting details may be arranged spatially, chronologically, in order of importance, from general to specific or vice-versa—or, in any arrangement that logically develops the main idea. Although writers will rarely follow a formula to create a paragraph, most abide by the rule of thumb that says that a paragraph of one or two sentences is too skimpy. To develop an idea thoroughly takes several sentences. At the same time, though, most modern writers of nonfiction avoid letting their paragraphs run for a dozen or more sentences. Between four and eight sentences is customary, but by no means universal. In the revision-in-context section of the SAT II, however, any paragraph that is substantially longer or shorter than the others in the essay may well be ripe for revision.

On the exam you may also be asked to identify a suitable plan for revising a particular paragraph. Therefore, you should know the most common patterns of paragraph development. Don't bother memorizing them for the exam, but your ability to recognize each pattern when you see it could be helpful.

1. *Argument and proof.* In this organizational plan, a paragraph's supporting sentences consist of arguments or examples meant to prove the validity of the topic sentence.

> Throughout the Vietnam war, military spokesmen invented a new way of speaking about combat in Southeast Asia. When your own troops were shelled by mistake, the event was called "accidental delivery of ordnance equipment." Soldiers didn't use shovels to dig holes, they used "combat replacement evacuators." Parachutes were "aerodynamic personnel accelerators." A "protective reaction strike" meant an invasion. Destroyed villages were not destroyed; they were "pacified." And the money paid to the family of a South Vietnamese civilian killed by mistake was a "condolence award."

The first sentence is the topic sentence. The rest of the paragraph consists of examples that illustrate the "new way of speaking."

2. *Definition.* The supporting details define or explain a general word, term, or idea. Ordinarily, such paragraphs consist of more than simple definitions like those found in a dictionary because broad and abstract ideas such as *loyalty, beauty, evil* and *success* are better defined by *example*, by *analogy*, or by *comparison and constrast*.

> Utopia is the name often given to a society in which everything is thought to be perfect. Everything in the society, from its economic policies to its social practices, is designed to keep the society functioning without difficulty. In Utopia all people are happy, wise, equal, prosperous, and well-educated. Utopia is an appropriate name. It comes from a Greek word meaning "no place."

The foregoing paragraph defines *utopia* by describing its characteristics and explaining the derivation of the word.

> To be in love with sailboats is to read books and magazines on sailboats, to paper your walls with sailboat pictures and posters, to keep lists of sailboats, and to study plans and blueprints of sailboats. It also means making models and dreaming someday of designing and building your own sailboat. It means that you also spend many hours of every day thinking about, looking at, and working on sailboats. And, of course, it means never letting a chance slip by to put on your shorts and sneakers, check the wind, and steer a sailboat out to open water.

The paragraph defines what it means to be "in love" with sailboats by citing examples of how sailors stricken with a nautical bug might spend their time.

> A spider's web is an exquisite musical instrument. It is constructed of many strings of different lengths under various degrees of tension. It is played upon by the rain and the wind, by other insects, and by the master musician herself, the spider. So sensitive is the spider's sense of touch that from one corner of the web she can locate a struggling victim, determine its size, and, by the rhythms and tempo of vibrations, judge it to be a moth, a hapless mosquito, housefly, or other insect.

The qualities of a spider web are here defined by drawing an analogy between the web and a fine musical instrument.

> Albert Perry may have been the model for Hal Roet in Thayer's new novel. Thayer calls Roet an "unpredictable farmer." The real-life Perry was a tobacco farmer for years and was known throughout Piedmont County as Peripatetic Perry. At 30, he unexpectedly left his wife and went to New York to become a rock and roll singer. Roet, too, left his farm in the hands of his wife and traveled around the country with a rodeo. But the similarity ends there. Perry was compulsively self-revealing, Roet quiet and unassuming. Perry was indifferent to his family, while Roet was torn, anguished and guilt-ridden about abandoning Marion and the three children. Finally, Perry craved fame. Roet, on the other hand, didn't care about becoming a well-known bronco rider. He was in it for the thrill of doing something dangerous.

In this paragraph the personalities of two men—one real and one fictional—are being defined by comparing and contrasting their characteristics.

3. *Cause and effect.* The details of a paragraph developed by means of cause and effect explain or demonstrate how one event or set of circumstances leads to, or causes, another event or set of circumstances.

> Because the moon has only one sixth the gravity of the earth, people on the lunar surface weigh only a fraction of their normal poundage. They walk easily, each step evolving into a rhythmic, bounding motion that feels like a stroll on a trampoline. At the same time, starting and stopping require unusual bursts of energy. To stop forward motion, they must dig their heels into the ground and lean backward. If they fall, they descend in slow motion, and the impact is no stronger than falling onto a feather bed. Getting up again is difficult and enervating, however.

In the cause-and-effect paragraph above, the consequences of one sixth gravity are described.

4. *Analysis.* In an analytical paragraph a general statement is divided into component parts. In a process analysis, for example, the steps in a procedure may be explained.

> When repainting a room, it's best to remove as much furniture and carpeting as possible. Be sure to cover everything left behind with a tarpaulin or plastic sheet. Using a roller, paint the ceiling first. While the ceiling dries, paint windows, doors, and trim, except for baseboards. Then paint the walls. Try to avoid changing cans in the middle of a wall because the paint color from two different cans may not match exactly. If you expect to finish a can before you finish a wall, pour the paint from two cans into a large bucket and mix well. One coat of paint is usually not enough, so be prepared to apply a second coat to all surfaces. Paint the baseboards last.

In the paragraph above, the steps in a process of repainting a room have been spelled out. Another kind of analytical paragraph classifies a general category by its component parts.

> Vegetables can be classified according to climate and growing requirements. Early vegetables like leaf lettuce, spinach, radishes, and peas grow best in cool weather and are planted shortly before the last frost. Moderately hardy vegetables, including potatoes and onions, should also be grown before the intense heat of summer. Late spring is the time to start hardy vegetables like carrots, beets, cabbage, and cauliflower because they easily endure the summer sun's heat. Some vegetables are extremely sensitive to cold and, therefore, can be planted only weeks after the last frost. These include soybeans, cucumbers, summer squash, and watermelons. Such plants as tomatoes, peppers, and eggplant are usually started indoors and transplanted outside in late spring or early summer.

Paragraphs need not be developed in only one way. Because purpose should dictate structure, you will often find effective paragraphs that combine two or more methods. To prove a point, for instance, a writer may combine facts with definition and analysis.

5. *The effectiveness of development.* The effectiveness of a paragraph sometimes depends on its organization—that is, on what comes first, what comes second, and so forth. Ideas can be arranged from general to specific or vice versa. Chronological and spatial arrangements make sense for narrative and descriptive paragraphs. In a cause and effect discussion, logic dictates that the cause precede the effect, but it may sometimes be preferable to reverse the order. Clarity and intent, as always, should govern the sequence of ideas. In an effective paragraph, each sentence has its place and purpose. Garbled paragraphs, on the other hand, often consist of sentences arranged in random order. On the SAT II you may be asked to identify and relocate sentences for more effective, coherent development.

In a well-knit paragraph, most sentences contain clues that situate them in a context. Although meaning is the primary clue, words and phrases like *for example, also, but, on the other hand,* and so forth link sentences to each other. In the following paragraph, for example, observe how the italicized words and phrases are clues to the arrangement of sentences:

> [1] Part-time jobs for high school students are a mixed blessing. [2] *They* help young people earn the value of money. [3] It is *also* satisfying for young people to help with their family finances. [4] *On the other hand*, jobs often

distract students from their schoolwork. [5] *Moreover*, many jobs are so boring that students get the idea that work is boring.

Sentence 1 expresses the most general idea in the paragraph and serves as the topic sentence. The pronoun *they*, which begins sentence 2, refers to *jobs*, a noun in the first sentence. Sentence 3 contains the connecting word *also*, indicating that a new thought will be added to one expressed in a previous sentence. Sentence 4 begins with *on the other hand*, a common transitional phrase, which signals the reader that a contrasting idea is about to be stated. The last sentence begins with *moreover*, another transitional phrase that signals the addition of still another idea. Because of the presence of linking elements, these five sentences cannot be arranged in any other way without destroying the paragraph's coherence.

## PRACTICE EXERCISE IN SENTENCE ARRANGEMENT

The sentences in each of the following groups belong to a well-written paragraph. They are not in the proper order, however. Rearrange the sentences into a logical order. In the blank spaces provided, write the number that represents each sentence's place in the paragraph.

1. _____ a. In the end, morale got so low that people started quitting the team.
   _____ b. Whether you were a pole vaulter, a sprinter, or a distance runner, practices were the same for everyone.
   _____ c. He was forcing the team to work out the same way every day.
   _____ d. Mr. Reese, the track coach, had been acting like a tyrant.

2. _____ a. First, put in the large, firm, and heavy items that won't be crushed or damaged by putting something on top of them.
   _____ b. Meanwhile, think of all the items that can be easily bruised, crushed, or broken, such as eggs, packages of bread, fruit, and lightbulbs.
   _____ c. To fill up a paper bag with groceries usually takes about fifteen seconds if you do it right.

   _____ d. Immediately after that, put in light, but firm items such as crackers, cereal, and butter.
   _____ e. Canned goods and bottles fit the bill perfectly.
   _____ f. Those should be saved for last.

3. _____ a. Then, too, I started feeling comfortable talking with adults.
   _____ b. Most people think of "maturity" in terms of responsibility, but I think it has more to do with learning to control one's actions.
   _____ c. I could actually talk to them instead of shutting up like a clam and just standing there like a dummy.
   _____ d. For example, I knew that I was more mature than others when I didn't laugh out loud in science class when the teacher talked about reproduction.

4. _____ a. As blood circulates, it cleans out body waste, like the collector who cruises the neighborhood picking up trash.
   _____ b. In return, it deposits oxygen and food in every body part, from the top of the head to the little toe.
   _____ c. Yet human life depends on those four quarts of blood that are pumped from the heart, flow to every cell in the body, and return to the heart to be pumped again.
   _____ d. If you drained the blood from the body of a girl weighing about 125 pounds, you would fill little more than a gallon milk container.

5. _____ a. His mistake was corrected fifty years later by Carl Blegen of the University of Chicago.
   _____ b. He figured out that every few centuries a new city had been built upon the ruins of an old.
   _____ c. In the 1870s, the archaeologist Heinrich Schliemann dug in the correct spot and discovered nine ancient cities of Troy, one lying on top of another.

_____ d. But without realizing it, Schleimann had dug right past the layer he had been seeking, the layer containing the ruins of the famous city of the Trojan Horse.

_____ e. By then, it was too late for Schliemann, who had been dead for fifty years.

6. _____ a. For months at a time Jerry's fans would devotedly follow his group around the country wherever it played in concert.

_____ b. Just two years after its debut, Jerry and his band left an indelible mark on millions of young fans.

_____ c. In spite of his family, who told him that he would never be a successful professional singer, Jerry decided to take up guitar and form a musical group.

_____ d. He did not only created a whole new subculture but developed a following.

7. _____ a. He felt terribly anxious about his wounded leg.

_____ b. The slightest movement of his knee caused a sudden and intense pain, unlike anything he had ever felt before.

_____ c. He could not sleep, in spite of the sedative administered to him by the British nurse.

_____ d. In Milan, the lieutenant lay in a hospital bed.

_____ e. It was even worse than the pain he recalled when, as a child, he had pulled a pot of steaming water over on himself.

8. _____ a. Each layer is another page that tells the story of volcanic eruptions, massive floods, and the advance and retreat of the Ice Age.

_____ b. Unfortunately, it also tells of the present day's pollution of the earth's air and lands.

_____ c. If you can read its language, the sediments contain a record of all the dramatic and catastrophic events that have occurred through the earth's history.

_____ d. The ocean floor is a diary of the earth.

9. _____ a. He became blind in 1652 and used his daughter as an instrument to write some of his finest poems.

_____ b. His daughter, with her quill pen in hand, sat with her father to record his thoughts, to read them back, to make revisions in whatever way Milton wanted.

_____ c. The first poet to use a word processor was John Milton.

_____ d. The actual processing of words went on in Milton's head.

10. _____ a. After winning two Critics' Circle awards and the Pulitzer Prize for drama, Tennessee Williams earned fame and lots of money.

_____ b. Usually, he's named with Eugene O'Neill and Arthur Miller as one of the leading American dramatists of the 20th century.

_____ c. They flocked to Broadway to see his plays and later swarmed to the movies to see filmed versions of his works.

_____ d. All of a sudden, the public began to view him as one of the best modern playwrights.

*Answers on page 160.*

### Review of Paragraph Structure

These are seven general principles of paragraph construction. Keep them in mind when answering questions in the revision-in-context section of the SAT II:

1. A paragraph usually contains two types of sentences: a topic sentence and supporting sentences. Occasionally, a paragraph may contain one or both of two other types: a transitional sentence and a sentence that announces the paragraph's purpose.

2. The intent of the paragraph is stated by the topic sentence. Sometimes the intent is not stated outright, but rather strongly implied by the content of the paragraph. When stated, the

topic sentence may be found anywhere in the paragraph as an independent sentence or as part of another sentence.

3. The idea stated or implied by the topic sentence is explained or illustrated by supporting sentences.

4. The topic sentence and supporting sentences are fused into a unit of communication by a particular underlying relationship such as that between argument and proof, cause and effect, definition, or classification and analysis, among others.

5. Unified paragraphs deal with only one major idea at a time.

6. Coherent paragraphs do not contain any extraneous or irrelevant material.

7. Coherence is further enhanced by verbal or logical links.

## Functions of Paragraphs

Some revision-in-context questions may single out a part or all of a paragraph and ask about its role in the given essay. You may be asked merely to identify the paragraph's function, or, if a particular sentence is flawed or weak, to determine which of five revisions would be preferable. To answer such questions, you should understand how various paragraphs generally function in an essay.

### First Paragraphs

Obviously, an effective introductory paragraph launches the essay and makes the intent of the essay clear to the reader. The essays you'll be given to read on the exam are rather brief, no more than three or four short paragraphs. Elaborate opening paragraphs written to grab a reader's attention are not appropriate. Nor is material that gradually leads to the essay's main point. You probably won't find vivid anecdotes, a snatch of conversation, an emphatic opinion, or any other popular gimmick—often called a *hook* in longer essays. Instead, look for succinct and straightforward introductions. Devoting a quarter or more of an essay to introductory material is bad form and reflects on the writer's sense of proportion.

When asked about the beginning of an essay on the exam, keep in mind that in a short essay, an introductory paragraph should get on with the essay's

main issue quickly. Material that fails to focus on the main point is ineffective and should be revised.

### Last Paragraphs

The final paragraph should leave a reader with a thought to remember. It should also give a reader a sense of completion. Because it comes last, the final paragraph often leaves an enduring impression on a reader's mind. A weak, apologetic, or irrelevant conclusion may dilute or even obliterate the effect that a writer tried hard to create earlier in an essay. A last paragraph that summarizes what came before may fit a long, complex essay, but not a brief one. Equally inappropriate is a conclusion that contains material that the writer has tossed in haphazardly because there is no place else in the essay to put it. In brief, the last paragraph, like the first, should be carefully constructed and sharply focused.

In a short essay no artificial ending is as effective and emphatic as one that grows out of a thoughtful arrangement of material. If the writer is trying to prove a point, for example, a perfect ending is that one irresistible piece of evidence that clinches the argument beyond dispute. If the essay is descriptive or narrative, the arrangement of details should lead to some sort of climax. A good last paragraph also may suggest a solution to a problem or call on the reader to think about an issue or to perform an action. On the SAT II any concluding paragraph that seems to end the essay very abruptly, that merely dissolves into irrelevancy, or that fits the essay too loosely needs revision.

### Developmental Paragraphs

Paragraphs are usually complex structures, too complex to perform only a single function in an essay's development. Most paragraphs play a primary role, however, and one or more secondary roles. For example, a paragraph may be used to carry forward the main point of the essay by contributing a solution to the problem being discussed. At the same time it may reinforce an idea proposed earlier and also supply background information for the next paragraph.

On the SAT II you may be asked to identify the main function of a particular paragraph or passage. Function has little to do with the meaning of the paragraph. Rather, it pertains to the role the paragraph plays in the journey from beginning to end of the essay. Developmental paragraphs often perform one or more of the following common functions:

- Reinforce an idea with a telling example
- Evaluate an opinion stated earlier
- Persuade the reader to believe or act in a certain way
- Continue the discussion begun in an earlier paragraph
- Add new ideas
- Provide a contrasting point of view
- Explain in more detail an idea presented earlier
- Summarize the argument made thus far
- Turn the essay in a new direction

- Describe the relationship between ideas presented earlier
- Provide background material
- Ask a hypothetical or rhetorical questions about the topic
- Serve as a transition between paragraphs (In essays as short as those on the SAT II, however, a whole paragraph is not likely to be devoted to such a function.)

To illustrate several of these functions, the three essays that follow are accompanied on the right side of the page by comments about paragraph function as well as structure, form, and development.

## Essay A

[1] Sled dogs seem to have been born for Antarctic expeditions. [2] Bellies flattened on the snow, they pant and claw their way across miles and miles of frozen landscape. [3] On downhills, they have to be braked and kept under control by winding ropes around the runners of the sled. [4] After a day's fun the dogs eat supper and sleep soundly. [5] In the morning, they bark and yip cheerfully, as though to shame their weary masters.

[6] Unlike dogs, humans often find Antarctica to be the most alien place on earth. [7] The scale is awesome, almost as if it were a landscape from another planet. [8] Away from the coast, there is no life, and therefore, no bacteria, no disease, no pests, no beasts of prey, no mobs, no human interference. [9] It is antiseptic and can be compared only with life under the ocean or in space.

[10] Snow in the Antarctic is an enemy to life and limb. [11] Although it offers shelter, insulation, drink, building material, and a highway, its friendliness is a dangerous illusion. [12] Ice blocks and sinister piles of snow tell a tale of avalanches tumbling regularly from the mountains all around. [13] A man on skis could suddenly disappear in a cavern of deep, glistening powder snow. [14] On foot, sunk to the hips in snow, a man might walk less than a mile before he drops from exhaustion. [15] Sudden snow squalls will blind a man, cause him to lose his bearings and his balance, trapping him hopelessly inside a drift that may soon serve as his burial mound.

The opening suggests that the essay will be about sled dogs.

The remainder of the paragraph supports the initial idea that sled dogs thrive in the Antarctic.

Sentences 4 and 5 are organized chronologically.

The end of sentence 5 alludes to humans, a reference that provides a lead-in to the next paragraph.

The essay is not only about sled dogs, after all, since the second paragraph begins by contrasting dogs' adaptability to the Antarctic to humans' alienation.

The remainder of paragraph 2 compares Antarctica to an alien place. By implication, Antarctica is being contrasted to other more conventional places.

Life under the ocean and in space is used as an example of comparably alien places.

The third paragraph continues to develop the idea that Antarctica is an alien place. Snow, in particular, is the greatest threat to humans in Antarctica.

Sentence 11 indicates that snow is useful, but one had better beware. The rest of the paragraph cites one example after another of the dangers to human beings of Antarctic snow.

By the end you may realize that the essay has no explicitly stated main idea. You may infer, however, that the essay's point is to explain the qualities of Antarctica, using factual evidence to show that Antarctica is hostile to men but not to dogs.

## Essay B

[1] On the water, sailboats and motor boats go faster than canoes. [2] They also go faster in stores. [3] People are buying them in greater numbers than ever before. [4] Not only are they more fashionable, but they give status to their owners. [5] Yet I'll take a canoe any time.

[6] For one thing, a canoe can last for more than thirty years. [7] Even if you get tired of it, you can sell it for a fairly large fraction of its original cost. [8] For example, a new aluminum canoe may cost about $500, but a used one costs about $400. [9] In addition, a canoe has no moving parts to wear out. [10] It requires almost no care, although you may have to paint it every few years or bang out some dents if you ride it through rapids.

[11] Besides being economical, a canoe can be used in a variety of ways. [12] In the first place, you can use it in the ocean as well as on a tiny lake. [13] You can use it on rivers, too, and in marshes and small streams. [14] As a result, wherever you go, there is bound to be a place for canoeing. [15] Not only can you take it anywhere, but you can go canoeing for a few hours or for weeks at a time. [16] In contrast to other boats, canoes don't depend on wind or fuel. [17] Furthermore, you don't have to waste time setting up or taking down a canoe. [18] Simply grab a paddle, and you're off on your own.

The very first sentence indicates that the purpose of this essay is to compare and contrast different kinds of boats.

Sentences 1–4 suggest that the writer favors sailboats and motorboats, but the fifth sentence undercuts what has gone before and introduces the main point of the essay: Canoes are preferable to other kinds of boats.

Very quickly the author has established an informal, person-to-person tone, using first person and addressing the reader directly as you.

The second paragraph begins with the transitional phrase For one thing, which provides continuity of thought between paragraphs.

An implied comparison and contrast is sustained throughout the remainder of the paragraph, and the author also weaves in a specific example to illustrate the value of canoes.

In sentence 9 still another transitional phrase, In addition, unifies the paragraph even further.

The transition to the last paragraph is particularly smooth.

Sentence 11 refers specifically to the discussion of economy in the second paragraph.

Sentence 11 also serves as the topic sentence of the last paragraph. It is a general statement followed by specific ways in which a canoe may be used.

Throughout the last paragraph almost every sentence is tied to the previous one by a transitional word or phrase.

Each paragraph cites facts and opinions in support of the writer's purpose—to convince the reader that canoes are better.

## Essay C

[1] John Steinbeck started getting ready to write The Grapes of Wrath when he was a small boy in California. [2] Much of what he saw and heard while growing up found its way into the novel. [3] On weekends his father took John and his three sisters on long drives out into the broad and beautiful valleys south of Salinas, the town where John was born in 1902. [4] John passed vast orchards and endless fields green with lettuce and barley. [5] He observed workers and the run-down shacks in which they lived. [6] And he saw, even before he was old enough to wear long pants, that the farmhands' lives differed from his own.

[7] Although the Steinbecks weren't wealthy (John's father ran a flour mill), they lived in a comfortable Victorian house. [8] John grew up on three square meals a day. [9] He never doubted that he would always have enough of life's necessities. [10] He even got a pony for his 12th birthday. [11] (The pony became the subject of one of Steinbeck's earliest successes, his novel The Red Pony.) [12] But don't think John was pampered; his family expected him to work. [13] He delivered newspapers and did odd jobs around town.

[14] Family came first in the Steinbeck household. [15] While not everyone saw eye to eye all the time, parents and children got along well. [16] His father saw that John had talent and encouraged him to become a writer. [17] His mother at first wanted John to be a banker—a real irony when you consider what Steinbeck says about banks in The Grapes of Wrath—but she changed her mind when John began spending hours in his room scrawling stories and writing articles for the school newspaper. [18] Later in life, Steinbeck denied that his family served as a model for the Joads in The Grapes of Wrath. [19] But both families understood well the meaning of family unity.

The first sentence introduces the topic of the essay. It promises the reader a discussion of Steinbeck's boyhood.

A relatively conversational tone is established early by using the young author's given name instead of his surname.

The rest of paragraph (sentences 2–6) consists of several general descriptions of what John saw and did as a boy. Each sentence supports the topic sentence.

The opening of the second paragraph is linked to the previous one by an allusion to the Steinbecks' economic situation. The dependent clause in sentence 7 is as much of a topic sentence as the paragraph gets. Yet, it is adequate, considering that the remainder of the paragraph paints the Steinbeck family's financial picture.

Sentence 11 is related directly to sentence 10, but since it obviously departs from the main subject of the paragraph, it is placed in parentheses.

Sentence 14 turns the focus of the essay to John's family. Because The Grapes of Wrath is the story of a family, the purpose of the final paragraph is to explain how the young author's real-life family may have influenced the creation of the fictional Joad family.

The last paragraph demonstrates clearly the validity of the essay's main idea, articulated by sentence 1. Although Steinbeck (surname is used here to refer to the author as an adult) denied the connection (18), the essay writer insists in sentence 19 that a connection between the real and fictional families exits.

From start to finish, the essay has focused squarely on the main idea.

## ANSWERS TO PRACTICE EXERCISES

### ⌐ Questions

#### Subject/Verb Agreement, page 61

1. talent. . .proves
2. book. . .was
3. team. . .is
4. you are
5. Correct
6. Correct
7. proceeds. . .are
8. team. . .is
9. Mr. McCallum
. . .was
10. Republicans are
11. (you) contact
12. Politics has
13. Darwin. . .is
14. Kate Green. . .and
accompanist. . .are
15. Nancy. . .appears
16. fact. . .makes
17. statutes. . .are (Here)
18. partners. . .are
19. parts. . .are
20. teacher. . .is
21. No one. . .wants
22. memories. . .are
23. shipment. . .was
24. Correct
25. recession. . .is

#### Verb Forms, page 63

1. eaten
2. caught
3. swam
4. drunk
5. gone
6. laid
7. shone
8. shrunk
9. sung
10. slew
11. stolen
12. strove *or* strived
13. wakened *or* waked
14. worn
15. broken
16. dived
17. crept
18. flung
19. swore
20. led

#### Verb Tense, page 67

1. came
2. brought
3. is
4. is
5. had reached
6. to spot
7. had finished
8. Correct
9. had given
10. Correct
11. stopped
12. pulls/gives *or* pulled/gave
13. Having worked
14. had taken
15. had seen
16. were
17. Having read
18. Correct
19. Having thought
20. has decided

#### Comparative Degree, page 69

1. richer
2. better
3. easier
4. greatest
5. most forgetful
6. Correct
7. more stubborn
8. worse
9. less hard
10. Correct
11. was sweeter
12. more profound
13. faster
14. more secure
15. unkind
16. Correct
17. was superior
18. the nicer
19. longer
20. Correct

#### Comparisons, page 71

*(These are suggested answers. Other answers may be equally valid.)*

1. Jane is more efficient than any other member of the committee.
2. Adam looks more like his father than his brother does.
3. When I went to see *Streetcar*, I disliked Stanley as much as I disliked Mitch.
4. Correct
5. Oscar was as tired as, if not more tired than, Pete.
6. To do the research for my paper, I had to do more reading than telephoning.
7. Although she's younger, Lillian looks older than Dorothy.

8. They talked more about Chekhov's stories than about his plays.
9. Allyn's canoe was destroyed in the rapids, just as his partner's was.
10. I read *The Great Gatsby* by Fitzgerald, an author I have come to love more than any other.
11. I am more interested in hiking than Peter is.
12. Biology is more popular than any other science.
13. It's been said that walking is better for you than jogging the same distance.
14. The students respect Mr. Phillip's teaching style more than they respect Mr. Green's.
15. His ears were bigger than Ross Perot's.
16. It took him longer to reach Trenton than to reach Camden.
17. Which is cheaper—flying to Washington or taking the train?
18. The lawyer insisted that she spent more hours on the job than a teacher does.
19. Wearing baseball caps is more popular now than wearing walkmans.
20. Cindy has applied to as many colleges as Joanne has, if not to more.

## Diction, page 78

1. Correct
2. Bruno failed
3. very scared
4. is identical to *or* is a replica of
5. about one another
6. at about six
7. he said
8. Correct
9. wanted to come in
10. from high school with strong feelings
11. because of the holiday
12. into the lake
13. off the dock
14. Used to
15. is a translation. . . regardless of
16. the facts *or* the truth
17. chose Friday
18. Correct
19. Correct
20. no one but
21. waited for
22. to clean
23. is hat
24. different from
25. Until

## Adjective/Adverb Use, page 81

1. bitter
2. Correct
3. smoothly
4. beautifully
5. slowly
6. cynically
7. Correct
8. smoothly
9. Correct
10. securely
11. oblivious
12. Correct
13. slowly
14. calm
15. easily
16. optimistic
17. badly
18. shy
19. sincerely
20. mischievously

## Pronoun Agreement, page 84

1. everyone. . .his physical
2. person. . .he collects
3. each. . .his
4. Somebody. . .her
5. you. . .you
6. Correct
7. one. . .his
8. trees. . .their
9. I have. . .I get
10. Neither. . .her
11. you. . .you
12. All those. . .their
13. library. . .its
14. Correct
15. I. . .myself

## Pronoun Reference, page 87

1. it
2. them
3. which
4. they
5. it
6. he
7. it
8. he
9. Correct
10. it
11. he
12. they
13. they
14. Correct
15. which
16. them
17. which
18. they
19. it
20. Correct
21. one
22. it
23. one
24. which
25. Correct

## Parallel Construction, page 90

*(These are suggested answers. Other answers may also be correct.)*

1. and inspirational
2. was accused not only of being a bigot but of being too stupid
3. and gone to fewer parties
4. preparing reports and placing various types of telephone calls
5. and to get up early
6. and she had a habit of disappearing
7. or a commercial artist
8. felt both pride and satisfaction
9. Correct
10. plans to live simply
11. not only all over the bus but also all over the sidewalk
12. have a good location, have land around it, and enjoy a view
13. Joan's broken yellow pencil came from this box
14. how to furnish and decorate the house simply
15. neither have a hotplate in his room nor take showers after 11:00 o'clock
16. and being miles from friends
17. either find a quick way into the attic or gnaw at the siding for days
18. and entertaining
19. and a job in the suburbs
20. that he'll defeat and that he'll emerge

## English Idiom, page 92

1. in battle
2. ascended the stairs
3. comply with
4. lose a lucrative business venture
5. OK
6. type your paper
7. independent of
8. pursuit of
9. interest in dinosaurs
10. arguing (with each other)
11. couldn't help seeing
12. doubts that
13. capable of doing
14. freedom of religion
15. type of student
16. with respect to
17. cases in which
18. in search of
19. that kind of pain
20. waiting for the bus

## Pronoun Choice, page 95

1. her and me
2. Sam and me
3. Gretchen and him
4. between you and me
5. We women
6. Johathan and him
7. Joe and he
8. He and I
9. Their singing
10. Correct
11. than she
12. as long as they
13. Correct
14. Tigers and them
15. as tall as I
16. sister and me
17. your questioning
18. their arguing
19. him and me
20. it was he
21. of their coming
22. Correct
23. Correct
24. his falling
25. He and I alternated
26. better than she
27. Roger and me
28. Mark and he
29. her nor her sister
30. us girls

## Misplaced and Dangling Modifiers, page 98

*(These are suggested corrections. Answers may vary because there is more than one way to rid a sentence of a misplaced or dangling modifier.)*

1. Norm and Matt served lunch while I watched the game on TV.
2. After I finished the math homework, that pizza tasted great.
3. Correct
4. Bob left the overcooked hamburger on the table.
5. After I ate a quick breakfast, the schoolbus picked me up.
6. Because Suzanne is so conceited and snobby, I cringe whenever I see her heading my way.
7. After his car was totaled beyond repair, Archie knew he'd have to buy a new one.

8. As I stopped to rest after the hike, a grizzly bear stood in front of me.
9. The story of the Donner Party has finally been told after 150 years.
10. After arriving from Honduras, Carlos described his ordeal to my class.
11. The police submitted a report about the bank robbery.

12. As I drove down the mountain road, a rock hit my windshield and smashed it.
13. Correct
14. Correct
15. Used all night long to illuminate the steps, my flashlight needed new batteries.

## Double Negatives, page 100

1. can hardly
2. museum had no/ didn't have any
3. any reason
4. Correct
5. had but
6. Correct
7. didn't have any/ had no cause
8. was scarcely
9. has but
10. has never/ hasn't ever

## Punctuation, page 103

1. While Bill was riding, his bike got a flat tire.
2. The mailman did not leave the package, for Jeff was not at home.
3. After doing her homework Millie, as you might expect, talked on the phone for an hour.
4. His work criticized many commonly held beliefs, however, and it was strictly censored.
5. Correct
6. Dad went to the airport to pick up Dave, and Ellie went to the train station to meet Debbie.
7. Correct
8. The boat was seventy-five feet long, eighteen feet wide, and it had a mast about eighty feet high.
9. To anyone interested in flying, planes hold endless fascination.
10. Jeff and Steve, left alone for the weekend, invited all their friends to a party.
11. I need street maps of Boston and Portland, Maine.
12. Some of theories dealt with the political, social, and religious ideas of the time.
13. Students who want to try out for the chorus have been asked to report to room 330.

14. Doug, for example, is both a scholar and an athlete.
15. Monica refused to go unless Phil went with her.
16. The author, Peter Jenkins, walked five thousand miles across the United States.
17. After all, she did for him what she could.
18. Starting in Minnesota, the Mississippi runs all the way to the Gulf of Mexico.
19. Harold Watkins, who comes from Chicago, won a full tuition scholarship to Columbia.
20. Although the characters in the book are stereotypes, they were interesting to read about.
21. Yo-Yo Ma, the famous cellist, will perform a recital on Saturday night.
22. This test covers Spanish literature, culture, and history, and it lasts for three hours.
23. Michelle is pretty, tall, and dark, but her older sister Norma is pretty, short, and light.
24. Sean, the twin brother of Ian, was struck by a car while crossing the street.
25. Correct

## Fragments, Run-ons, and Comma Splices, page 105

*(These are suggestions only. Answers will vary, especially for sentence fragments that have been transformed into complete sentences.)*

1. James finished writing the paper at 2:00 AM. Then he went to bed and slept through the class.
2. Open the door for the cat. She's been out all night.

3. Although she knows that she's stressed out about the SAT II, *she's confident.*
4. Having no more to do with the administration, despite twenty years of loyal service and

several prestigious awards for his research, *Abe declined the invitation to speak.*

5. Correct

6. *Steve found the book*, which the other members of the class were unable to find in the library.

7. Rose is a good friend. When she makes a promise she keeps it.

8. Though shoveling all the snow from the walk and the driveway took two hours, *Ray did not feel tired.*

9. When she laughs, I laugh; when I laugh, she laughs.

10. After the rain, the smell in the garden, as fresh as dew, *reminds me of England.*

11. My grandmother is 83 years old. Therefore, she walks very slowly.

12. Mark and Cathy went to San Diego for Christmas. They came back for New Year's, however.

13. Tony is the only freshman on the team, yet he was chosen as the most valuable player.

14. Ross edited the magazine for decades; he was followed by Shawn.

15. Correct

16. First try to do this exercise without looking in the book. If you can't do it, refer to page 56.

17. *It sounds like a* good idea, don't you think, to talk over the problem with his mother, father, and guidance counselor.

18. At the end of the course there is a test. It consists of three essays.

19. Huge redwood trees that had been alive for nearly 2,000 years *were being cut down.*

20. She asked the teacher for an extension on the assignment, *and* the teacher agreed.

## Possessives, page 107

1. Paul's
2. America's
3. Correct
4. women's
5. girls', boys'
6. Andersons', Year's
7. Correct
8. Morris's
9. computers'
10. months'

## Capitalization, page 108

1. After the Pilgrims crossed the ocean, they landed at Plymouth Rock.

2. The next President of the United States will probably be a westerner, or he might come from the South.

3. Yellowstone National Park is located in the western part of the state of Wyoming.

4. For Christmas he got a Black and Decker orbital sander from the Sears store next to the old Bedford courthouse.

5. The author of the brief on capital punishment in Missouri is Justice Andrew Ryan, Chief Judge of the Court of Appeals in the Ninth Circuit.

6. On Labor Day the Bennington County Fire Department plans to hold a turkey shoot on the field at Miller's Pond.

7. The medieval period is called the Dark Ages in Michael Crawford's textbook.

8. We expect to celebrate New Year's Eve again this year by renting a movie of an old Broadway musical and by settling down in front of the television set with some Canada Dry Ginger Ale and a box of Oreos.

9. The judge gave District Attorney Lederman a book entitled *Great Cases in Contract Law* and told her to take it with her on her European tour next summer.

10. According to Edith Nickerson, the principal of Parsons High School, Parsons attracts students from the whole West Coast. At Parsons students may major in drawing and painting, design, graphics, or sculpture. Ms. Nickerson said, "I attended a similar high school in New England just after the Second World War."

# Revision-in-Context Questions

## Topic Sentences, page 137

### Part A
1. Sentence 1
2. None. Implied topic sentence
3. Sentence 7
4. Sentence 10
5. Sentence 1
6. Sentence 1
7. Sentence 1
8. Sentence 3
9. Sentence 2
10. Sentence 6

### Part B Answers may vary.
1. Mother and Father are very different from each other.
2. In the past U.S. athletes dominated the Olympic Games.
3. Monopolies often destroy not only themselves but the incentive of businesses to change and make progress.
4. How little the aristocracy understood the needs of the masses.
5. Vera Simon wrote a gripping and realistic book.
6. Smoking in school is just not worth the trouble it can lead to.
7. But here are my requirements for the perfect roommate.
8. Age and experience have deprived me of courage and spirit.
9. *No topic sentence is needed.*
10. Although backward in some respects, a so-called primitive culture can be technologically sophisticated.

## Paragraph Unity and Coherence, page 141

1. Sentence 3 destroys the coherence of the paragraph. Delete it. There's no reason to save it because the idea is reiterated in sentence 7.
2. The paragraph lacks unity. It begins with a discussion of the consequences of smoking marijuana on young people, and ends by explaining the problems of parents. One solution is to divide the paragraph. Another is to expand the topic sentence to include parents, e.g.: *Under the present law, smoking marijuana can have serious consquences for both young people and their parents.* If this were done, however, the paragraph would need greater development.
3. The paragraph is coherent except for sentence 5, which should be deleted. Sentence 2 strongly supports the idea expressed in the topic sentence (1). The remaining sentences (except 5) support sentence 2, which is the major supporting sentence in the paragraph.
4. Although the entire paragraph discusses political parties, the discussion is not unified. Sentences 1–3 deal with the two-party system, while sentences 4–7 are about totalitarian countries. Either divide the paragraph, or add a topic sentence that justifies discussing both topics within a single paragraph.
5. Sentence 1 is the topic sentence. Sentence 4 is unrelated to the topic sentence. Delete it.
6. The paragraph's coherence is weakened by sentence 2, which digresses from the main topic, the intelligence of porpoises. Moreover, the initial pronoun *they* refers to *scientists,* not to *porpoises.* Delete sentence 2 or revise the topic sentence to include something about the human qualities of dolphins.
7. Although the opening sentence leads the reader to think that what follows will be about Robinson Crusoe, the paragraph is about the author, Daniel Defoe. To improve the coherence of the paragraph, delete or revise the misleading topic sentence.
8. The whole paragraph deals with ancient Greek philosophy, but it is extremely disjointed. Only sentences 3 and 4 connect with each other. All the others are independent thoughts, related in subject matter but not in style. To bring coherence to the paragraph, add a topic sentence, possibly using the material in sentence 5. The chronological fact that Socrates

taught Plato who taught Aristotle should serve as a guide in revising the paragraph.

9. The paragraph is coherent and unified until the last sentence. Delete sentence 6, but if the idea is too good to throw away, save it for another place in the essay or revise sentence 1, the paragraph's topic sentence.

10. The paragraph is unified and coherent. No revision is needed.

## Combining Sentences, page 143

*(Because many different answers are possible, these are suggestions only. As you compare your anwers to these, be sure that you have included all the information from each group of sentences.)*

1. At 13 she has already won recognition as an expert gymnast.

2. After the hit and run accident, broken glass lay on the road.

3. Aunt Ellen had a mess on her hands after she dropped a bag containing a glass bottle of tomato juice that she had bought at the grocery store.

4. The baseball hit Mr. Strickman's picture window, shattering it into a thousand pieces.

5. Since the storm dumped two feet of snow on the roads, I could not go out. I had nothing to do but watch TV and assemble a jigsaw puzzle. The time passed slowly.

6. The earth revolves around the sun every 365 days. At the same time, it rotates on its axis once every 24 hours. The earth's revolution around the sun determines the length of a year just as its rotation determines the duration of a day.

7. The 2,000-year-old tragedies of Euripides, an ancient Greek playwright, are still performed today.

8. Music has the unique power to transport people's minds. While listening, people often dream and think, and afterwards feel refreshed.

9. The skulls of humans consist of twenty-two bones: eight in the cranium, which protects the brain, and fourteen in the face and jaw.

10. The culture of the Hopi Indians, whose name means ''peaceful and happy,'' exemplifies peace and contentment. Lacking competitiveness, the people rarely feel tense. Material possessions are unimportant. What the Hopis value instead are self-discipline, restraint, and the welfare of others. But the highest value is the family, consisting of the entire Hopi tribe.

## Sentence Arrangement, page 147

| | | | | | |
|---|---|---|---|---|---|
| 1. a. 4, | b. 3, | c. 2, | d. 1 | | |
| 2. a. 2, | b. 5, | c. 1, | d. 4, | e. 3, | f. 6 |
| 3. a. 3, | b. 1, | c. 4, | d. 2 | | |
| 4. a. 3, | b. 4, | c. 2, | d. 1 | | |
| 5. a. 4, | b. 2, | c. 1, | d. 3, | e. 5 | |
| 6. a. 4, | b. 2, | c. 1, | d. 3 | | |
| 7. a. 3, | b. 4, | c. 2, | d. 1, | e. 5 | |
| 8. a. 3, | b. 4, | c. 2, | d. 1 | | |
| 9. a. 2, | b. 4, | c. 1, | d. 3 | | |
| 10. a. 1, | b. 4, | c. 3, | d. 2 | | |

# PART IV

# THE ESSAY QUESTION

# INTRODUCTION

What's wrong with this picture?

*A high school English classroom. Students are seated, quietly waiting for their teacher. Desks are clear, except for a pen or pencil. A whisper in the back of the room is followed by a quick, nervous giggle. Students exchange glances. One boy picks up pencil, drums the eraser on his desk. A girl sighs, audibly. The ensuing laughter is suddenly cut off when the door opens and the teacher enters, carrying a black attaché case. She places the briefcase on her desk, snaps open the locks, raises the lid, and takes out the day's essay assignment. When she starts to pass out the writing paper, the students clap, smile, and give three cheers.*

A pretty implausible portrait of a high school class, wouldn't you say? It's more like fantasy land or a Steven Spielberg movie, definitely not a real-life scene from the '90s, not the 1990s, anyway. In this era, nobody applauds the prospect of an essay assignment. More than likely, in fact, essay writing provokes catcalls and boos. Why? Because, frankly, most students hate to write essays.

That is not to say that students hate writing. Many students love to write—stories, personal remembrances, letters, poems, editorials, diary and journal entries—just not essays.

Essay writing has probably earned its reputation for several reasons. First, essays are assigned, and like all things forced on you, essay assignments breed resistance. Furthermore, essay writing is hard work, especially when you don't have much to say about the assigned topic. It also creates anxiety. There seem to be so many things that can go wrong, from faulty grammar to false logic. It's often hard to tell whether an essay is good or whether it's garbage. At times you may think you've handed in a respectable essay only to have it come back adorned with symbols and notations, including that most insidious of comments, ''See me!!!'' What an indignity! Small wonder that essay writing ranks with giving a speech and taking grammar tests as one of the least favorite things to do in school.

Of course, not everyone is vexed by essay writing. Innumerable students consistently write exemplary essays that are read aloud in class, printed in the school magazine, or come back with A's and a happy face. Yet even the most avid writers rarely choose to write essays in their spare time.

There's no danger that Part IV of this book will transform essay writing into your favorite pastime. Rather, the purpose of Part IV is to clear the air about essay writing, to take away its mystique. To be sure, every kind of writing is pitted with traps into which unwary students may stumble. But with this book as your trap detector, you'll learn both what to do and what to avoid as you write the SAT II essay, or any other essay for that matter.

No one should be intimidated by the SAT II essay question. Instead, be prepared, and view it as a chance to show your favorite colleges that they ought to let you in because you think worthwhile thoughts and know how to put them into clear, interesting, and correctly written words.

This part can probably be read in an hour or two, but you'll need more time to make it work for you. Unless you are a natural-born writer—in which case toss this book into the nearest recycling bin—keep these pages by your side. Let them nag you into seeking the three most basic and most desirable writing goals: clarity, interest, and correctness.

1. **Clarity** because your ideas probably need to be clear to you before you can make them clear to others.
2. **Interest** because readers will abandon your essay if you bore them.
3. **Correctness** because, whether it's fair or not, readers will judge you and your work according to how well you demonstrate the conventions of writing.

Clarity, interest, and correctness. After you've achieved them, you'll have found the secret of life. Well, maybe not life, but at least the essay writing part of it. The English language is rich with adjectives that describe good writing: *effective*, *eloquent*, *well-written*, *lively*, *stylish*, *polished*, *descriptive*, *honest*, *vivid*, *engaging*, and countless more. But in one way or other they all refer to clarity, interest, and correctness.

Essays rated ''6'' on the SAT II: Writing Test mean that the writers have sent out a clear statement about the assigned topic, presented it in an interesting manner, and made it conform to the standards of literate English. That's it—not altogether as formidable a task as the directions for writing the essay may seem:

---

*INSTRUCTIONS:* Plan and write an essay in response to the assigned topic. During the 20 minutes allowed, you should develop your thoughts clearly and effectively. A plain, natural style is probably best. Try to include specific evidence or examples to support your views.

The number of words is up to you, but quantity is far less important than quality. In general, however, a single paragraph may not give you the chance to develop your ideas sufficiently. You must limit your essay to the answer sheet. Please be advised, therefore, to write on every line, keep narrow margins, and write compactly enough to fit your essay on the page. Try to write as legibly as you can.

BE SURE TO WRITE ONLY ON THE AS-SIGNED TOPIC. AN ESSAY WRITTEN ON ANOTHER TOPIC WILL RECEIVE NO CREDIT.

---

On the actual SAT II the directions will be worded differently from these, but the message will always be the same. In fact, identical directions are used every time the exam is given. It would be smart to learn them. Then, on test day, when you reach the essay question, skip the directions and head right for the question. The 60 seconds you save might be more profitably spent on proofreading a paragraph or rephrasing an awkward sentence.

Knowing precisely what you're expected to do may well boost your essay score. With that in mind, take a closer look at the directions.

**Plan and write an essay in response to the assigned topic.**   The key word is **plan**. A plan is hardly more than a list of ideas arranged in the order you'll use them. In general, a planned essay is likely to be clearer than one without a plan. It speaks well of you as a writer that you present ideas in a thought-out sequence rather than spill them out as they happen to occur to you. Since time is brief, planning may consist of little more than jotting down a word or phrase to remind you of the gist of each paragraph and then numbering the paragraphs in the order you expect to use them.

Another important word in the instructions is **essay**.   When they say *essay*, they mean it. So don't write a play, poem, dialogue, fable, or anything other than an essay. If you have an irresistible urge to be creative, so be it, but adapt your creativity to the essay form.

**During the 20 minutes allowed, you should develop your thoughts clearly and effectively.** This sentence contains a host of messages. First, you have exactly 20 minutes to do everything, from reading and understanding the topic to revising and proofreading your completed essay. In effect, you are being forced to do in 1,200 seconds what would normally take far more time. A saving grace, however, is that the College Board's readers don't have unreasonable standards. They won't expect you to produce a polished piece of memorable prose, just a brief but competently written essay.

In the educational testing business, the essay question is sometimes called a ''prompt'' because it prompts, or inspires, you to take and defend a position on an issue. Your views on the prompt don't matter much. You won't be penalized for taking an unpopular, or politically incorrect position. But take a position you must. You could, of course, try straddling the fence with the ''it-all-depends'' argument. Such an approach is judicious and safe but not too interesting. It also could lead you to write an essay that merely describes or restates the prompt. If, in your judgment, however, the question warrants a middle-of-the-road response, don't hesitate to write one. In the end, readers won't be impressed by the position you take, but only by the forcefulness of your presentation.

The position to choose is the one about which you have the most compelling things to say. A simple way to decide is to make two lists. As quickly as you can, jot down all the arguments for and all those against the issue. Then decide which list holds the greater promise for an essay. From then on focus on the issue. Sharpen the focus at the beginning of your essay by stating outright what you think. Don't gum up the opening by restating or paraphrasing the question, and don't under any circumstances write one of those fuzzy, all-inclusive statements that try to encompass the history of mankind or the universe, such as, "Since time began, men have pondered moral questions, etc." Such overblown and pretentious writing has no place on the SAT II. Face it, you don't need to write the definitive essay on the subject. If you must state a universal truth just to get you started, by all means do so, but then cross it out and let your essay begin with a more down-to-earth idea.

Next, the instructions tell you to **develop your thoughts**, advice that you'd do well to heed while writing this or any other essay. Developing your thoughts means nothing more than backing up your opinion with illustrative material, which might take any number of forms. Use facts, statistics, common sense, historical background—anything, really, to demonstrate that your opinion is grounded on something more solid than a feeling or personal preference. The kind of writing expected on the SAT II is rational discourse, not emotional blabbering. The left side of your brain, the logical side, is being examined along with the right, creative side. The best essays reveal that both sides of your brain are in good working order.

Poor essays often suffer from lack of development. The writer states ideas and then drops them. You probably won't do that, however, if you think of your readers as skeptics or as natives of Missouri, the "Show-Me" state. They doubt your veracity unless you persuade them that their skepticism is unfounded, that what you have said is the truth. An undeveloped statement, no matter how strongly worded, usually won't suffice.

The instructions also say to write **clearly and effectively**. Clearly, **clearly** doesn't mean easy-to-read handwriting, although neat penmanship never hurts. Rather, it means choosing words that will convey exactly what you mean. Thinking is the first step to clarity. If you don't fully grasp the meaning of your own words, think some more. Since you can't expect readers to think for you, unscramble everything that might interfere with clear meaning. Read-

ers want to understand what you have to say. They need help, however, which only you can provide. Keep asking yourself, "What words must I use to be sure than my readers will grasp exactly what I mean?"

When it comes to making judgments about writing, the word **effectively** comes up repeatedly. It's popular because it's easy to use and hard to define. It means so much, and yet so little. Surely it connotes virtue, but virtues come in many stripes. You know effective writing when you see it, but what the SAT II people have in mind is good organization, choice of words, sentence structure, paragraphing, development of ideas, logic, and punctuation. It means everything, in fact, that might inspire the readers to declare, "A six, a very palpable six."

**A plain, natural style is probably best.** Don't be tempted to drag out your SAT vocabulary while writing the essay. The College Board readers are not world-class intellectuals who scoff at all but the most sophisticated prose. Rather, they're just high school and college teachers with plenty of experience teaching and evaluating students' writing. They won't be impressed by formal, pompous, or elegant writing. Think of them as everyday folks who appreciate straight, plain, everyday language, perhaps the kind of language you might use while talking to a college interviewer or the dean of your school. You have a natural voice. Use it. Don't try to pass yourself off as someone you are not. Readers can smell pretension a mile away.

**Try to include specific evidence or examples to support of your views.** Because the essay topic is likely to be rather general, your task is to make your response rather specific. Whatever your point of view, illustrate it with an example or two. Generalizations are easy. You hear them every day. (*Pollution is a problem. TV can be educational as well as entertaining. The country is going to the dogs. Good part-time jobs are hard to find.*) Such statements may be indisputable, but stated without any support, they are toothless. They don't leave an impression. To impress a reader, you have to say more. If pollution is a problem, for example, be sure the reader knows that you mean *dumping household trash, sewage, and factory waste into the bay.* Or if you truly think that the country is beset with crises, mention *AIDS, poor schools, racial intolerance, unemployment,* and the rest.

Not every statement you make requires a specific example for support, but any time you back up generalizations with details, you're definitely on the right track.

**The number of words is up to you, but quantity is far less important than quality.** The answer to the customary question, "How long does it have to be?" is usually something like, "Long enough to cover the subject, but brief enough to be interesting." On the SAT II, the answer differs because you won't be penalized for not completing your essay. It's acceptable not to cover the subject, provided that by the time you stop writing you've demonstrated your ability to develop ideas fully. The advice, "Write until you fill up the page" is also ludicrous because handwriting varies. Some people fit maybe five or six words on a line, while others squeeze twice as many into the same space.

In addition, most students use too many words in their prose. Given two essays on the same topic, one verbose and the other to the point, the tightly written one would come out ahead. In other words, economy is a virtue. If a point can be made with thirty words, don't use sixty, forty, or even thirty-five. Tight writing, with the verbiage squeezed out, is far more readable and interesting.

**In general, however, a single paragraph may not give you the chance to develop your ideas sufficiently.** Writing multiple paragraphs can show the depth of your thinking. A single paragraph is often pretty flimsy. Two is better, but three or more suggests that you have the capacity to probe pretty deeply into a subject. In addition, writing a multi-paragraph essay allows you to expand your thoughts about the subject. It allows you to use a variety of details in support of your main idea, but it shows particularly that you have the skill to present a complex subject clearly and logically. In the end, though, the actual number of paragraphs is far less important than what each paragraph says. Even a single paragraph could demonstrate that you are a first-rate essayist.

**You must limit your essay to the answer sheet. Please be advised, therefore, to write on every line, keep narrow margins, and write compactly enough to fit your essay in the space provided. Try to write as legibly as you can.** The College Board has a pragmatic reason for limiting the length of SAT II essays. It's cheaper. In a day's time, paid

readers can handle many more short essays than long ones. But more important, a brief sample of writing provides enough basic information about your writing ability for a reasonably accurate assessment to be made. Little more would be revealed by an essay twice or three times as long.

To some extent the SAT II tests your ability to control the small muscles in your hand and wrist to fashion small and neat letters. Sloppy, hard-to-read handwriting is not supposed to count against you. But think of it this way: the readers want to get the job done. Then they want to eat lunch, take a walk, or go home to dinner just like everyone else. If they are bogged down in a barely legible paper, they could develop a bias against you. They're not supposed to, but humans, being human, often can't help feeling irritated when their good intentions are being frustrated. Sloppy handwriting interferes with the rapid holistic reading of essays. Although they're not apt to admit to bias at the College Board, accept it as truth that handwriting counts! Messy handwriting works against you; a neat hand works in your favor.

If you have easily read handwriting, count your blessings, but if you write in a ragged scrawl, work at it. Your handwriting is a product of the way your brain connects with the small muscles in your fingers, hand, and wrist. Years of habit have given your handwriting its characteristic shape. Like any habit, it's hard to change. But unless your muscles are physically impaired, you can train yourself to write more neatly. A little practice prior to the SAT II could work to your advantage. Here's how: Give a sample of your handwriting to a friend to read aloud. Wherever your friend hesitates or stumbles over a word, your handwriting may be at fault. Pinpoint which letters or combinations of letters may be less than clear. Then practice forming those letters clearly, just the way you probably did back in elementary school. In case you don't remember, here is a basic handwriting checklist:

1. Check the shape of the most troublesome letters: *r, m, n, u,* and *w*.
2. Check the differences between open and closed letters, as in *e-i, l-t,* and *cl-d*.
3. Tall letters should stand out above the short letters.
4. Distinguish *a* and *e*; *g, q,* and *p*; and *h* and *k*.
5. Allow for sufficient space between words and sentences.

6. Indent generously at the start of each new paragraph.

Believe it or not, it's never too late to improve your handwriting. If your efforts fail, however, you can always print, although printing is a lot slower than cursive writing.

Finally, the instructions state emphatically that you must write on the assigned topic: **BE SURE TO WRITE ONLY ON THE ASSIGNED TOPIC. AN ESSAY WRITTEN ON ANOTHER TOPIC WILL RECEIVE NO CREDIT.** The College Board has never been known to use capital letters frivolously, so take the warning to heart, and write on the given topic. The test makers try to invent topics that are broad, open-ended, and easy enough for virtually any literate student. Since essays are evaluated holistically, which means that they are read quickly and compared to each other, all essays must be on the same topic. If everyone wrote on a different topic, valid comparisons would be impossible. Therefore, don't stray from the assigned topic.

Read the topic carefully. Read it twice or three times, underlining key ideas and words, until you are confident that you know *exactly* what you are being asked to write about.

For example, below are three different topics. After reading each one, write down what you must do in order to respond to the question. Then check the explanation.

*Topic A*

> Many thinkers believe that it is human nature to enjoy the struggles and labors of life more than to enjoy the achievements.
>
> Do you agree or disagree? Please comment, based on your observation, experience, reading, or study.

Required Task: _____
_____
_____
_____

**EXPLANATION:** The prompt is an observation about human nature. Do you agree with it? Do you agree that people find more pleasure in working and play-

ing hard than in enjoying the fruits or the victory of their struggles? Or do you disagree? Do you think that pleasure comes from the achievement of a goal or triumph, or, to put it another way, that the ends count for more than the means?

Your opinion on the issue is less crucial than your ability to draw specific examples from your knowledge and background to support your view. Examples may come from what you have observed in your personal life or from what you know about the lives of others. They may come from your reading of books, from the media, from any source whatever. The ticket to an interesting and readable essay might be a specific instance taken from your own experience. Perhaps you endured a struggle in a class or on a team. You emerged victorious, but where did you get the kick—in the struggle or in the triumph? Or think of lawyers, debaters, soldiers of fortune, mountain climbers, teachers, even essay writers, all of whom may enjoy the challenges of adversity. It's sweet to win, but much of the pleasure in their work must surely be derived from doing it. Obviously, there are at least two sides to the issue. Whatever your position, though, be sure to include more than a single example in your essay. One example will not suffice to prove your point.

*Topic B*

> The year is marked with many holidays, each with its traditional rites and customs. The Fourth of July, for example, is often celebrated with fireworks, while Mothers' Day means sending flowers or taking Mom out to dinner.
>
> If I could create a new holiday, it would be _____, and I would celebrate it by _____ _____.
>
> Complete the above statement by inventing a new holiday. In an essay, please explain your choice.

Required Task: _____
_____
_____
_____

*EXPLANATION:* This open-ended prompt invites you to invent a new holiday. Since holidays commemorate everything from granola to ground hogs, your invention cannot be wrong. It may be serious or fanciful, respectful or irreverent. Whatever your choice, though, name the holiday, explain why you picked it, and suggest some ways to celebrate it. The organization of the essay is suggested by the prompt. All you need to do is fill in the blanks and think about such issues as whether the day should be a national or a private holiday, whether schools and businesses should be closed, whether it should be celebrated annually, monthly, or daily. The topic allows you to be as imaginative as you can be. Remember that those who read your essay will not object to being entertained.

### Topic C

> Describing an acquaintance, the writer Anatole France said, "He flattered himself on being a man without any prejudices; and this pretension itself is a very great prejudice."
>
> Do you agree or disagree with the notion that a person cannot be free of some prejudice? Support your point of view with specific examples from your observation, from your reading, or from your own life's experience.

Required Task: _____
_____
_____
_____

*EXPLANATION:* What you write depends largely on your interpretation of the word *prejudice*. If you take it to mean ignorant bigotry toward a race, religion, age or any other group, you might disagree. Many people you know or have read about accept and respect all others equally, regardless of their backgrounds. On the other hand, you may think that no one can be completely free of bias for or against people of other groups. In fact, you could argue that it defies both logic and human nature to lack preferences and be immune from favoritism. As the topic says, examples to support your view may be drawn from various sources. The current world scene provides numerous examples. Or you may have observed prejudice in action closer to home or at school. Since you cannot know intimately the inner workings of others' minds, perhaps the best source is your own experience. Perhaps you have been a victim of prejudice because of your nationality, religion, race or age. Perhaps you feel prejudice yourself. If you do, it would be offensive and stupid to use this essay as a platform to preach hate or bigotry, but to admit to some doubts or fear of other groups is a very human thing to do.

## REVIEW OF INSTRUCTIONS FOR WRITING THE ESSAY

Now that the directions for writing the essay have been thoroughly dissected, read them once again:

> *INSTRUCTIONS:* Plan and write an essay in response to the assigned topic. During the 20 minutes allowed, you should develop your thoughts clearly and effectively. A plain, natural style is probably best. Try to include specific evidence or examples to support your views.
>
> The number of words is up to you, but quantity is far less important than quality. In general, however, a single paragraph may not give you the chance to develop your ideas sufficiently. You must limit your essay to the answer sheet. Please be advised, therefore, to write on every line, keep narrow margins, and write compactly enough to fit your essay on the page. Try to write as legibly as you can.
>
> BE SURE TO WRITE ONLY ON THE ASSIGNED TOPIC. AN ESSAY WRITTEN ON ANOTHER TOPIC WILL RECEIVE NO CREDIT.

At some point before you sit for the SAT II: Writing, review the foregoing explanation of the test directions. Having the directions fresh in your mind on test day will give you the confidence to ignore them on the test and permit you to set straight to work on the essay.

## SUMMARY OF THE MAIN POINTS

1. Once you understand the question, make a plan for organizing your essay.
2. Be sure to develop your thoughts and ideas with specific examples.
3. Write plainly. This test is not a place to flaunt your vocabulary, especially words you do not fully understand.
4. Write enough to demonstrate that you know how to develop ideas.
5. Write more than one well-developed paragraph.
6. Be prepared to write on no more than the space provided—about one and half sides of a sheet of lined paper.
7. Write legibly to avoid being unjustly penalized.
8. Write only on the assigned topic.

# HOW TO WRITE AN ESSAY IN 20 MINUTES

Don't be misled by the title of this section. It promises more than it can deliver. For one thing, writing an essay in 20 minutes may be a contradiction in terms. An essay is essentially the product of a writer's thinking about a topic. It expresses a point of view arrived at after reflection, analysis, or interpretation of a subject or issue. When you are given an assignment only 20 minutes before the essay is due, you can't expect to pore over the topic for long. If you think too deeply, before you know it you'll have thought the allotted time away.

A second reason to distrust the title is that no one learns to write well by reading a "how-to" book on the subject. You learn essay writing by taking a pen in hand, by messing around with ideas and words, by experimenting, practicing, and doing. Many of the in-class essays you've had to produce for science, social studies, and other courses have probably been good training for the kind of instant essay required by the SAT II: Writing Test. In your classes, though, success was often determined by how closely your essay resembled what the teacher had in mind. That's not true on the SAT II, which won't give you a topic with a predetermined answer. You can't study for this essay writing test the way you can study trig or Spanish. What you need to know is already lodged inside you. The task you face on test day is to organize your ideas and put them into readable form on a piece of paper, which takes practice, practice, practice. Just as athletic skills improve with repetition, so do essay writing skills. All you need each time you schedule a writing session is 20 minutes, hardly more time than it takes to get suited up for field hockey or basketball practice.

The next several pages will take you inside essay writing. By entering the territory, you won't become a world-class author of essays, but you'll see what most good writers do as they write essays. You'll be shown what works and what to watch out for. Basic principles of good writing will be discussed in detail and illustrated with sample essays written by students about to enter college. A book can do no more than keep you from falling flat on your face. The rest is up to you.

## A DOZEN PRINCIPLES OF GOOD WRITING

By this time in your education you've probably written enough essays to fill a fat book. Barely anyone escapes from an American high school without having written an essay on *Macbeth* or *Huckleberry Finn*, on the Civil War or civil rights, on the food chain or DNA, and perhaps even on "What I Did on my Summer Vacation." Although every essay topic offers writers a different challenge, the basic principles of writing remain constant. They apply to SAT II essays as well as to any others you'll ever be asked to write. Success in essay writing depends in large measure on how completely you can master these twelve guidelines:

1. Study the topic closely.
2. Narrow the topic.
3. Decide what point(s) to make about the topic.
4. Collect ideas and put them in order.
5. Start with an appealing and informative introduction.
6. Develop your ideas with specific examples and details.
7. Guide readers with transitions.
8. Use plain, precise, lively, and fresh words.
9. Omit needless words.
10. Vary your sentences.
11. End your essay unforgettably.
12. Follow the conventions of standard English.

Refer to it often. If your writing usually demonstrates mastery of these twelve principles, you're undoubtedly a terrific writer. To be a still better one, though, you must know that occasionally one or more of the principles ought to be set aside. When a principle leads you to say something barbaric, ignore it for the time being. Let your intuition and good judgment guide you instead. The principles, after all, merely describe what most good writers do; they are not commandments.

Most accomplished and experienced essayists hardly have to think about such practices while composing and editing their work. Through experience, they have absorbed good writing habits into their craft. Professionals needn't be reminded, for example, to cut needless words from their writing or to prefer the plain word to the pompous one. (That is why the twelve principles are reproduced in a handy wallet size. Photocopy the page, snip out the principles, and carry them with you or tape them to your wall. By referring to them often, let them become part of your life.)

---

**TWELVE BASIC PRINCIPLES OF GOOD WRITING**

1. Study the topic closely.
2. Narrow the topic.
3. Decide what point(s) to make about the topic.
4. Collect ideas and put them in order.
5. Start with an appealing and informative introduction.
6. Develop your ideas with specific examples and details.
7. Guide readers with transitions.
8. Use plain, precise, lively, and fresh words.
9. Omit needless words.
10. Vary your sentences.
11. End your essay unforgettably.
12. Follow the conventions of standard English.

---

## THE PROCESS OF WRITING AN ESSAY

Just as most people follow a ritual when they get up in the morning or walk their dogs, most writers adhere to a routine that helps them do their best work. The American poet Donald Hall, for example, says, "In summer I'll be up at 4:30, make coffee, let out the dog, go pick up *The Boston Globe*. Then I write." The daily routine of short story writer Flannery O'Connor was equally rigid: "Every morning between 9 and 12 I go up to my room and sit before a piece of paper. Many times I just sit for three hours with no ideas coming to me. But I know one thing: If an idea does come between 9 and 12, I am there

ready for it." And Ernest Hemingway, always one to pare his words to the bone, said, "My working habits are simple: long periods of thinking, short periods of writing."

Perhaps you follow a writing routine, too. Think about how you normally write an essay for a school assignment. Do you talk to others about the topic? Do you seek ideas or do they just come to you out of the blue? Do you preplan exactly what to say, or do you usually discover your point once the essay is underway? Before writing a draft, do you make notes or prepare an outline? Are you preoccupied with spelling and grammar as you write, or do you write freely? Do you reread as you go along or only at the end? How much do you actually write before revising anything? Do you habitually write in pencil, in ink, or on a computer? (By the way, on the SAT II, you must use a pen.) Whatever you usually do has become your personal writing process. Through trial and error you've probably found a procedure that works better than others but that may change from time to time according to the purpose and importance of the assignment and the amount of time you have to write it.

When your time comes to write the SAT II essay, it would be smart to have a well-rehearsed process in mind, since you won't have time to invent one on the spot. Try out several beforehand, practice them, and choose the techniques that enable you to work rapidly and efficiently while producing the best results.

To start, plan what to do during each stage of the process. The first stage, *prewriting*, consists of all you do before you actually begin writing the text of your essay. During the second stage, *composing*, you are choosing the words and forming the sentences that contain your thoughts. And finally, during the *revising and proofreading* stage, you polish and refine the text of your essay word by word, making it true, clear, and graceful. Actually, the lines between the stages are not at all distinct. Sometimes it helps to put words on paper during the prewriting stage. Writers compose, revise, and proofread simultaneously. New ideas may sprout at any time. No stage really ends until the final period of the last sentence is securely in place—or until time is up and test booklets are closed.

In spite of blurry boundaries between the stages of the writing process, it pays to keep the functions of each stage in mind as you study in detail how the dozen principles of good writing contribute to the growth of a successful essay.

## 1. Study the Topic Closely

Obviously, your work on the SAT II essay question should start with a meticulous reading of the topic. Read it more than once, underscoring key ideas and words until you know it intimately. If in doubt, read it again.

Here is a typical essay topic for your scrutiny. Because its prompt is a quotation by Robert Hutchings, the former president of the University of Chicago, let it henceforth be known as the Hutchings question.

> Concerned about the survival of democracy, the president of the University of Chicago, Robert Maynard Hutchings, once wrote, "The death of democracy is not likely to be an assassination from ambush. It will be a slow extinction from apathy, indifference, and undernourishment."
>
> While democracy may still be alive and well, situations often arise that do not coincide with the democratic principles on which America was founded. Using examples based on your studies, on reading, or on personal experience, write an essay that illustrates your view on the current health of democracy.

Before reading the explanation, briefly write your understanding of what the topic asks you to do:

_____

_____

_____

_____

_____

EXPLANATION: The basic task is clearly spelled out in the last clause: *write an essay that illustrates your view on the current health of democracy*. The prompt and everything else merely creates a context for the task and provides some general clues to the meaning of "health of democracy." Other essential information is that the essay must use examples drawn from your studies—that is, coursework or independent study; your reading, which includes fiction and non-fiction read for school or on your own; or relevant personal experiences.

All told, the topic gives students considerable leeway for interpretation. In fact, lengthy and complicated topics like this one often encourage students to blaze their own trails. Shorter topics, on the other hand, often tighten the reins on creativity.

. . . . . . . . . . . . . . . . . . . . . . . . . . . . . . . . . .

Taking advantage of the freedom inherent in this topic, two high school seniors, **Pat P** and **Chris H**, took different, but equally fruitful paths in handling the assignment. How each of them responded is presented below. Their unedited essays appear on pages 178 and 179 and will serve as samples for analysis through the balance of this chapter.

The first student, **Pat P**, read the whole question twice and thought, *"Hmm, an interesting quote.... I've never thought about the "survival of democracy.".... What in the world can I write about? ... Oh, I'm supposed to write about my view on the current health of democracy.... What is that supposed to mean? ... Is democracy sick? ... Not that I know of.... Well, what's democracy anyway? ... People participating in government ... choosing leaders ... government without dictators .... people not being afraid ... the opposite of communism.... Well, communism is dead, in Russia, at least .... Well, if communism is dead, then democracy must be pretty healthy.... I guess I'll write about that .... Now, I'll just have to think of some good examples of democracy."*

For **Chris H**, the other student, the assignment at first seemed to be light-years away from anything that he knew or cared about. That didn't deter him from writing an essay, however. He recalled the words of his writing teacher: "Don't think about the essay," Ms. Rogow had told him. "Think instead about the readers. What would they like to know? No, you can't predict exactly, but you can bet that, like most of us, they are crazy about stories, especially real-life, personal stories. So, find a connection between the topic and a situation in your life. Then, tell the reader your story. You can't lose."

Heeding that advice, Chris began to ponder the quotation: *"Apathy, indifference, undernourishment . . . that's what kills democracy. . . . Do I agree with that? . . . Let's see . . . apathy is a problem in this school . . . nobody cares . . . does that have anything to do with freedom? . . . With democracy? . . . Well, since nobody gives a damn, the teachers and administration can do whatever they want . . . they can be tyrants . . . like Mr. Finn . . . no one dares to fight back in his class . . . he's killed democracy, and the class just takes it . . . just like a flock of meek little sheep. . . . Now, that's the story to write!"*

• • • • • • • • • • • • • • • • • • • • • • • • • • • •

Although writing about one's experience has a lot of merit, not every SAT II essay question allows students to write a personal response. But when possible, it's an option that may be too good to refuse, especially when the topic leaves you cold. Students are leading authorities on their own life and times. With a little finesse, almost any topic on the SAT II can be shaped into an interesting and readable personal essay.

## 2. Narrow the Topic Unmercifully

Because an SAT II topic must suit a multi-ethnic, multi-cultural, and multi-talented student audience, it is bound to be very broad. Your first job is to reduce it to a size snug enough to fit your answer sheet. In fact, the quality of the essay you write could depend on how narrowly you define the topic. Think small. A cosmic approach won't work, and you are not likely to err by narrowing the topic too much. If you were to run out of things to say about a narrowed topic, the simple solution would be to expand the main idea in midstream, a far easier task than hacking away at a overweight topic after you're already filled most of a page.

It would be beyond the hope and talent of most students to compose a substantive 200 to 300 word essay on such topics as *democracy*, *psychology*, or *jazz*, subjects so vast you could probably fill a barn with books about them. The same holds true for any general subject, from *alcoholism* to *zoology*. Therefore, to keep your essay from being stuck in a mess of generalities, narrow the topic ruthlessly.

Try building a ladder of abstraction. Start at the top with the most general word. As you descend the ladder, make each rung increasingly specific. When you reach bottom, you may have a topic sufficient for a short essay. Here are some examples:

## SUBJECT: *Democracy*

| | |
|---|---|
| Democracy | *Highest level of abstraction* |
| Democracy in conflict with totalitarianism | *Too broad for a short essay* |
| People's rights vs. government control | *Still too broad* |
| Freedom of press vs. government restrictions | *Still too broad* |
| The right to print opinions vs. censorship | *Still broad, but getting there* |
| The right to print a scandalous story in a school newspaper | *Possible topic for a short essay* |
| What happened to Pete when *The Globe* published a story about incompetent teachers | *Distinct possibility for an essay* |

## SUBJECT: *Alcoholism*

| | |
|---|---|
| Alcoholism | *Highest level of abstraction* |
| The effects of alcoholism on society | *Extremely broad for a short essay* |
| Family problems resulting from alcoholism | *Still too broad* |
| Alcoholism as a cause of broken families | *Very broad, but getting closer* |
| The effects of alcoholism on children from broken homes | *Good only for a lengthy research paper* |
| The experience of Betsy G., the daughter of an alcoholic | *A definite topic for a short essay* |

## SUBJECT: *Zoology*

| | |
|---|---|
| Zoology | *Highest level of abstraction* |
| The study of mammals | *Too broad* |
| The study of primates | *Still very broad* |
| Researching the behavior of chimpanzees | *Still too broad* |
| Teaching of chimps | *Still rather broad* |
| Training chimps to distinguish colors | *A reasonable topic* |
| My job in the primate lab working on the color recognition project | *A fine topic for a short paper* |

Each subject has been pared down to a scale appropriate for an SAT II essay. Topics on the bottom rungs offer students a chance to write a thorough essay that will fit comfortably on a page. Focusing on a single idea may deny them the chance to demonstrate the scope of their knowledge. The SAT II, however, is not a place to show off breadth, but rather to display depth. College applications show breadth. For the present, it's depth that counts.

While contemplating the Hutchings question, both **Pat** and **Chris** instinctively began to peel away layers of abstraction, hoping to define the topic concisely enough for three- or four-paragraph essay. Pat arrived at the notion that democracy must be in

---

### Practice in Narrowing Topics

Reduce several of the following subjects to a level of specificity concise enough to be used for an SAT II essay. Try constructing a ladder of abstraction for each one. Put the broadest topic on the top. Don't stop descending until you have a topic suitable for a short essay.

| | |
|---|---|
| Youth and Age | Calamities |
| Procrastination | Probability |
| Jealousy | Truth |
| Taking Risks | Style |
| Change vs. Permanence | Wonder |

decent shape because in the 1980s and '90s the free nations of the world won the Cold War. To write something meaningful about the decades-long struggle between communism and democracy would probably take more than a page, so Pat had still more paring to do. This is not to say that a highly skilled writer couldn't compose a pithy essay on democracy. President Lincoln did it with 272 words for his speech at Gettysburg. But face it, Pat is no Abe Lincoln, and she knows it. So she dutifully kept searching for a narrower focus.

She considered the 1989 student uprising at Tiananmen Square, an event that surely illustrates the peerless power of freedom. She recalled the famous photograph of a young student standing face to face with a tank in the middle of the square. But the Tiananmen Square uprising took place when Pat was in junior high school, and now she couldn't remember anything else about it.

Her quest for a topic then turned to literature. In ninth grade she read *Animal Farm*, and the following year her class studied *1984*. Maybe a manageable topic could be extracted from Orwell's story of corrupt pigs or from the plight of Winston in the hands of the brutal Thought Police. She cast those ideas aside, though, after she recalled that in his novels Orwell didn't praise democracy, but rather condemned totalitarianism. She needed different examples to illustrate the health of democracy.

Each of Pat's false starts consumed less than a minute of her prewriting time. She then realized that much of her knowledge of democracy was acquired in history courses. So, she decided to illustrate the health of democracy by citing several historical events in which the forces of freedom prevailed over autocratic rule. If democracy always came out on top, she reasoned, it must be an inherently robust form of government.

In contrast to Pat's tortuous route to a sufficiently narrow essay topic, Chris made a quick decision. He would have no trouble squeezing the story of his math class onto a page. Chris knew that he would describe his math class and its tyrannical teacher. In just a few seconds the heart of the essay had come to him, but he didn't yet know what the point of his essay would be.

## 3. Decide What Point(s) to Make About the Topic

An essay needs a point. Nothing will disappoint a reader more than arriving at the end only to discover that the essay lacks a point. Essays may be written with beautiful words, contain profound thoughts, and make readers laugh or weep. But without a point, sometimes called a *main idea* or a *thesis*, an essay remains just words in search of a meaning. After they've finished, readers may scratch their heads, say "Huh?" and resent having wasted their time.

Don't confuse the topic of an essay with its point, for even a pointless essay is likely to be about something. It can be about seatbelts, war, business, sports, fax machines, France, stone walls—anything, really. But a topic isn't enough. An essay must also say something about its topic. Assume for a moment that one fine morning you inexplicably insisted on writing an essay on seatbelts. Your purpose might be to explain the use of seatbelts or to describe how they function. Or maybe you intend to recount the history and development of seatbelts, perhaps compare different types, or to discuss state laws that require occupants of a car to buckle up—all grist for an essayist's mill. Although the purpose of the essay may be clear, it still needs to make a point. An essay about seatbelt laws must lead to some sort of conclusion about those laws. It might make the point, for one, that seatbelt laws infringe on a driver's freedom of choice. Or its point might be that safety laws supercede a person's right to choose whether or not to wear seatbelts. Or the essay may simply prove that driving without seatbelts is dangerous and stupid.

As you have probably guessed by now, essays differ from reports. Reports simply give information about a topic. When you need information, you might read a newspaper or consult the great storehouse of factual reports, the encyclopedia. When you want to know what people think about a topic, though, you turn turn to the op-ed page and to essays. An essay, too, can be basically factual, but it usually expresses a point of view about an issue or topic.

---

### Finding a Point for Your SAT II Essay

TOPIC:  The topic will be given to you in the instructions for writing the essay.

PURPOSE:  The purpose of the essay will be explained by the wording of the topic. Look for such words as *describe*, *compare* and *contrast*, *persuade, explain*, *report*, *analyze*, and *interpret*. Each requires a slightly different response. Or the purpose of the essay may be left up to you.

POINT:  The point is the essay's main idea or thesis, or what the essay demonstrates, proves, or argues.

---

Although the SAT II topics are meant to be broad enough to elicit a response from almost every breathing soul, it could happen that, try as you might, you can't care a fig about the issue presented. What then? Can you still write an insightful essay? Is it possible without a sense of ennui screaming from your every sentence? The hard fact is that, even if you have no particular opinion on an issue or topic, you must still try to create the illusion that you care deeply about the issue. Doing so may rub your conscience the wrong way, but rather than raise a stink which won't get you anywhere, make the best of it. This time go along to get along. Don't regard it as a cop-out. Rather, consider it a survival tactic, a challenge to your resilience and creativity, qualities that colleges seek and admire.

Faced with the prospect of writing an essay about a topic that leaves you cold, you have some choices to make: Fake it, fight it, drop it, or psych yourself to do the best you can.

1. *Fake it.* Writing to say something even when you have nothing to say inevitably leads to words on a page that sound forced, like a conversation you might have with an aging aunt at Thanksgiving. Not a good choice.

2. *Fight it.* Some resentful students turn on the test or on the test makers by attacking the college admissions testing system in America. They write statements declaring their refusal to participate in a dehumanizing charade that fails to take into account each student as a unique individual. After the test, such students may feel relieved for having spoken their minds, but their position will also have irreparably damaged their chances of being admitted to the colleges of their choice. While college admissions officials generally approve of individual initiative and an independent spirit, they won't bother with students who respond defiantly to an SAT II essay question. Why invite trouble onto their campus? Not a good choice.

3. *Drop it.* Although this is the only foolproof way to keep yourself from writing a pointless essay, it's not a viable option when you're a junior or a senior and you're striving for good grades and high test scores. Not a good choice.

4. *Psych yourself.* This is the most promising solution. Begin by asking yourself ten or a dozen questions about the topic. Start with easy questions and work toward the harder ones.

Here, for example, are questions on the general topic *Dangerous Pursuits:*

*What are some dangerous pursuits?*
*Why do some people go bungee jumping?*
*Why don't I go bungee jumping?*
*Why does my cousin Henry go?*

After a while, the questions and answers become more provocative:

*When is it O.K. to gamble with your life?*
*Does the state have the right to forbid you from risking your life?*
*At what point in law-making does the government overstep its bounds?*

Obviously, at the beginning of a twenty-minute essay test, you won't have time to ask and answer dozens of questions, but the more thoughts you can generate, the richer your writing will be.

If self-psyching fails to work, try this alternative: As rapidly as possible write a list of anything, literally anything, that might qualify as a response to the topic. Like pulling a stopper, making a list often starts the flow of ideas. Your mind makes connections as one idea calls up memories of another, and then another. Don't be particular. After a short time, review the list and choose the idea that holds promise for your essay. Even if the list doesn't thrill you, pick the least objectionable item and begin to write on it. Who knows, you may have accidentally stumbled upon a rich lode of ideas. Writers often discover what they really want to say only after they've written for a while, even as long as 10 minutes. After that, time and space won't permit a complete rewrite, but a few crucial sentences could change the emphasis of what they've written, and they can quickly re-locate ideas and restructure their essays with neatly drawn arrows.

Sometimes a better thesis suddenly swims into the writers' view half way through the test. Should they change course or stick with what they have? It takes courage to return to "Go" and to start over. Because of time and space restraints on the SAT II, a switch could be fatal. In general, the new idea ought to be out of this world to justify trashing what they've written.

If you find yourself in such a predicament, don't switch unless you'll never again be able to look yourself in the eye. Grit your teeth and finish what you began. Resist the temptation to shift from your original idea even if you don't believe in it any more. You won't be penalized for hypocrisy, but you will surely damage your essay with a confusing or am-bivalent presentation.

Normally, the wording of an SAT II essay ques-tion forces you to take a position on the issue or topic. It might say to you directly, "State your opinion," or ask "Do you agree or disagree?" Your view then becomes the point, or thesis, of your essay. In the essay itself the thesis is usually stated outright in a simple declarative sentence, as in these examples:

| TOPIC: Democracy | Thesis: Democracy is a far more cumbersome form of government than dictatorship. |
| TOPIC: Psychology | Thesis: When disciplining children, instilling a fear of punishment is more effective than promising a reward. |
| TOPIC: War | Thesis: War is hell. |

On the other hand, the thesis of an essay may be so strongly implied by the cumulative weight of evi-dence that stating the thesis is unnecessary. Which-ever way you decide to inform the reader of your es-say's thesis—by announcing it directly or by weaving it subtly into the fabric of the text—be sure to lock onto it as you write. Let it guide you from the opening lines to your conclusion. Omit ma-terial that causes the essay to wander from its point. Readers will appreciate an essay that rarely deviates from a well-defined path.

### Pat P's Essay

Pat's reflections on the Hutchings question served her well. The failure of numerous dictatorial regimes throughout history seems to validate her thesis that democracy is, and always will be, the chosen form of government. Sticking to her thesis, Pat filled in details drawn from past and current events. Her essay is not perfect, but it contains many worthy qualities. It shows that Pat studied the topic carefully, narrowed it, and found a specific point to make. On the SAT II her essay would earn an above-average score. (*Note*: Sentences are numbered for convenient reference.)

(1) Rumors about the death of democracy have been greatly exaggerated. (2) All of Democracy's vital signs are stable. (3) It is the most popular kind of political system and has the best endurance record. (4) All the others, like socialism, communism, fascism, and monarchy come and go, but democracy goes for centuries. (5) This illustrates the health of democracy.

(6) In America, there have always been threats to democracy since the country was first settled. (7) The English, Spanish and French kings ruled at first, but their imperialism and oppression didn't last. (8) They were thrown out by the people of the colonies, that thought that they should decide how they wanted to live and to govern themselves. (9) The rule of monarchs in the Western Hemisphere was ended by the American Revolution. (10) In France a few years later the people threw out the king and his aristocracy and now there is hardly a country in the world where a king or queen has absolute power. (11) They are usually just figureheads. (12) Democracy has not died, but monarchy has instead.

(13) In 1917 the Russian communists overthrew the Csar. (14) Their regime lasted over seventy years. (15) In the late 1980s and early 1990s there was trouble in the country. (16) The communists were also overthrown by the will of the people. (17) Now the former Soviet Union is trying to establish democracy. (18) People have more freedom and they have a right to vote, to speak, to criticize the government and their leaders. (19) Countries that were taken over by the Soviet Union were let go and given the right to choose self-determination. (20) Even the Communist Party was outlawed. (21) When Boris Yeltsin took over from Mikhail Gorbachov, he declared communism officially dead as a doornail. (22) They had created a shambles of their economy. (23) Their money was worthless and the trepidation of mass starvation hung over millions of people.

(24) When the Berlin Wall was torn down and Germany was reunited, the Cold War was over. (25) America had won the war. (26) Our victory over the forces of the Communist menace means that democracy has the power to endure and is healthy.

### *Chris H's Essay*

Chris's essay is less scholarly than Pat's essay, but it nevertheless demonstrates his ability to write. On the SAT II the essay would be rated above average. Based on his careful reading of the topic, Chris wrote about a first-hand experience that illustrates the validity of the Hutchings quotation. The essay is not free of error, but it is well-organized and filled with details that hold the reader's interest. (*Note*: Sentences are numbered for convenient reference.)

(1) The quote, ''The death of democracy is not likely to be an assassination from ambush. It will be a slow extinction from apathy, indifference, and undernourishment,'' is relevant to my math class. (2) Room 202 of my high school is a totalitarian dictatorship in a world all by itself. (3) While democracy may still be alive and well in every other classroom in the school, a situation has arisen in Room 202 which doesn't fit with the democratic principles on which America was founded.

(4) Mr. Finn is the teacher. (5) He's a good teacher, but he runs the class like he never heard of democracy and the principles of freedom. (6) His policies and restrictions were told to us on the first day of class. (7) He won't allow you to have oral communion in class. (8) More prohibitions include chewing gum and wearing hats. (9) If you arrive after the bell, the door will be locked and you'll get detention. (10) If you don't do your homework, it is like the wrath of God on your head. (11) The first time somebody came to class without their homework, Mr. Finn yelled at him for twenty minutes. (12) The boy turned colors and practically cried. (13) After that no one comes to class without homework. (14) That is why people who take his class, know that they'll be well-prepared in math. (15) In Mr. Finn's favor, outside of class he is completely changed.

(16) As the pedagogue, Mr. Finn can run the class the way he wants, but does he have the right to be an inhuman, intimidating tyrant to the students?

(17) Basically, everyone is scared of him, which is why no one talks back or they say they don't care how he runs the class as long as they learn math. (18) That's where Robert Hutchings' quote is applicable. (19) The class is apathetic. (20) They won't stand up for their rights to be treated decently and humanely. (21) They have let Mr. Finn become a tyrant. (22) As long as people don't care or won't fight back, the potential for the demise of democracy is always a threat.

*(The pages that follow refer often to Pat's and Chris's essays. To find these essays quickly, please fold down a corner or insert a bookmark.)*

## 4. Collect Ideas and Arrange Them in Order

Unless you are blessed with a lightning-quick mind that instantly analyzes issues and draws conclusions in a logical sequence, you'll have to gather and organize ideas for your essay the way ordinary mortals do. You'll search your knowledge and experience for ideas and examples to support your thesis. You'll keep them in mind as you write, note them on paper as you think of them, or prepare a sketchy outline. Jotting down a brief list of ideas that occur to you, or possibly preparing a sketchy outline, is all it takes. Essay writers with more time than you'll have on the SAT II may write down key words, draw boxes around them, and connect them with arrows. Some prefer to draw circles within circles, as though to create a visual image of their essay before putting thoughts into words. No method excels another, as long as it helps the writer to collect and arrange ideas.

While you reflect on your jottings, a better thesis may come to mind, or you may run into new ideas that bolster your first one. On a roll, you might unleash a torrent of more great ideas than you can use. What a happy chore it will then be to pick only the best of the best for your essay. In other words, before you write a word on your answer sheet, you should probably devote at least a few minutes to collecting thoughts. Obviously, on the SAT II, you'll have to think rapidly, but better in haste than not at all.

### The Formula

Most essays are variations and adaptations of the formula. Using the formula will not make your prose immortal, but it could help turn a muddle of words into a model of clear thinking. The formula is simply an all-purpose plan for putting ideas into clear, easy-to-follow order. It uses a beginning, a middle, and an end. It's not sensational, but it works for virtually any essay. In fact, you've probably used it in school to answer a test question, analyze a story, or write a report on lab work. Its greatest virtue is simplicity. Each part has its place and purpose:

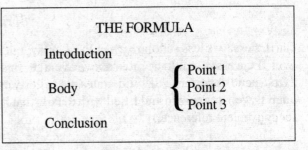

Writers rarely follow the formula letter by letter. Some compare this standard three- or five-paragraph format to painting by the numbers. It lacks creativity and originality. Yet many, many essays, even those that take circuitous paths from beginning to end, adhere to some sort of three-step organization. The introduction hooks the readers and promises them an essay on a particular topic. The body fulfills the promise and the conclusion sends readers off feeling glad that they read the essay to the end. Since all writers differ, however, the variations within each step know no bounds.

The formula prescribes a three-stage structure for an essay. It also requires a body consisting of three points. Why three? Mainly because three is a number that works. If you can make three different statements about a topic, you probably know what you're talking about. One is too simple, two is better but is still shallow. Three, however, is thoughtful. It suggests depth. Although every short essay needn't include three points to support its thesis, three carries a voice of authority. If you can't think of three, stick with two, and don't make up a third that is simply a rehash of one of the first two disguised as something new. Psychologically, three also creates a sense of wholeness for the reader, like the beginning, middle, and end of a story. It's no accident that the number three recurs in all literature, from *The Three Little Pigs* to *The Bible*.

The order of ideas is important, too. What comes first? Second? Third? The best order is the clearest order, the arrangement that readers can follow with the least effort. No plan is superior to another provided you have a valid reason for using it. The plan least likely to succeed is the aimless one, the one in which you state and develop ideas in the random order they happened to come to mind. It's better to rank your ideas in the order of importance. Decide which provides the strongest support of your thesis. Although your best argument may be listed first in your notes, save it for last on the essay. Giving it away at the start is self-defeating because everything that follows will be anticlimactic. In other words, work towards your best point, not away from it. An excellent way to plot three good ideas is to lead with your second best, save your best for the end, and sandwich your least powerful idea between the others. This structure recognizes that the end and the beginning of an essay are its critical parts. A good opening draws the reader in and creates an all-important first impression, but a memorable ending, coming last, is what readers have fresh in their minds when they assign you a grade.

As always, though, you mustn't follow these guidelines slavishly. **Pat P** didn't. Turn to her essay (page 178) to see a perfectly justifiable departure from the rule. Each of her paragraphs alludes to a different triumph of democracy over authoritarian rule. The first deals with the decline of monarchies, the second with the rise and fall of the Soviet Union, and the third with the end of the cold war. Because she structured her essay chronologically, Pat used up her strongest points before she got to the last paragraph.

## 5. Start With an Appealing and Informative Introduction

The opening lines of an essay tell readers what to expect. If the opening is dull or confusing, readers will brace themselves for a less than thrilling reading experience. Some essays become clear and engaging by the second paragraph, but an essay with an unimaginative start begins with a handicap, and the writer will have to work that much harder to overcome the readers' first impressions.

It pays, therefore, to write an opening that stops readers in their tracks. Begin with something to lure the reader into the piece. Use a hook—a phrase, sentence, or idea to grab your readers so firmly that they'll desperately want to read on. Hooks must be very crisp, very clean. They must surprise, inform, or tickle the reader in an instant, and say ''Read on; you'll be glad you did.'' A dull hook just won't do. In a short essay, a hook can't take up more than a couple of lines. Anything longer will erode the heart of the essay.

Let the opening sentences written by **Pat** and **Chris** serve as illustrations:

**Pat:**  Rumors about the death of democracy have been greatly exaggerated.

**Chris:**  The quote, ''The death of democracy is not likely to be an assassination from ambush. It will be a slow extinction from apathy, indifference, and undernourishment,'' is particularly relevant to my math class.

Pat's hook is sharper and cleaner. To introduce her essay, Pat cleverly alludes to a Mark Twain quotation, ''The reports of my death are greatly exaggerated.'' Pat's adaptation fits the topic, coincides with her tone and purpose, and suggests that she is a confident and literate writer. As a bonus, readers who know the Twain quotation may get a satisfying jolt of recognition and enjoy Pat's adaptation. In brief, she launched her essay stylishly. At the same time, though, she took a chance, because she could not know whether her audience would catch the allusion or let it fly right over their heads.

In contrast, Chris wrote a long and cumbersome opening sentence. He squeezed Hutchings' two-sentence quotation between the subject (*quote*) and its verb (*is*). It often works to begin an essay with an arresting quotation, but the quote must be brief. In spite of the awkwardness of Chris's long-winded opening, it is saved from disaster by awakening curiosity about the link between Hutchings' words and a high school math class.

A concise one-sentence opening is probably harder to write than a longer one. In other words, you can't fool around when space is tight. It's not unheard of for students, smitten with an inventive idea, to write half a page before they start to deal directly with the topic. Some students need that much space to put their thoughts in order. Either way, on the SAT II, beware of an introduction that drags on.

Beware also of openings that are too cute or precious, as in

Little did George Washington know as he sat sipping a brew on the veranda at Mount Vernon with his little woman Martha beside him, that . . . etc.

Be thoughtful and clever, yes, but not obnoxious. Above all, steer clear of an all-inclusive opening that grandiloquently reviews the history of mankind in fifteen words or less, as in

Throughout recorded time, man has struggled to keep the flame of freedom alive, etc.

Be intelligent and perceptive, yes, but not pompous.

Techniques for pulling readers into the body of an essay are unlimited. Yet many successful openings are merely unique variations of one of these popular formats:

1. Begin with an brief incident or anecdote that relates to the point of your essay.

When Joanne S entered Springdale High School early last September, she didn't know that she had left her constitutional rights at the schoolhouse gate.

2. State a provocative idea in an ordinary way or an ordinary idea in a provocative way. Either will arrest the readers' interest.

That a person is supposed to be innocent until proven guilty is an alien concept in Room 202 of my school.

3. Use a quote from the test question, from Shakespeare, Bruce Springsteen, or any other source—maybe even your grandmother. But be sure the quote relates to the topic of your essay and says it better than you can.

"Some animals are equal, but some are more equal than others." George Orwell said that.

4. Knock down a commonly held assumption or define a word in a new and startling way.

When Ivan Ulov, a Russian immigrant, arrived in Shaftsbury, Vermont, he learned that freedom does not mean cutting down a neighbor's maple tree.

5. Ask an interesting question or two, which you will answer in your essay.

Is true democracy possible? Or is it just an ideal to work for?

6. Make an unexpected connection between your topic and a bit of culture. By offering readers a second layer of meaning, your writing is enriched.

We'll get by with a little help from our friends. That, at least, was the hope of Hurricane Andrew's victims after the winds died down.

7. Create suspense by waiting until the end of the opening passage to reveal your topic.

Michael Jackson takes his everywhere, while Julia Roberts takes hers to bed. Rob Lowe keeps one in each Porsche, and Jennifer Jason Leigh has one made of gold. Happiness, for all these stars, depends on having a telephone at their fingertips.

If none of these techniques works for you, or if you don't have time on the SAT II to devise a good hook, rely on the direct approach. Just declare your thesis right up front. But don't phrase it like an announcement, as in, "In this essay, I am going to prove that democracy is not dead." State your point, as in "Democracy is far from dead," and take it from there.

If at first you can't find a suitable opening, don't put off writing the rest of your essay. Just skip a few lines and and begin with the body of your essay. As you write, a pleasing opening idea might strike you. Add it later. Whatever you do, though, be sure that your opening fits your writing style and personality. Work hard to get it right, but not so hard that it will seem forced or too cute or too long. Ideally, it should introduce your topic so naturally and unobtrusively that readers will not even realize that they are being enticed into reading past the first sentence.

## 6. Develop Your Ideas Fully With Examples and Details

No doubt you've heard people toss off opinions like, "We had an awesome vacation," or "That movie was terrible," or "Bob is a bore." Such remarks convey the speakers' general attitude toward their vacation, the movie, and Bob, and perhaps that's all you'd care to hear at the moment. But if it mattered to you why the vacation was great, why the movie stank, or why Bob is boring, you'd need details. You might ask, for example, what makes Bob dull? Is he a couch potato? Does he talk incessantly about tropical fish tanks? Maybe he doesn't talk at all, or maybe he does nothing but gripe about the SAT IIs. Whatever the reasons, a fuller explanation of why Bob induces widespread yawning might convince you, too, that the poor guy is indeed a hopeless bore. Or your informant might not give you enough data to really make up your mind about Bob. It would depend, wouldn't it, on the potency of the reasons and the way they are expressed? Precise, well-documented information is far more convincing than general and unsubstantiated opinion.

In an essay, the information used to give credence to the writer's main point is commonly called *development*. Because development indicates how deeply a student can think—a matter of great concern to colleges—it counts heavily in grading SAT II essays. Development does not mean number of words. An essay of a thousand words can still be underdeveloped. Some students, unaware of the difference between development and throwing the bull, fill their essays with verbal waste. They write even when they have nothing to say. Perhaps you've done it yourself on occasion. Be assured that essays short on development but long on refuse will be found wanting by SAT II readers, who know bull when they see it.

Nor is development simply the range of evidence summoned to uphold a thesis. Not every good essay needs, say, three or five or a dozen supporting ideas. The fact is that superior development skills can be demonstrated on the SAT II with a single vivid example. It's depth that counts.

• • • • • • • • • • • • • • • • • • • • • •

**Chris H**, addressing the Hutchings question, for example, successfully used only one compelling example to prove that apathy erodes democratic values. In telling the story of his math class, Chris detailed Mr. Finn's teaching style (sentences 4–12, 16) and described student reaction to Mr. Finn's tyrannical ways (sentences 13, 14, 17, 19–21). In other words, most of the Chris's sentences (16 of 21) in one way or other develop the proposition that democracy gets no respect in Room 202. The remainder of the essay introduces Chris's main idea (sentences 1–3) and draws a conclusion (sentence 22).

**Pat P**, in contrast to Chris, develops her essay with numerous examples that vouch for the staying power of democracy. Almost every sentence (7–25) contributes another supporting detail to her main point. Pat presents her thesis at the beginning of the essay (sentences 1–5) and reiterates it at the end (sentence 26). In between, the essay is nothing but development.

• • • • • • • • • • • • • • • • • • • • • • • •

Each paragraph in your essay should contribute to the development of the main idea. It should contain facts, data, arguments, examples—testimony of all kinds to corroborate the thesis. If you are unsure how a particular paragraph lends support to the thesis, cross it out or revise it. If you're perplexed, just imagine how your readers will feel. Be merciless with your writing. Even though you may admire a paragraph, give it the boot if it doesn't help to make your case.

A paragraph indentation ordinarily signals readers to get ready for a change in thought or idea, somewhat like the directional blinker telling other drivers that you're about to turn. Yet not every new paragraph signals a drastic change in direction. It may simply move the essay ahead one small step at a time. Paragraphs also permit readers to skim your writing. Readers in a hurry focus on opening and closing sentences and skip what lies between, but you can force readers to slow down by varying the location of the most important idea in each paragraph, usually called the *topic sentence*.

Not every paragraph requires a separate topic sentence. Sometimes the main point of a paragraph may be obvious without one. At other times two or more paragraphs may be united under a single, all-inclusive topic sentence. Occasionally, the main idea won't be apparent to readers until they reach the next paragraph. In short, the function of topic sentences varies.

• • • • • • • • • • • • • • • • • • • • • • • •

Some of the variations appear in the essays written by **Pat** and **Chris**. Pat's opening serves as both the thesis statement of her essay and the topic sentence of her first paragraph. The main topic of her next paragraph is not made clear until the end (sentence 12). Her third paragraph has no identifiable topic sentence, although the contents imply that it would be something like, "Democracy now prevails even in the former

Soviet Union, where dictators have long ruled." The fourth paragraph is so brief that a topic sentence seems superfluous. Yet the paragraph is unified under the thought contained in the second half of sentence 26, "democracy has the power to endure and is healthy," an idea that brings home the point not only of the paragraph but of Pat's entire essay.

Chris uses topic sentences more systematically. Each of his three paragraphs has one. Sentence 1, which contains the long quotation, conveys the main idea of both the paper and the first paragraph. The second paragraph is unified under sentence 5, and in the last paragraph, sentence 22 summarizes the point of the paragraph while also reiterating the thesis of the essay.

• • • • • • • • • • • • • • • • • • • • • • • • • • • • • • •

While topic sentences come in assorted guises, they share a common trait. They are helpful in keeping both writers and readers on the track. When you write, assume that readers have a poor sense of direction. Given half a chance, they'll lose their way. Therefore, remind them often of where they are. Lead them with topic sentences, but be sure that whatever you say in the rest of the paragraph supports what the topic sentence says. Oblivious to the needs of their readers, writers sometimes wander from their topic sentences, leaving readers bewildered

## 7. Guide Readers With Transitions

Readers need to be guided through an essay. Consider them visitors in a strange place. As the writer you must show them around by setting up verbal guideposts. Tell them where they are going, show them their progress, and remind them often of the destination. If you've done your job, they should be ready for what they find at the end.

In essays longer than the one you'll write for the SAT II, readers need to have their hands held more firmly. To do so, you needn't tell them again and again what you've already written, but rather restate key ideas, slightly rephrased. For instance, the main idea of this section (Guide Readers With Transitions) has thus far been that writers should guide their readers along. You'll find that idea stated in the opening sentence. You'll find the idea stated in new words at the start of the second paragraph by the phrase "readers need to have their hands held more firmly," which is meant to remind you of the main idea while also pulling you along to the next sentence, which discusses how to guide readers without repeating yourself. By repeatedly alluding to the main idea, you'll not only compel readers to focus on your point, but you'll keep readers at your side from start to finish. Watch out for detours. You may lose your reader if you suddenly step off the path you laid out at the start. (The sentence you just read is a detour. Of course it's related to the main topic of the paragraph, but it sets the paragraph on a new course.)

• • • • • • • • • • • • • • • • • • • • • • • • • • • • • • •

Refer to the essay by **Chris**. Notice that he set up several helpful guideposts to keep readers tuned to the issue. In the first paragraph he uses the phrases "death of democracy" (sentence 1) and "doesn't fit with the democratic principles" (sentence 3). In the second paragraph (sentence 5) he uses the phrase "never heard of democracy and the principles of freedom," and near the end (sentence 22) he refers to "the demise of democracy." At least four times in his short essay he has rephrased the main issue. Yet the refrain is not monotonous because different words are used each time.

Similarly, **Pat** keeps her readers in tow by the repeated references to the vitality of democracy, among them: "democracy's vital signs are stable" (sentence 2) "[democracy] has the best endurance record" (sentence 3), "democracy goes for centuries" (sentence 4), "democracy has not died" (sentence 12), "democracy has the power to endure" (sentence 26). There can't be any doubt, can there, that Pat has a powerful grip on her readers' hands?

• • • • • • • • • • • • • • • • • • • • • • • • • • • • • • •

Help readers along, too, by choosing words that establish relationships between one thought and the next. This can be done with words such as *this*, which happens to tie the sentence you are presently reading to the one before. (The word *too* in the first sentence of this paragraph serves the same function; it serves as a link between this and earlier paragraphs.) The English language is rich with words and phrases that serve to tie sentences and ideas together.

Here is a brief thesaurus of common transitions grouped according to their customary use. With a bit of thought, you probably can think of others.

When you **ADD** ideas: *in addition, furthermore, moreover, further, besides, too, also, and then, then too, again, next, secondly, equally important.*

When you **COMPARE or CONTRAST**: *similarly, likewise, in comparison, in like manner, however, in contrast, conversely, on the other hand, but, nevertheless, and yet, even so, still.*

When you cite an **EXAMPLE**: *for example, for instance.*

When you **REINFORCE** an idea: *indeed, in fact, as a matter of fact, to be sure, of course, in any event, by all means.*

When you show **RESULTS**: *as a result, as a consequence, consequently, therefore, thus, hence, accordingly.*

When you express a **SEQUENCE** or the passing of **TIME**: *soon after, then, previously, meanwhile, in the meantime, later, at length, after a while, immediately, next.*

When you show **PROXIMITY**: *here, nearby, at this spot, near at hand, in this vicinity, on the opposite side, across from, adjacent to, not far from.*

When you **CONCLUDE**: *finally, in short, in other words, in a word, to sum up, in conclusion, in the end.*

Not every sentence needs to be tied to the previous one with a particular transitional word or phrase. The ideas themselves sometimes create a natural link.

• • • • • • • • • • • • • • • • • • • • • • • • • • • • • •

In the following pairs of sentences taken from Chris's essay, notice how the italicized parts relate to each other.

**A.** (1) Room 202 of my high school is a totalitarian *dictatorship* in a world all by itself. (2) While democracy may be alive and well in every other classroom in the school, a situation has arisen in Room 202 which *doesn't fit with the democratic principles* on which America was founded.

**B.** (7) He *won't allow* you to have oral communion in class. (8) *More prohibitions* include no chewing gum and wearing hats.

**C.** (20) *They won't stand up for their rights* to be treated decently and humanely. (22) *As long as people don't care or won't fight back*, the potential for the demise of democracy is always a threat.

• • • • • • • • • • • • • • • • • • • • • • • • • • • • • •

Whenever you use a transition to tie one sentence to another, you do your readers a favor. You guarantee them a smooth trip through your essay. Otherwise, each sentence stands like a disconnected link in a chain, and readers bump along, often losing the point you are trying to make. Although many sentences won't contain transitions, three or four sentences in succession without a link of some sort may leave readers doubting that this trip is worth taking.

## 8. Choose Plain, Precise, Lively, and Fresh Words

### Use Plain Words

That's a principle easy to say but hard to live by when you're hoping to impress readers with your intellect and sophistication. Yet nothing, truly nothing, conveys your erudition better than plain words. However big your vocabulary, never use a complex word on the SAT II essay to show off or to make yourself sound mature for the readers. You'll get no extra credit for an essay crammed with ornate, multisyllabic words used for no other purpose than to sound ornate and multisyllabic. There's always a risk, in fact, that words that sound profound to you may seem pompous to your readers. Or worse, they could make you appear foolish.

The student who wrote "Parents usually inculcate their offspring like their own paters and maters inculcated them" knew more about how parents raise kids than about writing plainly. It would be better to have written, "Parents usually raise their children the same way they were raised," or "When bringing up children, parents usually do what was done to them." Likewise, the girl who wrote, "I am of the opinion that a prerequisite for parenthood includes disbursement of penal adjudication among siblings with an even, dispassionate hand," needs a basic lesson in plain writing. How much clearer to have written, "I think that good parents should know how to be fair in disciplining their children" or "I think that being equally strict with all their children is a prerequisite of being good parents." Words should be like gifts, carefully chosen to give pleasure to someone you like. High gloss is not a measure of value. You won't gain much by dressing ordinary ideas in fancy robes or from trying to appear more impressive than you already are.

This admonition to use plain words, however, shouldn't be regarded as a license to use current, everyday slang or street talk in your essays. Spoken language, which contains many colorful words and expressions like *chill*, *pig out*, *dissed*, and *freak out*, has its place, but its place is not in an SAT II essay unless you definitely need current lingo to create an effect that you can't get any other way. If you must write slang terms, fine, but don't highlight them with quotation marks. Why call attention to the fact that you can't think of standard or more original words?

Use plain words even for profound thoughts—correction, *especially* for profound thoughts. By writing, "I think. Therefore, I am," the seventeenth century philosopher Rene Decartes reshaped the way humans think about existence. He could have used more exotic words, of course, words more in keeping with the florid writing style of his time, but his statement probably derives its power from its simplicity. A sign of true intelligence is the ability to convey deep meanings with simple words.

Simple doesn't necessarily mean short. It's true that the plain words tend to be the short ones, but not always. The word *fid* is short, but it's not plain, unless you are a sailor, in which case you'd know that a fid supports the mast on your boat or is used to pry open a tight knot in your lines. On the other hand, *spontaneously* is five syllables long. Yet it is a plain and simple word because of its frequent use. It springs, well, spontaneously from the mouth.

For any SAT II essay, a plain, conversational style is appropriate. The language should sound like you. In formal writing, custom requires you to remove yourself from stage center and focus on the subject matter. At some point in your schooling, you may have been warned never to use "I" in an essay. That caveat may apply to some forms of exposition, but not to SAT II essays. In fact, SAT II topics encourage first-person responses by often asking you to state your opinion or preference. How do you do that without using "I"? It can be done, of course, by using pronouns like *one*, as in "When *one* is getting ready for college, *one* sometimes writes funny," or *you*, as in "Sometimes *you* feel like a dope" or by avoiding pronouns altogether. But an essay that expresses the writer's personal opinion will sound a lot more natural when cast in first-person singular.

• • • • • • • • • • • • • • • • • • • • • • • • • • • • • •

Refer now to the essays by **Pat P** and **Chris H**. In sentence 23 Pat said that "the trepidation of mass starvation hung over millions of people." She probably meant that Russians were scared of starving to death or that starvation threatened the Russian people. Pat deserves a hug for pulling *trepidation*, meaning *fear*, from her vocabulary storehouse, but in context, the word is used improperly. In standard English usage, *fear* may hang over people, a *threat* may hang over people, but *trepidation* may not. In this instance, a more common word would have been preferable.

Chris also used inflated language. In sentence 16, he calls Mr. Finn a *pedagogue*, an elaborate and increasingly old-fashioned word for *teacher*. Considering the informality of the rest of Chris' essay, the word seems pretentious and glaringly out of place.

• • • • • • • • • • • • • • • • • • • • • • • • • • • • • • • •

SAT II essay readers are old hands at rooting pretense out of student writing. Unless students are exceptionally astute, they usually give themselves away by using elaborate words that fall a mite short of precise diction. Writers who leave no clue that they are posing as bright, witty, clever, articulate people, on the other hand, are probably bright, witty, clever, and articulate enough to write essays in their natural voice, so why pretend?

The point is, don't be phony! Just let your genuine voice ring out, although the way you speak is not necessarily the way you should write. Most speaking is vague, clumsy, confused, and wordy. Consider writing as the casual speech of someone who speaks exceedingly well. It's grammatically correct and is free of pop expressions and clichés. Think of it as the kind of speech expected of you in a college interview or in serious conversation with the head of your school. Or maybe even the way this paragraph sounds. You could do a lot worse!

## Choose Precise Words

Hazy, vague, and abstract words fade as quickly from a reader's memory as last night's dream. They cover up lack of clear and precise thinking. How much easier it is to say that a book is *good*, *interesting*, or *exciting* than to search for words that will precisely describe the book's appeal. Similarly, it's more convenient to resort to words like *nice*, *fine*, *stupid*, *boring*, and *pretty* than to explain in detail what you mean by each word. But to write something that will stick in a reader's mind, use well-defined, hard-edged words. Exact words help you express exact thoughts. To write precisely is to write with pictures, sounds, and actions that are as vivid in words as in reality. Exact words leave a distinct mark; general ones, only a blurry impression.

Good writers often experience the world more intensely than other people. Like artists, they think visually. They listen hard to the sounds and voices around them and are extra-sensitive to smells, to tastes and to the feel of things. They keep their senses at full throttle in order, as the writer James Baldwin once said, "to describe things which other people are too busy to describe." They understand that much good writing must appeal to their readers' senses.

To evoke a strong response from your readers, make use of the principle that a picture is worth a thousand words. Actually, whether it's more or less than a thousand is debatable, but the point is clear: words should help readers *see*. Therefore, *show* more than you *tell*! Instead of describing your uncle as "absent-minded," show him stepping into his morning shower with his pajamas on. Rather than saying that your room is a "mess," show the pile of wrinkled clothes in the corner and the books and Snickers wrappers scattered on the floor next to your unmade bed. The same principle applies to smells: "Her breath was foul with a stale whiskey stench"; to sounds: "the hum and throb of big machines in the distance"; to touch: "the feel of cool, linen bedsheets"; and to tastes: "a cold, sweet drink of clear water on a hot day." In short, by writing vividly, you prevent readers from misinterpreting what you have to say.

• • • • • • • • • • • • • • • • • • • • • • • • • • • • • • • •

**Chris H** leaves his readers guessing in sentence 15 of his portrait of Mr. Finn. He observes that "outside of class he [Mr. Finn] is completely changed." The phrase "*completely changed*" is fuzzy. Does Chris mean that away from the classroom Mr. Finn smiles a lot and gives friendly pats on the back to all his students? Or does he become a bashful nerd who looks at his Reeboks when you meet him on the street? Chris disregards his readers' need for details by *telling* about his math teacher instead of *showing* him in living color. Had Chris been more alert to his readers, he might have created some illuminating pictures of Mr. Finn:

> TELL:  Mr. Finn possesses a variety of values.

SHOW: Mr. Finn insists that students study an hour every night. He prizes punctuality to class and regards math as the epitome of logical thought.

TELL: Mr. Finn doesn't care that I can't do math homework after school.

SHOW: When I explained to him that I'm kept from math homework by driving my brother Tommy to piano lessons or Little League, by yearbook meetings on Tuesdays, by work for Peer Leaders and Students Against Driving Drunk, by French tutoring, and a part-time job at the florist, Mr. Finn muttered, "That's your problem."

In sentence 15 of her essay on democracy, **Pat P** also leaves readers to puzzle out the exact meaning of the phrase ''trouble in the country.'' History shows that the Soviet Union was in deep trouble before the communists were removed from power, but readers are left in the dark about the nature of the trouble. Is Pat referring to ethnic unrest in several Soviet republics or to the failed political coup in August, 1991? Maybe she means the people's mistrust of President Gorbachev. Had Pat been more attuned to the needs of readers, such guesswork would be unnecessary. Other sentences in her essay could also benefit from more precise words:

TELL: The Cold War was over (sentence 24).

SHOW: Although there was no signing of an official truce, each Soviet republic declared independence, armies were disbanded, the Warsaw Pact was abolished, and Russia asked its former adversaries in the West for food and money.

TELL: The English ... were thrown out ... of the colonies (sentences 7, 8).

SHOW: The American colonists told King George to get out and defeated his army in the War for Independence.

• • • • • • • • • • • • • • • • • • • • • • • • •

Essays bogged down in detail no doubt grow tedious both to read and to write. Authors need to choose what readers need to see and know. Excessive analysis is boring, but so is too little. A balance is best. No one can tell you precisely how to achieve the balance. The feel of what seems right takes time and practice. In the end, the content and purpose of an essay will have to determine how detailed it needs to be. Every time you mention a meal, it's not necessary to recite the menu unless there's a good reason for doing so. When you use an abstract word, ask what is more important, to give details to readers or to push on to other matters? The context, as well as your judgment and experience as a writer, will determine what you can expect readers to understand. To get the knack a little more quickly, reread any interesting passage from a book or other publication. Pick out the details and the broad statements. What did the passsage show, and what did it tell? Since the passage held your interest, perhaps you will have found a model worth emulating in your own writing.

By no means does this plea for verbal precision suggest that abstract words be eliminated from the language. After all, we need them to talk to each other about *beauty, love, fairness, satisfaction, power, enlightenment*, and thousands of other notions that exist in our hearts and minds. The ability to think abstractly, to invent theories, to express feelings, and to articulate ideals and lofty principles is a gift that separates human beings from all other creatures, and we should delight in it, but remember that most readers are an impatient lot. They will reject essays that don't at some point, come down to earth.

### Use Lively Language

*Active and Passive Verbs:* Unlike the machine-scored multiple-choice questions, your SAT II essay will be read by people—real people with feelings, moods, likes and dislikes, and the capacity to laugh, grow angry, and be moved. They are usually teachers who know that high school writing can be lively, interesting, and clear. Like any readers, they will be put off by writing that is dull.

The most efficient way to inject life into your writing is to pay close attention to your choice of verbs. Verbs, as you've no doubt been taught, show action or state of being. To a writer, the fact that verbs show action is extremely important. Active verbs stimulate interest by waking up the language. They create movement, perform, stir things up, and move around. They excel all other words in their power to restore life to lifeless prose. They add energy and vitality to sentences, and, as a bonus, they help you to write more economically.

While *active* verbs are full of life, *being* verbs are not. They stagnate. They don't do anything but connect one thought to another, especially forms of the verb *to be*: *is, are, was, were, am, has been, had been, will be*. When used in sentences, each of these being verbs joins a subject to a predicate, and that's all. In fact, the verb *to be* in all its forms acts much like a verbal equal sign, as in "Seven plus three *is* ten" (7 + 3 = 10) or "Sam *is* a genius" (Sam = genius), or "Your SAT II score *is* going up" (That = good news!). Because being verbs (and equal signs) show little life, use active verbs whenever possible.

Here are some ways to pump life into sluggish sentences:

1. Try to substitute an active verb drawn from another word in the sentence.

BEING VERB:  Monica and Phil *were* the highest scorers on the SAT II practice test.

ACTIVE VERB:  Monica and Phil *scored* highest on the SAT II practice test.

The verb "*scored*" has been drawn from the noun "*scorers*."

Active verbs may also be extracted from adjectives:

BEING VERB:  Achievement *is* the determining factor in SAT II grades.

ACTIVE VERB:  Achievement *determines* SAT II grades.

The verb "*determines*" has been drawn from the adjective "*determining*."

2. Sometimes it's preferable to find an altogether new verb, as in:

BEING VERB:  It *is* logical that admission to college is the result of a student's effort and achievement.

ACTIVE VERB:  Logic *dictates* that a student's effort and achievement lead to college admission.

*Being* verbs are perfectly acceptable in speech and writing. We can hardly get along without them. But use them sparingly in your essays. As a rule of thumb, if more than one in four of your sentences relies on a form of the verb *to be* as its main verb,

you may be depending excessively on passive verbs.

• • • • • • • • • • • • • • • • • • • • • • • • • • •

For the record, **Pat P** used thirty-two verbs in her essay. Eight of them were forms of *to be*, but a few simple verb swaps might add still more energy to her writing.

BEING VERB:  " . . . the Cold War *was* over." (Sentence 24)

ACTIVE VERB:  " . . . the Cold War *ended*."

BEING VERB:  "Their money *was* worthless . . ." (Sentence 23)

ACTIVE VERB:  "Their money *lost* its value . . ."

**Chris** relies even more heavily on *being* verbs. Ten of his twenty-five sentences and clauses use some form of *to be*, a ratio that could be improved in the following ways:

BEING VERB:  "The quote . . . *is* relevant to my math class." (Sentence 1)

ACTIVE VERB:  "The quote . . . *applies* to my math class."

BEING VERB:  " . . . it *is* like the wrath of God on your head." (Sentence 10)

ACTIVE VERB:  " . . . the wrath of God *falls* on your head."

BEING VERB:  "Basically, everyone *is* scared of him . . . " (Sentence 17)

ACTIVE VERB:  "Basically, he *scares* everyone . . . "

• • • • • • • • • • • • • • • • • • • • • • • • • • •

When you start to weed *being* verbs out of your writing, you're likely to find that some sentences resist easy change. Some need to be thoroughly recast. Subjects become verbs, verbs turn into nouns, unnecessary phrases are eliminated entirely—alterations that result in sentences that bear little resemblance to the original. At the same time, though, your writing may get an unexpected lift. Verb-swapping tends to eliminate needless words, thereby improving your writing.

Once you get into the habit of clearing dead verbs out of your prose, you may notice that certain nouns limit your options for using active verbs. That is, certain nouns, when used as the subject of a sentence, determine your chances for finding a lively verb. Some abstract nouns, in fact, cut the choices drastically. Take, for example, sentences starting with "The reason," as in "The reason for taking the SAT II is . . ." How many verb choices do you have other than *is*, *was*, and other forms of *to be*? Not many. Verb choices are also severely reduced by subject nouns like *thought*, *idea*, *issue*, *way*, *notion*, *concept*, or any other essentially abstract nouns. The same holds true for sentences that begin with "There," as in "There are 2400 colleges in the USA," and often for sentences that begin with "It" as in "It is difficult to choose just one." On the other hand, nouns that name people, places, concrete objects, or events almost cry out for active verbs. When the subject can perform an action, like a person, for instance, you'll never run out of verb choices.

As these examples illustrate, whenever you insert a concrete, easy-to-define noun in place of an abstraction, you are apt to write a tighter, more energetic, and more readable sentence:

ABSTRACT:   The *cause* of the strike was the students' demand for freedom.

DEFINITE:   The *students* struck for freedom.

ABSTRACT:   The *way* to the deans's office is down the next corridor.

DEFINITE:   The next *corridor* goes to the dean's office.

ABSTRACT:   *There are* students who are good in chemistry but not in physics.

DEFINITE:   Some *students* excel in chemistry but not in physics.

*Being* verbs are not the only verbs that sap the life out of sentences. They share that distinction with several other verbs, such as any form of *to have, to come, to go, to make, to move,* and *to get.* We use such verbs all the time, almost without thinking. They are convenient and oh, so versatile. Webster's International Dictionary cites sixteen definitions alone for the verb *get,* not including such phrases as *get up, get around, get together,* and *get away.* Because of constant use, such verbs pale next to more animated verbs. But, like *being* verbs, they are indispensible. When they show up in your writing, stick with them only if you can swear that no other words will do. Unless they fit perfectly, however, trade them in for better, livelier ones, as in these examples:

DULL:   The line to the lunch counter *moved* very slowly.

LIVELY:   The line *crept* (crawled, poked, inched) to the lunch counter.

Note that by using a more animated verb, you eliminate the need for "very slowly," which would be redundant.

DULL:   The principal *gave* permission to the students to eat in the staff lunchroom.

LIVELY:   The principal *permitted* the students to eat in the staff lunchroom.

*Active and Passive Sentences:* To write lively prose, also keep in mind the distinction between *active* and *passive* sentences. A passive sentence is one in which the performer of the action is not mentioned until late in the sentence or is left out altogether. For example, in the following sentence, can you tell who is performing the action? *Six weeks were spent preparing for the SAT II.* OK, it was your English class, so you add a phrase: *Six weeks were spent preparing for the SAT II by our English class.* That's better, but it still obliges the reader to wait until the end to find out who has performed the action. Why keep the reader waiting? Not only that, but the folks who did the work—you and your English class—are mentioned almost begrudgingly, like an afterthought in the prepositional phrase that ends the sentence. Give credit where it's due. Put the performers of the action up front, as in *Our English class spent six weeks preparing for the SAT II.* This sort of revision not only eliminates passive verbs, but tightens and enlivens your writing. Any time you restructure passive sentences, you pep up the prose.

PASSIVE:   This book was recommended by my teacher.

ACTIVE:   My teacher recommended this book.

PASSIVE:   It was bought for me by my mother.

ACTIVE:   My mother bought it for me.

• • • • • • • • • • • • • • • • • • • • • • • • • • • •

The essay written by **Pat P** might be charged up by revising sentence 9:

ORIGINAL:   The rule of monarchs in the Western Hemisphere was ended by the American Revolution.

REVISED:   The American Revolution ended the rule of monarchs in the Western Hemisphere.

Stated in the active voice, the sentence is tighter. At least one sentence from **Chris H's** essay also needs a shot of energy.

ORIGINAL:    His policies and restrictions were told to us on the first day of class (sentence 6).

REVISED:    He told us his policies and restrictions on the first day of class.

• • • • • • • • • • • • • • • • • • • • • • • • • • • • • •

Although active sentences usually sound more natural and interesting, sometimes a passive sentence will work better. When it's immaterial who performed an action, for example, or when the actor can't be identified, passive voice makes perfect stylistic sense.

ACTIVE:    The exam proctor gave the starting signal at 8:30.

PASSIVE:    The starting signal was given at exactly 8:30.

In the passive version the important fact is the starting time. Who gave the signal is secondary.

ACTIVE:    Workers repaved this road with blacktop.

PASSIVE:    The road was repaved with blacktop.

The repaving material is the point of the sentence. Who performed the work is not.

*Use Fresh Language:* Here's your chance to do yourself and your readers a favor. Instead of relying on safe, customary language, take a chance now and then and give your readers a verbal surprise. SAT II readers, especially after reading hundreds of predictable essays on the same topic, will do cartwheels for something fresh, something new—a word, a phrase, a sentence still wet behind the ears. It's courageous to use fresh language. Living dangerously always takes mettle, but here's a guarantee: a pleasant verbal surprise or two will give your readers, as well as your essay, a boost.

A verbal surprise is simply a unique and interesting choice of words. You don't have turn exotic phrases in order to dazzle your reader. Common words, deftly used, will do the job just as well—better, probably, for they will sound more natural than something forced onto the page just to sound unusual. For example:

ORDINARY:    He wrote a magnificent essay on baseball.

SURPRISING:    He pitched a magnificent essay on baseball.

Since essays are not normally *pitched*, the unexpected shift from *wrote* to *pitched* is modestly surprising. The verb *pitched* works well only because the topic is baseball. It might be silly in an essay on another topic.

ORDINARY:    The shark bit the swimmers.

SURPRISING:    The shark dined on the swimmers.

Changing *bit* to *dined* suggests good manners and gentility, qualities that sharks rarely enjoy.

ORDINARY:    The gunshot frightened the pigeons, which flew away.

SURPRISING:    The gunshot filled the sky with frightened pigeons.

The ordinary sentence states literally what happened: The sound of the gunshot scared the pigeons silly. In the second version, though, the shot becomes a vital force with the power to fill the sky. Both the pigeons and the sentence have sprung to life.

The sound of words can also create modest surprises. Some words echo the sounds they describe. The word *bombard*, for instance, has an emphatically explosive sound. The sound of *yawn* is wide open and can be stretched indefinitely. *Choke* sticks in the throat. *Slogging* is slow, just like the action it describes, and *murmuring streams* evokes the sound of—what else?

Readers find unexpected pleasure from the repetition of sounds. *Alliteration*, the repetition of consonants, as in ''*Norman never knew*,'' pleases the ear and could make a common phrase uncommon. The appeal of such repetition is evidenced by the countless clichés that crowd much of our everyday speech and (regrettably) our writing, such as *footloose and fancy free*, *sink or swim*, and *helter-skelter*. *Assonance*, the term for vowel repetition, as in ''*The cold wind moaned over the ocean waves*,'' also promotes reading pleasure, but more subtlely. Use sound repetition only once in a while, though, because too much of it is distracting. An occasional treat for the ears will be a welcome diversion for your readers.

*Surprise with Comparisons:* Does this sound familiar? You can't find the words to express a feeling that you have inside you. You know what you want to say, but the words won't come. Although our language is filled with wonderful words to describe virtually anything, sometimes emotions and experiences seem almost inexpressible. How, for instance, do you show the look you got from the bus driver when you didn't have the exact fare? How do you describe street sounds at 5:00 o'clock on a summer morning or the feel of clean bedsheets?

Writers frequently depend on comparisons to catch those inexpressible details and fleeting sensations. A uniquely expressed comparison provides words to say the unsayable, and it also delights readers. That bus driver, for instance, may have looked "as though he'd just run over the carcass of a dead animal." The streets may have sounded "like an orchestra tuning up to play," and the bedsheets may have felt "like a drink of spring water on a sultry August afternoon."

Comparisons are economical. They condense a lot of thought and feeling into a few words. Ernie Pyle, a famous newspaper correspondent in World War II, reported his stories as though they were being told by the average GI lying in a foxhole. He said, "I write from a worm's eye point of view." What a terrific comparison! Who ever thought that worms have eyes, much less a point of view? The idea gives a fresh slant to an old expression, "bird's eye view" and cleverly emphasizes Pyle's position on the battlefield.

*Similes* ("Norma babbles like a brook") and *metaphors* ("Norma is a babbling brook") compare something known (a babbling brook) to something unknown (Norma). Little kids use such figures of speech instinctively. Because their vocabularies are limited, they compare what they know with what they can't yet express. "When my foot is asleep, it feels like seltzer," says a boy to his daddy, or "Today is chocolate sunshine." As people grow up, they lose the knack of making colorful comparisons and have to relearn it. When you actively look for comparisons, they sprout, like weeds in the garden, all around. Compare the smell in the locker room to rotting hay, the sound of your science teacher's voice to a foghorn, the tension in a room to a stalking cat.

• • • • • • • • • • • • • • • • • • • • • • • • • • •

Both **Chris** and **Pat** make an effort to clarify their thoughts with comparisons. Chris compares his math class to a "totalitarian dictator-

ship." He also compares Mr. Finn's ire to "the wrath of God" falling on hapless students' heads. Although neither comparison is particularly fresh, both convey Chris's message more succinctly than if he had fully spelled out what he meant. Pat uses a more striking comparison by declaring that "democracy's vital signs are stable." By comparing democracy to a sick person, Pat suggests that, despite reports to the contrary, the patient is still kicking. Later, Pat claims that communism is "as dead as a doornail." She deserves credit for the comparison but not for enlisting an old and worn-out simile. American English is littered with hundreds of such metaphors and similes, once fresh and surprising, but now dried out and lifeless, as dead as, er, well, doornails, whatever they are.

• • • • • • • • • • • • • • • • • • • • • • • • • • •

At one time, an expression like "dead as a doornail" may have been illuminating, but repeated use has dimmed its effect, and doornails (nails with oversize heads) are as obsolete as 78-rpm recordings. Every familiar combination of words, such as "I could care less," or "you've got to be kidding," or "what a bummer," was once new, cool, or poetic. Trying to be clever, cool, or poetic, people dug them. But constant repetition turned them into clichés, and clichés, by definition, have lost their zing and their power to surprise.

Still, clichés crowd our conversations, swamp our air waves, and deluge the media. Like the air we breathe (a cliché), we hardly notice them. In an essay, however, especially one that is supposed to demonstrate your unique cast of mind, you must avoid clichés like the plague. "*Like the plague*," in fact, is one you should avoid, along with other secondhand phrases and expressions like *the bottom line, how does that sit with you, to touch base with, off the top of my head, I'm outta here, a point well taken, two sides of the same coin, getting psyched, go off the deep end, life in the fast lane, for openers, flipped out, get off my back, get a life! super, so amazing, at the cutting edge of ___, no way, José,* and would you believe, *would you believe*? Using such trite phrases and expressions declares that you'd rather borrow what someone else has said than think of something on your own. Spewing one cliché after another is also the sign of a poverty-stricken mind. How can people hooked on clichés ever express their unique thoughts and feelings when they depend on others' words? How honest is the man who, just after his home has been blown down by a tornado, sings out to a TV camera, *"Such is life. I guess it's just one of of those things"*? Custom may expect a man to accept setbacks without being destroyed, but the poor fellow sheds no light on what he felt during what must have been one of life's devastating moments. He might just as well have used any number of other meaningless expressions that people use to mask life's disappointments and tragedies: *it just goes to show you, that's the way the cookie crumbles, you can't win 'em all, win some, lose some,* and *you have to take the good with the bad.*

*"You can say that again,"* agrees the cliché-monger. But don't you believe it. You don't have to put up with bad writing. Expunge clichés that sneak into your prose *when your back is turned, when your defenses are down,* and *when you least expect them.* Be vigilant, and purge them from your prose. Don't use an expression that you've ever heard or seen before. If you've written a phrase with a familiar ring, drop it, not *like a hot potato,* but just as quickly.

Your SAT II essay won't be penalized for an absence of inventive and scintillating expressions, but it is sure to suffer if infested with clichés. Get into the habit of expelling all trite phrases from your writing vocabulary. *Half the battle,* as they say, is knowing a cliché when you see one. The other half—removing them—is still to be fought and won.

## 9. Omit Needless Words

In *Hamlet*, the old windbag Polonius knew what he was talking about when he said "Brevity is the soul of wit." What he meant, in brief, is that Brief is Better. Never use two words when one will do. Readers want to be told quickly and directly what you have to say. They value economy and resent reading more words than necessary. Excess verbiage is a pain in the neck. So cut out unnecessary words.

(Stop! Go back to the last paragraph. Did you notice the needless words? Did you see that the last sentence is redundant? It's short, yes, but is it needed? Does it merely add fat to the paragraph?) Sentences, like muscles, should be lean and tight. Needless words are flabby. So, trim the fat. Exercise those writing muscles.

Here's a word to the wise:

Work through all the sentences you write by examining each one and crossing out all the words you don't definitely need.

Actually, that's twenty-one words to the wise—probably more than are needed.

Go through every sentence you write and cross out unecessary words.

That's better—eleven words of free advice, but still too many. The sentence could be trimmed still further:

Cut extra words out of every sentence.

Aha! This streamlined version contains just seven words, one-third of the original. If you can regularly trim that proportion of words from your writing without changing meaning or intent, you will have gone about as far as you can to make your writing interesting, although a ruthless, sharp-eyed editor might to cut even more: Omit unnecessary words. The ultimate goal in economical writing is to make every word count, so that omitting a single word will alter or distort the meaning.

Sentences are trimmed by squeezing them through various wringers:

*Wringer #1.* Look for repetition. Then combine sentences.

FAT: In his last and final year in high school, Bill was elected to be the head of the statewide SADD organization. As the head of the statewide organization, he learned about the details of laws dealing with DWI convictions and had many experiences talking in public to large groups of people. (51 words)

TRIMMED: Elected head of the statewide SADD organization in his senior year, Bill learned about DWI laws and spoke often to large groups. (21 words)

FAT: (From **Pat's** essay) They were thrown out by the people of the colonies, that thought that they should decide how they wanted to live and to govern themselves. (25)

TRIMMED: Demanding self-government and freedom, the colonists threw them out. (10)

*Wringer #2.* Look for telltale words like *which, who, that, thing, all.* They sometimes indicate the presence of fat.

FAT:    Football is a sport *that* millions of fans enjoy. (9)

TRIMMED:    Millions of fans enjoy football. (5)

FAT:    (From **Chris's** essay) Basically, everyone is scared of him, *which* is why no one talks back . . . (13)

TRIMMED:    Feeling scared of him, no one talks back . . . (9)

*Wringer #3.* Look for phrases that add words but little meaning.

FAT:    *By that point in time,* people will be ready for a change. (12)

TRIMMED:    By then, people will be ready for a change. (9)

FAT:    Hamlet returned home *as a result of* his father's death. (10)

TRIMMED:    Hamlet returned home because his father died. (7)

| Fat phrases | Trimmed |
|---|---|
| what I mean is | I mean |
| on account of, due to the fact that | because |
| in the final analysis, the bottom line is | finally |
| few and far between, insignificant in number | few |
| each and every one | each |
| this is a subject that | this subject |
| ten in number | ten |
| at the age of six years old | at age six |
| most unique | unique |
| true fact | fact |
| biography of his life | biography |
| in regard to, with regard to, in relation to, with reference to | about |

*Wringer #4.* Search for redundancies. Countless words are wasted on reiteration of what has already been said, on restating the obvious, on repeating ideas, on saying the same darn thing again and again and again until readers scream, "Stop! I can't take it any more."

FAT:    While carefully scrutinizing her patient's medical history, the doctor seemed fully absorbed by what she was reading. (17)

Because *scrutinize* means "to study carefully," the word "carefully" is unnecessary. Also, *absorbed by what she was reading* repeats what has already been stated.

TRIMMED:    While scrutinizing her patient's medical history, the doctor seemed absorbed. (10)

FAT :    (From **Chris's** essay) Room 202 of my high school is a totalitarian dictatorship.

Since a dictatorship has come to mean total control by the person in charge, the phrase *totalitarian dictatorship* contains a redundancy.

After you've pared your sentences to the bone, study the remains. Cut away still more by tracking down little words like *the, a, an, up, down,* its, and *and.* Don't remove whatever gives writing its energy and character, but neither should you spare yourself the pain of removing what you worked hard to put in. Throwing away your precious words may feel sometimes as though you are chopping off your hand, but count on it, your writing will gain life and strength without unnecessary words.

## 10. Vary Your Sentences

Repetition is boring. Yes, repetition is boring. A diet of nothing but unsalted mashed potatoes dulls the taste buds. A 200-mile stretch of straight road takes the pleasure out of driving. Yes, repetition is boring.

In writing, it's easy to fall into a rut by repeatedly using the same sentence pattern. To avoid boring your readers to death, serve them a variety of sentences. Your prose will be invigorated and your readers will be happy. Because English is such a pliant language, sentences can be endlessly revised until you've got a mix that works. Variety for its own sake, however, is hardly better than assembly-line writing in which every sentence follows the exact same pattern. On the other hand, variety to clarify meaning or to accentuate an idea is another story.

You probably know that most simple declarative sentences start with the subject, followed by the verb, as in:

*The peaches* (subject) *are* (verb) not yet ripe or ready to eat.

*They* (subject) *left* (verb) for the airport at dusk.

*This policy* (subject) *is* (verb) not easy to enforce.

Several sentences in a row with this subject-verb pattern will make writing sound like a chapter from a grade school primer. Take steps to more mature prose by checking an essay you've recently written. If several of your sentences lead off with the subject, try starting some of them with a prepositional phrase, with an adverb or adjective, or with some other grammatical unit. By varying sentence openings, you make your writing bolder and more readable.

The following pairs of sentences illustrate ways in which a subject can be shifted from its customary position:

BEFORE THE SHIFT:  Poison ivy thrives in the woods

AFTER THE SHIFT:  In the woods and meadows poison ivy thrives.

After a prepositional phrase the subject of the sentence appears.

BEFORE:  Poison ivy is apparently one of the most poisonous plants.

AFTER:  Apparently, poison ivy is one of the most poisonous plants

Obviously, the revised sentence begins with an adverb.

BEFORE:  Many people still don't know what it looks like.

AFTER:  Still, many people don't know what it looks like.

Well, here the sentence subject is snuck in after an opening connective.

BEFORE:  People should keep their eyes peeled for an innocent-looking three-leaved plant on a single stem whenever they go out to the country.

AFTER:  Whenever people are out in the country, they should keep their eyes peeled for an innocent-looking three-leaved plant on a single stem.

After introducing this sentence with a dependent clause, the writer named the subject and then added the rest of the sentence.

BEFORE:  A prudent person should take a shower with plenty of soap and water as soon as possible after brushing up against the plant to guard against infection.

AFTER:  To guard against infection after brushing up against the plant, a prudent person should take a shower with plenty of soap and water as soon as possible.

To revise this sentence the writer began with a *verbal*, in this case "to guard," the infinitive form of the verb. Verbals look and feel a lot like verbs (hence, their name), but are not. (The infinitive form of any verb, for example, cannot serve as the main verb of a sentence.) Verbals, though, come from verbs, which explains the resemblance.

BEFORE:  Some people walk through patches of poison ivy without worrying, thinking that they are immune.

AFTER:  Thinking that they are immune from poison ivy, some people walk through patches of the stuff without worrying.

Hoping to add diversity to sentence openings, the writer began this sentence with another kind of verbal, known as a *participle*. Most of the time the *-ing* ending is a clue that the word is a participle.

BEFORE:  Such people, who were unconcerned about becoming infected, may be shocked to discover that their immunity has suddenly disappeared.

AFTER:  Unconcerned about becoming infected, such people may be shocked to discover that their immunity has suddenly disappeared.

Determined to try something different, the writer picked an adjective that happens to sound like a verb because of its *-ed* ending.

Another variation to try occasionally is the sentence with a paired construction. Two equal and matched ideas are set against each other, often differing by only one or two words, as in:

It wasn't that David caught poison ivy, it was poison ivy that caught him.

"Ask not what your country can do for you, ask what you can do for your country."
—John F. Kennedy, January 20, 1961

The strength of such a sentence lies in the balance of parallel parts. Each part could stand alone, but together the thought is expressed more vigorously.

On occasion, an idea can be expressed powerfully by reversing the usual order of words. Out of context, such a sentence might sound almost like non-English, but in the right place such a sentence can pack a wallop. For example, "A brain he is not" is a far more forceful statement than "He is not a brain." Similarly, in the proper context, "Dangerous are the woods in the dead of winter" may sound more ominous than "The woods in the dead of winter are dangerous." Use inverted sentences only rarely, though. Frequent use will sound affected and silly.

No rule of thumb governs the proportion of sentences in an essay that should depart from the usual subject-verb word order. Much depends on the intent and content of the essay.

. . . . . . . . . . . . . . . . . . . . . . . . . . . . . . . . . .

In **Chris H's** essay, ten of twenty-two sentences begin with the subject, and in **Pat P's**, fourteen of twenty-four. Do those numbers indicate that one is superior to the other? Not at all, but the ratio shows that both Chris and Pat realize the value of sentence diversity.

. . . . . . . . . . . . . . . . . . . . . . . . . . . . . . . . . .

The English language offers writers a spectacular variety of sentence types. In most essay writing, declarative sentences predominate. (To refresh your memory, a *declarative* sentence, like the one you are now reading, simply makes a statement.) But you can create all sorts of fascinating effects with *interrogative* sentences. (Did you remember that they ask questions?) Or *imperative* sentences. (Remember that they give commands or make requests.) And *exclamatory* sentences. (What strong feelings they can express!) Furthermore, you can write sentences interrupted in midstream by a dash—although some people will tell you that it's not quite proper to do so in formal prose—and you can use direct and indirect quotations. Once in a while, you can drive home a point with a single emphatic word. Super!

Again, though, don't deliberately scramble up sentence types just to make a sentence potpourri, for you may end up with a mess on your hands. Be guided always by what seems clearest and by what seems varied enough to hold reader interest.

*Use of Repetition:* Contrary to what this book has stated previously, repetition deserves a place in an essay writing repertoire. Some kinds of repetition are boring, true, but adept use of repetition lets a writer stress important ideas in an unusual way. People naturally repeat words for emphasis, anyway, as in "I love you. I love you very much" and "Knock it off. I said knock it off!"

At first glance, the passage that follows may seem awfully repetitious:

> This school is in dire straits. It needs a new vision of education. It needs an administration and faculty devoted to learning. The science department needs more materials, textbooks, and equipment. The English department needs more books, supplies, and more teachers. The gym needs a new floor, and the students, the life-blood of the school, need an enormous transfusion of school spirit.

Every sentence but the first uses the same verb, but the passage is anything but monotonous. What impresses the reader is not repetition, but relentlessness. The writer used the verb *needs* six times to point out her school's shortcomings. She wouldn't have achieved the same emphasis by using a different verb in each sentence.

Or take this passage written by an incorrigible Oreo freak:

> My love for Oreos knows no bounds. My breakfast consists of cereal and three Oreos. My lunch is a peanut butter and banana sandwich with five Oreos. At snack time I devour ten Oreos straight. After dinner I have ten more. Before bed I wash down a half dozen Oreos with a glass of milk, and in case I have insomnia, I stash a handful of Oreos in my room for a small middle-of-the-night feast.

That's strong repetition with a purpose. The writer pounded Oreos into the reader's brain. Even if nothing else in the passage is worth remembering, a reader won't forget the cookie—not Fig Newtons or Animal Crackers, but good old Oreos!

While effective repetition leaves its mark, accidental repetition can be annoying. Watch out for avoidable repetitions:

> At the end of the hall stood a clock. The clock said five o'clock.

> Columbus made three voyages. The voyages took him across the Atlantic.

Usually, combining such sentences will keep you from ending one sentence and starting the next one with the same words:

The clock at the end of the hall said five.

Columbus made three voyages across the Atlantic.

Occasionally sentences are plagued by a word or sound that won't let go. One student wrote:

Maybe some people don't have as much free-dom as others, but the freedom they do have is given to them for free. Therefore, freedom is proof enough that the best things in life are free.

Another student wrote,

The members of the assembly remembered that November was just around the corner.

These authors weren't listening to the sound of their own words. Had they read their sentences aloud, their ears would probably have noticed that the record seemed to be stuck. In fact, reading your work aloud allows you to step back (Hold it! Those two words—aloud and allows—should not be al-lowed to stand. They sound sour, don't you agree?). Anyway, when you say your written words out loud, you gain perspective and notice repetitive bumps that need repair. Or better still, let your essay cool for a spell, then recruit a friend to read it to you. That's how to achieve real objectivity.

*Short and Long Sentences:* Sentences can be written in any length, from one word to thousands. A long sentence demands more from readers because, while stepping from one part of the sentence to the next, they must keep track of more words, modifiers, phrases (not to speak of parenthetical asides), and clauses without losing the writer's main thought, which may be buried amid any number of secondary, or less important, thoughts. Short sentences are easier to grasp. A brief sentence makes its point quickly and often with considerable force, as in this passage about a family trip:

For three days, my parents and I sat in our Toyota and drove from college to college, look-ing for the perfect place for me to spend the next four years. For 72 hours we lived as one person, sharing thoughts and dreams, stating opinions about each college we visited, taking guided tours, interviewing students and college officials, asking directions a hundred times, eating to-gether in town after town, and even sleeping in the same motel rooms. But mostly, we fought.

The blunt closing sentence, particularly after a windy forty-six word sentence, produces a mild jolt. To be sure, it's meant to shock, but placing a tight, terse sentence against a long one intensifies the ef-fect. Like all stylistic techniques, this one mustn't be used too often. Overuse dilutes its impact, but when it works well, it's indelible.

Short and long sentences create the rhythm of writing. Because readers usually pause, subcon-sciously at least, at every period, short sentences slow the tempo. Long sentences may speed it up, but the pace depends a lot on the placement of clauses, the amount of parenthetical matter, and word choices. Although essays are usually meant for silent reading, writers can slow the pace by carefully se-lecting difficult-to-pronounce words or words with a great many hard consonants. *The squad plodded across the ugly swamp* is an illustration. Likewise, speed increases with sentences like *While shaving and dressing and combing his hair, he scanned his face in the mirror.*

In any case, a string of short, simple sentences can be as tiresome to read as series of long, complex ones strung end to end. A balance is best. A sequence of four or five equally short (or long) sentences should be given the fission-or-fusion treatment. That is, split the big ones and combine the others. To illus-trate, here is an elongated sentence that, like the situ-ation it discusses, needs improvement:

Because the federal government spends money for a vast number of programs that seem to me, a high school senior living in a town in a North-east industrial state, to be wasteful and extrava-gant, especially when it makes a lot more sense to put money into education, helping the poor, and fixing up the environment, which has been sadly neglected for many years, mostly in the northwestern United States, where animals are in danger of extinction as thousands of acres of old-growth forest are being clearcut every year for the benefit of private lumber companies, I will not support the present administration in the next election.

The sentence is perfectly grammatical, but it car-ries a big load, 105 words to be exact. To overhaul the monster, break it into pieces, rearrange it, add verbs, drop ideas, change the emphasis and trim words. In the end, the refurbished sentence might sound something like this:

I cannot support the present administration in the next election. The federal government spends too much money on a vast number of programs that, to me, seem wasteful and extravagant. It makes a lot more sense to put money into education, helping the poor, and fixing up the environment, which has been sadly neglected for many years. Environmental problems in the northwestern United States are exceptionally severe because animals are in danger of extinction as thousands of acres of old-growth forest are being clearcut every year for the benefit of private lumber companies

Whether or not you accept the writer's opinion, you'll probably agree that the revision, consisting of four sentences, from ten to thirty-six words, is clearer and easier to read.

Passages consisting of short sentences can also be made more readable by fusing ideas.

My high school is segregated. The different ethnic groups are separated. Whites have their territory. The black students also have an area. The Hispanic students also have their area. Some classes are integrated. History and gym classes are mixed. Most math classes are not. Foreign language classes are not integrated at all. Discussions about this problem have occurred many times in school. No one is sure it can be solved. It's hard to change people's views. I'd love to see prejudice end. Not everyone sees it the same way.

Although fourteen terse sentences may convey feelings of tension in the school, the writing calls to mind the style of grade school reading books, in which every sentence is equally important. A revised version might sound like this.

In my high school, black, white, and Hispanic students are set apart from each other. Each group has its own turf. Although history and gym classes are well-integrated, math and foreign language classes are not. Discussions about this problem have occurred many times in school, but not everyone agrees that it can be solved. Although I'd love to see prejudice end, some students refuse to change their views.

When sentences are combined, words are excised and the writing often becomes livelier. Not only that, but when some ideas are subordinated to others, not every thought receives equal emphasis. Overall, the revised version is more thoughtful and mature.

Neither **Pat** nor **Chris** included any excessively long sentences in their essays, but both tend to use short sentences that could be revised to advantage. For example, Pat wrote:

''(13) In 1917 the Russian communists overthrew the Csar. (14) Their regime lasted over seventy years . . . . (16) The communists were also overthrown by the will of the people.''

Pat's essay would flow more smoothly by combining sentences 14 and 16 in this manner:

''In 1917 the Russian communists overthrew the Csar. After seventy years the communists in turn were overthrown by the will of the people.''

This from Chris's essay:

''(6) His policies and restrictions were told to us on the first day of class. (7) He won't allow you to have oral communion in class. (8) More prohibitions include chewing gum and wearing hats.''

Sentences 7 and 8 might easily be combined to read this way:

''Prohibitions include oral communion [talking out], gum chewing, and wearing hats.''

---

### To Vary Your Sentences—A Summary

Start sentences with:
1. A prepositional phrase: *In the beginning, From the start, In the first place*
2. Adverbs and adverbial phrases: *Originally, At first, Initially*
3. Dependent clauses: *If you follow my lead, When you start with this*
4. Conjunctions: *And, But, Not only, Either, So, Yet*
5. Verbal infinitives: *To launch, To take the first step, To get going*
6. Adjectives and adjective phrases: *Fresh from, Introduced with, Headed by*
7. Participles: *Leading off, Starting up, Commencing with*
8. Inversions: *Unique is the writer who embarks . . .*

Use a variety of sentences types.
Balance long and short sentences.
Combine series of very short sentences.
Dismember very long sentences.

## 11. End Your Essay Unforgettably

When you reach the end of your SAT II or any other essay, you can lift your pen off the paper and be done with it, or you can leave your readers a little gift to remember you by. What you leave can be a little piece of insight, wisdom, or humor to make readers glad that they stayed with you to the end. It may be something to tease their brains, tickle their funny bones, or make them feel smart.

Whatever you give, choose it carefully, and let it spring naturally from the text of your essay. A good essay can easily be spoiled by an ill-fitting ending. Also, don't be tempted to use an ending that's too coy, corny, or cute, such as: *that's all, folks; it was a dream come true; a good time was had by all; tune in next week—same time, same station; or a nice place to visit, but I wouldn't want to live there.* These are outrageously trite endings that leave behind an impression that the writer was either too cheap to leave a better gift or too dull to think of something classier. Readers will appreciate almost any gift you give them, provided you've put some thought into its selection. Don't spoil a fresh essay with a stale conclusion.

Nor must you tack on an ending just for the sake of good form. The best endings grow organically out of the essay's content. Endings are so crucial in works of creative art that specific words have been designated to name them. A piece of music has a *coda*; a story or play, a *dénoument*, a musical show, a *grand finale*. When an ending approaches, you sense it at hand and expect soon to be bathed with a feeling of satisfaction. Good endings please both heart and mind.

Choose the gift judiciously. Leave behind a memento of your thinking, your sense of humor, or your vision. Even an ordinary thought, uniquely presented, will shed an agreeable afterglow.

1. Have some fun with your ending. A reader may remember your sense of humor long after forgetting the essay that struck his funny bone.

   SUBJECT: Stricter gun control laws

   GIFT: On this issue, the legislature has taken a cheap shot at many law-abiding citizens.

   SUBJECT: The nomenclature of college admissions

   GIFT: But the definition of "early action" that I prefer is "instant winner."

2. End with an apt quotation taken from the essay, from the assigned topic or from some other source.

   SUBJECT: The nobility of the teaching profession

   GIFT: As a wise person once said, "Catch a fish and you feed a man his dinner, but teach a man to fish, and you feed him for life."

   SUBJECT: The costs of racial disharmony

   GIFT: Now, more than ever, Rodney King's question, "Can we all get along?" has a new meaning.

3. Finish by reviewing the paper's main point, but with new words. Add a short tag line, perhaps.

   SUBJECT: The low quality of art supplies used in school, arguing that money should be devoted to support the art program

   GIFT: Colors fade rapidly when exposed to sunlight, a true indication of the paint's poor quality. How frustrating!

   SUBJECT: (**Pat's** essay) The purported death of democracy

   GIFT: Our victory over the forces of the communist menace must mean that democracy has the power to endure and must mean that it is healthy.

4. Project your readers into the future. What will happen in the months or years ahead?

   SUBJECT: Being adventurous

   GIFT: By late spring I had my fill of studying the river; it was time to get a raft and try the rapids myself.

   SUBJECT: The misuse of our environment

   GIFT: We must all do our part to save the planet, or there won't be a planet left to save.

A catchy conclusion isn't always needed, but some sort of ending is necessary to make readers feel they've arrived somewhere. They won't be satisfied with an essay that just evaporates. A short one is better than none at all. Stay away from summary endings, particularly when the essay is short, as on the SAT II . It's insulting, in fact, to review for the readers what is evident on the page in front of them. Readers are intelligent people. Trust them to remember what the essay says.

## PAT P AND CHRIS H GO FOR A "6"

Taking into account many of the recommendations made during the discussion of the first eleven principles of good essay writing, Pat and Chris turned their essays into exemplary pieces of writing, worthy of the highest score of the SAT II. With the major weaknesses eliminated, the essays turned out like this:

*Pat's "6"*

Rumors about the death of democracy have been greatly exaggerated. All the other political systems—socialism, communism, fascism, and monarchy—come and go, but democracy endures. Not only are its vital signs stable, but it is at the peak of health.

Since America was settled, democracy has always been threatened. At first English, Spanish, and French kings ruled, but their imperialism and oppression didn't last. Thinking that they themselves should choose how to live and to be governed, the colonists expelled the monarchs. The American Revolution ended monarchy in the Western Hemisphere forever. In France a few years later the people overthrew the king and his aristocracy. Now most monarchs are figureheads. There is hardly a country in the world where a king or queen rules with absolute power. Monarchy has died, not democracy.

In 1917 the Russian communists overthrew the czar. Seventy years later the communists, unable to control people's desire for independence, were also overthrown following several years of ethnic unrest. Its economy in shambles, with a worthless monetary system and the threat of mass starvation, the Soviet Union gave all its republics the right of self-determination. The Communist Party was outlawed. When Boris Yeltsin took Mikhail Gorbachev's place as the head of the Russian government in 1991, he declared communism officially dead. Now the former Soviet Union is trying to establish democracy. People have freedom and the right to vote, to speak, and to criticize the government and its leaders.

The breakup of the Soviet Union, combined with the destruction of the Berlin Wall and the reunification of Germany, signaled the end of the cold war. America and its democratic allies had won. Victory over the communist menace indicates the health and strength of democracy.

### Chris's "6"

``The death of democracy is not likely to be an assassination from ambush. It will be a slow extinction from apathy, indifference, and undernourishment.'' This quotation applies directly to my math class. While democracy may still be alive and well in every other classroom in the school, the situation in Room 202 doesn't fit with the democratic principles on which America was founded. Room 202 of my high school is a dictatorship.

Mr. Finn is the teacher. He's a good teacher. People who take his class know that they'll be well-prepared in math, but he runs the class as though he has never heard of democracy and the principles of freedom. On the first day of class he told us his policies and restrictions. He won't allow talking out loud, chewing gum, or wearing hats. Late arrivals will be greeted by a locked door and a detention. If you don't do your homework, the wrath of God falls on your head. The first time somebody came to class without homework, Mr. Finn yelled at him for twenty minutes. The boy turned colors and practically cried. Since then, no one has come to class without homework.

Outside of class Mr. Finn is a nice guy. He coaches hockey, and he regularly jokes and talks with students in the cafeteria and in the halls of the school. He is like a different person.

As the teacher, Mr. Finn can run his classes the way he wants, but does he have the right to be an inhuman, intimidating tyrant? Basically, he scares everyone, which explains why no one talks back. Or students say that they don't care how he runs the class as long as they learn math.

The class is apathetic. They won't stand up for their rights to be treated decently and humanely. They have let Mr. Finn tyrannize over them. As long as people don't care or won't fight back, the potential for the demise of democracy exists. Could Robert Hutchings's have been thinking of a class like mine when he made the quoted statement?

## 12. Follow the Conventions of Standard English

This book is too lean to house a complete handbook of standard English usage, although a good many usage problems are discussed in Part III. For a full treatment of English usage, however, go to the library and check out one of the hefty books on the subject. Look, for instance, at H. W. Fowler's *Modern English Usage*, the definitive reference work, in which you can find a page-long discussion of such arcane usage questions as the difference between *farther* and *further*, or when to use *that*, as in "Is it my Mazda Miata *that* is parked illegally?" and when to use *which*, as in, "Yes, your Mazda Miata, *which* is now being ticketed, is parked illegally." Numerous other books, such as the *The New York Times Manual of Style and Usage* and *The Careful Writer* by Theodore M. Bernstein are packed with solutions to literally thousands of usage problems.

Unhappily, there is no particular logic to standard English usage. Like the famous definition of pornography, it's hard to define but easy to spot when you see it. Standard English is merely a badge of an educated person, the level of writing and speech expected of people who are literate and who, to some degree, must depend on their language skills to help them make their way in the world.

The following pages present information on standard usage that every decent writer needs to know. Although the essentials won't surprise you— to write complete sentences, to choose words judiciously and accurately, to know how to spell, punctuate, and capitalize—some of the finer points may give you pause. Because usage is only a distant cousin of grammar, this section contains only a few rudimentary grammatical terms and rules. For a more concentrated dose of grammar, turn back to Part III or find a good grammar textbook and read, read, read.

## Standard English

### Complete Sentences

Formal writing usually requires complete sentences. Words can be arranged in so many ways that a defi-nition of a complete sentence covering all possibilities hasn't yet been devised. Nonetheless, most complete sentences do have certain characteristics that distinguish them from non-sentences, often called *sentence fragments*. For one, they start with capital letters and end with a period, a question mark, or an exclamation point. Beyond that, they're likely to have four qualities that identify them as complete grammatical sentences:

**1. Look for a *subject*.** It will be a noun or pronoun.

> The *lawyer* cross-examined the witness.
> *She* asked hard questions.

Every sentence has a stated subject unless it gives commands or make a request.

> Make mine without mayonnaise.
> Please be ready at six.

In such sentences, the noun or pronoun is omitted.

**2. Look for a *verb*.** Every sentence needs one. The verb tells what the subject does or did.

> Lucy *eats* raw onions by the pound.
> Her boyfriend, Frank, *smelled* the onions on Lucy's breath.

Or it tells what happened to the subject.

> Lucy *reeked* for a week.
> Frank's eyes *watered*.

Or it tells what the subject is or was.

> Frank *is* an onion hater.
> Lucy *was* an onion eater.

Some verbs end with the letters *-ing*. Examine them carefully because they may not be what you're looking for. You need a verb that goes with the subject of the sentence:

> *Waiting* for the odor to subside, Frank grew impatient.
> While *waiting* for Frank to settle down, Lucy stayed at home.

The word *waiting* looks and sounds like a verb. But it isn't. It's a verbal, a word derived from a verb. In fact, no word ending in *-ing*, except one-syllable words like *sing* and *ring*, can be the verb of a complete sentence unless it's preceded by *is*, *are*, *was*, or some other being verb, as in *was skating* or *were spelunking*.

**3. Look for statements (not questions) that start with certain words** as *when*, *where*, *which*, *who*, *what*, *while*, *because*, *that*, *although*, *in*, and *to*. These words often introduce phrases and clauses, which are never complete sentences.

> Because she missed her ride to school
> While Lucy waited for the bus on the corner
> Although it was 8:35 and the bus did not come

To make these partial sentences whole, add a comma and then another clause:

> Because she missed her ride to school, Lucy decided to take the day off.
> While Lucy waited for the bus on the corner, she made plans for a day in town.
> Although it was 8:35 and the bus had not come, Lucy remained mellow, as usual.

**4. Listen to your voice.** When speaking or reading aloud, most people pause for a split second at the end of each sentence. Unless the sentence asks a question, the pitch of their voices also drops slightly. Listen to yourself read aloud an essay you've written. Read it slowly. If the pitch of your voice does not descend slightly when you come to a period, you may have written an incomplete sentence, or you may have picked up the '90s habit of letting your voice rise slightly at the end of a sentence, causing your sentences to sound simultaneously like a statement and a question. For example, "This is Su*san*?" says the girl on the phone, uncertain whether Arnie would remember her. "I'm going *home*?" says Kevin, as though he knows it's not yet time to leave the meeting and hopes that Mr. King won't object. If you have adopted that speech pattern, listen for a rise rather than a lowering of pitch. Either way, a momentary pause and a change in the pitch of your voice may signal the end of a sentence.

Because of endless variations in the structure of sentences, you may occasionally write a perfect sentence in which only one or two of the aforementioned characteristics are apparent. At such times, go with your instinct. It may be a good guide.

# Word Choice

The number of words available in English is incalculable—some say up to a million. Yet most people have no more than a few thousand different words in their writing and speaking vocabularies. In this section you'll find a select sample of commonly abused and confused words. Because language keeps changing, a few of these usages may someday become standard English. In the meantime, however, use the proper words in any writing that's important to you.

## *Frequently Misused Words and Phrases*

### aggravate

Contrary to popular usage, *aggravate* does not mean *to anger* or *to annoy*. Its standard meaning is *to make worse*, as in "Stumbling over the dog *aggravated* Don's back pain." True, Don may be mad at Fido, but he's not "*aggravated*."

### amount, number

Use *amount* to refer to a mass or quantity—an *amount* of money, for instance. Use *number* to refer to anything that can be individually counted—*number* of dollars, number of people. Items that come in *amounts* include wheat, water, land, noise, sleep, and shrimp dip. Items that come in *numbers* include members, crackers, classes, trees, volts, rules and cans of soup. For example:

> From a large *number* of cans you can make a large *amount* of soup.
> People who read a *number* of newspapers every day pick up an enormous *amount* of information.
> An *amount* of insecticide has polluted a *number* of wells.

### and/or

This phrase, found most often in legal writing, makes even the most charming words sound like a manual for vacuum-cleaner maintenance. "Empty and/or clean your machine after every use," says the instruction booklet. Such a phrase has no business in an essay.

**bad, badly**

As an adjective, *bad* describes anything evil, tainted, corrupt, or disagreeable, as in *bad* apple, *bad* blood, *bad* day. Unwell people feel *bad*. They do not feel *badly* (an adverb) unless their sense of touch has gone *bad*. Cars run *badly*, investments turn out *badly*, and a person may want something *badly* enough to kill for it, which would probably be a *bad* move.

**between, among**

Use *between* to refer to anything split into two or divided by two, like, the Milky Way that Barbara split *between* George and herself. Use *among* for a division by more than two. For example, the seven famished kids divided the Doritos *among* themselves. Also:

> Among the three of us, we should figure out the answer.

> We should probably choose *between* Katie's and Sam's answers.

**data**

*Data* is a synonym for facts and statistics and is always plural, although it is increasingly used as a singular noun.

> The *data* show that few drivers observe posted speed limits any more.

> A single fact is a *datum*, but the word is rarely used. Rather, "a piece of *data*" would do just fine.

**different from, different than**

Republicans are *different from* (not different *than*) Democrats because one political party differs *from* another. Since the phrase *to differ than* is not English, different than is not standard usage. Use *different from*.

**due to, owing to**

These phrases are often used interchangeably, but in standard usage, *owing to* means "*because of*," as in "*Owing to* the strike, the milk was not delivered." *Due to* means the "result of," as in "That the milk was finally delivered was *due to* the contract settlement." *Owing to* may begin a sentence, but *due to* may not.

**etc.**

This abbreviation for the Latin word *etcetera* (meaning other things) is a way for writers to fool readers into believing that there's plenty more to say, but it's a bother to spell it out. Because it's easier to write *etc.* than it is to think, *etc.* is a lazy person's word. Avoid it if you can, unless the unwritten part of the list would be so obvious that it's not worth writing out, as in *first, second, third, etc.* Instead of *etc.*, consider using *and so forth, and so on, and other things, and the rest.*

**good, well**

*Good* is an adjective. Like any adjective it can be used before a noun, as in *good* apple, *good* grief, and *good* night. That's easy.

*Good* sometimes causes bad trouble when it's used after a verb. Good should not be used after most verbs, so avoid *talks good, drives good, writes good,* and so on.

*Good*, however, may be used after some verbs (called linking verbs), such as *looks, smells, sounds, feels,* and all forms of *to be*. So it's perfectly correct to say, "That idea sounds *good*." If you're not sure whether a verb is a linking verb, substitute a form of the verb *to be* in its place. If the sentence keeps its basic meaning, the verb might well be a linking verb. For example,

> The apple *tastes* good. = The apple *is* good.

(Replacing *tastes* with *is* preserves the basic meaning. Therefore, *tastes* must be a linking verb.) Other common linking verbs: *appear, stay, remain, grow,* and *become*.

Where *good* is not correct, use *well*—as in *talks well, drives well,* and *writes well*.

**he or she (he/she)**

Traditionally, the masculine pronoun *he* was the pronoun of preference for writers. *He* was used regardless of sex, as in

> When a person asks a favor, *he* should say "please."

To avoid masculine bias, the phrases *he or she* and sometimes *he/she* have come into everyday usage. Both are cumbersome, wordy, and slightly tacky. Don't use them. Instead, make your nouns plural, as in

> When people ask favors, *they* should say "please."

Or if appropriate, switch to second person pronouns (you), as in

When *you* ask a favor, please say "please."

## hung, hanged

Both *hung* and *hanged* are past tense of the verb *to hang*. But *hanged* refers only to executions, as in

They *hanged* poor Tom in Texas.

After the attempted coup, the rebels were *hanged*.

Everything else in the world is *hung* (posters, coats, effigies, mistletoe, mobiles, and blame.)

## kind of, sort of, type of

The phrase *kind of* is informal except when it is used literally, as in

Backgammon is a *kind of* board game. (Not a *kind of a* board game)

Few knew that Harold was that *kind of* man. (Not that *kind of a* man)

*Kind of* is used with singular nouns, while *kinds of* is used with plural, as in

That *kind of animal* lives in the jungle.

Those *kinds of animals* live in the jungle.

It's not proper to mix singular and plural words as in

Those *kind of animals* live in the jungle.

Everything noted about *kind of* also applies to *sort of* and *type of*.

## less, fewer

Use *less* to refer to a mass or quantity—*less* talent or air, for instance. Use *fewer* to refer to anything that can be individually counted—*fewer* tests, airplanes, and calories. One can have less wheat, water, land, noise, sleep, and shrimp dip, but fewer crackers, classes, trees, volts, rules, and cans of soup. For example:

Fewer cans make *less* soup.

Less garbage is generated by *fewer* people.

## like, as

*Like* and *as* are used for comparisons, as in

Barney walks *like* a duck.

I wish he'd walk *as* his brother does.

*Like* introduces a phrase; *as* introduces a clause. Phrases usually end with a noun or pronoun, as in Alice talks *like* her father. Clauses also contain nouns

or pronouns, but they are often followed by a verb as in Alice talks *as* her father did.

When you are uncertain whether to use *like* or *as*, look for a verb. If you see a verb at the end, you'll know that *as* is the word to use. For instance

Every day, the child acts more *like* her mother.

Do *as* I say, not *as* I do.

## only

*Only* has a way of popping up almost anywhere in a sentence.

They *only* went to the mall to buy ice cream.

They went *only* to the mall to buy ice cream

They went to the mall *only* to buy ice cream

They went to the mall to buy *only* ice cream.

Because of the position of *only*, each sentence says something different. To avoid confusion, *only* should appear only before the word or phrase it modifies. "I *only* love you" and "I love *only* you" make a world of difference. Put *only* only where it belongs.

## media

Officially, *media* is a plural noun. The news *media* are television, newspapers, radio, and magazines. Each of these sources of news is officially a *medium*. But only officially. In reality, *media* is being increasingly used as a singular noun, as in "According to the mayor, the *media* is biased." Using media as a singular noun lumps all the media into one unit, a perfectly logical notion, but still not grammatically correct.

## numerals

Spell out numerals of three words or less: *two*, *thirty-five*, *five hundred million*, *nineteenth*, and so on. Writing out longer numbers becomes a burden, so use the actual figures: *$4, 376*, a population of *94, 897*.

Also use figures for dates, street numbers, telephone numbers, decimals, and percentages. A number that starts a sentence, however, should be spelled out, no matter how long it is, as in "Nineteen ninety two went by very quickly." If the number is too long, try to start your sentence with a different word.

## real, really

The word *real* is an adjective that means "genuine." In formal writing *real* should not be used before another adjective, as in *real good* or *real fast*. *Really* (an adverb) could serve as a stand-in for very, as in *really fast*, but maybe another word entirely, such as *speedy* would really be more interesting. Here are two *real* examples that *really* illustrate proper usage:

> For the first time, we had a *real* vacation.

> We never *really* worried about getting home on time.

### reason is because, reason is that

In formal writing, the locution *the reason is that* is preferable to the *reason is because*. The reason for that preference is that *the reason is because* contains a redundancy. The word *because* means *for the reason that*. Therefore, there's no reason to say it twice.

### shall, will

*Shall* was once considered the acceptable form to express intent in the first person future tense.

> "I *shall* return," said General MacArthur.

Now the word is used interchangeably with *will* in the speech and writing of literate people. Perhaps the only subtle distinction that remains between *shall* and *will* boils down to the difference between force and free will. "Betty *will* do her homework" means that Betty has decided on her own to sit down and do her work. "Betty *shall* do her homework" suggests that she's being forced in some way to do it. In common usage, the distinction has grown muddy. Therefore, when Jimmy says "I *shall* call you tomorrow," he has said that he feels obligated to call. In fact, though, he may want very much to talk to you. Although it may sound picky, *shall* and *will* will continue to have distinct functions among guardians of the language.

### that, which

In everyday usage, little distinction is made between *that* and *which*. No one would argue seriously that "This is the face *that* launched a thousand ships" is superior to "This is the face *which* launched a thousand ships." To be precise, however, *that* is the pronoun reserved for restrictive clauses:

> The battle *that* ended the war was fought in Troy.

*Which*, on the other hand, is used for nonrestrictive clauses:

> The battle, *which* ended the war, was fought in Troy.

### that, who

Both *who* and *that* are relative pronouns that introduce subordinate clauses, as in

> Meet John, the engineer *who* designed the bridge across the bay.

> This is the bridge *that* John designed.

No one would ever substitute *who* for *that*, as in "This is the bridge *whom* John designed," but the reverse—substituting *that* for *who*—is becoming increasingly widespread: "Meet John, the engineer *that* designed the bridge across the bay."

John, a person, ought to be introduced by the pronoun *who*, which is reserved for people. The pronoun *that* is reserved for things. Don't dehumanize people by referring to them as objects.

### try to, try and

How often ordinary idiom defies logic. Literally, "*Try and* come to the meeting," and "*Try and* stop me," both suggest two separate actions when only one is intended. Instead of *try and*, write *try to*.

### you

Some people think that the word *you* (when it is used to refer to people in general) should not be used in formal writing. Others say it's acceptable. But it's never, never acceptable in a piece of writing to suddenly switch to the pronoun *you* after you had begun it using pronouns like *he* or *she* or the impersonal *one*. In other words, be consistent.

With some kinds of statements—formal or informal— *you* is out of place. Don't use it unless you are writing a set of instructions, such as how to twirl, toss a salad, or write an SAT II essay. You have to decide whether *you* is appropriate for whatever you're writing.

## Spelling

When people say that someone is a poor writer, they often mean he's a poor speller, but as you know by now, there's a lot more to writing than spelling words without error. Just as some people are born with an eye for color, and others have an innate sense of design, some people are natural spellers. They see a word once or twice, and it sticks. They never spell it wrong. Other people master spelling by memorization and practice. Still others may memorize words on a list, but when they write the words, they spell them incorrectly. Psychologists are stymied about why this occurs. They know, however, that the ability to spell has little to do with intelligence. Many brilliant people are hopeless spellers.

Spelling counts on the SAT II, and counts heavily, because spelling carries an inordinately powerful influence on readers. You won't earn credit for spelling everything correctly, but you'll lose it by turning in an essay crowded with misspellings. Poor spelling detracts from and weakens good writing.

In spelling, there are literally millions of ways to make mistakes. Considering how many chances there are to slip up, you can still take pride in being a near-perfect speller even if you err now and again. Many unusual words offer spelling challenges. You won't be faulted for spelling *hemmorhoids* or *silhouette* with a misplaced letter or two, but beware of the many ordinary words that plague many high school students' writing.

The list that follows contains the most popular words to misspell. A few of the words may surprise you, especially if you're already a pretty good speller. Some people claim that they see some of these words misspelled so often they hardly know right from wrong any more. Take the word *all right*, for example. The majority of Americans spell it *alright*. A few years ago the rock group The Who issued a popular album called "The Kids Are Alright." Promoters put the album name in ads, on t-shirts, windshield stickers, and posters. They probably did more to undo the work of English teachers than anyone since advertisers claimed that "Winston tastes good, like a cigarette should." Anyone on the verge of taking the SAT II in writing, of course, might recognize the grammatical flaw faster than it takes to light up a Winston. The ad was highly successful and probably would fallen flat had it been phrased properly, "Winston tastes good, *as* a cigarette should."

Here are several dozen of the words most likely to be mispelled, er, . . . misspelled.

**a lot**

*A lot* is two words, not one, as *a lot* of people think.

**accidentally**

This word is *accidentally* spelled *accidently* because of its *-ally* ending

**accommodate**

Because of two *c*'s and two *m*'s, this word is often misspelled. The word *accommodate* is long enough to *accommodate* two pairs of double letters.

**acquaintance**

Some people stumble over the *-ance* ending, but more troublesome is the *c* after the initial *a*. The rule is that words starting with the combination *a-q* refer always to water, as in *aqueduct* or *aquatic*. All others include *c* between the *a* and the *q*, as in *acquaint* and *acquiesce*.

**affect, effect**

*Affect* is a verb, *effect* is a noun, except in a rare instance. Spelling *affect* (verb) when you mean *effect* (noun) will *affect* your reputation as an accurate speller. The *effect* on the SAT II may be a lower score. Then again, your score may not be appreciably *affected*. The rare case: when *effect* means to bring to pass or to accomplish, as in "Study hard to *effect* a change in your spelling performance."

**all right**

*All right* is two words; it's never one. It's not like *already* and *altogether*, which can be either one word or two, depending on your meaning. Remember that and you'll do all right.

**already**

Like *altogether*, *already* is one word unless used in the sense of "The dinner is *all ready* to eat." *Already* as a single word is an adverb referring to a prior, present, or future time, as in "Enough, *already*."

**altogether**

*Altogether* is one word, except when referring to a group, as in, "The family was *all together* at Thanksgiving." Otherwise, *altogether* (as one word) means thoroughly or completely, as in "Spelling is *altogether* too complicated."

**athlete**

Because *athlete* is often pronounced *ath-a-lete*, as though the word has three syllables, the word is improperly spelled *athelete*.

## breath, breathe

It takes your breath away to see how often the final *e*, which changes the noun to a verb, is omitted.

## conquered

This word is often spelled *conquored* because the related word *conqueror* has both an *e-r* and an *o-r* to reckon with.

## conscience, conscious, conscientious

*Conscience*, composed of *con* and *science*, refers to a sense of moral righteousness. Spell it correctly so you won't feel pangs of *conscience* about spelling it incorrectly.

*Conscious*, an antonym for unconscious, means being mentally awake, a condition that aids in spelling *conscious* as well as many other devilishly difficult words.

*Conscientious* looks like a blend of conscience and conscious, but it means hard working, an attribute of a *conscientious* speller.

## could've (could of), could have

*Could've* unites two verbs, *could* and *have*. The phrase *could of* is sometimes mistakenly used for *could have*. But *could of* is not standard English. Don't use it or any of its relatives, *should of*, *might of*, and *would of*. Instead, write *should have*, *might have*, and *would have*.

## desert, dessert

This famous spelling bugaboo may remind you of your third grade teacher, who must have told you that, because kids like two helpings of *dessert*, spell the word with two *s*'s, not one, like its dry and arid homonym, which has only one.

## doesn't

*Doesn't* combines *does* and *not*. The apostrophe takes the place of the *o* in *not*. That's the only difference between spelling *does not and doesn't*. Therefore, it doesn't make sense to write *dosen't*, as many people do.

## dying, lying

Since *dying* comes from the verb *to die*, and *lying* comes from the verb *to lie*, they are sometimes spelled *dieing* and *lieing*. Don't confuse *dying* with *dyeing*, the word for changing the color of hair, t-shirts, shoes, or anything else.

## effect, affect

See *affect*, *effect* above.

## embarrassed

One of the two *r*'s or the two *s*'s often gets lost in the spelling of this word. To avoid embarrassment, just remember the two pairs of double letters.

## etc.

*Etc.* is the abbreviation for *etcetera*. People rely on *etc.* when they can't think of what else to say or when subsequent items on a list are too obvious to spell out, as in "A, B, C, D, *etc.*" Notice that because *etc.* is an abbreviation, it is always followed by a period, even in midsentence. Why so many students write *ect.* is a puzzle.

## exercise

Numerous ways have been devised to misspell *exercise*, from *excercise* to *exersize*. Exorcize all those incorrect ways and spell it in the one and only proper way.

## forty

Because *forty* is derived from four, the word is sometimes misspelled *fourty*. Why the *u* has been dropped from *forty* but retained in *fourteen* is a linguistic puzzlement.

## grammar

Grammar rhymes with hammer and with other words, too, which leads to the spelling of grammar with *er* at the end. To hit the nail on the head, spell it with *ar*.

## harass

Authorities don't agree whether *harass* should be pronounced with an accent on the first or on the second syllable. They agree completely on its spelling, though. It's not *harrass*, regardless of how you say it.

## its, it's

*It's* is a marriage of *it* and *is*. The apostrophe stands for the missing letter. That's the only way it's correct. *Its* (without the apostrophe) indicates possession, as in "The cat chased *its* tail." You won't go far writing *her's* or *his's*, so don't write *it's* unless you mean *it is*.

## jewelry

Pronunciation is at the core of why *jewelry* is often spelled *jewlery* or *jewelery*.

## judgment, judgement

This word is a gift from the spelling god. Both

versions are perfectly acceptable. Keep the first *e* or leave it out, as you please.

### loneliness

Anyone who writes *lonliness* doesn't know the spelling rule which says, keep the final *e* before a suffix beginning with a consonant.

### lose, loose

One letter, the "o," makes a difference. Don't confuse *lose* with *loose*, which rhymes with goose. *Loose* things include rules, shoelaces, screws, and escaped killers "on the loose." Among other things, you can *lose* in Monopoly, *lose* your way, and *lose* your mind. Be careful with *loose* change in your pocket, or you may *lose* it.

### mileage

*Mileage* is one of the exceptions to the spelling rule that says, drop the final *e* before a suffix beginning with a vowel. If the *e* were left out, the pronunciation of the word would change to something like "millage," whatever that is.

### misspell

Ha!

### ninety

Omitting the *e* violates the rule about adding suffixes that start with a consonant. Please see *loneliness* above.

### occasion, occasionally

Both *occasion* and *occasionally* have two *c*'s and only one *s*. Don't sneak in a double *s*. One will do, thank you.

### perform

Because *pre-* is a common prefix, it is attached to many words, such as *predict*, *prevent*, and *prejudice*. *Pre* means before as in prewar (before the war.) Perform is unrelated. Why the word is often misspelled *preform* remains a mystery worth pondering.

### playwright

A *playwright* writes plays. Yet the word is not "playwrite." In the old days a wright made things. A cartwright made carts, a wheelwright made wheels, and a *playwright* made . . . you guessed it. Nevertheless, *playwrights* engage in *playwriting*, not "playwrighting."

### precede

Three words in the English language end with the letters -*ceed*: *exceed*, *proceed*, and *succeed*. Obviously, *precede* is not one of them.

### preferred

This word illustrates the following long-winded spelling rule: Double the final consonant when adding a suffix that starts with a vowel, such as -*ed* or -*ing*, but only if the word has one syllable (like *run*, or *plan*), and it ends with a single consonant (also like *run* or *plan*), or if it's a two-syllable word with the accent on the second syllable (like *prefer* and *occur*). If this rule is baffling, work at it and keep it mind next time you spell *occurred*, *preferred*, *deferred*, *benefitting*, and *propelling*, among other words.

### prejudice, prejudiced

*Prejudice* is a noun. Its relative, *prejudiced*, is an adjective. The two words are not interchangeable. A *prejudiced* person suffers from *prejudice*.

### principal, principle

In grade school you may have been told that the *principal* of your school is your *pal*. That's why you spell the word *principal* . One would hope that principals have noble principles, but that may not always be the case.

### privilege

This word is often saddled with a *d* as in *priviledge*, which has the same ending as knowledge. But, please, no *d*! Nor should it be burdened with an additional *e* as in *privelege*. Two *e*'s are enough.

### professor, profession

*Professors* are sometimes called "Prof," a title with one *f* and the grade one deserves for spelling *professor* and *profession* with two.

### psychology

The *p* in *psychology* is tormenting.

### quite, quiet

The difference between these two words lies in the order of the last two letters. *Quite* has a silent *e* while *quiet*, ironically, doesn't. The *e* in *quiet* is *quite* evident when you say the word aloud.

### restaurant

Sometimes the *u* in *restaurant* is shifted from the

second to the third syllable, giving the word a French look. But even in Paris, they spell the word *restaurant*.

### rhythm

Notice that this word consists of six consonants in a row. That's why it may be hard to spell. It's rumored that every word needs at least one vowel, but linguists call the letter *y* a *semi vowel,* meaning that, although it's not a vowel, it acts like one.

### separate

Always look for *a rat* in *separate*.

### schedule

*Schedule* is a two-syllable word sometimes given a third by people who pronounce it "sched-u-al" and spell it as they hear it—*scheduAl*. If pronounced "sched-yule," it will probably be spelled as it should.

### scissors

Fifty percent of the letters in *scissors* are *s*'s. Never write *scissor*, a useless object if ever there was one. What can one do with half a pair of scissors? Probably the same thing that one does with a plier, a shear, and a pant.

### should've (should of), should have

*Should've* is OK. So is *should have*. But *should of* is not. See **could have** for the reasons why.

### similar

Because *similar* resembles *familiar*, people sometimes write *similiar*. Don't be deceived by the similarity of the two words.

### skiing

It's very uncommon for an English word to be spelled with double *i*'s. *Skiing* is spelled that way because it consists of *ski* and an *-ing* ending. Let the two i's remind you of tracks left behind by a passing skier.

### supposed to

The past tense of most verbs is formed by adding *-d* or *-ed* to the present tense form. *Supposed*, therefore, is the past tense of the verb *suppose*. Even though you may not hear the *d* in the phrase *supposed to*, it's supposed to be there when you spell it. Avoid writing *suppose to*.

### than, then

Use *than* rather than *then* when making a comparison (Phil eats faster *than* Fido.) *Then* is a time word, like the word *when*. Both contain the letter e. Remember this tale: Phil eats faster than his dog. First Phil finishes, then Fido. The end.

### their, they're, there

Don't confuse these three words. Each has its own separate use and meaning:

*Their* indicates possession, as in "*Their* spelling is getting better all the time."

*They're* combines *they* and *are*, as in "*They're* words that can easily be combined."

*There* is the opposite of here. Both are places. This word is used whenever *their* and *they're* don't fit. *There* are numerous places to use this word.

### tragedy

How sad that writers sometimes add an extra *d* to *tragedy*. If you write *tradgedy*, it's not a tragedy, but it is dead wrong.

### used to

If you're *used to* writing this phrase, you probably know that the correct way to spell it is *used to*, not use to.

### vacuum

*Vacuum* may be unique—the only word in the language that sports double *u*'s. Deposit that fact in your trivia bank, and you won't write *vacume*.

### villain

*Villain* is a treacherous word to spell because of confusion between the *-ia* combination found in such words as *brilliant* and *machiavellian* and the *-ai* combination in words like *pain* and *gain*.

### Wednesday

The first *d* in *Wednesday* causes problems. Most people have no trouble spelling the abbreviation for the third day of the week, *Wed.*, but when it comes to spelling the whole word, the third letter, *d*, falls into fourth place or is left out altogether.

### weird

The preeminent spelling rule of our time is, "Put *i* before *e* except after *c*." *Weird* is one of the exceptions to the rule, along with *foreigner*, *seize*, *neither*, and *either*.

### woman, women

Isn't it odd that few people err when it comes to spelling *man* (singular) and *men* (plural), but when the gender is changed, they make a mess of it. Adding *w-o* shouldn't mean woe and confusion. *Woman* is singular; *women*, plural.

### whether, weather

It's often said that everyone talks about *weather*, but no one does anything about it. Not true! What you can do is spell *weather* correctly, and don't write *whether* when you mean rain, sleet, or sunshine. And vice versa.

### who's, whose

Like every contraction, *who's* is a marriage of two words, in this case *who* and *is*, as in " *Who's* going to spell *who's* correctly from now on?" Answer: You! *Whose*, on the other hand, is a type of pronoun indicating possession, as in "You're a person *whose* spelling is getting better."

## Punctuation

Many people punctuate the way they play the lottery—hit or miss. Using the scatter-shot approach, they pepper their writing with commas and apostrophes and hope for the best. A lucky shot will land a comma in the right place.

Cracking the punctuation code is not all that difficult. A few basic rules cover ninety percent of everyday punctuation. The rest can be learned by curling up with a good book on the subject or by studying well-written, carefully edited magazines and books. Punctuation rules are surprisingly flexible. They bend easily to support greater clarity and accurate expression.

### Apostrophes

Apostrophes are used in only three places:

1. In a **possessive noun**, as in *Annie's* grades, *women's* rights and *class's* attitude. When the noun (singular or plural) ends with any letter except *s*, put the apostrophe at the end of the word and add *s*, as in

| | |
|---|---|
| *child's* games | *women's* rights |
| *Tim's* lesson | *Sarah's* bike |

When the noun (singular or plural) ends in *s*, the apostrophe goes after the *s*, as in:

| | |
|---|---|
| *leaves'* (pl.) color | the *Smiths'* (pl.) house |
| *class'* (sing.) attitude | |

| | |
|---|---|
| *horses'* (pl.) stable | *Silas'* (sing.) barn |
| *classes'* (pl.) attitude | |

In punctuating possessive nouns that end with *s*, some writers prefer to be guided by pronunciation. If the *s* adds a syllable to the word, as in *Chris's* boots, they write *Chris's* instead of *Chris'* or *waitress's* instead of *waitress'*. Both forms are acceptable.

2. In a **plural** of a letter, a sign or a number, as in *A's* and *B's*, the *1980's*, and *6's* and *7's*. This usage is changing, and many authorities now prefer 1980s, Ps and Qs.

3. In **contractions** like *can't*, *would've*, and *where's*. The apostrophe marks the place where letters have been left out. In spoken language, letters are sometimes dropped at the end of words. Therefore, words like *goin'*, *comin'*, *ma'm* and *o'*, *as in two feet o'* snow, get apostrophied.

### *Commas*

When properly used, commas prevent confusion and misunderstanding. They divide sentences into parts, making meaning clearer by separating groups of words that belong together from those that don't. They often tell readers to pause as they read. Occasionally, commas are needed only to conform to customary usage. In many situations, a comma may be optional. When the choice is yours, leave it out. That's the modern way, especially in informal writing.

1. Commas are used to signal **pauses between parts** of a sentence:

NO PAUSE:  While Melissa rowed the boat started to sink.

PAUSE:  While Melissa rowed, the boat started to sink.

A comma is necessary to separate the subordinate clause, *While Melissa rowed*, from the main clause.

NO PAUSE:  After brushing his teeth gleemed.

PAUSE:  After brushing, his teeth gleamed.

In this example, the comma separates a phrase, *after brushing*, from a clause, and is necessary to avoid confusion. Ordinarily, a sentence composed of phrases and clauses may be written without commas:

On the desk lay a letter from the admissions office.

Over the river and through the woods to grand-mother's house we'll go.

No Pause:  Mom may I have the car?
   Pause:  Mom, may I have the car?

Commas are needed after some introductory words and in various forms of address:

No, I need it myself.

Well, I can't lend it to you today.

It will be available tomorrow, John.

2. Commas are used to set off words that **interrupt the flow** of a sentence:

Howard, however, was left off the list.

Janet, on the other hand, was included.

Conjunctive adverbs inserted between the subject and the verb of each of these sentences need to be set off by commas.

The hikers, who had been lost for two days, found their way home.

The bikers, whose tires were flat, also found their way home.

When a subordinate clause containing information not essential to the meaning of the main idea (sometimes called a *nonrestrictive modifier*) is embedded in the main clause, commas are needed.

Sally, the pilot, re-entered the cockpit.

The co-pilot, Harry, was missing.

In these examples, *the pilot* and *Harry*, are appositives, which identify or explain a noun and which need commas unless they are needed to identify the noun.

3. When writing a **compound sentence**, one constructed from a pair of shorter sentences and joined by *and*, *but*, *for*, *or*, or *nor*, use a comma to separate the parts:

Don't tease the dog, and she won't bite you.

The competition is stiff, but it won't keep Mark from winning.

In addition to *and* and *but*, words that often join sentences to each other are *for*, *or*, *nor*, and *so*:

It was an emergency, so I came without my shoes.

Harvey better call my mother, or I'll be in big trouble.

Some experts claim that, when a compound sentence is extremely short, a comma is superfluous and should be omitted unless essential for clarity.

4. Use commas in a **series**:

Rosie's car needs new tires, a battery, a tailpipe, and a tune-up.

History, English, math, and science are my easiest courses.

It was a wonder that Mike endured the long, boring, infantile, and ridiculous lecture.

You may skip the comma before the last item in the series if the meaning is clear without it.

5. Commas are used to separate parts of **addresses, dates, and place names**. For example:

Who lives at 627 West 115th Street, New York, NY?

Ileen was born on May 27, 1977, the same day as George.

David lived in Madison, Wisconsin; Seattle, Washington; and Portland, Oregon.

Notice that, because each item in that last example already contains a comma, semicolons are needed to avoid confusion.

6. Commas are used generously in writing **dialogue**:

She seemed to be asleep. Her breath was slow and even. I tiptoed out, thinking that I'd leave her a note before I left.

"Bye-bye," she said. "Don't forget to call when you get there."

"I thought you were sleeping."

"I am," she giggled. Then she turned over on her stomach, punched her pillow, and pulled the quilt over her head.

"Talk to you later," I said through the closed door.

Dialogue on the printed page has a distinct look. Without reading a word, you probably recognize it. At a glance, you probably see its profusion of punctuation, lines that stop short of the righthand margin, indentations whenever the speaker changes, and quotation marks all over the place. In dialogue commas are used in place of periods at the end of utterances when the sentence continues beyond the spoken words:

"Close the window," said Jacqueline.

"Come on, Ellie, tell me who called," said Scott.

### Semicolons

Semicolons are handy when you've written two sentences that are so closely linked in meaning that to separate them into two distinct units would destroy their integrity. By inserting a semicolon instead of a period, in effect, the pause that readers would ordinarily make between two separate sentences is shortened:

Management and the union reached an impasse; neither side would give in.

His mother was worried; Jake never stayed out this late.

Momentum was building; she couldn't be stopped now.

Notice that the words grouped on either side of the semicolon are really complete, independent sentences that could as easily have been punctuated with a period. Avoiding the common error of using a semicolon in place of a comma; use a semicolon as a substitute for a period only.

Semicolons are used also to avoid confusion in sentences that may contain too many commas. In this example, did Allyn meet three people on a hike, or did he meet five?

Hiking up Mount Ranier, Allyn met Dr. Jones, a pediatrician from St. Louis, Captain Scotch, an airline pilot, and me.

Inserting semicolons makes clear that Allyn met only three:

Hiking up Mount Ranier, Allyn met Dr. Jones, a pediatrician from St. Louis; Captain Scotch, an airline pilot; and me.

### Quotation Marks

Quotation marks usually surround direct quotations, as in

"I'm crazy about you," whispered Rita to Bob.

Frost's poem repeats the line, "And miles to go before I sleep."

Or they call attention to certain technical or unusual words and phrases:

Begin your essay with a "hook."

Much to Mary's dismay, her computer "crashed."

Or they enclose the titles of short works—stories, poems, chapter headings, and magazine articles. On the other hand, titles of books, plays, magazines, and films are underlined when they appear in handwritten or typed essays. (Underlining is a custom derived from the publishing business. When preparing manuscripts for the press, editors underline titles and any other words they want printed in *italics*. A line drawn beneath the word instructs the typesetter to change the style of type. With italic type now available to anyone with a word processor, the custom is honored in the breach but lingers on in handwritten schoolwork and on the SAT II essay.)

Don't use quotation marks for indirect quotes.

WRONG:    Jan said "that John's car will be ready at noon."

RIGHT:    Jan said that John's car will be ready at noon.

Jan said, "John's car will be ready at noon."

Please don't call attention to your use of trite expressions and slang terms by highlighting them with quotation marks. Rewrite instead, using your own original words.

Finally, quotation marks may enclose words that express the silent thoughts of a character:

Maryanne glanced at her watch. "I've got to walk faster," she thought.

To avoid confusing the reader, don't use this technique when a narrative includes both silent thoughts and spoken words.

In most instances, periods and commas are placed inside close-quotation marks. Other marks of punctuation are placed inside only when they are part of the quotation itself. Otherwise, they follow the close-quotation marks.

"Are we going to allow this?" Lorraine asked.

Do you understand what Wilson meant by "normalcy"?

## Capital Letters

While capitalization isn't completely standardized, it's not a free-for-all, either. It follows conventions that most people learned early in their writing lives, such as to begin sentences with capital letters and to capitalize proper names—names of people, places, organizations, religions, titles, and many other things, as well as words derived from proper names.

It stands to reason that capitalization skills develop with writing experience. Even polished writers, though, may now and then refer to a book to make sure they've got it right. The list of what to capitalize is long. Included here are capitalization guidelines that a student might regularly use while writing an essay. For unusual capitalization problems, consult a dictionary or a grammar and usage handbook.

Capitalize:

1. The first letter of a sentence or group of words that ends with a period or other final mark of punctuation.

2. Proper names (*Eddie, Georgia, Shakespeare, United Nations, the Bible, the Civil War, Yellowstone Park, Southern Baptist, Lake Moosilauke, Cheerios, the Midwest*). Don't capitalize north, east, south and west, however, unless you are referring to the particular region of the country, as in "They go to college in the *West*."

3. Derivatives of proper names (*Edwardian, New Yorker, Shakespearian, Lutheran, British*). Some words that originated from proper names have evolved into common nouns (*kleenex, corn flakes, venetian blinds, machiavellian, band-aid*).

4. Days of the week, months, holidays, and historical periods (*Monday, May, Mother's Day, Middle Ages*). The seasons of the year are not capitalized unless given an identity like Old Man Winter.

5. The various names for God and pronouns referring to *Him* or to *Her* (*Holy Spirit, the Almighty, the Lord, His or Her love*).

6. The important words in the titles of books, stories, plays, magazines, articles and literary works of every kind.

7. Titles and forms of address that precede the name of the person (*King Charles, Commissioner Burke, Dean Chambers*). When a title follows the name, the guidelines are fuzzy. Some experts say that you should capitalize the titles of people with particular stature or distinction, but not the titles of more ordinary folks. Thus *Nicholas, Czar of Russia* is capitalized but not *Mary Clark, clerk of the highway department*. Ordinarily *President of the United States* is capitalized, but it's a judgment call whether to capitalize president of the Jack Youch Fan Club.

   The same rule applies to words used as substitutes for a proper noun (*the Superintendent, the King, the treasurer of the class, the backfield coach*), except when the word is being used as a form of address ("I'll do it, *Mother*;" "Hi, *Coach*;" "Of course, *Doctor*"). Such capitalized names need to be distinguished from the same words used in a general way (Her *mother* is strict; the *coach* is on the field; he went to the *doctor*).

8. The names of specific courses and schools (*American History, Biology, Ridgemont High School*). While course names are capitalized, subjects are not. Therefore, one studies *history* in *American History* and learns *biology* in *Biology*. Similarly, one goes to *high school* at *Ridgemont High School*.

# ESSAY WRITING PRACTICE

Here is your chance to use the essay writing principles reviewed in this chapter. Each of five topics is followed by a page of blank lines on which to write your essay. Allow yourself 20 minutes from the time you begin reading the topic. After you have planned, written, and proofread your own essay, read the unedited text of six students' responses to the same topic. Rate them on a scale of 1 (worst) to 6 (best), and write a comment about your impressions in the spaces provided. Then compare your impression with that of a rater's. Finally, reread and score your own essay, or better yet, find someone impartial to do it for you.

The essays written in response to Topic 1 appear in best to worst (6 to 1) order. Responses to the other topics (2 through 5) appear in random order.

## TOPIC 1 WITH SIX STUDENTS' RESPONSES

### *Topic 1*

A wealthy donor has promised to give your school $1 million to be used either for the advancement of science or for promoting the arts and humanities.

The donation cannot be divided; it must be all or nothing.

If the issue were to be put to the students of your school to decide, which would you support? In an essay, please explain the reasons for your choice.

Limit your essay to the space provided.

## Six Students' Responses

 *Paul F's Essay*

If a donation were to be given to the school, I think the money should go to the sciences. This may seem like an odd choice for me to make because I am a drama and theater freak, and $1 million dollars would do a great deal for the drama program. But I think that the funds would do more for the sciences.

In numerous science classes I have taken, we have always talked about experiments, but we couldn't do them properly because equipment was too expensive. We had to make do with old, tired, worn-out equipment. Scientific theories that we were taught in class were not practiced or demonstrated in the labs. One million dollars could refurbish the science labs with sinks that work, proper safety equipment and scientific apparatus to strengthen our understanding of basic concepts in the field.

In the arts, funds are sorely needed too. Artists usually don't have $10,000 to build a set or huge amounts of money to hire professional theater directors or to rent or buy state of the art lighting equipment. Artists, therefor, are often forced to work within financial constraints. Sometimes, however, this produces incredible creativity. One of the best design concepts I have ever seen was built for under $100. It was a set for "Godspell" and basically consisted of junk and garbage from area dumps and yards and platforms built from recycled lumber. Some of the best directors I have worked with have been volunteers or people who were goven a token payment. The lack of funds may have pushed them to work harder than if the money had been handed over to them.

The students in this school are much more apathetic about science than about the arts. Science interests a smaller group of people than the arts and humanities. If teachers could show students actual genetics taking place or show students how to apply all the laws of chemistry, or if they could show how light and lasers follow the laws outlined on the blackboard, then interest in scientific fields would rise. That's why the money should go to science.

*Your Impressions:* _____

_____

_____

_____

_____

*A Rater's Impressions: You hook your reader almost immediately by claiming to make an unexpected choice, thereby compelling the reader to find out why. Each paragraph of explanation is unified and well developed with supporting arguments. You vary your sentences, make some interesting word choices, and write in a readable, natural style. All told, the essay creates a favorable impression of you as a writer. Your essay is rated "6."*

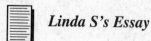

## Linda S's Essay

If a donor gave the school $1 million, the money should be used for promoting the arts and humanities. Too often these subjects are rejected by people who think that the arts are not "academic" enough for serious minded students. Sciences need lab equipment and up to date text books, and money has been channeled into science area consistently for many years. The arts and humanities now should receive their share of funds.

Children need to be taught from an early age that expression through art is not only an acceptable thing but also a good medium for communication. Placing emphasis on sciences and deemphasizing the arts is not a good idea because this breeds linear thought in too many students. With the help of theater class, for example, a person learns to diversify their thoughts. By expanding their thought processes, a student learns to express themselves more clearly, work with others, think ahead, etc.

Everyone who goes through high school will most likely take biology, chemistry, and physics. It has become expected. Many students will miss out on courses like poetry, creative writing, and British literature. If these courses had more funding, enabling them to have more books or teachers, students would experience so much more.

Speaking about books, I'll give you an example of how skewed funding and support is at the moment. In my French class, we work from a text book that was first used in the 1960s. All of our books are missing covers and pages and must be held together by rubber bands. This should not be the case.

*Your Impressions:* _____

_____

_____

_____

_____

_____

*A Rater's Impressions:* With the exception of a few minor lapses in English usage, your command of writing skills is evident throughout your essay. A strong opening paragraph states your position clearly. In the remainder of the essay, you present varied kinds of evidence to support your opinion. The last paragraph, though, seems considerably less persuasive than the others because you offer a fairly trivial reason for supporting the arts. Also, the argument in the third paragraph raises the question whether students are missing out on humanities courses because of insufficient funds or because they take science courses. Your essay is rated "5."

## *Nat H's Essay*

If a donor were to give $1 million for either science advancement or for promoting the arts and humanities, I would support giving it to the arts. Though science is a necessity to today's society, I feel the promotion of arts and humanities would be more beneficial.

Though science gives us reasons for ailments, both human and technological, arts and humanities give us more. They give us understanding of culture, human nature and beauty. Without these things, it would not be worth caring aobut society and its ailments.

Without art of any kind the world would lack something. It would lack the ability to appreciate beauty. It would also lack the ability to interpret things in more than one way.

Bacon's scientific process was a breakthrough of thought. It gave us a way to logically deduce conclusions through hypothesis and observations. However, the world and human nature is not always as logical.

In science there is one concrete solution to one problem. In life there are many abstract solutions to any one problem, and many problems overlap. The study and promotion of the humanities help us as humans with feelings and emotions understand ourselves better. Emotion is one thing science can not take into account, as it is an ever changing variable.

Science is a wonderful thing, but it would mean nothing if we could not appreciation. Through our learning of appreciation which comes through art, and our ability to understand people and other forms of reasoning, which come through the humanities, we can truly appreciate what science does for us. Arts and humanities are tools for evolution, teaching us new ways of thought. Science is a great way to understand this evolution.

*Your Impressions:* _____

_____

_____

_____

_____

_____

*A Rater's Impressions: Your essay's greatest strength lies in its profundity. You offer several thoughtful comments about the importance of art. You also know how to write interesting and varied sentences. Your use of repetition and some of your unusual word choices give the essay a good deal of energy—more energy than clarity, however. Because you skip from topic to topic rather rapidly the essay seems disjointed. Notice that every paragraph is short, no more than two or three sentences. Also, imprecise expression sometimes interferes with meaning, and a few usage errors weaken the overall effect of the writing. Your essay is rated ''4.''*

*Jane O's Essay*

If a wealthy person decided to donate $1 million to my school I would want the money to be used for the advancement of science.

I feel this way because science and life are in conjunction, and by improving science and making new discoveries and advancement, we can improve life. It is important for young people to have a sound scientific education. Children are America's future, and by having much scientific knowledge, the people of my generation may develop a cure for AIDS, cancer, and other diseases threatening the lives of the people.

I am not a scientist. Although I enjoyed Chemistry and biology, I can rarely pass a test in Physics. and have realized that I have a greater interest in other areas as opposed to the scientific world. I do feel though, that another advantage to furthering the advancement of science is that science provides explanations for most natural occurrences and why the environment around us is the way it is. It is important for young people to understand how they were conceived and how the universe developed. My generation also needs to know how to handle disasters like earthquakes. Occurences like this can be handled and understood through scientific means.

It is a wonderful feeling to be able to look at somethiing and because of knowledge I obtained through my years of high school science, be able to explain it. I feel that by improving the scientific knowledge of young people, the lives of the people of future generations will benefit.

*Your Impressions:* _____

_____

_____

_____

_____

_____

*A Rater's Impressions: Your essay shows that you know how to vary your sentences and that you have command of basic writing skills. You cite some specific examples of how science serves mankind but neglect to explain clearly why science is a better choice than the arts to receive the donated money. In your paragraphs, instead of developing a single idea, you skip rather quickly from subject to subject. You fail to explain, for instance, why it's necessary for young people to know how they were conceived and how to ''handle'' earthquakes. Although your personal conviction is evident throughout the essay, the overall presentation lacks freshness. You've dragged out some fairly banal reasons for studying science, and your use of language is rarely more than mildly interesting. Your essay is rated ''3.''*

### *Carole R's Essay*

If a wealthy donor has promised to give $1 million to my school to be used for only one purpose, I will choose for it to go toward the advancement of science. There are several reasons why I feel this way.

First of all, many things can be discovered with improved labs and technological devices. Cures to diseases such as AIDS or cancer can possibly be discovered.

Secondaly, if kids were given the chance to work with new and improved scientific devices, there's more hope for the future. Kids will learn how to perform studies that they had never done before. If kids are more experienced now, the better our future will be. Kids will be more educated and more aware of issues if they learn more now.

Lastly, kids should be exposed to the world around them at an early age. A microscope can broaden their interest in astrology. They would see that there are really planets out there and that there is no "man in the moon." It's really craters. A compound microscope can make them aware of all of the living things on earth, including cells and bacteria.

In conclusion, I feel that the money should go toward the advancement of science. There is no limit to science. There are still mysteries to be discovered, and it would be up to the young people of today to discover them.

*Your impressions:* _____

_____

_____

_____

_____

_____

*A Rater's Impressions: Your point of view is clearly expressed, and you organized ideas logically. The essay reads much like a list, however, because of the repetition of such transitional words and phrases as First of all, Secondly, and Lastly. The reasons you cite for choosing science over the arts are fairly mundane and receive minimal development. While your sentences are basically correct, there is little variety in their structure, and verb tenses are consistently erratic. Your essay is rated "2."*

## Mickey M's Essay

A donation of one million dollars to this school could be put to use in an infinite number of ways. But the benefactor set guidelines, the task of alloting the money could become difficult. The money could only be used for the advancement of science or promoting for the arts and humanities, there would be many conflicting opinions as to how the money should be used. One way to solve the problem would be to let the students decide.

I would have quite a hard time casting my vote. I, myself, am torn between my love of art and my love of animals. I have always been sure of my plans for the future—a vetrinarian. I am working towards being accepted into the states vetirenarian college. Yet, in the back of my mind, I dream of being an artist. I take every scince class and every art class I can in high school.

Weighing the two options, the money should be used for sciences. I cannot support my decision one way or the other but to say - It is my preference. I would rather be involved in a new science program or use new equiptment than improve my art supplies.

*Your Impressions:* _____

_____

_____

_____

_____

_____

*A Rater's Impressions: Much of your essay restates the question and explains how hard it is to decide how spend the $1 million. You don't address the question until the last paragraph, where you state your opinion on the use of the funds. Much of the material in the essay is irrelevant. Numerous sentence and usage errors suggest serious deficiencies in your writing skills. Your essay is rated "1."*

# TOPIC 2 WITH SIX STUDENTS' RESPONSES

## *Topic 2*

The world is an imperfect place, and one could throw the stone of criticism in many different directions. One direction in which I would throw a stone is

_____.

Complete the above statement by choosing a school, local, national, or world condition that, in your opinion, deserves to be criticized. In an essay, please explain why you chose it.

Limit your essay to the space provided.

_____

_____

_____

_____

_____

_____

_____

_____

_____

_____

_____

_____

_____

_____

## Six Students' Responses

### *Rose S's Essay*

One direction in which I would throw a stone is at divorce. Even though you can't taste, touch, or smell divorce, you can still feel it. Divorce is a concept which many American children have been made to understand by bitter experience; divorce has forced the progeny of broken marriages to suffer in this imperfect world.

Why do people get married and repeat vows, such as "until death do us part," if they end up terminating the relationship? Where's the logic to this? not to mention, their children suffer. While many of their friends are entering the three-legged contest at family picnics, they end up sharing chicken pot pie with one of their parents. This may sound a bit extreme, for all divorces don't end up this way. However, there are more that do.

Institutions, such as churches and synogogues, shouldn't allow people to be "joined in matrimony" if the people don't seem right for each other. Doesn't the divine being know whether a man and woman would remain married or not? Can't He give the priest or rabii a sign? If it's sacriligious to separate from your mate, why does He allow such things?

Divorce is almost as difficult as marriage. The fusion of two people may seem to be one of success, however when the "lawfully wedded" couple splits - the fission is one of disaster.

*Your Impressions:* _____

_____

_____

_____

_____ *Score:* _____

*A Rater's Impressions: There's a lot of emotional fervor in your writing, which makes the essay very readable, but also may interfere with its clarity. The development of the second paragraph, for instance, suffers from disjointedness. In the third paragraph you ask a question that seems out of place in a rational discussion of an issue. Your essay is soundly organized, and although the meaning of some of your ideas is fuzzy, you have made an effort to use interesting language. Several sentence errors weaken the essay. Overall, the faults outweigh the merits. Your essay is rated ''3.''*

### *Martha B's Essay*

Television commercials. You're sitting there watching TV, really getting into the plot of the show, when suddenly the story is interrupted by some innane jingle about a soap detergent. Such interuptions are especailly bad with movies. Movies are not made to be cut into 20 minute interrupted segments. When you see a movie in a theater, you go to see the whole movie, not the previews or the advertisements for the local dry cleaners or Chrysler cars. It is the same with movies on television. They often show commercials at the worst times, such as in the middle of a tension filled scene, for instance, just when the hero is about to walk into an ambush. Sometimes the timing is bad and the network cuts off the last few lines and when the movie comes back you don't know what is going on.

Made for TV movies are a bit different. They are made in sections deliberately for commercials, but the interuptions are still annoying.

To solve the problem, I propose creating new network, CTN - Commerical Television Network, where they will run television commercials 24 hours a day. The programming schedule would be easy: 6:00 - food commercials; 7:00 - clothing commercials; 8:00 - toy commercials; 9:00 - cosmetics commercials, etc, throughout the day. Then people addicted to commercials would be satisfied. Also, I would be happy because I wouldn't have to watch them, and my favorite movies would never be interrupted.

*Your Impressions:* _____

_____

_____

_____

_____

_____ *Score:* _____

*A Rater's Impressions: Using humor and a natural style, you have written a readable and imaginative essay. You provide interesting and specific material in support of your position. You've chosen a sensible organization, first to explain the issue, then to propose a solution. Lapses in mechanics and English usage, along with an underdeveloped second paragraph, prevent your essay from earning the highest rating. Your essay is rated "5."*

*Charles D's Essay*

The world is an imperfect place, and one can throw the stone of criticism in many different directions. One direction is Brookdale. Its a small school with alot of people and it (illegible) learning styles.

Brookdale has grades from six to tweve; Junior High and High school are together. It like one hallway; To have all those people in there is absurd. They need more space. They have to build another building or something like that.

People say they don't have the acidemic learning stimulation like this school. Some classes are not challenging. If a student were challenged they would be alot more people going to college. They have a small gym, it's floor is all messed up with warped boards on the basketball court. The board of education hired teachers who are not competent teachers. What I mean by this is a lot of times a teacher could mess up a kids academic career. For example, if Jane was an excellent math student and she got Mr Smith for a math teacher (who did not teach anything the whole year) she could fail the math SAT and leave a bad mark on her record.

I think it is important to check the qualifictions of a teacher before hiring them.

*Your Impressions:* _____

_____

_____

_____

_____

_____ *Score:* _____

*A Rater's Impressions: The main thrust of your essay is clear enough. You cite several reasons why Brookdale deserves to be criticized, but you neglect to support most of your complaints. Writing errors of many kinds abound, weakening the effectiveness of your argument. Expression is awkward and ungrammatical. Overall, the essay demonstrates a severe deficiency in basic writing skills. Your essay is rated "1."*

## Tracy W's Essay

The world is an imperfect place, and one could throw the stone of criticism in many different directions. One direction in which I would throw a stone is my high school. There are many improvements to be made in our school system, because it is not one that suits the needs of everyone.

One thing wrong with this school is that there is not enough leeway for us to take all the classes that we want. For example, if someone is taking a music class and also wants to take art, it is impossible to do so without dropping a required course - such as Gym. Gym takes up so much of our school week, and although physical exercise is important, there should be a better arrangement so that we can study things we really want to.

Another criticism I have about this school is the way certain classes operate. There are many unnecessary rules, and many teachers treat students as infants that need basic instructions. They spend too much time on inane things such as handing in homework on time, being on time to class, a neat notebook, and a cover on your textbooks instead of focusing on the more important issues - making sure that students get the information and the experience they need for a good education. If teachers could make the rules as a given, and trust the students, they might be able to get a better attitude back.

*Your Impressions:* _____

_____

_____

_____

_____

_____ *Score:* _____

*A Rater's Impressions: The purpose of your essay is clearly stated. You chose two excellent examples to support the main idea, but they are only loosely tied to your main complaint that the school fails to serve everyone's needs. Development of each paragraph is sufficient, although not very compelling or convincing. Use of langauge is rarely interesting and almost consistently awkward. The essay also contains some minor lapses in grammar and usage. Your essay is rated ''4.''*

### *David L's Essay*

One direction in which I would cast a stone is in the world's mistreatment of the environment. Without improvement in environmental conditions, future generations will suffer in ways we cannot even imagine. In fact, their survival literally hangs in the balance.

Many countries overuse the Earth's resources. In some countries, millions of acres of rainforests are being razed every year to make room for more farmland or to cut lumber for export. Not only does this destroy the habitats of many animals, but it kills species of trees and plants that may someday be found to cure cancer, AIDS, or other diseases. Not only this, but the rainforests produce most of the oxygen in the Earth's atmosphere.

Still other nations exploit the oceans. By dumping garbage, sewage and other hazardous waste products into the oceans, they pollute the water. Eventually, the garbage washes back on shore, making beaches filthy and swimming dangerous. The pollutants also kill or taint fish in the ocean with toxic materials. When we end up eating these fish, the toxins enter our bodies. Also, pollutants kill many yet undiscovered species of fish which might help us in the future.

Yet another way the world misuses the environment is its treatment of the atmosphere. Until recently, there were no laws in the U.S. governing the amount of harmful gases given off by cars and trucks. Some countries still do not have laws governing car emissions. Governments around the world need to press corporations to reduce their burning of fossil fuel so that less smoke mixes with clouds to form acid rain, which harms almost everything it falls on.

These are just a few ways in which the world mistreats the environment. All people must try to do their part to leave the world a better place for their children and grandchildren.

*Your Impressions:* _____

_____

_____

_____

_____

_____ *Score:* _____

*A Rater's Impressions: Your essay is extremely well focused, admirably organized and clearly presented. You develop your examples fully and appropriately. The essay is consistently informative and effectively written. It demonstrates your maturity and control as a writer. Your essay is rated "6."*

## Peter B's Essay

If I was to throw a stone of critizism in some direction, it would be aimed at school sport teams and the way coaches run them.

The amount of time you play at the position should be determined by your play on the field that year. Not the year before or from your reputation that precedes you. If you are slumping you should sit on the bench. If you are on a tear at whatever sport you are playing, you should play. But that is not what happens on many teams.

I don't think it is fair when coaches play favorites. If he or she does that they should be fired. It doesn't help the team to win or look good for the school or the coach. They should have no problem with sidelining any player because of poor play.

Slumps last from a week to the whole season. But a good coach knows a player will come back next year and show he's got good stuff. That's the fair way to run a team.

In conclusion, I beleive sport teams are run poorly and it will never change for the better.

*Your Impressions:* _____

_____

_____

_____

_____

_____ *Score:* _____

*A Rater's Impressions: Much of your essay seems to be a generalization drawn apparently from a negative experience of one athlete with his coach. Based on the evidence you present, your conclusion that all sports teams are run poorly is not justified. The development of ideas in the second paragraph is appropriate, but the third paragraph jumps from topic to topic. The essay shows some degree of writing competence, but is heavily flawed. Overall use of language is limited. Your essay is rated "2."*

## TOPIC 3 WITH SIX STUDENTS' RESPONSES

### *Topic 3*

Many students claim that if they work very hard in a course, they should earn very high grades. Others claim that achievement rather than effort should determine student grades.

Please write an essay in which you explain your position on this issue.

Limit your essay to the space provided.

## Six Students' Responses

### *Janice L's Essay*

Students should earn grades which reflect their achievement. There are many students who work hard, yet do not receive high grades. However, if they are unable to retain the knowledge they have been taught, then they should receive the grade that they deserve. If the system were to change and every student who tried hard received a high grade, how would we differentiate between those who are truly gifted and those who merely make an effort? This is especially important in high school and college, where intelligence matters a lot. I, for one, would not want to go to a dentist or a doctor who got good grades in dental or medical school because they tried hard. I would want the best there is to take care of me.

In the younger years of schooling, on the other hand, effort should be given some credit, but as junior high school approaches, students should be divided by ability. This division should be made apparent within their grades.

The system of high grades for achievement should apply in every academic subject. When electives are involved, a different process could be used. If someone is not artistic or athletic, but tries hard, they should be awarded a grade for effort. However, their artistic and athletic classmate should be awarded a grade for ability. If we were to change this efficient system, the determination of placement of all students would be disrupted.

*Your Impressions:* _____

_____

_____

_____

_____ *Score:* _____

*A Rater's Impressions: The essay is unified and generally readable. You back up your opinions with interesting and specific supporting material. You maintain a consistent point of view and organize your ideas in a logical fashion. Sentences are varied and well-structured. Some imprecise language, awkward wording, and an enigmatic final sentence take away from the overall quality of the piece. Your essay is rated "5."*

## Phil R's Essay

I feel that the issue here and where I stand depends on alot. For example, I think it depends on what kind of student you are, what kind of classes you are in and if your an all around prepared student. Your grade really depends on what kind of person you are. If your lazy and take everything as a joke. Never hand in work. Late a lot. Fail tests, then that's the grade you deserve.

If you are all around prepared student and you really try hard you should give someone high grades I have had this kind of expirience thru high school I have tried hard but haven't achieved alot through my effort. In Math Class I had in my freshman year but I did't do so good so I had to go to summer school but did very well on it. I think that during summer school I set a goal for myself. That's why I did good I think if people set a goal for themself they would try even in any subject.

*Your Impressions:* _____

_____

_____

_____

_____ *Score:* _____

*A Rater's Impressions: The error-filled usage and the confusing presentation of ideas suggest that you have severe problems with basic English expression. Your writing suggests that English may be your second language. Including a personal anecdote (about your math class) to support your point of view is a worthwhile technique in essay writing. The numerous problems demonstrated in your writing point to a need for remedial work in writing before you attend college. Your essay is rated "1."*

## *John E's Essay*

Ever since there were schools there has been controversy over grades, because grades in school in some ways determine the course of your life. Which is more important, achievement or effort? In which situations is one more important than the other?

I believe that a student who works very hard in a very difficult course, but doesn't quite make it into the ninety range, should be rewarded for their effort. On the other hand, a student who is naturally gifted in the area of the hard course and achieves say a ninety five test average with little or no work, should remain with their test grades for their final average.

As must be evident to any one, a child in elementary school should be graded differently than a student in Harvard Law. Effort should be regarded as the basis for grading of a very young student, because grades K - 6 are crucial years when children must be shown the importance of effort. Students at Harvard Law are different. They should be graded with emphasis on achievement rather than effort, because trying hard doesn't matter if when they go out into the real law world, their effort is not irrelevant. If they don't win the case, no one cares about how hard they tried.

It is ridiculous to expect that we can use the same basis for everyone in the educational world. Everyone is individual and should be treated like one.

*Your Impressions:*  _____

_____

_____

_____

_____

_____  *Score:* _____

   *A Rater's Impressions: You open your essay with an unnecessarily broad and pointless generalization about grades. The second paragraph contains good thoughts but they could be more clearly and economically expressed. The remainder of the essay consists of vivid examples to support your opinion. Your sentences are varied but only sometimes effective. The concluding idea is not altogether justified by the content of your essay. Your essay is rated ''4.''*

## *Mark D's Essay*

Many students work very hard in school courses. I beleive they deserve high grades for their efforts. If a student does not work hard and does not make an effort to do well, I believe that the student deserves a low grade. If they like a certain subject they tend to make an effort and do well in the class. This type of student deserves a high grade. If the subject is disliked, the student still should strive and make an effort to do well. They could have an attitude problem. If this student does badly, even if they try their best, I beleive they deserve a high grade anyway.

If a student is behind in their educational careers, it does not make any difference. If this type of student tries hard they should receive a high grade. People who don't work hard normally get low grades anyway. Grades are not very important for this type of student. All they want is graduate. They don't go to college. They are usually at the bottom of the class academically. Studying is the last thing they do. If they apply for a job, their employers won't ask to see their transcript. All they want to know about the student is whether they were able to pass their courses and get a diploma.

*Your Impressions:* _____

_____

_____

_____

_____

_____ *Score:* _____

*A Rater's Impressions: Your essay focuses on the issue, and your discussion of different types of students is reasonably well-developed. Expression is often quite awkward, and the repeated use of sentences beginning with "If" suggests a limited awareness of sentence variety. In a few places, the essay suffers from incoherence, and throughout demonstrates little mastery of some principles of basic usage, especially regarding pronouns. Your essay is rated "3."*

## *Frank A's Essay*

I believe that in the ideal educational system students should be rewarded with high grades for their effort. Not necessarily for their achievements. I believe that a system such as one based on effort would decrease the motivation for cheating. However, a system based entirely on effort might allow for an illiterate child who tries very hard to read to get excellent marks yet never learn to read. A common analogy might be a player on a team. Some players try hard, but they shouldn't earn a starting position and cause the team to lose just for that. Realizing this discrepancy, I feel that if a "reward by effort" system was to be intituted, then students would still be required to maintain appropriate grades on exams in each subject. These exams would allow for regular "checks" on what a student's actual understanding of the "concepts at hand" were. Without appropriate grades on these "understanding exams" a student would not be allowed to advance through the educational process. On the aspect of lessening the motive to cheat, this "reward by effort" system could have great advantages. Because ones effort, not achievement, would be rewarded, a student would have to display their own effort in their work, but more importantly, in the classroom. It would be really very difficult to copy someone else's effort during a student's "lunch period."

*Your Impressions:* _____

_____

_____

_____

_____

_____ *Score:* _____

*A Rater's Impressions: Your essay starts well and contains some interesting, although awkwardly expressed, ideas about the subject. You present examples to support your view, but they are not clear or effective. Toward the end, your point is lost in a puzzling array of quotation marks and a hard-to-follow structure. Had you used more than one paragraph, the meaning of the essay might be more transparent. Based on a reasonably solid opening, your essay is rated "2."*

## Janet R's Essay

Education today has turned into a race for the highest numbers. It doesn't matter how hard you work or how much you learn. What is important is the number at the top of the paper. In my opinion, this is the wrong way to look at education.

If grades only reflected achievement, there would be almost no point to going to school because almost every student would take the easiest courses, or they would cheat, or find some other way—any way at all—to get that good grade. Meanwhile, they would learn nothing. On the other hand, if students know that a good grade will come only after put effort into their classes, not only will they work harder, but they would also learn something. In such cases, students will determine to put all they can into their studies. The easy way out will not pave the way to a high quality transcript.

Therefore, grades should indicate neither achievement nor effort alone, but a combination of the two criteria. Also, their natural intelligence should count. Granting good grades for the effort they put into their work will force them to use their minds. Granting good grades for what they achieve will give them a realistic picture of their academic ability. Students will be less frightened by challenges and more ready to take them, no matter what their age or what stage they are in their educational career. Also, if students are very intelligent, they should not expect high grades unless they also work very, very hard. They should get a lower grade than someone who is less intelligent than they are but who works harder. This may seem unfair to someone who thinks that the grade should only be for achievement. Very intelligent people, though, should be penalized for showing little effort. As they say, "A mind is a terrible thing to waste."

*Your Impressions:* _____

_____

_____

_____

_____

_____ *Score:* _____

*A Rater's Impressions: This is a well-reasoned argument for learning. Your opening is appealing, and you've supported your viewpoint with clear observations about how students might respond to changes in grading policies. The presentation is interesting and well-expressed. The ending, although a cliché, sums up your point nicely. Your essay is rated "6."*

## TOPIC 4 WITH SIX STUDENTS' RESPONSES

### *Topic 4*

"WANT TO GET AHEAD? TRY LYING" says a headline, with the idea that those who always tell the truth, or tell too much of the truth, are doomed to fail.

Does this statement accurately describe the way things are? Or is it a cynical distortion of the the truth? Evaluate the validity of the statement according to your experience, observation, or study.

Limit your essay to the space provided.

# Six Students' Responses

### *Mary Ann M's Essay*

"Want to get ahead? Try lying" is described as a truthful statement in our society today. Usually good things happen when people who do not lie, but today it is more likely that good things will happen to people who refrain from telling the truth.

For example, in our society insider trading tips in the stock market can make an investor pay off faster than another investor who is playing by the rules. Another example of how this statement is correct is when a person is applying for a job. He usually tries to exaggerate, in other words, lying, on their resumé so that he will be a more enticing employee. If he told the truth he might not be hired as readily.

Lying may get a person ahead, but they must also live with a conscious. Perhaps in the long run it isn't worth it because he will have to face the fact that the reason he is "ahead" is because he lied. He did not "get ahead" based on skills or knowledge but on the lie.

Severe lying is considrerd a psychological disease, like addiction, they even lie when there is no reason. Dependancy on lying can be cured by therapy.

*Your Impressions:* _____

_____

_____

_____

_____

_____ *Score:* _____

*A Rater's Impressions: Your essay develops its main idea rather haphazardly and is generally awkward and crowded with usage errors. The third paragraph contradicts the earlier statement that "good things happen to people" who lie. Although your essay shows some command of a rich vocabulary, expression is awkward, and the last paragraph seems irrelevant. Your essay is rated "2."*

## Don P's Essay

To get ahead in this world, you have to be realistic as well as honest. In the real world there is no simple application of being the "good" or the "bad," there's only reality. A real human being can not be portrayed as a simple mind person with one quality of either being either the good or the bad. Everyone has somewhat of a devil in him/her, we better have kindness and humanity. The world we live on would not [illegible] without either of these qualities.

Lying is important aspect to some success. There are no Saints in this world, so why try to be one. I will state that honesty is not always the best policy but our conscious will not allow the destruction of our morals. I guess in our imperfect world we imperfect to be successful. Conclusion is lying wil get you to a point of success, but our conscious minds will really be guilty all about it.

*Your Impressions:* _____

_____

_____

_____

_____ *Score:* _____

*A Rater's Impressions: Your essay reveals that you have little awareness of sentence structure and English usage. Ideas are cumbersomely expressed and obscure in meaning. The first paragraph has no discernible relation to the topic. The second paragraph has no discernible relation to coherent thought. Your essay is rated "1."*

### *Enid K's Essay*

Lying is something many people fall prey to. The biggest attraction of lying is that it is so easy to do. There is no physical labor, no strenuous activity. All you have to do is open your mouth and let the words fall out.

Trying to get ahead by lying is something that might be associated with trying to get a job. You write up your nice little resumé with all the details of your life, most of which don't pertain to the job at all, such as, for instance, your marital status or that you won the Noble Serf Award in eleventh grade. Also, you might not have quite enough experience for the job you are trying to get. So you fabricate a little more on your resumé. After all, there's no harm in telling a little white lie.

While it's true enough that this will have no immediate effect, what will happen if your lie is checked up on, when your prospective employer finds out that there is no such thing as the Noble Serf Award, and that you were not the assistant manager of the supermarket at all but just the stock boy who retrieved baskets from the parking lot. This is when you face the consequences of your "harmless" little lies. If you are caught lying, after your face goes back to its normal color, you will mostly likely looking for another job.

Another effect of lying can be more serious. If you claim credit for something that is not yours and you hurt somebody, then you have stepped over the line. You have become not only a liar but a thief, and you have lost your integrity. So, while lying may be as easy as breathing, it may have far more harmful results.

*Your Impressions:* _____
_____
_____
_____
_____
_____ *Score:* _____

**A Rater's Impressions:** *Your essay combines a serious message with a bit of humor. The examples used to support your thesis are well-written and sufficiently detailed. The overall presentation is lively, interesting, and free of error. Your essay is rated "6."*

## Harvey R's Essay

I once saw a billboard which stated, "Want to Get Ahead? Try Lying!" I assumed this to mean that people who always tell the truth are doomed to fail. I pondered the idea for a while and realized how ridiculous the statement was.

Thinking back on my own life, I realized that everytime I have tried to lie I have gotten caught. Once when I was very young, I told my parents that I was too sick to go to school. As I look back, I realize that they knew I was lying. My father suggested that I go the doctor to get some medicine. I told him that I better not go, or the doctor would get my illness. My mother and father began to laugh and proceeded to dress me for school.

Another time, when I was in high school, I told my parents that I was sleeping over at a friend's house. This would enable me to stay out later. The next morning when I came home my parents found out that I had lied. I don't know how, I was grounded for the next month.

There are many other times where my attempts at lying backfired in my face. I read the billboard again to myself and laughed, "I bet the person who wrote that never lied once in his life."

*Your Impressions:* _____

_____

_____

_____

_____

_____ *Score:* _____

*A Rater's Impressions: Your essay is lively and generally well-written in a natural, easy-to-read style. Examples are pertinent but barely sufficient to support the assertion that you were caught "every time" you told a lie. The ending cleverly brings the essay back to the starting place, giving the essay a sense of unity. Lapses in verb tense and in expression keep your essay from earning the highest rating. Your essay is rated "5."*

## *John K's Essay*

Through Hollywood and hundreds of television shows, we definitely get the impression that the liar often wins. The liar wins the girl (or man), the liar makes the money, and the liar goes free. I don't think that it means that every liar becomes a hero or that lying is the right thing to do. However, I am very sure that the impression left in the audience's mind is that by telling the truth you could be "doomed to fail."

Experience tells me that a lot of people lie, some even without reason. Therefore, I always seek some fact to back up what I've been told, especially by people who I may have caught lying before. Every where I look I see liars. Why even I lie.

I know that I would never make a habit of it. The belief that lying will take you farther than telling the truth may be a delusion of compuslsive liars who have been caught, either by realizing it themselves or being caught by others, and need a reason and justification for what they do. Going out to succeed amid thinking that the only way to do it is to lie, is a lie in itself, in my opinion.

(They probably told this lie just so they could write a headline.)


*Your Impressions:* _____

_____

_____

_____

_____

_____ *Score:* _____


*A Rater's Impressions: The essay is divided into two halves. The first half is coherent, well-written and effective. The second half, especially the third paragraph, is couched in obscure and hard-to-follow language. You must know how to develop an idea and present it forcefully, but the inconsistency between the two halves of your essay is curious and perplexing. Based mainly on the strength of your first paragraph, your essay is rated "4."*

## Hal R's Essay

The statement, "Want to get ahead? Try lying." accurately describes the way things are. Those who always tell the truth or tell too much of the truth are asking for trouble every time they open their mouth.

The truth tellers get stomped on by all the liars. When you are honest, you may never get hired for a job because there are many liars out there who can convince the employer that they are more qualified for the job. Heck, they can say anything, they are liars! Do not be a fool and think that this world is fair because it is not. Liars get ahead and those who tell the truth stay behind.

People may even hate you for telling the truth because the truth sometimes hurts. Just try telling someone you do not think is very good looking that they are as ugly as a pig and see where it gets you. Honesty gets you in trouble. If you commited a crime and are accused and told the truth about how you did it, you'd be sent to jail. See how far the truth gets you? Instead, tell a few lies, go to trial, you might be aquited. In social relations, you have to lie a lot. If you don't you'll be considered obnoxious and soon have no friends. You have to tell little while lies to survive.

In conclusion, do not tell the truth because you are just going to be left behind.

*Your Impressions:* _____

_____

_____

_____

_____

_____ *Score:* _____

*A Rater's Impressions: Your essay fails to maintain a consistent purpose. At the start, it supports the validity of the quotation but then turns into a bitter sermon of the value of lying. Nevertheless, the essay is well-focused on the main point and is full of interesting examples of the need to lie. Imprecise usage weakens the effort, however. Your essay is rated "3."*

## TOPIC 5 WITH SIX STUDENTS' RESPONSES

### Topic 5

"The American Dream" is an often-used phrase in our culture. The meaning of the phrase has kept changing, however, as our society has changed. The earliest settlers dreamed of religious, political, and personal freedom. Millions of immigrants dreamed of economic opportunity. Native Americans, perhaps, dreamed of being left alone on their land, and African-Americans of full and equal participation in society.

Write an essay in which you discuss "The American Dream" of the 1990s. Please don't comment on your personal dream (college, a good job, marriage), but rather on what you see as a collective American dream, based on your observation, study, or reading.

Limit your essay to the space provided.

## Six Students' Responses

 *Ileen G's Essay*

The American Dream means many different things to many different people, depending upon where someone is coming from, what their background is and what they want from life will change the meaning of "The American Dream."

Someone who has spent their entire life under the unjust rule of a dictator, or perhaps a racially biased society, will look upon "The American Dream," and dream of freedom. A dream to be able to do whatever they want, whenever they want to. These people want a fair government who cares about them, and once they find that, they have found what they consider "The American Dream."

Many people come from what might be considered very stringent family or social systems. These people want only to break free of such unwritten laws that their ancestors have followed for so long and be able to go their own ways. To these people, "The American Dream" would simply be the freedom to make your own decisions in life. Not to have to follow a presettled course, to pave your own road!

Money is one of the most magnetic things in the world. Many people live life with the sole intention of making more and more money. America has a very open economy, one good business move may turn out to be very lucrative. These people who love money, look at "The American Dream" as a dream of starting at the bottom, starting with nothing, and making millions of dollars.

*Your Impressions:* _____

_____

_____

_____

_____

_____ *Score:* _____

*A Rater's Impressions: Although you focus sharply on the topic, and the essay is rich with ideas, the writing rarely reaches the degree of specificity needed to be effective. To your credit, the essay is clearly organized, and each paragraph adds to the development of your main point. A considerable number of usage errors, however, prevents the essay from being any better than mediocre. Your essay is rated "3."*

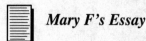

*Mary F's Essay*

When you open a newspaper or watch the TV news, all you see is stories news, murders, rape, babies dying, corrupt governments, war, bloodshed and debt, debt, debt. Then you wonder, is there any hope for our "America, the beautiful?" You feel like closing the newspaper and switching off the TV, when you hear about such blood-curdling and devastating events, they just make you sick. What happened to the American Dream of peace, love, equality and justice?

If you look closely enough at the newspaper in that little corner on page seventeen, you read about that boy scout that got an award for saving the life of a little girl that was being beaten up. He called the police. Then you hear stories of brave policemen and firemen risking their lives for the safety of others. Then you have to say to yourself, "Maybe there is still hope."

The American Dream today should be peace on earth, acceptance of people for who they are and not what they are, and justice for all. When one looks at American today, one can see that each day we are coming closer to these ideals. The cries for tolerance are being heard. If you watch any talk shows there are usually some people that are not the same as everyone else trying to make the public understand and accept them. So it seems that we may not be so far away from the "American Dream."

*Your Impressions:* _____

_____

_____

_____

_____

_____ *Score:* _____

*A Rater's Impressions: The essay starts off vividly. The first two paragraphs are coherent, detailed, and well-developed. A change occurs in the third paragraph, however, which weakens the essay considerably. You say that increased tolerance is bringing us closer to the American Dream but present no evidence to support that viewpoint. Except for the puzzling third paragraph, you seem to have command of essay-writing skills. Your essay is rated ''4.''*

## *John P's Essay*

The American Dream can have different meanings to many people. However, on the whole, people have a few specific American Dreams now during the 1990's And one example is world peace. People don't want fighting to be the answer to their problems. They'd rather talk than put young men and women out on the battlefield. Americans don't beleive in that. We didn't condone Saddam Hussein's actions in Kuwait, but we had to go to war to protect our ally.

Another American Dream could be the desire for racial equality. The Los Angeles riots proved that people feel that racism still plays a large part in our society. Didn't Martin Luther King have any effect on us? He had a dream - and look how far we've come up until this point. There's no more segregation between blacks and whites in public places. If we keep this up, we'll have us all living in harmony.

The American Dream of the 1990's cannot be classified as being one specific dream because of the ethnic diversity of American people today. Every different race and religion have their own dreams and goals. I believe that if all the different groups could act reasonably together to create a peaceful state then a common American dream would be possible again and maybe it would deal with cleaning America up.

*Your Impressions:* _____

_____

_____

_____

_____

_____ *Score:* _____

*A Rater's Impressions: The essay's thesis is stated clearly at the beginning, but its support, rendered with vague and sweeping assertions, is ineffective. Ideas abound in your essay, but none is coherently developed. By keeping related material together, you show an ability to organize material, but the essay demonstrates a lack of discipline. Your essay is rated "2."*

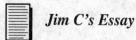

### Jim C's Essay

"The American Dream" has been forever changing, as the world changes. In recent years the American people have become more diverse which has intern changed the dream. Since America is a "melting pot" of other cultures, it has not only focused on the hopes of this country. An American Dream as turned toward a world hope. The American people have changed since the freedoms which they dreamed of earlier have been taken for granted, and now the people have moved to bigger hopes and aspirations.

Recently the world has seem to become more unified, with such events as the fall of comunism in Russia, which has ended the long cold war America fought, and the financial unification of Europe is another step towards world unification. People hope or dream for world peace. But with in America the people also hope for a freedom from the prejudious that has torn America apart over the Two Hundred years of existance.

*Your Impressions:* _____

_____

_____

_____

_____

_____ *Score:* _____

*A Rater's Impressions: Your essay attempts to develop a reasonable thesis, but the supporting ideas are poorly expressed and often not logically connected to each other. Expression is awkward, sentence structure is frequently faulty, and your mechanics need a lot of work. Your essay is rated "1."*

## Rita P's Essay

Specific aspects of "The American Dream" have changed dramatically from the time of the earliest settlers until now, the 1990's. For centuries, people from other lands have dreamed of coming to America to improve their lives and find freedom.

Yet, the basic idea of the "American Dream" has not changed. People still long to find peace among themselves and with other Americans, although what needs to be done to achieve this goal has changed. Not only do the majority of people want to stop pollution, put an end to racism, provide economic opportunity for the poor and homeless, continue to practice our freedoms, but part of the American Dream today is to help other nations achieve their dreams as well. American has a history of generosity and helping other nations. Immigration from Third World countries has grown. Asians and Hispanics are coming to the U.S. in record numbers. The U.S. freed Kuwait from Saddam Hussein and helped Somalia which was starving to death. It is only recently that this has really touched the hearts of many people who have made it a part of this dream. I don't believe that Americans will rest until South Africa is free and Russia is secure, and maybe even China becomes a complete democracy with a stable government.

Many people think of Americans as being selfish and wanting economic prosperity without having to work for it. Wanting this basic dream of peace and freedom to include everyone of all creeds, races and nationalities is what the American Dream is all about. In the upcoming decade, I believe Americans will work hard for this dream to come true.

*Your Impressions:* _____

_____

_____

_____

_____

_____ *Score:* _____

*A Rater's Impressions: Your essay is generally unified and well-written, although it contains some lapses in logical connections between ideas. Evidence in support of your thesis is sufficiently developed. The ending is weaker than it should be and not substantiated by the content of your essay. The essay demonstrates that your have mastered basic writing skills. Your essay is rated "5."*

### Lorraine D's Essay

"The American Dream" has different meanings for everyone. In the past some people thought that it was to find a good job, marry, have kids, buy a house with a white picket fence, to own two cars (one Volvo, one BMW), and to live happily until retirement at age 65. Others thought that to achieve the American Dream you needed a large family. Still other people said that we have already accomplished the dream with freedom of speech and religion, the right to choose our government, and economic opportunity (except during a recession). No one had the exact same view.

In the 1990's this view may have changed. From the present recession to the Gulf War to the riots in Los Angeles, people have been seeing their dreams ripped to shreds. The good job that they one held has been eliminated and they have been "excessed." Their kids joined the peacetime army but were sent away to the desert to fight the enemy, and they were shocked to see that in Los Angeles stores were being looted and innocent people were being beaten because of their skin color. Now they are looking for a job, not one for $100,000 a year, but a job that pays $6.00 an hour. They have moved out of their house or condo into a cheap apartment, or out of their cheap apartment into the streets.

Because the dream was not coming true, it has changed. Now people dream of peace at home and in the world. No more wars, no more killing, no more racism. They've had enough with economic problems. They are heading toward the social way of thinking. I don't mean going to parties and talking about the stock market. I mean getting along with and helping your neighbor, to live in peace with the people around you, and just talking to them or inviting them over to be with them. It's the "Family of Man," as John Steinbeck said in *The Grapes of Wrath*.

Now, as much as I think that this is the new American Dream, I don't think that it will ever be accomplished. It is only something to hope and strive for, but it probably won't happen. Eventually, out of work people will find a good job and move back to their houses in the suburbs. They will soon forget everything that economic hardship taught them.

*Your Impressions:* _____

_____

_____

_____

_____ *Score:* _____

*A Rater's Impressions: Your essay contains a compelling analysis of the changing American dream. It is well-organized, consistently readable, and interesting. Aside from the material about the Gulf War, which seems slightly beside the point, the essay is unified and reveals a high level of writing skills. The essay is rated "6."*

# ESSAY TOPICS FOR FURTHER PRACTICE

In case you've just turned to this page without having read the preceding chapter, here for the last time (whew!) are the directions for writing the essay on the SAT II: Writing Test:

---

INSTRUCTIONS: Plan and write an essay in response to the assigned topic. During the 20 minutes allowed, you should develop your thoughts clearly and effectively. A plain, natural style is probably best. Try to include specific evidence or examples to support your views.

The number of words is up to you, but quantity is far less important than quality. In general, however, a single paragraph may not give you the chance to develop your ideas sufficiently. You must limit your essay to the answer sheet. Please be advised, therefore, to write on every line, and write compactly enough to fit your essay in the space provided. Try to write as legibly as you can.

BE SURE TO WRITE ONLY ON THE ASSIGNED TOPIC. AN ESSAY WRITTEN ON ANOTHER TOPIC WILL RECEIVE NO CREDIT.

---

As the directions say, set aside 20 minutes for writing an essay on each of these topics. Twenty topics are suggested for practice, but if you write on the same topic again and again, the number of topics is two, three, or even ten times twenty. Since it's virtually impossible to write the same essay twice, you could try the same topic over and over without repeating yourself. Each time you write on the same topic, choose another point of view to defend. They say that one sign of erudition is the ability to argue both sides of an issue equally well. Then compare the results.

1. Adlai Stevenson once commented, "It is often easier to fight for principles than to live up to them."
   Based on your reading, observation, or experience, to what extent do you agree or disagree with Stevenson's words? Please give examples that support your point of view.

2. Most of us go through life handicapped by old myths rather than inspired by current realities.
   To what extent do you agree or disagree with this observation of human behavior? In supporting your point of view, please cite examples from your experience, observation, reading or study.

3. The former Secretary General of the United Nations, Dag Hammerskjold, wrote, "Never look down to test the ground before taking your next step: only he who keeps his eye fixed on the far horizon will find his right road."
   While such a philosophy may be appropriate for the leader of the United Nations, it may not be an acceptable practice for ordinary individuals to follow as they go about their daily lives. What is your opinion? Support your position with illustrations from your observation, study, reading, or personal experience.

4. The German poet Goethe once wrote, "Treat people as if they were what they ought to be and you help them to become what they are capable of being."
   Goethe's statement could probably apply to schools, government, social services, busi-

ness, even to families—anyplace, really, where people interact with each other. Is Goethe just expressing pretty-sounding, idealistic nonsense, or does his idea have real-life applicability? Based on your experience, observation, or reading, please comment on the usefulness of Goethe's statement as a realistic guide to human relationships.

5. "The best things in life are free," says a refrain from an old song.
   Do you agree or disagree with this sentiment? Based on your experience, observation, or reading, either defend the truth of the statement, or show why it is invalid.

6. Some cultures view life as a line, extending from point A to point B. Others view life as a circle.
   Explain which of these two views coincides with yours. If neither, what shape or form would you propose? Please explain.

7. After rescuing a child from a burning building, Jim Smith, a fireman, commented, "Courage is just a matter of luck—of being in the right place at the right time."
   Do you think that courage is common to most of us, but that most of us never have an opportunity to show it? Or is physical courage like Jim Smith's an unusual quality in most of us?

8. Why are you such an awful procrastinator? Or why doesn't this question apply to you?
   Explain your answer to one of the above questions. Use illustrations from your personal experience to support your views.

9. "Ignorance of the law is no excuse for breaking it."
   Do you agree or disagree with this legal principle? If you do, should there ever be exceptions made? Under what circumstances? If you don't, why do you suppose such a principle exists? What would you propose as an alternative?

10. There's an old proverb, "Spare the rod and spoil the child." To put it another way, fear of punishment keeps people in line. Do you agree or disagree with this view of human nature? Is the hope of reward ever a better way to control behavior?

11. There's an old proverb, "There's no great loss without some gain." Another way to put it is, "Every cloud has a silver lining."
    Do you agree or disagree with this observation? Support your position with illustrations from your observation, studies, reading, or personal experience. (*Note:* Sample essays written in response to this question appear in Part 1.)

12. An old English proverb says, "What you don't know can't hurt you."
    Do you think that this proverb is generally true or generally false, or do think that its validity lies somewhere in between? Defend you opinion using examples from life, literature, or your studies.

13. Thomas Jefferson said, "When a man assumes a public trust, he should consider himself public property." In other words, public figures, such as a president and other government officials, should not expect to have the same right of privacy as ordinary citizens.
    To what extent do you support or oppose this point of view? Be as specific as you can in explaining your position.

14. On whom should the moral responsibility for battlefield atrocities lie? Does it rest on military leaders, political leaders, soldiers who carry out orders, the makers of weapons, or on the people as a whole? Or do you think that no person has the right to hold another person morally responsible for anything—in wartime or any other time?
    Where do you stand on this issue? Please explain and defend your position.

15. It has been said that a great man cannot be overly cautious.
To what extent do you agree or disagree with this statement? Support your point of view using examples from your observation, experience, reading, or study of history.

16. By law, cigarettes and liquor may not be advertised on television. Some people think there should also be an advertising ban on foods that are unhealthy for children, such as candy and heavily sugared cereals. Opponents view such a ban as an infringement of basic freedoms.
What is your opinion? Explain and defend your viewpoint, using examples from your observation, study, or experience.

17. Two existing government organizations are the National Endowment for the Humanities, which supports art and culture, and the National Academy of the Sciences, which supports endeavors in the sciences. If you had the opportunity to propose the creation of a new organization to support a cause, it would be the National _____.
Fill in the blank and explain why you would support such a venture.

18. After a dozen years of schooling, you are likely to have had some good teachers. In your view what makes a good teacher?

19. In some high schools and most colleges, students who fail a certain number of academic courses are ineligible to participate in interscholastic or intercollegiate athletics until their grades have improved. Do you believe it is proper to link participation in athletics to classroom performance? Write an essay in which you defend or criticize this policy.

20. As a visitor from another planet, you have been observing humankind and its behavior on Earth. One of the oddest features you have observed is _____.
Fill in the blank, and explain why you singled out that particular feature.

# PART V

# TESTS FOR PRACTICE

Practice Test A

Practice Test B

Practice Test C

Practice Test D

Practice Test E

# ANSWER SHEET FOR
# PRACTICE TEST A

## Usage

1. Ⓐ Ⓑ Ⓒ Ⓓ Ⓔ
2. Ⓐ Ⓑ Ⓒ Ⓓ Ⓔ
3. Ⓐ Ⓑ Ⓒ Ⓓ Ⓔ
4. Ⓐ Ⓑ Ⓒ Ⓓ Ⓔ
5. Ⓐ Ⓑ Ⓒ Ⓓ Ⓔ
6. Ⓐ Ⓑ Ⓒ Ⓓ Ⓔ
7. Ⓐ Ⓑ Ⓒ Ⓓ Ⓔ
8. Ⓐ Ⓑ Ⓒ Ⓓ Ⓔ
9. Ⓐ Ⓑ Ⓒ Ⓓ Ⓔ
10. Ⓐ Ⓑ Ⓒ Ⓓ Ⓔ
11. Ⓐ Ⓑ Ⓒ Ⓓ Ⓔ
12. Ⓐ Ⓑ Ⓒ Ⓓ Ⓔ
13. Ⓐ Ⓑ Ⓒ Ⓓ Ⓔ
14. Ⓐ Ⓑ Ⓒ Ⓓ Ⓔ
15. Ⓐ Ⓑ Ⓒ Ⓓ Ⓔ
16. Ⓐ Ⓑ Ⓒ Ⓓ Ⓔ
17. Ⓐ Ⓑ Ⓒ Ⓓ Ⓔ
18. Ⓐ Ⓑ Ⓒ Ⓓ Ⓔ
19. Ⓐ Ⓑ Ⓒ Ⓓ Ⓔ
20. Ⓐ Ⓑ Ⓒ Ⓓ Ⓔ
21. Ⓐ Ⓑ Ⓒ Ⓓ Ⓔ
22. Ⓐ Ⓑ Ⓒ Ⓓ Ⓔ
23. Ⓐ Ⓑ Ⓒ Ⓓ Ⓔ
24. Ⓐ Ⓑ Ⓒ Ⓓ Ⓔ
25. Ⓐ Ⓑ Ⓒ Ⓓ Ⓔ
26. Ⓐ Ⓑ Ⓒ Ⓓ Ⓔ
27. Ⓐ Ⓑ Ⓒ Ⓓ Ⓔ
28. Ⓐ Ⓑ Ⓒ Ⓓ Ⓔ
29. Ⓐ Ⓑ Ⓒ Ⓓ Ⓔ
30. Ⓐ Ⓑ Ⓒ Ⓓ Ⓔ

## Sentence Correction

31. Ⓐ Ⓑ Ⓒ Ⓓ Ⓔ
32. Ⓐ Ⓑ Ⓒ Ⓓ Ⓔ
33. Ⓐ Ⓑ Ⓒ Ⓓ Ⓔ
34. Ⓐ Ⓑ Ⓒ Ⓓ Ⓔ
35. Ⓐ Ⓑ Ⓒ Ⓓ Ⓔ
36. Ⓐ Ⓑ Ⓒ Ⓓ Ⓔ
37. Ⓐ Ⓑ Ⓒ Ⓓ Ⓔ
38. Ⓐ Ⓑ Ⓒ Ⓓ Ⓔ
39. Ⓐ Ⓑ Ⓒ Ⓓ Ⓔ
40. Ⓐ Ⓑ Ⓒ Ⓓ Ⓔ
41. Ⓐ Ⓑ Ⓒ Ⓓ Ⓔ
42. Ⓐ Ⓑ Ⓒ Ⓓ Ⓔ
43. Ⓐ Ⓑ Ⓒ Ⓓ Ⓔ
44. Ⓐ Ⓑ Ⓒ Ⓓ Ⓔ
45. Ⓐ Ⓑ Ⓒ Ⓓ Ⓔ
46. Ⓐ Ⓑ Ⓒ Ⓓ Ⓔ
47. Ⓐ Ⓑ Ⓒ Ⓓ Ⓔ
48. Ⓐ Ⓑ Ⓒ Ⓓ Ⓔ

## Revision-In-Context

49. Ⓐ Ⓑ Ⓒ Ⓓ Ⓔ
50. Ⓐ Ⓑ Ⓒ Ⓓ Ⓔ
51. Ⓐ Ⓑ Ⓒ Ⓓ Ⓔ
52. Ⓐ Ⓑ Ⓒ Ⓓ Ⓔ
53. Ⓐ Ⓑ Ⓒ Ⓓ Ⓔ
54. Ⓐ Ⓑ Ⓒ Ⓓ Ⓔ
55. Ⓐ Ⓑ Ⓒ Ⓓ Ⓔ
56. Ⓐ Ⓑ Ⓒ Ⓓ Ⓔ
57. Ⓐ Ⓑ Ⓒ Ⓓ Ⓔ
58. Ⓐ Ⓑ Ⓒ Ⓓ Ⓔ
59. Ⓐ Ⓑ Ⓒ Ⓓ Ⓔ
60. Ⓐ Ⓑ Ⓒ Ⓓ Ⓔ

# PRACTICE TEST A

## USAGE

INSTRUCTIONS: The underlined and lettered parts of each sentence below may contain an error in grammar, usage, word choice (diction), or expression (idiom). Read each sentence carefully, and identify which item contains the error. Indicate your choice by filling in the corresponding space on your answer sheet. Only the underlined parts contain errors. Assume that the rest of each sentence is correct. No sentence contains more than one error. Some sentences may contain no error, in which case the correct choice will always be (E) (No error).

SAMPLE QUESTIONS

1. Because Mr. Peters suddenly lost his job, the family
   (A)

   hasn't ate out in a year's time. No error
   (B) (C)        (D)              (E)

2. The police responded quick to the call after
                   (A)       (B)             (C)
   Raul dialed 911 to report the fire. No error.
                   (D)              (E)

SAMPLE ANSWERS

1. Ⓐ Ⓑ ● Ⓓ Ⓔ

2. Ⓐ ● Ⓒ Ⓓ Ⓔ

---

1. It was upsetting to Tim to find his classmates

   responding so sarcastic to his presentation,
   (A)           (B)
   on which he had worked diligently and seri-
   (C)         (D)
   ously for days. No error.
                   (E)

2. In big cities like Detroit and Houston, there
                 (A)
   isn't hardly a day that goes by when there are
   (B)                              (C)
   no homicides, according to the report of the
   (D)
   commissioner. No error.
                 (E)

   *double negative*

3. At seven, when Martha went to the circus and
   (A)
   saw the clown act, she knew immediately that
                          (B)
   when she grew up she would like to be one,
                                          (C)
   too. No error.
   (D)    (E)

4. Dame Sophie runs what has been called a tea

   room, but it is really a mecca in which to
                                 (A)
   pause from a day of running around the city
         (B)
   or shopping, to buy a sandwich and a cup of
                (C)
   tea, and to have their palms read. No error.
                       (D)              (E)

   *her*

5. <u>After all</u>, Elizabeth is the strongest candidate
   (A)

   for the job, <u>since</u> her looks, experience, and
   (B)

   natural intelligence <u>attracts</u> voters <u>toward</u>
   (C)            (D)

   her. <u>No error</u>.
   (E)

6. History <u>tells</u> us that the Cossacks were
   (A)

   nationalistic and ruthless people, <u>usually men</u>
   (B)

   having <u>little or no</u> concern <u>of</u> their wives.
   (C)            (D)

   <u>No error</u>.
   (E)

7. I fully agree with Bertram's idea that each

   person is in <u>themselves</u> a complex puzzle
   (A)

   and that all of us need to set <u>aside</u> time in our
   (B)

   hectic lives <u>for</u> trying <u>to</u> solve the puzzle.
   (C)        (D)

   <u>No error</u>.
   (E)

8. Because the rescuers <u>had been</u> beset with doubt
   (A)

   <u>that</u> anyone could have survived the mudslide,
   (B)

   it was all the <u>more nicer</u> for them <u>to have found</u>
   (C)            (D)

   the old man and the child unharmed. <u>No error</u>.
   (E)

9. Although the passage fails to state opinions <u>of</u>
   (A)

   the speaker <u>in</u> which I can agree, I am thankful
   (B)

   that Mr. Foley <u>has given</u> me an opportunity
   (C)

   <u>to think</u> about the issues in a fresh and
   (D)

   illuminating manner. <u>No error</u>.
   (E)

10. The smoke alarm, coincidentally,

    <u>had been repaired</u> only the day before <u>it</u> sounded
    (A)                        (B)

    at 3:00 o'clock in the morning and <u>awakened</u>
    (C)

    <u>up</u> the whole family. <u>No error</u>.
    (D)                (E)

11. <u>Although</u> a teenager may think that <u>their</u> parents
    (A)                            (B)

    are often overprotective, parents think <u>that</u>, by
    (C)

    shielding their offspring from harm, they are

    merely demonstrating how much they love <u>their</u>
    (D)

    child. <u>No error</u>.
    (E)

12. The orchestra played <u>so</u> <u>loudly</u>, and there was
    (A)  (B)

    such a din in the ballroom throughout the

    wedding reception, that <u>it</u> was <u>hardly possible</u> to
    (C)            (D)

    hold a conversation without shouting. <u>No error</u>.
    (E)

13. According to the conservative view espoused

    <u>by</u> Harrington, a woman is assigned a role in
    (A)

    life, <u>is to be</u> treated with respect, <u>and is</u>
    (B)                        (C)

    constantly to be reminded that <u>they are</u>
    (D)

    appreciated and loved. <u>No error</u>.
    (E)

14. As a meek and humble clerk, Melvin never

    asked for anything, never raised his voice,

    never taunted anyone <u>or</u> made a <u>scenario</u> <u>about</u>
    (A)        (B)    (C)

    what was happening to <u>him around</u> the
    (D)

    office when the boss was not present. <u>No error</u>.
    (E)

15. After his death *it* had been rumored that
(A)
Akaky's ghost *is* seen spooking around the city,
(B)
stripping overcoats from passers-by and

*creating* havoc and fear *among* the bureaucrats
(C)                          (D)
in the ministry of courts and justice. No error.
(E)

16. Watching television at eleven in the evening,

*they always* give a summary of the day's
(A)   (B)
important news, an editorial *on* a current issue
(C)
and the weather forecast *for* the next few days.
(D)
No error.
(E)

17. If you expect to be absent from school when

the senior paper is due, you should hand *it* in
(A)
early or, *if necessary*, *one* should arrange for an
(B)            (C)
extension *with* an advisor or teacher. No error.
(D)                                    (E)

18. *Considering* the frailty of *his* health, the old
(A)                        (B)
man should not have descended the subway

stairs as *rapid* as he *did*. No error.
(C)              (D)    (E)

19. If Tom Cruise *was* alive *during* the heyday of
(A)         (B)
Hollywood's glamorous and debonair leading

actors, he probably would have been

*thought to be* too naive and boyish *to become*
(C)                              (D)
a big star. No error.
(E)

20. *Agreeing* with Mr. Hearn's assessment of two
(A)
Hemingway novels, *A Farewell to Arms* *is* by
(B)
far the *better*, not only because of its structure
(C)
*but also because* of the fascinating story it tells.
(D)
No error.
(E)

21. Many people are taught *when very young* that
(A)
no matter what they are feeling they should

always wear a smile, *and* that is why one
(B)
person's sadness can look exactly *like*
(C)
someone *else's* happiness. No error.
(D)              (E)

22. The settlement of the health-care issue *between*
(A)
the union and the management came just at the

moment *when* all parties were *on the verge* of
(B)                          (C)
throwing their hands up and *quitting*. No error.
(D)                          (E)

23. Because he was more than five years older

than *me* and a hundred years smarter, I never
(A)
felt comfortable in his presence, not, *at least*,
(B)
until the evening *when* he told me *that* he
(C)                        (D)
loved me. No error.
(E)

24. Though the peasants did not raise <u>any</u> political
                                        (A)
demands, they suffered <u>from</u> severe economic
                        (B)
oppression and were willing to appropriate

<u>by direct action</u> the land that they believed was
    (C)
theirs by right. <u>No error.</u>
(D)              (E)

25. Henry's heroism was demonstated when <u>he</u> was
                                          (A)
being hunted because, <u>as an officer</u>, he was
                       (B)
expected to be <u>on</u> the front lines, not strolling
                (C)
<u>around the streets</u> of Milan with a woman at his
 (D)
side. <u>No error.</u>
      (E)

*Subject is about the
heroism, not Henry.*

26. <u>While</u> they were crossing the lake in a small
    (A)
dinghy, Catherine was scared, but <u>after</u> they
                                   (B)
arrived on the opposite shore she said <u>that</u> she
                                         (C)

*had*        *been*

<u>was not frightened</u> at all during the trip.
       (D)
<u>No error.</u>
    (E)

27. His career of <u>killing and causing mayhem</u> and
                   (A)
his murder of more than one FBI agent <u>is</u> proof     *wel*
                                        (B)
that he is one of the most <u>notorious</u> criminals
                            (C)
in the <u>annals of</u> American justice. <u>No error.</u>
        (D)                              (E)

28. At the close of the season Sarah <u>was promised</u>
                                       (A)
                *she*
that <u>it</u> was <u>her</u> who <u>was</u> to receive the MVP
      (B)         (C)      (D)
Award at the fall sports dinner. <u>No error.</u>
                                  (E)

29. <u>Having been</u> brought up <u>differently</u>, I cannot
     (A)                          (B)
approve of Taras's choice of killing his own

son rather than <u>betray</u> his people, <u>regardless</u> of
                 (C)                      (D)
his oath of allegiance. <u>No error.</u>
                         (E)

*Whether*

30. <u>If</u> <u>their</u> newborn infant is breathing or not
    (A)(B)
becomes an obsessive concern to many parents

<u>who</u> are afraid of SIDS, the unexplainable
 (C)
disease that claims the lives of thousands of

healthy babies <u>each year</u>. <u>No error.</u>
                (D)         (E)

**DON'T STOP.   PLEASE CONTINUE WITH THE NEXT QUESTIONS.**

## SENTENCE CORRECTION

INSTRUCTIONS: The underlined sections of the sentences below may contain errors in standard English, including awkward or ambiguous expression, poor word choice (diction), incorrect sentence structure, or faulty grammar, usage, and punctuation. In some items, the entire sentence may be underlined. Read each sentence carefully and identify which of the five alternative versions most effectively and correctly expresses the meaning of the original. Indicate your choice by filling in the corresponding space on your answer sheet. Choice (A) always repeats the original. Choose (A) if none of the other choices improves the original sentence.

SAMPLE QUESTION

Adopted children often want to know who <u>its natural parents are</u>.

(A) its natural parents are
(B) it's natural parents are
(C) their natural parents is
(D) their natural parents are
(E) his or her natural parents are

SAMPLE ANSWER

Ⓐ   Ⓑ   Ⓒ   ●   Ⓔ

31. Neither visiting the school nor spending time with the students and teachers <u>has prevented Mr. Ranalli to criticize</u> the manner in which education is conducted in the local district.

(A) has prevented Mr. Ranalli to criticize
(B) have prevented Mr. Ranalli criticizing
(C) have kept Mr. Ranalli from expressing opinions about
(D) has kept Mr. Ranalli expressing opinions of
(E) has prevented Mr. Ranalli from criticizing

32. <u>Funds that are earned as tips and personal sales of goods and services is</u> one of the most difficult sources of income for the IRS to monitor.

(A) Funds that are earned as tips and personal sales of goods and services is
(B) How money that gets earned as tips and personal sales of goods and services is
(C) Earning tips and funds from personal sales of goods and services are
(D) Money earned from tips and from personal sales of goods and services is
(E) The funds raised by tipping and by selling goods and services is

33. October 15th will mark the second anniversary <u>of us coming to live in Allentown and it's flown by.</u>

(A) of us coming to live in Allentown and it's flown by.
(B) of our coming to live in Allentown, and the time has flown by.
(C) of our arriving to live in Allentown and it has flown by.
(D) of living in Allentown, and its flown by.
(E) of us coming to live in Allentown, and the time has flown by.

34. <u>The editorial, demanding the reversal of the Supreme Court's decision, brutally attacking the liberal justices, exemplifying flammatory journalism at its worst.</u>

(A) The editorial, demanding the reversal of the Supreme Court's decision, brutally attacking the liberal justices, exemplifying flammatory journalism at its worst.
(B) The editorial, an example of flammatory journalism at its worst, demands the reversal of the Supreme Court's decision and brutally attacks the liberal justices.

(C) The editorial demands the reversal of the Supreme Court's decision, brutally attacking the liberal justices and an example of flammatory journalism at its worst.

(D) An example of an editorial demanding the reversal of the Supreme Court's decision, and brutally attacking the liberal justices, is flammatory journalism at its worst.

(E) An example of flammatory journalism at its worst demands the reversal of the Supreme Court's decision, brutally attacking the liberal justices.

35. The far right Libertarian <u>Party, usually by fairly simple electronic hookups, has tried to preach their</u> ideology on the closed-circuit TV systems of small, often rural, colleges.

(A) Party, usually by fairly simple electronic hookups, has tried to preach their

(B) Party uses fairly simple electronic hookups to preach its

(C) Party, using fairly simple electronic hookups, preaches their

(D) Party, preaching via fairly simple electronic hookups has sent out its

(E) Party, usually by fairly simple electronic hookups, it has tried to preach its

36. <u>Applications and interest in Mrs. Clinton's college, Wellesley, has risen</u> because she often mentions her undergraduate days in public statements.

(A) Applications and interest in Mrs. Clinton's college, Wellesley, has risen

(B) Applications to and interest in Mrs. Clinton's college, Wellesley, have raised (risen)

(C) A rise in applications and an increased interest in Wellesley are attributed to Mrs. Clinton

(D) Mrs. Clinton is responsible for raising applications and increasing interest in Wellesley

(E) Mrs. Clinton is blamed for the increasing popularity of Wellesley

37. Obviously, today a great deal more violence occurs in the United States <u>than fifty years ago</u>, when guns were not so pervasive as they are now.

(A) than fifty years ago

(B) there was fifty years ago

(C) than occurred fifty years ago

(D) there occurred fifty years ago

(E) then did occur there fifty years ago

38. Religious fundamentalism has become a major factor in modern Iranian <u>society, now almost every woman</u> follows its dress code.

(A) society, now almost every woman

(B) society; this being evident in how almost every Iranian woman now

(C) society, so now that almost every woman

(D) society; in fact, almost every woman

(E) society, making now almost every woman

39. <u>Janet felt elated to find the book she had been looking for walking by the window of the used book shop of High Street.</u>

(A) Janet felt elated to find the book she had been looking for walking by the window of the used book shop of High Street.

(B) Feeling elated, Janet found the book she had been looking for walking outside the window of the used book shop of High Street.

(C) Walking by the used book shop on High Street, the book Janet had been looking for appeared in the window, much to her delight.

(D) Janet, feeling elated over finding the book she had been looking for while walking outside the window of the used book shop of High Street.

(E) Walking by the used book shop on High Street, Janet was elated to find in the window the book for which she had been looking.

40. Dale Zheutlin, a popular contemporary ceramic <u>artist, with sculptures mounted in homes and office buildings across the country, but her studio is in New Rochelle, New York.</u>

(A) artist, with sculptures mounted in homes

and office buildings across the country, but her studio is in New Rochelle, New York.

(B) artist, has mounted sculptures in homes and office buildings across the country, and her studio is in New Rochelle, New York.

(C) artist with a studio in New Rochelle, New York, has mounted her sculptures in homes and office buildings across the country.

(D) artist, has a studio in New Rochelle, New York, meanwhile her sculptures are mounted in homes and office buildings across the country.

(E) artist, whose sculptures are mounted in homes and office buildings across the country; New Rochelle, New York, is the location of her studio.

41. When Beethoven's music was first introduced to the public, they had found it difficult to understand and unpleasant to listen to.

(A) When Beethoven's music was first introduced to the public, they found it

(B) When it was first introduced to the public, they found Beethoven's music

(C) When the music of Beethoven was introduced, the public found it

(D) To be introduced to Beethoven's music, the public found it

(E) The public, being first introduced to Beethoven's music, found it

42. Novels which were not customarily written at the time, began to be received more favorably in Russia because of Pushkin's efforts to tell extended stories in prose.

(A) Novels that were not customarily written

(B) Novels which had not been written by custom

(C) Novels, not customarily written

(D) Novels, which having not been customarily written

(E) Novels, which were not written according to custom

43. As a student at Yale, Julie Ledbetter grew to love history with a passion that ultimately led to an appointment as Ohio State Historian, a position she held for nearly two decades.

(A) Julie Ledbetter grew to love history with a passion that ultimately led

(B) where Julie Ledbetter grew to love history with a passion, ultimately leading

(C) where she grew to love history passionately, as a result leading ultimately

(D) Julie Ledbetter's love for history grew with a passion and it ultimately led her

(E) where Julie Ledbetter grew to passionately love history, ultimately leading her

44. A biotechnology company in New Jersey got a patent for xenografting, a technique for developing animals to supply organs like hearts, livers, or kidneys for human transplant recipients.

(A) xenografting, a technique for developing animals

(B) xenografting, which is a technique for the development of animals

(C) xenografting, which is when scientists use a technique for developing animals

(D) xenografting, in which animals are developed using a technique

(E) xenografting, a technique for animals to be developing

45. Since dolphins are social animals, it is possible for Atlantic dolphins to speak the same basic ''language'' as Pacific dolphins although not being able to communicate exact nuances and subtleties of meaning.

(A) although not being able

(B) but not having the ability

(C) even as their ability is lacking

(D) although they are not able

(E) even though being unable

46. Two-thirds of the schools in New York City, a mecca for the arts, have no art or music teachers, they have been cut from the program because of fiscal belt-tightening.

(A) a mecca for the arts, have no art or music teachers, they have been cut

(B) an artistic mecca that has no art or music teachers have been cut

(C) a mecca for the arts; they have no art or music teachers, who have been cut

(D) a mecca for the arts, have no art or music teachers; they have been cut

(E) a mecca for the arts, have cut art or music teachers out

47. There is plenty of Thoreau's practical advice about life which every reader can benefit from in his *Walden*.

(A) There is plenty of Thoreau's practical advice about life which every reader can benefit from in his *Walden*.

(B) In Thoreau's *Walden*, he gives the reader plenty of practical and beneficial advice about life.

(C) Reading Thoreau's *Walden*, plenty of practical advice is offered to the benefit of readers.

(D) In *Walden*, Thoreau offers readers plenty of practical and beneficial advice about life.

(E) Plenty of beneficial and practical advice about life is offered to readers by Thoreau's *Walden*.

48. Another dimension of Pugachev's personality, which was indeed crafty, was if he found himself in trouble, he would drag someone down with him to share the blame and endure the punishment.

(A) was if he found himself in trouble, he would drag someone down with him

(B) was his need to drag someone down with him, when he found himself in trouble,

(C) was that when he found himself in trouble, he will drag someone down with him

(D) was when he got nailed, he will always drag someone down with him

(E) came about when he was in trouble; he would drag someone down with him

**DON'T STOP.   PLEASE CONTINUE WITH THE NEXT QUESTIONS.**

## REVISION-IN-CONTEXT

INSTRUCTIONS:  The passages below are the unedited draft of two students' essays. Some of each essay needs to be rewritten to make the meaning clearer and more precise. Read the essays carefully.

Each essay is followed by six questions about changes that might improve all or part of its organization, development, sentence structure, use of language, appropriateness to the audience, or use of standard written English. Choose the answer that most clearly and effectively expresses the student's intended meaning. Indicate your choice by filling in the corresponding space on the answer sheet.

### ESSAY A

*[1] Much of Russia lies under a cover of snow and ice for most of the year. [2] Permafrost covers the tundra. [3] Ports in northern Russia are not navigable for most of the year simply because they are frozen in. [4] In the south, the Black Sea gives Russia access to warm water ports. [5] The reason that the Black Sea is important is because it gives them the ability to export timber, furs, coal, oil, and other raw materials that are traded for food and manufactured goods. [6] The Black Sea will continue to help their economic growth.*

*[7] The English Channel has served as a barrier between Great Britain and the rest of Europe. [8] It has prevented attacks on Great Britain for hundreds of years. [9] Except for the Norman invasion over 900 years ago. [10] This allowed the nation to develop economically and remain politically stable. [11] The isolation of Great Britain allowed the industrial revolution to begin in England.*

*[12] Much of Egypt is covered by desert. [13] The desert is irrigated by the Nile River. [14] It is longer than any river in the world. [15] The land along the river has historically been the site of farms and other settlements. [16] For centuries, the river has deposited rich particles of soil for growing crops along its banks. [17] Since building the Aswan High Dam in 1968, the farmers downstream from the dam have been using artificial fertilizer. [18] The banks of the Nile and the river's delta are among the most productive farming areas in the world. [19] Therefore, Egypt's people depend on the Nile.*

*[20] Russia, Great Britain, and Egypt are only three countries that have been shaped and developed by bodies of water.*

49.  Which is the best revision of the underlined segment of sentence 5 below?

*The reason that the Black Sea is important is <u>because it gives them the ability to export</u> timber, furs, coal, oil, and other raw materials that are traded for food and manufactured goods.*

(A)  that it enables Russia to export

(B)  its ability to allow exports of

(C)  the ability of Russia to export

(D)  because of exporting opportunities of

(E)  for Russian exports of

50.  In the context of the second paragraph, which is the best revision of sentences 8 and 9?

(A)  The English Channel has prevented Great Britain's being attacked for hundreds of years; except for the Norman invasion in 1066.

(B)  It has prevented attacks, except for the Norman invasion in 1066, on Great Britain for hundreds of years.

(C)  Except for not preventing the Norman invasion over 900 years ago, the English Channel has prevented attacks on Great Britain for hundreds of years.

(D)  It has prevented attacking Great Britain for 900 years, except the Normans.

(E)  For hundreds of years it has prevented attacks on Great Britain, except for the Norman invasion in 1066.

51. Which is the best way to combine sentences 12, 13, and 14?

    (A) The Nile, the longest river in the world, irrigates the desert that covers much of Egypt.
    (B) Egypt, which is covered by desert, is irrigated by the Nile, which is longer than any river in the world.
    (C) The desert, which covers much of Egypt, is irrigated by the Nile, which is longer than any river in the world.
    (D) The longest river in the world, the Nile River, irrigates the Egyptian desert, which means that the river irrigates most of the country.
    (E) Much of the desert covering much of Egypt lies alongside the Nile, the longest river in the world, and much of it is irrigated by it.

52. To improve the coherence of paragraph 3, which of the following sentences would be the best to delete?

    (A) Sentence 15
    (B) Sentence 16
    (C) Sentence 17
    (D) Sentence 18
    (E) Sentence 19

53. Which of the following sentences is most in need of further support and development?

    (A) Sentence 1
    (B) Sentence 2
    (C) Sentence 5
    (D) Sentence 11
    (E) Sentence 14

54. Considering the essay as a whole, which one of the following least accurately describes the function of paragraph 4?

    (A) It summarizes the essay's main idea.
    (B) It serves to unify the essay.
    (C) It proves the validity of the essay's main idea.
    (D) It defines the purpose of the essay.
    (E) It gives a sense of completion to the essay.

## ESSAY B

*[1] Although some people believe that certain celebrations have no point, celebrations are one of the few things that all people have in common. [2] They take place everywhere. [3] Listing all of them would be an impossible task. [4] People of all kinds look forward to celebrations for keeping traditions alive for generation after generation. [5] Those who criticize celebrations do not understand the human need to preserve tradition and culture.*

*[6] In the Muslim religion, the Ead is a celebrated. [7] It begins as soon as Ramadan (the fasting month) is over. [8] During the Ead, families gather together. [9] New clothes are bought for children, and they receive money from both family and friends. [10] Also, each family, if they can afford it, slaughters a sheep or a cow. [11] They keep a small fraction of the meat, and the rest must give to the poor. [12] They also donate money to a mosque.*

*[14] Many celebrations involve eating meals. [15] In the United States, people gather together on Thanksgiving to say thank you for their blessings by having a huge feast with turkey, sweet potatoes, and cranberry sauce. [16] Christmas and Easter holiday dinners are a custom in the Christian religion. [17] They have a roast at Christmas. [18] At Easter they serve ham. [19] The Jewish people celebrate Passover with a big meal called a Sedar. [20] They say prayers, drink wine, and sing songs to remember how Jews suffered centuries ago when they escaped from slavery in Egypt.*

*[21] A celebration is held each year to honor great people like Dr. Martin Luther King. [22] His birthday is celebrated because of this man's noble belief in equality of all races. [23] People wish to remember not only his famous speeches, including "I Have A Dream," but also about him being assassinated in Memphis in 1968. [23] He died while fighting for the equality of minorities. [25] Unlike religious celebrations, celebrations for great heroes like Martin Luther King are for all people everywhere in the world. [26] He is a world-class hero and he deserved the Nobel Prize for Peace that he won.*

55. To improve the unity of the first paragraph, which of the following is the best sentence to delete?

(A) Sentence 1
(B) Sentence 2
(C) Sentence 3
(D) Sentence 4
(E) Sentence 5

56. Which is the best revision of sentence 9 below?

*New clothes are bought for children, and they receive money from both family and friends.*

(A) New clothes are bought for children, and money is received from both family and friends.
(B) The children receive new clothes and gifts of money from family and friends.
(C) Receiving new clothes, money is also given by family and friends.
(D) Gifts are given to the children of new clothes and money by family and friends.
(E) Parents buy new clothes for their children, and family and friends also give money to them.

57. In the context of the third paragraph, which is the best way to combine sentences 16, 17, and 18?

(A) A roast at Christmas, ham at Easter—that's what Christians eat.
(B) Christians customarily serve a roast for Christmas dinner, at Easter ham is eaten.
(C) At customary holiday dinners, Christians eat a roast at Christmas and ham is for Easter dinner.
(D) Christians often celebrate the Christmas holiday with a roast for dinner and Easter with a traditional ham.
(E) Christmas and Easter dinners are the custom in the Christian religion, where they have a roast at Christmas and ham at Easter.

58. In an effort to provide a more effective transition between paragraphs 3 and 4, which of the following would be the best revision of sentence 21 below?

*A celebration is held each year to honor great people like Dr. Martin Luther King.*

(A) There are also some celebrations to honor great people like Dr. Martin Luther King.
(B) Martin Luther King Day is also celebrated in the United States.
(C) In the United States, celebrating to honor great people like Dr. Martin Luther King has become a tradition.
(D) In addition to observing religious holidays, people hold celebrations to honor great leaders like Dr. Martin Luther King.
(E) Besides holding religion-type celebrations, celebrations to honor great people like Dr. Martin Luther King are also held.

59. Which is the best revision of the underlined segment of sentence 23 below?

*People wish to remember not only his famous speeches, including "I Have A Dream," but also about him being assassinated in Memphis in 1968.*

(A) that his assassination occurred
(B) about his being assassinated
(C) the fact that he was assassinated
(D) about the assassination, too,
(E) his assassination

60. Considering the essay as a whole, which of the following best explains the main function of the last paragraph?

(A) To summarize the main idea of the essay
(B) To refute a previous argument stated in the essay
(C) To give an example
(D) To provide a solution to a problem
(E) To evaluate the validity of the essay's main idea

**PLEASE STOP WORK.   USE WHATEVER TIME IS LEFT BEFORE THE 40-MINUTE TEST PERIOD EXPIRES TO CHECK YOUR ANSWERS.**

# ESSAY

## Time allowed: 20 minutes

INSTRUCTIONS:  Plan and write an essay in response to the assigned topic. During the 20 minutes allowed, you should develop your thoughts clearly and effectively. A plain, natural style is probably best. Try to include specific evidence or examples to support your views.

The number of words is up to you, but quantity is far less important than quality. In general, however, a single paragraph may not give you the chance to develop your ideas sufficiently. You must limit your essay to the answer sheet. Please be advised, therefore, to write on every line and write compactly enough to fit your essay in the space allowed. Try to write as legibly as you can.

BE SURE TO WRITE ONLY ON THE ASSIGNED TOPIC. AN ESSAY WRITTEN ON ANOTHER TOPIC WILL RECEIVE NO CREDIT.

---

In ancient Greece a "hero" was a man who won glory on the field of battle. Since then heroes have taken many shapes, from astronauts to Mother Theresa to just plain folks caught up in unusual circumstances. Who would be your nominee to be put in a Hall of Heroes? Your hero may be real or fictional, living or dead, and of any species, human or nonhuman.

In an essay, please explain the reasons for your choice.

---

This space reserved for your personal bar code

## SAT II: WRITING
### ESSAY
**Time allowed: 20 minutes**

FOR OFFICE USE

First reader _____

Second reader _____

Third reader (if needed) _____

Topic:   **HEROS**

The space below is for your essay. Please restrict your writing to the designated area.

Please continue your essay on the next page if you need more room.

# ANSWERS

| | | | | | |
|---|---|---|---|---|---|
| 1. B | 11. B | 21. E | 31. E | 41. C | 51. A |
| 2. B | 12. E | 22. E | 32. D | 42. C | 52. C |
| 3. C | 13. D | 23. A | 33. B | 43. A | 53. D |
| 4. D | 14. B | 24. E | 34. B | 44. A | 54. C |
| 5. C | 15. B | 25. A | 35. B | 45. D | 55. C |
| 6. D | 16. A | 26. D | 36. C | 46. D | 56. B |
| 7. A | 17. C | 27. B | 37. C | 47. D | 57. D |
| 8. C | 18. C | 28. C | 38. D | 48. B | 58. D |
| 9. B | 19. A | 29. C | 39. E | 49. A | 59. E |
| 10. D | 20. A | 30. A | 40. C | 50. E | 60. C |

# PERFORMANCE EVALUATION CHART

## I. Self-rating Chart

Usage, Questions 1–30                           Number correct _____

Sentence Correction, Questions 31–48            Number correct _____

Revision-in-Context, Questions 49–60            Number correct _____

Subtotal _____

_____

*Penalty.* Subtract 1/4 point (.25) for each incorrect answer.

(No penalty for unanswered questions)

TOTAL SCORE _____

## II. Key to Self-rating

| | Usage | Sentence Correction | Revision-in-Context | Total |
|---|---|---|---|---|
| Excellent | 27–30 | 17–18 | 11–12 | 55–60 |
| Very good | 23–26 | 14–16 | 9–10 | 46–54 |
| Good | 19–22 | 11–13 | 7–8 | 37–45 |
| Fair | 15–18 | 9–10 | 5–6 | 29–36 |
| Poor | 10–14 | 6–8 | 3–4 | 19–28 |
| Very poor | 0–9 | 0–5 | 0–2 | 0–18 |

# ANSWERS EXPLAINED

## Usage

1. **B** Diction error. An adverb is needed to modify the verb *responding*. Use *sarcastically*.
2. **B** Double negative. Both *isn't* and *hardly* are negative. Change *isn't* to *is*.
3. **C** Pronoun reference error. The pronoun *one* fails to refer to any specific noun or pronoun.
4. **D** Pronoun reference. The pronoun *their* does not refer to any specific noun or pronoun.
5. **C** Subject-verb agreement. Compound subjects need plural verbs. Use *attract*.
6. **D** Idiom error. In standard usage the phrase is *concern for*.
7. **A** Pronoun-antecedent agreement. The antecedent *person* is singular; the pronoun *themselves* is plural. Use *himself*.
8. **C** Faulty comparison. The phrase *more nicer* is redundant. Use *nice* in place of *nicer*.
9. **B** Idiom error. In standard usage, the phrase is *with which I can agree*.
10. **D** Idiom error. The word *up* is unnecessary. Delete it.
11. **B** Pronoun-antecedent agreement. *Teenager* is singular, *their* is plural. Use *his*.
12. **E** No error.
13. **D** Pronoun-antecedent agreement. The antecedent *woman* is singular; the pronoun *they* is plural. Use *she* is.
14. **B** Faulty diction. Use *scene* instead of *scenario*.
15. **B** Verb tense. Because the sentence is cast in the past perfect tense, use *was* instead of *is*.
16. **A** Dangling Participle. The phrase beginning *Watching television* lacks a noun or pronoun to modify.
17. **C** Shift in pronoun person. The sentence begins in the second person, *you*. To be consistent, use pronouns of the same person throughout.
18. **C** Diction error. An adverb is needed to modify the verb *descended*. Use *rapidly*.
19. **A** Verb tense. The past perfect tense refers to action completed before some specific time in the past. Use past. Use *had been* instead of *was*.
20. **A** Dangling participle. The phrase beginning *Agreeing with* lacks a noun or pronoun to modify.
21. **E** No error.
22. **E** No error.
23. **A** Pronoun choice. In comparisons with *than*, complete the comparison with the verb that would follow naturally: "older than *I* (am)."
24. **E** No error.
25. **A** Pronoun reference. The pronoun *he* should not be used to refer to a possessive noun.
26. **D** Verb tense. The past perfect tense refers to action completed before some specific time in the past. Use *had not been frightened* instead of *was not frightened*.
27. **B** Subject-verb agreement. The compound subject *career and murder* requires a plural verb. Use *are*.
28. **C** Pronoun choice. Pronouns in the nominative case are used in predicate nominatives. Use *she*.
29. **C** Faulty parallelism. In a comparison, coordinate ideas should be in the same grammatical form. Use *betraying*.
30. **A** Idiom error. In standard usage the phrase is *whether or not*.

## Sentence Correction

**Note:** *Although many choices contain multiple errors, only one error is listed for each incorrect answer.*

31. **E** A. Idiom error. In standard usage, the phrase should be *from criticizing*.
    B. Subject-verb agreement. Spending is singular; *have* is plural.
    C. Subject-verb agreement. Spending is singular; *have* is plural.
    D. Idiom error. In standard usage, the phrase is *from expressing*.

32. **D** A. Subject-verb agreement. *Funds* is plural; *is* is singular.
   B. Mixed construction. The construction that begins *personal sales* has no grammatical relationship to the earlier part of the sentence.
   C. Faulty parallelism. The phrase *Earning tips* lacks a grammatical parallel.
   E. Idiom error. In standard idiom the phrase is *earned from tips*.

33. **B** A. Pronoun choice. Use a possessive pronoun (*our*) before a gerund (*coming*).
   C. Pronoun reference. The pronoun *it* has no specific referent.
   D. Diction error. The word *its* is a possessive pronoun, not a contraction for *it is* or *it has*.
   E. Pronoun choice. Use a possessive pronoun (*our*) before a gerund (*coming*).

34. **B** A. Sentence fragment. The construction lacks a main verb. The *-ing* form of a verb (*demanding, attacking, exemplifying*) may not be used as the main verb without a helping verb, as in *was demanding* and *is attacking*.
   C. Faulty parallelism. The phrase *brutally attacking* lacks a grammatical parallel.
   D. Mixed construction. The construction that begins *is flammatory* has no grammatical relationship with the earlier part of the sentence.
   E. Misplaced modifier. The phrase that begins *brutally attacking* modifies *decision* instead of *journalism*.

35. **B** A. Pronoun-antecedent agreement. *Their* is plural; *party* is singular.
   C. Pronoun-antecedent agreement. *Their* is plural; *party* is singular.
   D. Punctuation error. A comma between *hookups* and *has* is needed to set off nonessential information.
   E. Mixed construction. The construction that begins *it has tried* lacks a grammatical relationship with the earlier part of the sentence.

36. **C** A. Subject-verb agreement. The subject, *applications and interest*, is plural; the verb, *has* is singular.
   B. Faulty verb form. *Risen* is the perfect form of the verb *to rise*.
   D. Diction error. *Raising* is an inappropriate word choice.
   E. Diction error. *Blamed* is an inappropriate word choice.

37. **C** A. Faulty comparison. *Violence* is compared to *years*, an illogical comparison.
   B. Faulty parallelism. The phrase *violence occurs* is not grammatically parallel to *there was*. In the former, the subject precedes the verb; in the latter it follows the verb.
   D. Incomplete construction. The word *than* has been left out.
   E. Diction error. Use *than* instead of *then*.

38. **D** A. Comma splice. A comma may not be used to separate two independent clauses.
   B. Sentence fragment. The construction lacks a main verb. The *-ing* form of a verb (*being*) may not be used as the main verb without a helping verb, as in *is being*.
   C. Incomplete construction. The coordinating conjunction *so* introduces an incomplete coordinate clause.
   E. Clumsy construction. The phrase that begins *making now* is awkward.

39. **E** A. Misplaced modifier. The phrase *walking by the window* modifies *book* instead of *Janet*.
   B. Misplaced modifier. The phrase *walking by the window* modifies *book* instead of *Janet*.
   C. Dangling participle. The phrase that begins *Walking by* modifies *book* instead of *Janet*.
   D. Sentence fragment. The construction lacks a main verb. The *-ing* form of a verb (*feeling*) may not be used as the main verb without a helping verb, as in *was feeling*.

40. **C** A. Faulty coordination. The coordinating conjunction *but* fails to create a reasonable relationship between the clauses.
   B. Faulty coordination. It is inappropriate to assign equal importance to the material in the coordinate clauses of the sentence.

D.  Comma splice. A comma (between *York* and *meanwhile*) may not be used to separate two independent clauses.

E.  Semicolon error. A semicolon is used to separate two independent clauses. The clause that begins *Dale Zheutlin* lacks a main verb.

41.  **C**  A.  Redundancy. The phrase *first introduced* is redundant.

B.  Ambiguous pronoun reference. The pronoun *they* lacks a specific referent.

D.  Faulty verb tense. Replace the infinitive form *To be* with *Having been* in order to keep the verb tense consistent with the rest of the sentence.

E.  Clumsy construction. The phras*e being first introduced* is awkwardly worded.

42.  **C**  A.  Punctuation error.  A nonessential dependent clause (*which were not . . .*) must be set off by commas when embedded in the main clause.

B.  Misplaced modifier. The phrase *by custom* modifies *written* instead of *not*.

D.  Clumsy construction. The construction that begins *which having* is awkward.

E.  Misplaced modifier. The phrase *according to custom* modifies *written* instead of *novels*.

43.  **A**  B.  Sentence fragment. The construction lacks a main clause.

C.  Mixed construction.  The phrase that begins *as a result* has no grammatical relationship with the earlier part of the sentence.

D.  Misplaced modifier. The phrase *As a student at Yale* modifies *love*, not *Julie Ledbetter*.

E.  Ambiguous reference. The phrase that begins *ultimately leading her* has no specific referent.

44.  **A**  B.  Wordy. The phrase *which is* is unnecessary.

C.  Idiom error.  The phrase *which is when* is nonstandard.  When defining a noun (*xenografting*), use another noun, not a clause.

D.  Change in meaning. This sentence alters the meaning of the original.

E.  Faulty verb form. The verb should be *to be developed*.

45.  **D**  A.  Faulty parallelism. The infinitive verb *to speak* lacks a grammatical parallel.

B.  Faulty parallelism. The infinitive verb *to speak* lacks a grammatical parallel.

C.  Clumsy construction. The entire construction borders on the incomprehensible.

E.  Clumsy construction. The contruction is awkwardly worded.

46.  **D**  A.  Comma splice.  A comma (between *teachers* and *they*) may not be used to separate two independent clauses.

B.  Mixed construction. The phrase that begins *have been cut* lacks a grammatical relationship with the the earlier part of the sentence.

C.  Semicolon error. A semicolon is used to separate two independent clauses.

E.  Idiom error. By adding *out*, standard idiom is violated. *Out from the program*, should be *out of the program*.

47.  **D**  A.  Pronoun reference. The pronoun *his* cannot refer to a possessive pronoun.

B.  Pronoun reference. The pronoun *he* cannot refer to a possessive pronoun.

C.  Dangling participle. The phrase *Reading Thoreau's* <u>Walden</u> should modify *reader* instead of *plenty*.

E.  Passive construction. An active sentence is preferable.

48.  **B**  A.  Mixed construction.  The clause that begins *if he found* lacks a grammatical relationship with the earlier part of the sentence because a predicate nominative should be a noun or pronoun, not a dependent clause.

C.  Shift in verb tense. The sentence, cast in the past tense, shifts to the future tense.

D.  Diction error. The use of *nailed* is not consistent with the tone and mood of the sentence.

E.  Clumsy construction. The phrase *came about* is awkward in this context.

### Revision-in-Context

49.  **A**  Only Choice A is concisely expressed in standard English. All the other choices are awkward or non-standard.

50.  **E**  Choice A has a sentence fragment after the semicolon.
Choice B divides the main clause awkwardly.
Choice C is wordy and repetitious.  It unnecessarily repeats *the English Channel,* the subject of sentence 7.
Choice D is an unclear, awkwardly constructed sentence.
Choice E is an accurate and logical revision. It is the best answer.

51.  **A**  Choice A succinctly and effectively combines the three sentences. It is the best answer.
Choice B contains a faulty comparison. The Nile cannot be longer than itself.
Choice C is similar to B.
Choice D is accurate but wordy and repetitious.
Choice E is awkwardly expressed.

52.  **C**  Although it is related to the topic of the paragraph, sentence 17 steers the discussion away from the paragraph's main topic, Egypt's dependence on the Nile. Therefore, C is the best answer.

53.  **D**  Sentence 11 states a complex idea that needs further explanation. The other sentences are facts that stand on their own. Therefore D is the best answer.

54.  **C**  Choice C does not describe the function of the last paragraph.  The essay's main idea is validated by the contents of the essay's three main paragraphs, not by the final paragraph.

55.  **C**  All sentences except sentence 3 contribute to the paragraph's main point, that celebrations help to unite people and keep traditions alive. Therefore, C is the best answer.

56.  **B**  Choice A is grammatically correct but is awkwardly expressed in the passive voice.
Choice B is clearly written and to the point. It is the best answer.
Choice C contains a dangling participle.  The phrase *Receiving new clothes* should modify *children,* not *money*.
Choice D is awkwardly  expressed.
Choice E is needlessy wordy and awkward.

57.  **D**  Choice A is fresh, but its tone is not consistent with the rest of the essay.
Choice B contains a comma splice between *dinner* and *at*.
Choice C emphasizes the idea properly, but contains an error in parallel construction.
Choice D places the emphasis where it belongs and expresses the idea effectively. It is the best answer.
Choice E is repetitious, and it contains an error in pronoun reference.  The pronoun *they* has no specific referent.

58.  **D**  Choice A does not provide a significantly better transition.
Choice B does nothing to improve the relationship between paragraphs 3 and 4.
Choice C is awkwardly worded and does not include transitional material.
Choice D provides an effective transition between paragraphs. It is the best answer.
Choice E tries to provide a transition, but it is wordy and it contains a dangling participle.

59.  **E**  Choice A places emphasis on the location of the assassination instead of the event itself, an emphasis that the writer did not intend.
Choice B contains a nonstandard usage. The phrase to *remember about* is not standard.
Choice C is grammatically correct but wordy.
Choice D is the same as B.
Choice E is a succinct and proper revision. It is the best answer.

60.  **C**  The main purpose of the last paragraph is to provide an example of a celebration that unites people and preserves tradition. Therefore, C is the best answer.

# SELF-SCORING GUIDE FOR THE SAT II ESSAY

## PRACTICE TEST A

**Using this guide.** Rate yourself in each of the six categories on the left. Circle the item that most accurately describes your performance. Enter the numbers on the rating guide below. Then calculate the average of the six ratings to determine your total score. On the SAT II itself, two readers will rate your essay on a scale of 6 (high) to 1 (low). The score will be reported to you as the sum of the two ratings, from 12 (best) to 2 (worst).

Note that on the SAT II, essays are judged in relation to other essays written on the same topic. Therefore, this Self-Scoring Guide may not yield a totally accurate prediction of the score you can expect to earn on the actual exam. Because it is difficult to achieve objectivity when assessing your own writing, you may improve the validity of your score by having a trusted friend or teacher read your essay and rate it using this scoring guide.

| | 6 | 5 | 4 | 3 | 2 | 1 |
|---|---|---|---|---|---|---|
| **PURPOSE OF THE ESSAY** | Very clear and insightful; fresh and engaging | Quite clear and insightful; interesting | Fairly clear and with some insight; marginally interesting | Somewhat clear but some confusion, too; fairly dull | Largely unclear and confusing | Extremely confusing |
| **ORGANIZATION AND DEVELOPMENT** | Meticulously organized and thoroughly developed; coherent and unified | Well organized and sufficiently developed; basically coherent and unified | Reasonably organized and developed; mostly coherent and unified | Somewhat organized and developed; some incoherence and lack of unity | Little organization and meager development; mostly incoherent and void of unity | No apparent organization or development; incoherent and lacking unity |
| **USE OF SENTENCES** | Effectively varied and engaging; essentially error-free | Varied and interesting; one or two minor errors | Adequately varied and interesting; some errors | Somewhat varied and marginally interesting; one or more major errors | Little variation and basically dull; some major errors | Uniformly repetitious and dull; numerous major errors |
| **CHOICE OF WORDS** | Interesting, sensitive, and effective; basically error-free | Generally interesting, clear and effective; one or two inaccuracies | Occasionally interesting and effective; one or two errors in diction or idiom | Somewhat dull and ordinary; some errors in diction or idiom | Mostly dull and conventional; several errors | Dull, immature; numerous errors in diction and idiom |
| **GRAMMAR AND USAGE** | Error-free | Occasional minor errors | Several minor errors | Some major errors | Frequent major errors | Severely flawed |
| **OVERALL IMPRESSION** | Demonstrates excellent skills and writing competence | Demonstrates good skills and competence | Demonstrates adequate skills and competence | Suggests fair skills and competence | Demonstrates poor skills and competence | Demonstrates lack of skill and competence |

For rating yourself

*Rating Guide*
Each category is rated 1 (low) to 6 (high)

Purpose of the Essay          _____
Organization and Development  _____
Use of Sentences              _____
Choice of Words               _____
Grammar and Usage             _____
Overall Impression            _____
TOTAL                         _____
  Divide total by 6 to get final score: [    ]

For a second opinion

*Rating Guide*
Each category is rated 1 (low) to 6 (high)

Purpose of the Essay          _____
Organization and Development  _____
Use of Sentences              _____
Choice of Words               _____
Grammar and Usage             _____
Overall Impression            _____
TOTAL                         _____
  Divide total by 6 to get final score: [    ]

# ANSWER SHEET FOR
# PRACTICE TEST B

## Usage

1. Ⓐ Ⓑ Ⓒ Ⓓ Ⓔ
2. Ⓐ Ⓑ Ⓒ Ⓓ Ⓔ
3. Ⓐ Ⓑ Ⓒ Ⓓ Ⓔ
4. Ⓐ Ⓑ Ⓒ Ⓓ Ⓔ
5. Ⓐ Ⓑ Ⓒ Ⓓ Ⓔ
6. Ⓐ Ⓑ Ⓒ Ⓓ Ⓔ
7. Ⓐ Ⓑ Ⓒ Ⓓ Ⓔ
8. Ⓐ Ⓑ Ⓒ Ⓓ Ⓔ
9. Ⓐ Ⓑ Ⓒ Ⓓ Ⓔ
10. Ⓐ Ⓑ Ⓒ Ⓓ Ⓔ
11. Ⓐ Ⓑ Ⓒ Ⓓ Ⓔ
12. Ⓐ Ⓑ Ⓒ Ⓓ Ⓔ
13. Ⓐ Ⓑ Ⓒ Ⓓ Ⓔ
14. Ⓐ Ⓑ Ⓒ Ⓓ Ⓔ
15. Ⓐ Ⓑ Ⓒ Ⓓ Ⓔ
16. Ⓐ Ⓑ Ⓒ Ⓓ Ⓔ
17. Ⓐ Ⓑ Ⓒ Ⓓ Ⓔ
18. Ⓐ Ⓑ Ⓒ Ⓓ Ⓔ
19. Ⓐ Ⓑ Ⓒ Ⓓ Ⓔ
20. Ⓐ Ⓑ Ⓒ Ⓓ Ⓔ
21. Ⓐ Ⓑ Ⓒ Ⓓ Ⓔ
22. Ⓐ Ⓑ Ⓒ Ⓓ Ⓔ
23. Ⓐ Ⓑ Ⓒ Ⓓ Ⓔ
24. Ⓐ Ⓑ Ⓒ Ⓓ Ⓔ
25. Ⓐ Ⓑ Ⓒ Ⓓ Ⓔ
26. Ⓐ Ⓑ Ⓒ Ⓓ Ⓔ
27. Ⓐ Ⓑ Ⓒ Ⓓ Ⓔ
28. Ⓐ Ⓑ Ⓒ Ⓓ Ⓔ
29. Ⓐ Ⓑ Ⓒ Ⓓ Ⓔ
30. Ⓐ Ⓑ Ⓒ Ⓓ Ⓔ

## Sentence Correction

31. Ⓐ Ⓑ Ⓒ Ⓓ Ⓔ
32. Ⓐ Ⓑ Ⓒ Ⓓ Ⓔ
33. Ⓐ Ⓑ Ⓒ Ⓓ Ⓔ
34. Ⓐ Ⓑ Ⓒ Ⓓ Ⓔ
35. Ⓐ Ⓑ Ⓒ Ⓓ Ⓔ
36. Ⓐ Ⓑ Ⓒ Ⓓ Ⓔ
37. Ⓐ Ⓑ Ⓒ Ⓓ Ⓔ
38. Ⓐ Ⓑ Ⓒ Ⓓ Ⓔ
39. Ⓐ Ⓑ Ⓒ Ⓓ Ⓔ
40. Ⓐ Ⓑ Ⓒ Ⓓ Ⓔ
41. Ⓐ Ⓑ Ⓒ Ⓓ Ⓔ
42. Ⓐ Ⓑ Ⓒ Ⓓ Ⓔ
43. Ⓐ Ⓑ Ⓒ Ⓓ Ⓔ
44. Ⓐ Ⓑ Ⓒ Ⓓ Ⓔ
45. Ⓐ Ⓑ Ⓒ Ⓓ Ⓔ
46. Ⓐ Ⓑ Ⓒ Ⓓ Ⓔ
47. Ⓐ Ⓑ Ⓒ Ⓓ Ⓔ
48. Ⓐ Ⓑ Ⓒ Ⓓ Ⓔ

## Revision-In-Context

49. Ⓐ Ⓑ Ⓒ Ⓓ Ⓔ
50. Ⓐ Ⓑ Ⓒ Ⓓ Ⓔ
51. Ⓐ Ⓑ Ⓒ Ⓓ Ⓔ
52. Ⓐ Ⓑ Ⓒ Ⓓ Ⓔ
53. Ⓐ Ⓑ Ⓒ Ⓓ Ⓔ
54. Ⓐ Ⓑ Ⓒ Ⓓ Ⓔ
55. Ⓐ Ⓑ Ⓒ Ⓓ Ⓔ
56. Ⓐ Ⓑ Ⓒ Ⓓ Ⓔ
57. Ⓐ Ⓑ Ⓒ Ⓓ Ⓔ
58. Ⓐ Ⓑ Ⓒ Ⓓ Ⓔ
59. Ⓐ Ⓑ Ⓒ Ⓓ Ⓔ
60. Ⓐ Ⓑ Ⓒ Ⓓ Ⓔ

# PRACTICE TEST B

## USAGE

INSTRUCTIONS: The underlined and lettered parts of each sentence below may contain an error in grammar, usage, word choice (diction), or expression (idiom). Read each sentence carefully, and identify which item contains the error. Indicate your choice by filling in the corresponding space on your answer sheet. Only the underlined parts contain errors. Assume that the rest of each sentence is correct. No sentence contains more than one error. Some sentences may contain no error, in which case the correct choice will always be (E) (No error).

SAMPLE QUESTIONS

1. At which point does the people in the
   (A)            (B)
   audience stand for a moment of
                   (C)
   silence? No error.
     (D)       (E)

2. She and me earned certificates of
        (A)  (B)
   appreciation from the town's daycare
        (C)                  (D)
   center. No error.
               (E)

SAMPLE ANSWERS

1. (A) ● (C) (D) (E)

2. ● (B) (C) (D) (E)

---

1. To sing a song good, you must focus your
        (A)            (B)
   attention not only on the music but on the
                                      (C)
   words as well. No error.
        (D)        (E)

2. Victor's parents can't afford to lay aside funds
                                (A)
   for luxuries such as a new car or a vacation,
                   (B)
   but rather must save it for their son's college
                  (C)        (D)
   education. No error.
                (E)

3. Every morning the scouts gathered at the
   flagpole to listen to the announcements for the
            (A)
   day being read aloud from a clipboard by the
                          (B)
   head counselor and to salute the flag as
                                       (C)
   it was risen over the camp. No error.
        (D)                    (E)

4. Young children should not be urged into

   activities before they are ready <u>for them</u>, <u>for</u>
                                      (A)        (B)
   pushing them prematurely often proves to be a

   waste of time and may cause <u>children</u> <u>to feel</u>
                                 (C)        (D)
   failure and frustration. <u>No error</u>.
                              (E)

5. The opposing attorneys, Mr. Kourabas and

   Mr. Martin, <u>had gone</u> to the courthouse that
               (A)
   morning determined <u>to take full advantage</u> of
                       (B)
   the situation <u>in order to</u> promote <u>his</u> client's
                  (C)                    (D)
   interests. <u>No error</u>.
              (E)

6. Since <u>nihilists</u> neither valued nationalism nor

   patriotism, <u>nor</u> committed <u>themselves</u> to any
                (A)               (B)
   cause <u>whatever</u>, they believed it was wrong to
          (C)
   join the army or to serve <u>your</u> country in any
                              (D)
   way. <u>No error</u>.
         (E)

7. The class <u>especially</u> enjoyed the talk <u>by the man</u>
              (A)                              (B)
   who <u>has been</u> in Russia during the 1991
       (C)
   coup that <u>overthrew</u> the Communist regime of
              (D)
   Mikhail Gorbachev. <u>No error</u>.
                        (E)

8. The <u>womens</u> movement was <u>thought to have</u>
        (A)                      (B)
   come <u>of age during</u> the 1992 elections,
         (C)
   when four women were elected <u>to the</u> United
                                 (D)
   States Senate and a record number won seats in

   the U.S. House of Representatives. <u>No error</u>.
                                       (E)

9. A large formation of geese, in addition to one

   pure-white <u>and</u> graceful swan, <u>were swimming</u>
               (A)                     (B)
   peacefully on the surface of the lake <u>when the</u>
                                          (C)
   report of a rifle shot sent them <u>aloft</u>. <u>No error</u>.
                                     (D)       (E)

10. Chekhov's eye <u>for detail</u> and use of cogent
                   (A)
    language <u>make</u> <u>his</u> short stories and plays
              (B)     (C)
    popular the world over, even among people

    who know little about literature or <u>care little</u>
                                          (D)
    for serious theater. <u>No error</u>.
                          (E)

11. <u>Throughout</u> the year, the park attracts tourists
     (A)
    and campers who come <u>for</u> hiking the
                          (B)
    unspoiled wilderness, climbing the mountains,

    <u>water sports</u>, and catching trout and
     (C)
    other prized game fish. <u>No error</u>.
     (D)                     (E)

12. Carolyn's mother was born and raised in the

    mainly residential area of the Bronx, where
    (A)

    she went to high school, got married, and gave
                   (B)           (C)          (D)

    birth to Carolyn on October 20, 1979. No error.
                                          (E)

13. Tolstoy said that happiness derives from living
                                              (A)

    for others and that, if one fails to serve
              (B)

    others in some fashion, when life's end
                               (C)

    approaches, they will die with regrets. No error.
          (D)                              (E)

14. On her application to Rutgers, Carole wrote that
    (A)

    medical technician had always been an idea that
                       (B)   (C)         (D)

    that attracted her. No error.
                       (E)

15. Work in specialized fields like bacteriology,
                               (A)

    nutrition, horticulture, public health, and animal

    husbandry require at least a bachelor's degree,
             (B)

    and for a job in management and research, a
            (C)

    master's degree or even a doctorate. No error.
                    (D)                  (E)

16. Chilblains is a skin condition that stings, itches,

    and burns, it affects the feet particularly, mostly
              (A)                              (B)

    after they have been exposed to the cold or after
         (C)                                      (D)

    being cold and wet. No error.
                        (E)

17. Baker, in his memoir, tells stories about the time
                          (A)          (B)

    before high school when he worked as a paper
                                (C)

    boy and delivered newspapers to the huge

    estates and mansions that used to line the
                             (D)

    riverfront. No error.
               (E)

18. Although Martin Luther King's birthday is on
    (A)                                    (B)
    January 15th, it is celebrated on the third
                 (C)
    Monday of January, regardless of the date.
                       (D)

    No error.
    (E)

19. In the fifteenth century the French king, Charles

    VIII, flexed his army's muscles in what are now
                                           (A)

    Naples and Brittany; the latter of the two turned
              (B)

    out to be the weakest, and soon became a part
       (C)        (D)

    of France. No error.
               (E)

20. The collective thoughts, reflections, memories,

    and opinions expressed by the seniors in the
                 (A)

    pages of the student magazine represent the
               (B)                (C)

    diversity and uniqueness that characterizes
                                 (D)

    Brookdale High School. No error.
                          (E)

21. A good motorcycle rider like Johnny is

    someone who knows how to switch gears at the
            (A)

    right moment, can downshift on a berm,

    obeys the law, and controls their bike at all
    (B)               (C)      (D)

    times. No error.
          (E)

22. When Annie <u>set out</u> to find the <u>best</u> automobile
                    (A)

    at a price she could afford, she decided that

    she'd look <u>for</u> something different <u>than</u> the
                (B)                    (C)
    typical models that her friends <u>were driving</u>.
                                        (D)

    <u>No error</u>.
     (E)

23. It was improper for <u>an owner to beat</u> <u>his</u> slaves
                        (A)

    at that <u>time, however</u>, there actually <u>were</u>
                (B)                              (C)
    laws <u>on the books</u> that specified the
            (D)
    circumstances when slavebeating was justified.

    <u>No error</u>.
     (E)

24. The award-winning *Sound of Music*

    <u>has been seen</u> by <u>more</u> moviegoers <u>than</u>
        (A)              (B)
    <u>any musical</u> film <u>in</u> the history of the movies.
        (C)              (D)
    <u>No error</u>.
     (E)

25. In all of <u>Carson McCullers'</u> stories, <u>she</u> probes
                (A)                              (B)
    the minds and the hearts of the characters,

    <u>leaving</u> no detail unnoticed, no expression or
     (C)
    gesture <u>unobserved</u>. <u>No error</u>.
            (D)              (E)

26. When he walked <u>in</u> the classroom from the
                    (A)
    corridor, all the students <u>rose as one</u> and
                                (B)
    applauded <u>him</u> for <u>having run</u> in the New York
              (C)           (D)
    Marathon and finishing in under three hours.

    <u>No error</u>.
     (E)

27. As an indication of the <u>play's</u> power to hold <u>its</u>
                            (A)                        (B)
    audience, when the final curtain descended,

    there <u>was</u> only one man and one woman
           (C)
    <u>remaining</u> in the theater. <u>No error</u>.
     (D)                            (E)

28. <u>As</u> implied in the author's biography, to show
     (A)
    <u>how</u> the tenant farmers <u>had been</u> exploited by
     (B)                          (C)
    the owners was the whole point <u>of him</u> writing
                                        (D)
    the book. <u>No error</u>.
              (E)

29. <u>Despite</u> exploitation by gold-seeking
     (A)
    marauders, the tribe survived and <u>even</u>
                                        (B)
    flourished because their pride in themselves

    was <u>stronger than almost</u> any <u>other</u> people.
         (C)                          (D)
    <u>No error</u>.
     (E)

30. Neither the chameleon, a lizard known for <u>its</u>
                                                (A)
    ability to change color, nor many other lizards

    <u>having</u> the same attribute, <u>is</u> able to assume
     (B)                              (C)
    more than a few green and brown shades when

    the temperatures <u>fall</u> below freezing. <u>No error</u>.
                      (D)                      (E)

**DON'T STOP.    PLEASE CONTINUE WITH THE NEXT QUESTIONS.**

## SENTENCE CORRECTION

INSTRUCTIONS: The underlined sections of the sentences below may contain errors in standard English, including awkward or ambiguous expression, poor word choice (diction), incorrect sentence structure, or faulty grammar, usage, and punctuation. In some items, the entire sentence may be underlined. Read each sentence carefully and identify which of the five alternative versions most effectively and correctly expresses the meaning of the original. Indicate your choice by filling in the corresponding space on your answer sheet. Choice (A) always repeats the original. Choose (A) if none of the other choices improves the original sentence.

SAMPLE QUESTION

The kindness <u>he was showed</u> as a child led him to the priesthood as an adult.

(A) he was showed
(B) he was shown
(C) that shown to him
(D) that he was showed
(E) which had been showed

SAMPLE ANSWER

Ⓐ ● Ⓒ Ⓓ Ⓔ

31. The strength and appearance of denim fabric <u>account for its appeal</u> among campers, hikers, and other outdoor enthusiasts.

(A) account for its appeal
(B) accounts for its appeal
(C) account for their appeal
(D) explains why it is appealing
(E) are the reasons for their appeal

32. Although dinosaurs were the hugest animals ever to roam the earth, many modern-day whales <u>are as equal in their dimensions to</u> many prehistoric dinosaurs.

(A) are as equal in their dimensions to
(B) are as large or equal to
(C) are as large as
(D) are as equally large in their dimensions as
(E) are as equal in dimensions with

33. The dilemma of loyalty to one's country versus loyalty to one's family is exemplified in the story when Thomas must decide whether to kill his own son, Andy, who had betrayed family tradition <u>by joining the Union army for a woman.</u>

(A) by joining the Union army for a woman.
(B) for a woman joining the Union army.
(C) by, for the reason of a woman, joining the union army.
(D) by for a woman joined the Union army.
(E) for a woman, for joining the Union army.

34. Soviet Olympians were supposed to be more than <u>athletes they were</u> also meant to be symbols of the greatness of the socialist system.

(A) athletes they were
(B) athletes and were
(C) athletes; they were
(D) athletes, although they were
(E) athletes; being that they were

35. Like Jasper Johns, Pop artist Ed Ruscha was fascinated by <u>words, and have consistently formed the principal subject matter</u> of his paintings and graphics.

(A) words, and have consistently formed the principal subject matter
(B) words, and words have consistently formed the principal subject matter

(C) words which have consistently formed the principal subject matter

(D) words, consistently they have formed the principal subject matter

(E) words, which have consistently formed the principal subject matter

36. The telling of tales is one of the earliest forms of human pastime, and they increased in complexity as well as sophistication as time went on.

(A) pastime, and they increased in complexity as well as sophistication

(B) pastime, they both increased in complexity and sophistication

(C) pastime, which both increased in complexity as well as in sophistication

(D) pastime, and it increased their complexity and sophistication

(E) pastime, an activity that increased in complexity as well as sophistication

37. Cervantes, the sixteenth-century Spanish author, was so far ahead of his day that, despite the instant popularity of his *Don Quixote*, no immediate successors had come into being during his lifetime.

(A) no immediate successors had come into being during his lifetime

(B) he had no immediate successors during his lifetime

(C) the coming of a successor was not to be during his lifetime

(D) there was not a coming of a successor during his lifetime

(E) during his lifetime it had no immediate successors

38. Howard stepped briskly to the counter and bought a cup of black coffee with Janet's money, which he drank quickly before hurrying back downtown.

(A) and bought a cup of black coffee with Janet's money, which he drank quickly

(B) and buying a cup of black coffee with Janet's money, drank it quickly

(C) and using Janet's money and buying a cup of black coffee that he drank quickly

(D) and, with Janet's money, bought a cup of black coffee, which he drank quickly

(E) and, using the money from Janet, buys a cup of black coffee which he drinks quickly

39. Subjecting laboratory rats to cold temperatures change the ratio of brown fat cells to white fat cells in the animal's body.

(A) change the ratio of brown fat cells to white fat cells

(B) produce a change in the ratio between brown fat cells and white fat cells

(C) change the ratio between brown fat cells to white fat cells

(D) produce changes in the ratios between white and brown fat cells

(E) changes the ratio of brown fat cells to white fat cells

40. Another of the common characteristics of the bulimic is their dependence on the good opinion of others.

(A) of the bulimic is their dependence on

(B) of the bulimic is their reliability on

(C) of bulimia is her reliance on

(D) of bulimia is their reliability on

(E) of bulimics is their dependence on

41. My grandfather owned a watchmaker's shop in South Philadelphia, and it was burglarized at least once a month, and he loved the place.

(A) My grandfather owned a watchmaker's shop in South Philadelphia, and it was burglarized at least once a month, and he loved the place.

(B) My grandfather loved his watchmaker's shop in South Philadelphia, in addition to being burglarized at least once a month.

(C) Although his watchmaker's shop in South Philadelphia was burglarized at least once a month, my grandfather loved the place.

(D) Although my grandfather owned a watchmaker's shop in South Philadelphia which was burglarized at least once a month, but he loved the place.

shop in South Philadelphia, my grandfather loved the place even though it
was burglarized at least once a month.

42. Geneticists, in a relatively short time, have
uncovered vast amounts of information about
human heredity despite the fact of human
generations being separated by twenty or
more years.

(A) despite the fact of human generations being
separated by twenty or more years
(B) despite the fact that a human generation has
been separated by twenty or more years
(C) despite human generations are separated by
twenty or more years
(D) even though human generations are separated by twenty or more years
(E) even though a period of twenty or more
years separate human generations

43. Paying for a college education in this decade is
more difficult for the average family than it
was in the past.

(A) than it was in the past
(B) than for past families
(C) than the past
(D) than families in the past
(E) than it used to be in the past

44. If you wish to truly understand Jefferson's
notion of ''the pursuit of happiness,'' a person
should read his letters to his son.

(A) a person should read his letters to his son
(B) you should read his letters to his son
(C) you should read the letters Jefferson wrote
to his son
(D) the letters Jefferson wrote to his son should
be read
(E) Jefferson's letters to his son should be read

45. It is the sort of an offer that no one but him
would refuse.

(A) the sort of an offer that no one but him
(B) the sort of offer that no one but he
(C) sort of an offer that no one but him
(D) a type of an offer that only him
(E) the type of offer only he

46. Having studied the works by the ancient physicians of Greece helped to kindle a rebirth of
the biological sciences during the Renaissance.

(A) Having studied the works by the ancient
physicians of Greece
(B) By studying the works by the ancient
physicians of Greece
(C) Knowledge of the ancient physicians of
Greece
(D) Studying and knowing the works by the
ancient physicians of Greece
(E) Having known and studied the works by
the ancient physicians of Greece

47. In most of the cults studied by sociologists, they
practice a studied deception to attract young
people, for example, inviting them to share a
meal and to be ''friends.''

(A) they practice a studied deception to attract
young people, for example, inviting
them to share a meal and to be ''friends.''
(B) they practice a studied deception to attract
young people; for example, they invite
them to share a meal and to be ''friends.''
(C) a studied deception is practiced; for example, young people are invited to share a
meal and to be ''friends.''
(D) members, to attract young people, practice
a studied deception, for example, to invite them to share a meal and to be
''friends.''
(E) young people are attracted by being invited
and being ''friends,'' for example, or
sharing a meal with members who practice a studied deception

48. Kate complained to her father that she ought to
be able to date any boys she wanted and become as good of friends with them as she
wished.

(A) as good of friends with them
(B) as good a friend to them
(C) as good as friends to them
(D) a good friend of theirs
(E) as good as friends with them

**DON'T STOP.   PLEASE CONTINUE WITH THE NEXT QUESTIONS.**

## REVISION-IN-CONTEXT

<u>Instructions</u>: The passages below are the unedited draft of two students' essays. Some of each essay needs to be rewritten to make the meaning clearer and more precise. Read the essays carefully.

Each essay is followed by six questions about changes that might improve all or part of its organization, development, sentence structure, use of language, appropriateness to the audience, or its use of standard written English. Choose the answer that most clearly and effectively expresses the student's intended meaning. Indicate your choice by filling in the corresponding space on the answer sheet.

### ESSAY A

*[1] At the beginning of the twentieth century, no one knew the technological developments that would be made by the 1990s. [2] The area of communication media is one of the significant developments in the twentieth century. [3] Also nuclear energy and great advancements in medicine and the treatment of disease.*

*[4] One important development was the invention of communication satellites which allow images and messages to be sent wirelessly around the world. [5] One advantage is that current events can be sent worldwide in seconds. [6] News used to travel by boat and take weeks or months to get overseas. [7] When a disaster struck the World Trade Center, the world saw it immediately and condemned the terrorists' actions. [8] One weak aspect of communication satellites is that they are launched from a space shuttle, and that is an extremely costly operation. [9] They also they cost millions of dollars to build and operate. [10] Therefore, many poor countries are left out of the so-called "Global Village."*

*[11] The invention and use of nuclear energy is another important technological development. [12] One positive feature of nuclear energy is that energy is cheaper, and can be made easy. [13] This is important in countries like France where almost all of the electricity is nuclear. [14] A negative consequence of nuclear energy is the probability of major nuclear accidents. [15] Watch out for human error and careless workmanship. [16] They were the cause of the meltdown in Chernobyl, which killed hundreds or maybe even thousands, and radiated half the Earth.*

*[17] There have been many significant technological advances in medicine in the twentieth century. [18] One development was the invention of the CAT scan. [19] The CAT scan allows doctors to make a picture of your brain to see if there is a growth on it. [20] One positive effect of the CAT scan is that doctors can diagnose brain tumors and brain cancer at an early stage. [21] Many lives have been saved. [22] One negative effect is that CAT scans are costly, so they are not used in third world countries.*

49. Considering the main idea of the whole essay, which of the following is the best revision of sentence 1?

    (A) In 1900 no one could anticipate the technological developments in the 1990s.

    (B) Recent technological achievements would blow the mind of people at the beginning of the twentieth century.

    (C) The twentieth century has seen remarkable technological achievements, but there has also been a price to pay for progress.

    (D) No one knows if the twenty-first century will produce as much technological progress as the twentieth century did.

    (E) Technological progress in communications, nuclear energy, and medicine is wonderful, but in the process we are destroying ourselves and our environment.

50. Which is the best revision of the underlined segment of sentence 12 below?

    *One positive feature of nuclear energy is that <u>energy is cheaper, and can be made easy</u>.*

(A) energy is cheaper and can be made easily

(B) energy is made cheaper and more easily made

(C) it is cheap and easy to make

(D) it is both cheap as well as made easily

(E) it's more cheaper and easier to make

51. To improve the coherence of paragraph 2, which of the following is the best sentence to delete from the essay?

(A) Sentence 5

(B) Sentence 6

(C) Sentence 7

(D) Sentence 8

(E) Sentence 9

52. In the context of the sentences that precede and follow sentence 15, which is the best revision of sentence 15?

(A) Human error and careless workmanship are almost unavoidable.

(B) Especially human error and careless workmanship.

(C) There's hardly no foolproof way to prevent human error and careless workmanship.

(D) You must never put down your guard against human error and careless workmanship.

(E) Accidents can happen accidentally by human error and careless workmanship.

53. With regard to the entire essay, which of the following best explains the writer's intention in paragraphs 2, 3, and 4?

(A) To compare and contrast three technological achievements

(B) To provide examples of the pros and cons of technological progress

(C) To analyze the steps needed for achievement in three areas

(D) To convince the reader to be open to technological change

(E) To advocate more funds for technological research and development

54. Assume that sentences 17 and 18 were combined as follows: *A significant advance in medicine has been the invention of the CAT*

*scan.* Which of the following is the best way to continue the paragraph?

(A) The CAT scan allows your doctors to make pictures of a brain to see if it has a growth on it, a cancer is growing, or tumors at an early stage.

(B) The CAT scan permits your doctors to make a picture and see if your brain has a growth on it, or whether or not you have brain tumors or brain cancer at an early stage.

(C) Taking pictures with a CAT scan, your brain is studied by doctors for growths, brain tumors, and cancer at an early stage.

(D) Doctors may make pictures of your brain to see if there is a growth, a tumor, or cancer at an early stage on it.

(E) With this device a doctor may look into a patient's brain to check for growths and to detect cancerous tumors at an early stage.

## ESSAY B

*[1] Members of our community have objected to the inclusion of various pieces of art in the local art exhibit. [2] They say that these pieces offend community values. [3] The exhibit in its entirety should be presented.*

*[4] The reason for this is that people have varied tastes, and those who like this form of art have a right to see the complete exhibit. [5] An exhibit like this one gives the community a rare chance to see the latest modern art nearby, and many people have looked forward to it with great anticipation. [6] It would be an unfortunate blow to those people for it not to be shown.*

*[7] The exhibit may contain pieces of art that tend to be slightly erotic, but what is being shown that most people haven't already seen? [8] So, give it an R or an X rating and don't let small children in. [9] But how many small children voluntarily go to see an art exhibit? [10] The exhibit includes examples of a new style of modern art. [11] The paintings show crowds of nude people. [12] The exhibit is at the library's new art gallery. [13] For centuries artists have been painting and sculpting people in the nude. [14] Why are these works of art*

*different? [15] Perhaps they are more graphic in some respects, but we live in a entirely different society than from the past. [16] It is strange indeed for people in this day and age to be offended by the sight of the human anatomy.*

*[17] If people don't agree with these pieces, they simply should just not go. [18] But they should not be allowed to prevent others from seeing it.*

55. Taking into account the sentences which precede and follow sentence 3, which of the following is the best revision of sentence 3?

   (A) On the other hand, the whole exhibit should be presented.
   (B) The exhibit, however, should be presented in its entirety.
   (C) The exhibit should be entirely presented regardless of what the critics say.
   (D) But another point of view is that the exhibit should be presented in its entirety.
   (E) Still other members also say the whole exhibit should be presented in its entirety.

56. In the context of paragraph 3, which of the following is the best revision of sentence 8?

   (A) So, an R or X rating will warn people with small children to keep them out.
   (B) Therefore, giving it an R or an X rating and not letting small children in.
   (C) To satisfy everyone objecting to the exhibit, perhaps the exhibit could be given an R or an X rating to advise parents that some of the art on exhibit may not be suitable for young children.
   (D) Let an R or an X rating caution the public that some of the art may be offensive and be unsuitable for young children.
   (E) In conclusion, small children will be kept out by giving it an R or an X rating.

57. In the context of paragraph 3, which of the following is the best revision of sentences 10, 11, and 12?

   (A) Paintings on exhibit at the library showing crowds of nude people and done in a new style of modern art.
   (B) The exhibit, on display at the library, in-

cludes paintings of crowds of nude people done in a new style of modern art.
   (C) The exhibit includes paintings in a new style of modern art, which shows crowds of nude people at the library.
   (D) The library is the site of the exhibit which shows a new style of modern art, with paintings showing crowds of nude people.
   (E) The new style of modern art includes examples of paintings showing crowds of nude people on exhibit in the library.

58. To improve the clarity and coherence of the whole essay, where is the best place to relocate the ideas contained in sentences 10, 11, and 12?

   (A) Before sentence 1
   (B) Between sentences 1 and 2
   (C) Between sentences 8 and 9
   (D) Between sentences 15 and 16
   (E) After sentence 18

59. Which of the following is the best revision of the underlined segment of sentence 15 below?

   *Perhaps they are more graphic in some respects, but we live in a entirely different society than from the past.*

   (A) an entirely different society than of the past
   (B) a completely different society than the past
   (C) a society completely different than from past societies
   (D) a society which is entirely different from the way societies have been in the past
   (E) an entirely different society from that of the past

60. Which of the following revisions of sentence 17 provides the best transition between paragraphs 3 and 4?

   (A) If anyone doesn't approve of these pieces, they simply should not go to the exhibit.
   (B) Anyone disagreeing with the pieces in the exhibit shouldn't go to it.
   (C) Anyone who disapproves of nudity in art simply shouldn't go to the exhibit.
   (D) If anyone dislikes the sight of nudes in art, this show isn't for them.
   (E) Don't go if you disapprove of nudity in art.

**PLEASE STOP WORK.   USE WHATEVER TIME IS LEFT BEFORE THE 40-MINUTE TEST PERIOD EXPIRES TO CHECK YOUR ANSWERS.**

# ESSAY

**Time allowed: 20 minutes**

INSTRUCTIONS: Plan and write an essay in response to the assigned topic. During the 20 minutes allowed, you should develop your thoughts clearly and effectively. A plain, natural style is probably best. Try to include specific evidence or examples to support your views.

The number of words is up to you, but quantity is far less important than quality. In general, however, a single paragraph may not give you the chance to develop your ideas sufficiently. You must limit your essay to the answer sheet. Please be advised, therefore, to write on every line, keep narrow margins, and write compactly enough to fit your essay in the space allowed. Try to write as legibly as you can.

BE SURE TO WRITE ONLY ON THE ASSIGNED TOPIC. AN ESSAY WRITTEN ON ANOTHER TOPIC WILL RECEIVE NO CREDIT.

---

> Given the chance to pick from one to three items for a time capsule to be opened in a thousand years, what would you choose to represent the way of life in America in the last decade of the twentieth century? In an essay, please explain the reasons for your choice(s).

This space is reserved for your personal bar code.

## SAT II: WRITING
## ESSAY
### Time allowed: 20 minutes

FOR OFFICE USE

First reader _____

Second reader _____

Third reader (if needed) _____

Topic:  **TIME CAPSULE**

The space below is for your essay. Please restrict your writing to the designated area.

Please continue your essay on the next page if you need more room.

_____

_____

_____

_____

_____

_____

_____

_____

_____

_____

_____

_____

_____

_____

_____

_____

_____

_____

_____

_____

_____

_____

## ANSWERS

| | | | | | |
|---|---|---|---|---|---|
| 1. A | 11. C | 21. D | 31. A | 41. C | 51. B |
| 2. C | 12. E | 22. C | 32. C | 42. D | 52. A |
| 3. D | 13. D | 23. B | 33. A | 43. A | 53. B |
| 4. E | 14. D | 24. C | 34. C | 44. C | 54. E |
| 5. D | 15. B | 25. B | 35. E | 45. E | 55. D |
| 6. D | 16. A | 26. A | 36. E | 46. C | 56. D |
| 7. C | 17. E | 27. C | 37. B | 47. C | 57. B |
| 8. A | 18. E | 28. D | 38. D | 48. B | 58. A |
| 9. B | 19. D | 29. C | 39. E | 49. C | 59. E |
| 10. C | 20. D | 30. C | 40. E | 50. C | 60. C |

## PERFORMANCE EVALUATION CHART

### I. Self-rating Chart

Usage, Questions 1–30                      Number correct _21_

Sentence Correction, Questions 31–48       Number correct _13_

Revision-in-Context, Questions 49–60       Number correct _8_

Subtotal _____

*Penalty.* Subtract 1/4 point (.25) for each incorrect answer.  _9 +5+4_

(No penalty for unanswered questions)

TOTAL SCORE _37.5_

### II. Key to Self-rating

| | Usage | Sentence Correction | Revision-in-Context | Total |
|---|---|---|---|---|
| Excellent | 27–30 | 17–18 | 11–12 | 55–60 |
| Very good | 23–26 | 14–16 | 9–10 | 46–54 |
| Good | 19–22 | 11–13 | 7–8 | 37–45 |
| Fair | 15–18 | 9–10 | 5–6 | 29–36 |
| Poor | 10–14 | 6–8 | 3–4 | 19–28 |
| Very poor | 0–9 | 0–5 | 0–2 | 0–18 |

# ANSWERS EXPLAINED

## Usage

1. **A**  Diction error. Adverbs modify active verbs. Use *well* in place of *good* to modify the verb *to sing*.
2. **C**  Pronoun reference. The pronoun *it* doesn't refer to any specific noun or pronoun.
3. **D**  Verb form. The past perfect form of *raise* (to lift) is *raised*.
4. **E**  No error.
5. **D**  Pronoun-antecedent agreement. The antecedent *attorneys* is plural; *his* is singular. Use *their*.
6. **D**  Pronoun shift. The sentence is cast in third person. Use *their* instead of *your*.
7. **C**  Verb tense.  The past perfect tense is used to refer to action completed prior to a specific time in the past. Use *had been* in place of *has been*.
8. **A**  Punctuation. The possessive *women's* needs an apostrophe.
9. **B**  Subject-verb agreement. The subject *formation* is singular; the verb *were* is plural. Use *was*.
10. **C**  Pronoun reference. The pronoun *his* cannot be used to refer to a possessive noun.
11. **C**  Faulty parallelism.  Coordinate elements in a series should be in parallel grammatical form.  *Water sports* is not parallel.
12. **E**  No error.
13. **D**  Pronoun-antecedent agreement.  The antecedent *one* is singular; the pronoun *they* is plural. Use *he* or *one*.
14. **D**  Diction error. Medical technician is not an *idea*. Use *job* or *position*.
15. **B**  Subject-verb agreement. The subject *work* is singular; the verb *require* is plural. Use *requires*.
16. **A**  Comma splice. Separate two independent clauses with a period or a semicolon.
17. **E**  No error.
18. **E**  No error.
19. **D**  Comparative degree.  A comparison of two requires an adjective in the comparative degree.  Use *weaker* in place of *weakest*.
20. **D**  Subject-verb agreement.  The subject *diversity and uniqueness* is plural;  the verb *characterizes* is singular. Use *characterize*.
21. **D**  Pronoun-antecedent agreement. The pronoun *their* is plural; the antecedent *rider* is singular. Use *his*.
22. **C**  Idiom error. Standard usage is *different from*.
23. **B**  Comma splice.  Don't use *however* as a conjunction between two independent clauses.  Use a semi-semicolon or a period.
24. **C**  Faulty comparison. The word *other* or else must be included in a comparison of one thing with a group group of which it is a member. Use *any other musical film*.
25. **B**  Pronoun reference. The pronoun *she* cannot refer to a possessive noun.
26. **A**  Diction error. Use *into* in place of *in*.
27. **C**  Subject-verb agreement. Compound subjects need plural verbs. Use *are*.
28. **D**  Pronoun choice. A possessive pronoun is needed before a gerund. Use *his*.
29. **C**  Faulty comparison. Two unlike ideas—*pride* and *people*—may not be compared.  Use *stronger than that of*.
30. **C**  Subject-verb agreement. Verbs following compound subjects joined by *nor* get their number from the the closer noun (*lizards*). Use *are* in place of *is*.

## Sentence Correction

**Note**: *Although many choices contain multiple errors, only one error is listed for each incorrect answer.*

31. **A**  B.  Subject-verb agreement. *Strength and appearance* is plural; *accounts* is singular.

C. Pronoun reference. The pronoun *their* should refer to *fabric*, but because *their* is plural, it seems to refer to *strength and appearance*.

D. Subject-verb agreement. *Strength and appearance* is plural; *explains* is singular.

E. Pronoun reference. The pronoun *their* should refer to *fabric*, but because *their* is plural, it seems to refer to *strength and appearance*.

32. **C**  A. Faulty comparison. The comparison requires the *as equal . . .as* construction.

B. Redundancy. The phrases *as large* and *or equal* are redundant.

D. Redundancy. The word *large* and the phrase *in their dimensions* are redundant.

E. Idiom. In standard idiom *equal with* should be *equal to*.

33. **A**  B. Misplaced modifier. This version says the woman joined the Union army.

C. Clumsy construction. The phrase that begins *for the reason* is awkward.

D. Faulty idiom. The phrase *by for a woman* is non-English.

E. Mixed construction.  The phrase *for joining the Union army* is grammatically unrelated to the previous part of the sentence.

34. **C**  A. Run-on sentence. End punctuation is needed between *athletes* and *they* to separate the two independent clauses.

B. Faulty coordination.  The conjunction *and* fails to create a meaningful relationship between the clauses.

D. Faulty subordination.  The subordinating conjunction *although* fails to establish a logical relationship between the clauses.

E. Semicolon error. A semicolon may not be used to separate an independent clause from a dependent clause.

35. **E**  A. Mixed construction.  The construction that begins *and have* is grammatically unrelated to the earlier part of the sentence

B. Needless repetition. The second *words* is excessive.

C. Punctuation error.  The absence of a comma between *words* and *which* creates a restrictive clause that changes the meaning of the sentence.

D. Comma splice. A comma may not be used to separate two independent clauses.

36. **E**  A. Pronoun-antecedent agreement. *They* is plural; *telling* is singular.

B. Comma splice. A comma may not be used to separate two independent clauses.

C. Faulty parallelism. The verb *increased* lacks a grammatical parallel.

D. Pronoun reference. The pronoun *it* lacks a specific referent.

37. **B**  A. Faulty verb tense. The verb *had come* should be in the simple past tense (*came*).

C. Clumsy construction. The entire clause is awkwardly worded.

D. Wordy. The phrase *not a coming of a successor* could easily be *no successor*.

E. Pronoun reference. The pronoun *it* lacks a specific referent.

38. **D**  A. Misplaced modifier. The phrase *which he drank quickly* modifies *money* instead of *coffee*.

B. Pronoun reference. The pronoun *it* refers to *cup*, not to *coffee*.

C. Sentence fragment.  The construction lacks a main verb.  The *-ing* form of a verb (*using, buying*) may not be used as the main verb without a helping verb, as in *was using, is buying*.

E. Shift in verb tense. The sentence is cast in the past tense. The verb *buys* is in the present tense.

39. **E**  A. Subject-verb agreement. *Subjecting* is singular; *change* is plural.

B. Subject-verb agreement. *Subjecting* is singular; *produce* is plural.

C. Idiom error. In standard idiom *to* should be *and*.

D. Subject-verb agreement. *Subjecting* is singular; *change* is plural.

40. **E** A. Pronoun-antecedent agreement. *Their* is plural; *bulimic* is singular.
    B. Diction error. *Reliability* should be *reliance*.
    C. Pronoun reference. The pronoun *her* lacks a specific referent.
    D. Pronoun reference. The pronoun *their* illogically refers to *characteristics*.

41. **C** A. Faulty coordination. The three coordinate clauses contain ideas of unequal importance.
    B. Mixed construction. The phrase that begins *in addition to* is grammatically unrelated to the previous part of the sentence.
    D. Faulty subordination. The conjunction *but* fails to create a logical relationship between the two clauses in the sentence.
    E. Shift in verb tense. The tense shift between past perfect (*had owned*) and simple past *(was)* is inconsistent.

42. **D** A. Clumsy construction. The construction *the fact of human generations being* is awkwardly worded.
    B. Verb tense. The present tense is used to express statements of general truth.
    C. Faulty verb form. *Are* should be *being*.
    E. Subject-verb agreement. *Period* is singular; *separate* is plural.

43. **A** B. Faulty comparison. *Paying* is compared to *families*, an illogical comparison.
    C. Faulty comparison. *Paying* is compared to *past*, an illogical comparison.
    D. Faulty comparison. *Paying* is compared to *families*, an illogical comparison.
    E. Redundancy. The phrases *used to be* and *in the past* are redundant.

44. **C** A. Shift in pronoun person. The sentence begins in second person (*you*), but shifts to third person.
    B. Pronoun reference. The pronoun *his* has no specific referent.
    D. Passive construction. Also, the subject shifts from *you* to *letters*.
    E. Passive construction. Also, the subject shifts from *you* to *letters*.

45. **E** A. Idiom error. The standard idiom is *sort of offer*.
    B. Pronoun choice. Use an objective case pronouns (*him*) following *but*.
    C. Idiom error. The standard idiom is *sort of offer*.
    D. Pronoun choice. Use a nominative case pronoun (*he*) as the subject.

46. **C** A. Dangling participle. The phrase that begins *Having studied* has no noun or pronoun to modify.
    B. Dangling participle. The phrase that begins *By studying* has no noun or pronoun to modify.
    D. Dangling participle. The phrase that begins *Studying and* has no noun or pronoun to modify.
    E. Dangling participle. The phrase that begins *Having known* has no noun or pronoun to modify.

47. **C** A. Mixed construction. The phrase that begins *inviting them* is not grammatically related to the earlier part of the sentence.
    B. Pronoun reference. The pronoun *they* lacks a specific referent.
    D. Mixed construction. The phrase that begins *to invite* is not grammatically related to the earlier part of the sentence.
    E. Clumsy construction. The portion of the sentence that begins *being invited in* is awkward.

48. **B** A. Clumsy construction. The construction is awkwardly worded.
    C. Clumsy construction. The construction is awkwardly worded.
    D. Faulty comparison. The *as . . . as* construction used to make comparisons is not complete.
    E. Faulty comparison. Repeating *as* makes the comparison confusing.

*Revison-in-Context*

49. **C**   Choice A implies that the essay's purpose is to admire the technological achievements of the twentieth century. The essay, however, has another purpose.

Choice B is similar to A and also contains an inappropriate colloquialism.

Choice C accurately captures the essay's theme—that technological progress is neither all good nor all bad. It is the best answer.

Choice D suggests that the essay will discuss the prospects for continued technological progress, but the essay has a different purpose.

Choice E names the three areas discussed in the essay but, contrary to the point of the essay, suggests that we would be better off without technological progress.

50. **C**   Choice A unnecessarily repeats *energy* and contains an incomplete comparison. Energy is cheaper than what?

Choice B contains an incomplete comparison. Energy is cheaper than what? It also contains an error in parallel construction.

Choice C is succinct and accurately expressed. It is the best answer.

Choice D contains an error in parallel construction.

Choice E also contains a faulty comparison. Cheaper and easier than what?

51. **B**   Although related to communications, the information contained in sentence 6 is not germane to the discussion of communication satellites. Therefore, B is the best answer.

52. **A**   Choice A is consistent in style and tone to the sentences preceeding and following sentence 15. It is the best answer.

Choice B is a sentence fragment.

Choice C contains the nonstandard usage, *hardly no*, which is a double negative.

Choice D contains a sudden shift to second person, which does not fit the tone and style of the preceding and following sentences.

Choice E is needlessly repetitious.

53. **B**   Choice A does not accurately describe either the paragraph structure or the point of the essay.

Choice B precisely describes the structure of each paragraph. It is the best answer.

Choices C and D describe neither the paragraph structure nor the point of the essay.

Choice E is an inference that might be drawn from the essay, but the writer never says so.

54. **E**   Choice A unnecessarily repeats *CAT scan* and contains faulty parallelism.

Choice B unnecessarily repeats *CAT scan* and is needlessly wordy.

Choice C contains a dangling participle. The phrase that begins *Taking pictures* should modify *doctors*, not *brain*.

Choice D has no discernible connection with the previous sentence.

Choice E is a succinct and error-free follow-up to the previous sentence. It is the best answer.

55. **D**   Choices A, B, and C abruptly state the contrasting point of view without regard to the context.

Choice D takes the context into account and provides for a smooth progression of thought. It is the best answer.

Choice E is confusing. It is unclear until the end of the sentence whether the *other members* support or oppose the exhibit.

56. **D**   Choice A is not consistent in style and mood with the rest of the paragraph.

Choice B is a sentence fragment.

Choice C is excessively wordy.

Choice D fits the context of the paragraph and expresses the idea correctly. It is the best answer.

Choice E inappropriately uses *in conclusion* and contains the pronoun *it,* which lacks a specific referent.

57. **B**  Choice A lacks a main verb; therefore, it is a sentence fragment.

Choice B accurately combines the sentences. It is the best answer.

Choice C expresses the idea in a way that the writer could not have intended.

Choice D subordinates important ideas and emphasizes a lesser one.

Choice E restates the idea in a manner that changes the writer's intended meaning.

58. **A**  Choice A is the best choice because the sentences contain basic information about the topic. Readers are left in the dark unless the information appears as early as possible in the essay.

59. **E**  Choice A contains faulty idiom; the phrase *than of the past* is nonstandard usage.

Choice B contains a faulty comparison; *society* and *the past* cannot be logically compared.

Choice C contains an error in idiom; the phrase *than from* is redundant.

Choice D is correct but excessively wordy.

Choice E is the best answer.

60. **C**  Choice A provides a reasonable transition, but it contains an error in pronoun-antecedent agreement. The pronoun *they* is plural; its antecedent *anyone* is singular.

Choice B contains an error in diction. One can *disapprove of* but not *disagree with* a piece of art.

Choice C alludes to the content of the previous paragraph and is clearly and succinctly expressed. It is the best answer.

Choice D contains an error in pronoun-antecedent agreement. The pronoun *them* is plural; the antecedent *anyone* is singular.

Choice E is inconsistent in tone and mood with the rest of the essay.

# SELF-SCORING GUIDE FOR THE SAT II ESSAY

## PRACTICE TEST B

**Using this guide.** Rate yourself in each of the six categories on the left. Circle the item that most accurately describes your performance. Enter the numbers on the rating guide below. Then calculate the average of the six ratings to determine your total score. On the SAT II itself, two readers will rate your essay on a scale of 6 (high) to 1 (low). The score will be reported to you as the sum of the two ratings, from 12 (best) to 2 (worst).

Note that on the SAT II, essays are judged in relation to other essays written on the same topic. Therefore, this Self-Scoring Guide may not yield a totally accurate prediction of the score you can expect to earn on the actual exam. Because it is difficult to achieve objectivity when assessing your own writing, you may improve the validity of your score by having a trusted friend or teacher read your essay and rate it using this scoring guide.

*Remove scoring guide by cutting on dotted line*

| | 6 | 5 | 4 | 3 | 2 | 1 |
|---|---|---|---|---|---|---|
| **PURPOSE OF THE ESSAY** | Very clear and insightful; fresh and engaging | Quite clear and insightful; interesting | Fairly clear and with some insight; marginally interesting | Somewhat clear but some confusion, too; fairly dull | Largely unclear and confusing | Extremely confusing |
| **ORGANIZATION AND DEVELOPMENT** | Meticulously organized and thoroughly developed; coherent and unified | Well organized and sufficiently developed; basically coherent and unified | Reasonably organized and developed; mostly coherent and unified | Somewhat organized and developed; some incoherence and lack of unity | Little organization and meager development; mostly incoherent and void of unity | No apparent organization or development; incoherent and lacking unity |
| **USE OF SENTENCES** | Effectively varied and engaging; essentially error-free | Varied and interesting; one or two minor errors | Adequately varied and interesting; some errors | Somewhat varied and marginally interesting; one or more major errors | Little variation and basically dull; some major errors | Uniformly repetitious and dull; numerous major errors |
| **CHOICE OF WORDS** | Interesting, sensitive, and effective; basically error-free | Generally interesting, clear and effective; one or two inaccuracies | Occasionally interesting and effective; one or two errors in diction or idiom | Somewhat dull and ordinary; some errors in diction or idiom | Mostly dull and conventional; several errors | Dull, immature; numerous errors in diction and idiom |
| **GRAMMAR AND USAGE** | Error-free | Occasional minor errors | Several minor errors | Some major errors | Frequent major errors | Severely flawed |
| **OVERALL IMPRESSION** | Demonstrates excellent skills and writing competence | Demonstrates good skills and competence | Demonstrates adequate skills and competence | Suggests fair skills and competence | Demonstrates poor skills and competence | Demonstrates lack of skill and competence |

| For rating yourself | | For a second opinion | |
|---|---|---|---|
| ***Rating Guide***<br>Each category is rated 1 (low) to 6 (high) | | ***Rating Guide***<br>Each category is rated 1 (low) to 6 (high) | |
| Purpose of the Essay | _____ | Purpose of the Essay | _____ |
| Organization and Development | _____ | Organization and Development | _____ |
| Use of Sentences | _____ | Use of Sentences | _____ |
| Choice of Words | _____ | Choice of Words | _____ |
| Grammar and Usage | _____ | Grammar and Usage | _____ |
| Overall Impression | _____ | Overall Impression | _____ |
| TOTAL | _____ | TOTAL | _____ |
| Divide total by 6 to get final score: | ☐ | Divide total by 6 to get final score: | ☐ |

# ANSWER SHEET FOR PRACTICE TEST C

## Usage

1. Ⓐ Ⓑ Ⓒ Ⓓ Ⓔ
2. Ⓐ Ⓑ Ⓒ Ⓓ Ⓔ
3. Ⓐ Ⓑ Ⓒ Ⓓ Ⓔ
4. Ⓐ Ⓑ Ⓒ Ⓓ Ⓔ
5. Ⓐ Ⓑ Ⓒ Ⓓ Ⓔ
6. Ⓐ Ⓑ Ⓒ Ⓓ Ⓔ
7. Ⓐ Ⓑ Ⓒ Ⓓ Ⓔ
8. Ⓐ Ⓑ Ⓒ Ⓓ Ⓔ
9. Ⓐ Ⓑ Ⓒ Ⓓ Ⓔ
10. Ⓐ Ⓑ Ⓒ Ⓓ Ⓔ
11. Ⓐ Ⓑ Ⓒ Ⓓ Ⓔ
12. Ⓐ Ⓑ Ⓒ Ⓓ Ⓔ
13. Ⓐ Ⓑ Ⓒ Ⓓ Ⓔ
14. Ⓐ Ⓑ Ⓒ Ⓓ Ⓔ
15. Ⓐ Ⓑ Ⓒ Ⓓ Ⓔ
16. Ⓐ Ⓑ Ⓒ Ⓓ Ⓔ
17. Ⓐ Ⓑ Ⓒ Ⓓ Ⓔ
18. Ⓐ Ⓑ Ⓒ Ⓓ Ⓔ
19. Ⓐ Ⓑ Ⓒ Ⓓ Ⓔ
20. Ⓐ Ⓑ Ⓒ Ⓓ Ⓔ
21. Ⓐ Ⓑ Ⓒ Ⓓ Ⓔ
22. Ⓐ Ⓑ Ⓒ Ⓓ Ⓔ
23. Ⓐ Ⓑ Ⓒ Ⓓ Ⓔ
24. Ⓐ Ⓑ Ⓒ Ⓓ Ⓔ
25. Ⓐ Ⓑ Ⓒ Ⓓ Ⓔ
26. Ⓐ Ⓑ Ⓒ Ⓓ Ⓔ
27. Ⓐ Ⓑ Ⓒ Ⓓ Ⓔ
28. Ⓐ Ⓑ Ⓒ Ⓓ Ⓔ
29. Ⓐ Ⓑ Ⓒ Ⓓ Ⓔ
30. Ⓐ Ⓑ Ⓒ Ⓓ Ⓔ

## Sentence Correction

31. Ⓐ Ⓑ Ⓒ Ⓓ Ⓔ
32. Ⓐ Ⓑ Ⓒ Ⓓ Ⓔ
33. Ⓐ Ⓑ Ⓒ Ⓓ Ⓔ
34. Ⓐ Ⓑ Ⓒ Ⓓ Ⓔ
35. Ⓐ Ⓑ Ⓒ Ⓓ Ⓔ
36. Ⓐ Ⓑ Ⓒ Ⓓ Ⓔ
37. Ⓐ Ⓑ Ⓒ Ⓓ Ⓔ
38. Ⓐ Ⓑ Ⓒ Ⓓ Ⓔ
39. Ⓐ Ⓑ Ⓒ Ⓓ Ⓔ
40. Ⓐ Ⓑ Ⓒ Ⓓ Ⓔ
41. Ⓐ Ⓑ Ⓒ Ⓓ Ⓔ
42. Ⓐ Ⓑ Ⓒ Ⓓ Ⓔ
43. Ⓐ Ⓑ Ⓒ Ⓓ Ⓔ
44. Ⓐ Ⓑ Ⓒ Ⓓ Ⓔ
45. Ⓐ Ⓑ Ⓒ Ⓓ Ⓔ
46. Ⓐ Ⓑ Ⓒ Ⓓ Ⓔ
47. Ⓐ Ⓑ Ⓒ Ⓓ Ⓔ
48. Ⓐ Ⓑ Ⓒ Ⓓ Ⓔ

## Revision-In-Context

49. Ⓐ Ⓑ Ⓒ Ⓓ Ⓔ
50. Ⓐ Ⓑ Ⓒ Ⓓ Ⓔ
51. Ⓐ Ⓑ Ⓒ Ⓓ Ⓔ
52. Ⓐ Ⓑ Ⓒ Ⓓ Ⓔ
53. Ⓐ Ⓑ Ⓒ Ⓓ Ⓔ
54. Ⓐ Ⓑ Ⓒ Ⓓ Ⓔ
55. Ⓐ Ⓑ Ⓒ Ⓓ Ⓔ
56. Ⓐ Ⓑ Ⓒ Ⓓ Ⓔ
57. Ⓐ Ⓑ Ⓒ Ⓓ Ⓔ
58. Ⓐ Ⓑ Ⓒ Ⓓ Ⓔ
59. Ⓐ Ⓑ Ⓒ Ⓓ Ⓔ
60. Ⓐ Ⓑ Ⓒ Ⓓ Ⓔ

# PRACTICE TEST C

## USAGE

INSTRUCTIONS: The underlined and lettered parts of each sentence below may contain an error in grammar, usage, word choice (diction), or expression (idiom). Read each sentence carefully, and identify the item that contains the error. Indicate your choice by filling in the corresponding space on your answer sheet. Only the underlined parts contain errors. Assume that the rest of each sentence is correct. No sentence contains more than one error. Some sentences may contain no error, in which case the correct choice is (E) (No error).

SAMPLE QUESTIONS

SAMPLE ANSWERS

1. At the conclusion of the ceremony, the
        (A)
   new members sweared that they would never
              (B)              (C)
   reveal the secret handshake. No error.
   (D)                         (E)

1. Ⓐ ⬤ Ⓒ Ⓓ Ⓔ

2. John could hardly do no better than
                      (A)       (B)
   to have caught a bass of such
   (C)                      (D)
   dimensions. No error.
               (E)

2. ⬤ Ⓑ Ⓒ Ⓓ Ⓔ

1. No matter how self-deluded one may be,
                                (A)
   there's no getting around the fact that there is no
   (B)
   person who can be held responsible for one's
          (C)
   sad fate except themself. No error.
                      (D)        (E)

2. I get along reasonably good with my parents,
                          (A)
   but I know that when you have somebody who
                        (B)
   loves you and honestly supports everything you

   do, it makes you all the more happy.  No error.
   (C)              (D)                  (E)

3. From the students' point of view, the new rules
                 (A)
   regarding class attendance were more  stricter
   (B)                              (C)
   than the old ones. No error.
              (D)     (E)

4. The speaker won applause by emphasizing the
                            (A)
   point that a woman must not be held back by
                            (B)
   custom and tradition and by the preference of

   male politicians when they make the difficult
                        (C)
   decision whether to run for high public office.
            (D)
   No error.
   (E)

5. When <u>one</u> works as a census taker, you become
        (A)

    an <u>employee</u> of the United States government,
        (B)

    but you don't get the health and other benefits

    that others <u>do</u> because you have the status of
        (C)

    <u>only</u> a temporary employee. <u>No error</u>.
    (D)                              (E)

6.  <u>At</u> the prearranged signal from
    (A)
    <u>Andy, the chief editor of the newspaper,</u> all the
                    (B)
    members of the the staff <u>raised up</u> from <u>their</u>
                              (C)           (D)
    chairs and silently filed out of the meeting room.

    <u>No error</u>.
      (E)

7.  <u>To grasp</u> the enormity of the crime <u>that</u>
       (A)                                    (B)
    <u>has been</u> committed against nature, imagine
      (C)
    every square inch of the Taj Mahal or

    St. Peter's Square covered <u>with</u> spray paint and
                                (D)
    graffiti.  <u>No error</u>.
               (E)

8.  Don had <u>little or no</u> interest <u>in</u> <u>listening</u> to
              (A)                      (B)
    another lecture <u>on</u> tobacco, drug, and alcohol
                    (C)
    <u>abuse, therefore,</u> he declined to participate in
      (D)
    the conference. <u>No error</u>.
                      (E)

9.  <u>A person's behavior</u> can be <u>effected</u> by outside
       (A)                          (B)
    influences, but it is a fallacy <u>to believe</u> that
                                     (C)
    <u>in the long run</u> there will always be someone to
      (D)
    blame for personal misfortune. <u>No error</u>.
                                      (E)

10. They <u>had had</u> the foundation of their house
          (A)
    sealed, but <u>that</u> proved no defense against the
                 (B)
    water that squeezed through the windowsills

    <u>and filled</u> the basement <u>to a depth</u> of four feet.
      (C)                        (D)
    <u>No error</u>.
      (E)

11. Once the vacation starts, I will <u>have</u> a chance
                                      (A)
    to prepare my art project <u>by</u> choosing the
                               (B)
    paintings, cutting some mats, and <u>to find</u> frames
                                        (C)
    of the right size for the pictures <u>to be hung</u>
                                         (D)
    in the exhibition. <u>No error</u>.
                         (E)

12. When the story <u>begins</u>, Don Benedetto, a young
                    (A)
    clergyman, is on his way home when he <u>met</u> a
                                            (B)
    pair of hoodlums <u>who</u> threaten to harm him
                      (C)
    physically if he allows the imminent marriage

    of Renzo and Lucia <u>to take place</u>. <u>No error</u>.
                         (D)             (E)

13. It turned into an adventure of a lifetime, a

    sometimes <u>dangerous but never tedious</u> three-
                        (A)
    week trip, <u>during</u>  <u>which</u> we spent virtually
                 (B)        (C)
    every hour <u>of it</u>  together. <u>No error</u>.
                 (D)                   (E)

14. Prior to her exposing the scandal, an attitude
    (A)   (B)
    of cockiness and carelessness were widespread
                                  (C)
    throughout the industry, and safety rules were

    hardly taken seriously.  No error.
                 (D)          (E)

15. While visiting my family in Italy last summer,

    I saw that following traditional family values
                 (A)
    have become one of the distinct differences
    (B)
    between the members of the older generation
    (C)
    and me. No error.
        (D)     (E)

16. Because of a dog's more lively disposition and
                         (A)
    aggressiveness, animal trainers prefer dogs

    over cats as subjects to work  with. No error.
    (B)                  (C)   (D)      (E)

17. To be a real cowboy takes particular qualities of
                        (A)
    endurance and tolerance for discomfort , and I
                                            (B)
    believe that Dan would have failed miserably

    in an attempt to become like them. No error.
    (C)                            (D)      (E)

18. The scandal reveals that elected officials,

    who are chosen to represent us citizens,
                               (A)
    when granted political power, feel nothing but
    (B)                          (C)
    disdain of the common people. No error.
          (D)                      (E)

19. Bartleby was a copying clerk in the office of a

    counselor-at-law, and it was all he intended to
                        (A)
    do, regardless of the effort by his employer to
        (B)                     (C)
    alter Bartleby's assignment. No error.
    (D)                          (E)

20. Neither of the candidates are yet to take a
                            (A)     (B)
    position on what to do about racial strife in the

    inner city, even though the issue is foremost in
                                         (C)
    the voters' minds. No error.
        (D)            (E)

21. By the end of the month the contractors,

    much to the owner's surprise, had already laid
    (A)      (B)                        (C)
    out the site, cleared the land, and began to dig
                                       (D)
    the excavation. No error.
                    (E)

22. There isn't any justification for you becoming
                                   (A)
    so angry with Jason and him that you can hardly
                          (B)              (C)
    deal rationally with the problem of their lost
         (D)
    passports. No error.
               (E)

23. If she only had done like I told her, what should
                 (A)      (B)
    have been an ordinary day at school would not

    have turned into a regrettable dilemma that will
                       (C)
    remain unsolved for a long time. No error.
           (D)                       (E)

24. When my five-year-old brother put a frog in
    (A)
my grandfather's bed, he only acted
           (B) (C)
surprised and laughed at the little fellow's
        (D)
impish nature. No error.
        (E)

25. Reading about the chemistry of the sun in
        (A)
Knox's book will provide her with information
            (B)
similar to that which she would have heard if
        (C)
she would have attended the physics class on
     (D)
Tuesday. No error.
      (E)

26. The garage attendant yelled that he does not
             (A)     (B)
want me to park too close to the black

Mercedes, a car I later found out
           (C)
had been stolen in Riverdale. No error.
  (D)          (E)

27. The false alarm had frightened everyone in the
           (A)
condo, and she more than the other residents
       (B)
who lived there, since she had once been living
  (C)       (D)
in a building that was destroyed by fire. No error.
                (E)

28. It's not the end result of the trial that may
  (A)     (B)
forever damage a defendant's reputation; it's
           (C)
the fact that he went to trial in the first place that
        (D)
could cause him irrevocable harm. No error.
             (E)

29. Ever since the beginning of the year, the
  (A)
shelter, like the cardboard shack the homeless
    (B)
man had been forced nightly to sleep in,
        (C)
has been rather cold comfort for him. No error.
  (D)            (E)

30. During the war in Vietnam, American troops

observed that the local mountain tribesman made
  (A)   (B)
an excellent soldier—loyal, and always ready
             (C)
and willing to die for their cause. No error.
      (D)    (E)

**DON'T STOP.   PLEASE CONTINUE WITH THE NEXT QUESTIONS.**

## SENTENCE CORRECTION

INSTRUCTIONS: The underlined sections of the sentences below may contain errors in standard English, including awkward or ambiguous expression, poor word choice (diction), incorrect sentence structure, or faulty grammar, usage, and punctuation. In some items, the entire sentence may be underlined. Read each sentence carefully and identify which of the five alternative versions most effectively and correctly expresses the meaning of the original. Indicate your choice by filling in the corresponding space on your answer sheet. Choice (A) always repeats the original. Choose (A) if none of the other choices improves the original sentence.

SAMPLE QUESTION

Karen told her mother that the car
had been scratched in the parking lot.

(A) the car had been scratched
(B) Karen's mother's car was being scratched
(C) her car was now scratched
(D) Karen's car is now scratched
(E) the car has been scratched

SAMPLE ANSWER

Ⓐ  Ⓑ  Ⓒ  Ⓓ  Ⓔ

31. Public transportation in the suburbs and outlying areas is generally not as convenient and reliable as it is in the city.

(A) as it is
(B) as they are
(C) as those
(D) as buses
(E) since it's

32. While passing the fire department building, the siren began to screech loud, which scared me.

(A) the siren began to screech loud, which scared me
(B) the siren began screeching loudly, which scared me
(C) the screech of the loud siren scared me
(D) I was scared by the loud screech of the siren.
(E) I heard the siren screech loudly and scare me

33. The public is welcome to visit the cemetery where famous and well-known composers, artists, and writers are buried every day except Thursday.

(A) The public is welcome to visit the cemetery where famous and well-known composers, artists, and writers are buried every day except Thursday.
(B) The cemetery where the public, every day except Thursday, famous composers, artists, and writers are buried, is open.
(C) Every day except Thursday the public is welcome to visit the cemetery where well-known composers, artists, and writers are buried.
(D) The public is welcome to visit the cemetery every day except Thursday where famous composers, artists, and writers are buried.
(E) The cemetery where famous and well-known composers, artists, and writers are buried welcomes the public every day except Thursday.

34. <u>My grandfather was the kind of a man that worked</u> long hours for the welfare of his family and the benefit of the community.

    (A) My grandfather was the kind of a man that worked
    (B) My grandfather, the kind of a man that worked
    (C) My grandfather was the kind of man who works
    (D) My grandfather was a man, the type of which works
    (E) My grandfather was the sort of a man that would work

35. <u>You challenging the authority of the administration has brung</u> about a change in policy.

    (A) You challenging the authority of the administration has brung
    (B) Your challenging the authority of the administration has brought
    (C) Your challenge of the authority of the administration has brung
    (D) By your challenging the authority of the administration has brought
    (E) The challenge by you to the administration's authority has brought

36. The principal interrupted classes this morning to announce that Casey McDermott <u>was in an accident yesterday and was needing</u> blood donations this afternoon.

    (A) was in an accident yesterday and was needing
    (B) was in an accident yesterday and is needing
    (C) was in an accident yesterday and needs
    (D) having been in an accident yesterday and needing
    (E) had been involved in an accident yesterday and he will have a need for

37. The senator cared about neither what happened to his constituency, <u>nor how tax money was spent and keeping appointments</u> that he thought were unimportant.

    (A) nor how tax money was spent and keeping appointments
    (B) nor how tax money was spent, nor the keeping of appointments
    (C) nor how tax money was spent, nor the need for keeping appointments
    (D) and how tax money was spent, nor keeping appointments
    (E) nor how tax money was spent; nor did he care about keeping appointments

38. Constantly encountering resistance from surrounding material, <u>variations in the speed of underground water flows</u> from a fraction of an inch to a few feet per day.

    (A) variations in the speed of underground water flows
    (B) underground water varies in its flowing distance
    (C) the speed of underground water varies
    (D) underground water has flown
    (E) the flow of underground water varies

39. In the Pacific Northwest, <u>waste products from cutting lumber, such as wood chips and sawdust, are one of the ingredients</u> of waferboard panels used in residential construction instead of plywood.

    (A) waste products from cutting lumber, such as wood chips and sawdust, are one of the ingredients
    (B) waste products from cutting lumber, such as wood chips and sawdust, is one of the ingredients
    (C) wood chips and sawdust, waste products from cutting lumber, makes one of the ingredients
    (D) lumber-cutting waste products like wood chips and sawdust is used as an ingredient
    (E) the waste from cutting lumber as wood chips and sawdust, for example, is an ingredient

40. <u>Melody is the most directly appealing element in pieces of music and are what we sing and hum and whistle.</u>

    (A) Melody is the most directly appealing element in pieces of music and are what we sing and hum and whistle.

(B) Melody is the most directly appealing element in a piece of music, this explains why we sing and hum and whistle it.

(C) Melody, as the most directly appealing element in a piece of music, but it is what we sing and hum and whistle.

(D) Melody, being both the part we sing and hum and whistle, and the most directly appealing element in a piece of music.

(E) Melody, the part we sing and hum and whistle, is the most directly appealing element in a piece of music.

41. Although the novel is not lengthy, it contains several subplots <u>as well as a daring and irresistible heroine which weakens the story</u>.

(A) as well as a daring and irresistible heroine which weakens the story

(B) which weakens the story, as well as a daring and irresistible heroine

(C) which weaken the story, who's heroine is daring and irresistible

(D) which weaken the story. It also has a daring and irresistible heroine.

(E) which not only include a daring and irresistible heroine but also weaken the story

42. If anyone wishes to research the techniques of transcendental meditation, <u>which is when a person completely relaxes their mind and body, they</u> will find several relevant books on the shelf.

(A) which is when a person completely relaxes their mind and body, they

(B) which is when a person completely relaxes his mind and body, he

(C) which is when someone completely relax their minds and bodies, they

(D) the complete relaxation of the mind and body, he

(E) which completely relaxes your mind and body, you

43. Even if nursing homes follow state regulations to the letter of the law, <u>it doesn't guarantee an efficient, cordial, well-trained staff and atmosphere on hand</u>.

(A) it doesn't guarantee an efficient, cordial, well-trained staff and atmosphere on hand

(B) it doesn't guarantee neither an efficient, well-trained staff nor a cordial atmosphere on hand

(C) they don't guarantee either the efficiency and good training of its staff nor the cordiality of its atmosphere

(D) there's no guarantees of an efficient, well-trained staff and cordial atmosphere

(E) they can't guarantee an efficient, well-trained staff and a cordial atmosphere

44. Since some expansion of government is inevitable, governors often convince themselves that extending their powers, <u>even if not having the desire</u>, is justifiable.

(A) even if not having the desire

(B) without it being something to desire

(C) although it not being a desirable action

(D) although their desire can be contrary to it

(E) while undesirable

45. Women in a hunter-gatherer society had to spend much of their time collecting plant <u>food, while carrying her baby with her she also had to be ready to run or otherwise protect herself from</u> wild animals.

(A) food, while carrying her baby with her she also had to be ready to run or otherwise protect herself from

(B) food, while carrying her baby with her; she also had to be ready to run or otherwise protect herself from

(C) food, while carrying their babies with them; they also had to be ready to run or otherwise protect theirselves from

(D) food while carrying their babies with them; they also had to be ready to run or otherwise protect themselves from

(E) food; while carrying their babies with them; they also had to be ready to run or otherwise protect themselves from

46. Therefore, I tip my hat to anyone who speaks up for democratic principles, <u>even if it's for their own personal gain</u>.

    (A) even if it's for their own personal gain
    (B) even if his motive is personal gain
    (C) even if the motive is to be for his own personal gain
    (D) whether or not it's for their own personal gain
    (E) whether the motive is for their own personal gain or not

47. Although young children have higher metabolic rates than adults, <u>there is hardly no data that shows human infants surviving longer in severe cold compared to adults</u>.

    (A) there is hardly no data that shows human infants surviving longer in severe cold compared to adults
    (B) there is hardly no data showing human infants surviving longer than adults in severe cold
    (C) data hardly exists to show human infants surviving longer in severe cold compared to adults

    (D) there is hardly any data that shows human infants surviving longer in severe cold in comparison to adults
    (E) there are hardly any data that show human infants surviving longer than adults in severe cold

48. <u>Should a college application essay be required</u>, one should probably set aside a large block of time and avoid doing it at the last minute.

    (A) Should a college application essay be required
    (B) Should you need to write a college application essay
    (C) If you need to write a college application essay
    (D) In an event that one needs to write a college application essay
    (E) If a college application essay is necessary for anyone to write

**DON'T STOP.    PLEASE CONTINUE WITH THE NEXT QUESTIONS.**

# REVISION-IN-CONTEXT

INSTRUCTIONS:  The passages below are the unedited draft of two students' essays. Some of each essay needs to be rewritten to make the meaning clearer and more precise. Read the essays carefully.

Each essay is followed by six questions about changes that might improve all or part of its organization, development, sentence structure, use of language, appropriateness to the audience, or its use of standard written English. Choose the answer that most clearly and effectively expresses the student's intended meaning. Indicate your choice by filling in the corresponding space on the answer sheet.

## ESSAY A

*[1] For two hundred years United States citizens have taken for granted their right to life, liberty, and the pursuit of happiness. [2] From the experiences in the former Yugoslavia to the repressive regime in the People's Republic of China, Americans should know, however, that human rights are always in danger.*

*[3] During the period of the conquistadores and Spanish colonial rule of Latin America, for example. [4] Latin American natives were often violated and repressed by European settlers, an example of this is the fact that the land formerly owned by the native Latin Americans was taken away from them so the people lost the right to own land. [5] Secondly, the Latin American people were forced to work this land as slaves on their own land. [6] These human rights violations were overcome by the independence movements led by such freedom fighters as Bolivar and San Martin in the late 1800s.*

*[7] In the Soviet Union, the extremely repressive Stalinist regime after WW II violated the rights of the Russian peasants, known as kulaks. [8] Collectivizing their farmlands by force, their rights were violated by Stalin. [9] Therefore, their private possessions were lost. [10] Another way by which they had their human rights violated was by forcing political opponents to remain silent, to work in labor camps, or to be killed. [11] After Stalin's death in 1953, one of his successors, Nikita Khruschev, attempted to denounce the Stalinis regime. [12] However, it took another thirty years and the collapse of the Soviet Union to bring about basic human rights in Russia.*

*[13] About the history of human rights violations, the Serbs in the former Yugoslavia and the leaders of Communist China should know that they can't go on forever. [14] Eventually, their power will be usurped, or the people will rise up to claim their God-given human rights.*

49. Taking into account the sentences which precede and follow sentence 3, which of the following is the best revision of sentence 3?

    (A) As an example, the time that the Spanish were expanding their empire and searching for gold.
    (B) Take, for example, during the era of the conquistadores and Spanish colonial rule in Latin America.
    (C) Consider, for example, the period of the conquistadores and Spanish colonial rule in Latin America.
    (D) The Spanish expanded their empire into Latin America in the 16th century.
    (E) For instance, the period of Spanish colonialism in Latin America, for example.

50. Which of the following is the best revision of sentence 4?

    (A) The land of Latin American natives was confiscated by European settlers. In fact, the rights of the natives to own land was violated and repressed.
    (B) European settlers in Latin America have seized the land and the natives had repressed the right to own property.
    (C) The colonial rulers confiscated the natives' property and denied them the right to own land.

(D) Having their rights violated, the natives of Latin America had their land taken away. Then the European settlers repress their right to own any land at all.

(E) The rights of the Latin American natives were violated and repressed. For example, they took their land and they prohibited them from owning land.

51. In the context of paragraph 3, which is the best revision of sentences 8 and 9?

(A) Forcing them to collectivize their farmlands, Stalin confiscated their private property.

(B) One of the ways by which Stalin violated their rights was by forcing people to collectivize their farmlands, thus, causing them to lose their right to hold private possessions.

(C) One way in which the kulaks had their rights violated was Stalin forcing them to collectivize their farmlands and therefore, surrender private property.

(D) Having lost the right to own private property, Stalin collectivized the kulaks' farmland.

(E) The loss of private property and the collectivization of farmland was one way by which Stalin violated their rights.

52. Which of the following is the best revision of the underlined segment of sentence 10 below?

*Another way by which they had their human rights violated was by forcing political opponents to remain silent, to work in labor camps, or to be killed.*

(A) A second method at which political opponents had their human rights violated was

(B) Stalin also violated the human rights of political opponents

(C) Stalin also violated human rights

(D) Stalin's violation of the human rights of political opponents was

(E) Political opponents' human rights were also violated by Stalin

53. Considering the content of the entire essay, which revision of the underlined segment of sentence 13 below, provides the best transition between paragraphs 3 and 4?

*About the history of human rights violations, the Serbs in the former Yugoslavia and the leaders of Communist China should know that they can't go on forever.*

(A) In conclusion,

(B) Finally,

(C) Last but not least,

(D) Based on the history of international agreements on human rights,

(E) If the experience of Latin America and the Soviet Union means anything,

54. Based on the essay as a whole, which of the following describes the writer's intention in the last paragraph?

(A) To draw a conclusion based on the evidence in the passage

(B) To prepare readers for the future

(C) To instruct readers about the past

(D) To offer solutions to the problem posed by the essay

(E) To give an example

## ESSAY B

*[1] Teenagers under eighteen can now receive a major credit card as long as the credit card's use is supervised by a parent or guardian. [2] This is a good idea since it gives these teenagers the responsibility of managing their money. [3] Another is because teenagers can develop good habits of spending that will be useful later in life.*

*[4] A teenager can legally hold a job at age sixteen. [5] This means that many teenagers have a steady income, which they should be able to spend as they wish. [6] Being in control of their own finances not only teaches them the value of money but how to spend it wisely.*

*[7] An example of a teenager with a credit card is Bonita Robbins. [8] Bonita is junior in high school. [9] She is seventeen years old. [10] She works after school in a real estate office. [11] She earns about $100 a week. [12] After three months of work she applied for a credit card. [13] Her bank gave her one but said that there will be a "trial period" in which her parent will be responsible. [14] Most of the time Bonita paid her bills punctually and on time. [15] However, during one month Bonita charged more*

*charged more than she could pay, so her parents loaned her the money. [16] The next month Bonita saved her income and paid it back. [17] This was a good lesson for Bonita, because next time she'll probably be more careful about spending money.*

*[18] This plan also lets the parents and the teenagers plan how the credit card will be used. [19] Teenagers might use the card freely to buy things for less than $25. [20] For items costing more, talk to your parents before buying them. [21] Parents could help their teenager to plan a budget or set priorities for spending money. [22] Since parents are going to assume responsibility for the card's use or abuse, they will want to have some input on how it will be used.*

55. Which is the best revision of the underlined segment of sentence 3 below?

    *Another is because teenagers can develop good habits of spending that will be useful later in life.*

    (A) reason is because teenagers develop
    (B) reason is that teenagers may develop
    (C) idea is due to the fact that teenagers may develop
    (D) may come about due to teenagers' developing
    (E) idea may be because teenagers develop

56. Given the context of paragraph 3, which revision of sentences 8, 9, 10, and 11 is the most effective?

    (A) Bonita, a junior in high school, earning about $100 a week by working after school in a real estate office, is seventeen years old.
    (B) As a junior in high school and being seventeen, she works after school in a real estate office, earns about $100 a week.
    (C) A seventeen-year old high school junior, she earns $100 a week at an after-school job in a real estate office.
    (D) Bonita Robbins earns about $100 a week, being employed after school in a real estate office; she is seventeen and is a high school junior.
    (E) Being a junior in high school, Bonita, seventeen years old, earning about $100 a week in a real estate office at an after-school job.

57. Which of the following is the best revision of sentence 14?

    (A) Bills were paid punctually.
    (B) Usually Bonita had paid her bills on time.
    (C) Most of the time the bills were paid by Bonita on time.
    (D) Usually Bonita paid her bills punctually and on time.
    (E) Usually Bonita paid her bills when they were due.

58. With regard to the whole essay, which of the following best describes the function of paragraph 3?

    (A) To summarize the discussion presented in earlier paragraphs
    (B) To persuade readers to change their point of view
    (C) To provide an example
    (D) To ridicule an idea presented earlier in the essay
    (E) To draw a conclusion

59. Which revision of the underlined segment of sentence 18 below provides the best transition between the third and fourth paragraphs?

    *This plan also lets the parents and the teenagers plan how the credit card will be used.*

    (A) Another advantage to this plan is that it
    (B) Another advantage of a "trial" credit card program like Bonita's is that it
    (C) A different advantage to Bonita's experience
    (D) All of a sudden, it
    (E) Together, it

60. In the context of the fourth paragraph, which is the best revision of sentence 20?

    (A) Before buying items worth more, teenagers might consult a parent.
    (B) Teenagers should be talking to their parents before buying something that costs more than $25.
    (C) But first talking about things costing more than $25 between parents and teenagers.
    (D) First teenagers and parents must talk before buying something that costs more than $25.
    (E) Buying something that costs more than $25 to purchase must be talked over between parents and teenagers beforehand.

**PLEASE STOP WORK.   USE WHATEVER TIME IS LEFT BEFORE THE 40-MINUTE TEST PERIOD EXPIRES TO CHECK YOUR ANSWERS.**

# ESSAY

## Time allowed: 20 minutes

INSTRUCTIONS: Plan and write an essay in response to the assigned topic. During the 20 minutes allowed, you should develop your thoughts clearly and effectively. A plain, natural style is probably best. Try to include specific evidence or examples to support your views.

The number of words is up to you, but quantity is far less important than quality. In general, however, a single paragraph may not give you the chance to develop your ideas sufficiently. You must limit your essay to the answer sheet. Please be advised, therefore, to write on every line, keep narrow margins, and write compactly enough to fit your essay in the space allowed. Try to write as legibly as you can.

BE SURE TO WRITE ONLY ON THE ASSIGNED TOPIC. AN ESSAY WRITTEN ON ANOTHER TOPIC WILL RECEIVE NO CREDIT.

---

The Russian poet Alexander Pushkin once wrote that "the most lasting social changes are those that result from gradual improvements rather than from violent upheaval."

Do you believe that Pushkin's observation is valid? Write an essay in which you support or oppose Pushkin's view, using evidence drawn from your studies, reading, personal observation, or experience.

---

---

**This space is reserved for your personal bar code.**

---

## SAT II: WRITING
## ESSAY
**Time allowed: 20 minutes**

Topic:  **CHANGE**

FOR OFFICE USE

First reader _____

Second reader _____

Third reader (if needed) _____

The space below is for your essay. Please restrict your writing to the designated area.

_____

_____

_____

_____

_____

_____

_____

_____

_____

_____

_____

_____

_____

_____

_____

_____

Please continue your essay on the next page if you need more room.

# ANSWERS

| | | | | | |
|---|---|---|---|---|---|
| 1.  D | 11. C | 21. D | 31. A | 41. D | 51. A |
| 2.  A | 12. B | 22. A | 32. D | 42. D | 52. C |
| 3.  C | 13. D | 23. B | 33. C | 43. E | 53. E |
| 4.  C | 14. C | 24. B | 34. C | 44. E | 54. A |
| 5.  A | 15. B | 25. D | 35. B | 45. D | 55. B |
| 6.  C | 16. B | 26. B | 36. C | 46. B | 56. C |
| 7.  E | 17. D | 27. B | 37. E | 47. E | 57. E |
| 8.  D | 18. D | 28. B | 38. E | 48. A | 58. C |
| 9.  B | 19. A | 29. E | 39. A | 49. C | 59. B |
| 10. E | 20. A | 30. D | 40. E | 50. C | 60. A |

# PERFORMANCE EVALUATION CHART

## I.  Self-rating Chart

Usage, Questions 1–30                                          Number correct _____

Sentence Correction, Questions 31–48                 Number correct _____

Revision-in-Context, Questions 49–60               Number correct _____

Subtotal _____

*Penalty.* Subtract 1/4 point (.25) for each incorrect answer. _____

(No penalty for unanswered questions)

TOTAL SCORE _____

## II. Key to Self-rating

| | Usage | Sentence Correction | Revision-in-Context | Total |
|---|---|---|---|---|
| Excellent | 27–30 | 17–18 | 11–12 | 55–60 |
| Very good | 23–26 | 14–16 | 9–10 | 46–54 |
| Good | 19–22 | 11–13 | 7–8 | 37–45 |
| Fair | 15–18 | 9–10 | 5–6 | 29–36 |
| Poor | 10–14 | 6–8 | 3–4 | 19–28 |
| Very poor | 0–9 | 0–5 | 0–2 | 0–18 |

# ANSWERS EXPLAINED

## Usage

1. **D** Diction error. *Themself* is nonstandard usage. Use *themselves*, or if a singular pronoun is needed, use *himself*, *herself*, or, as in this case, *oneself*.

2. **A** Diction error. An adverb is needed to modify *get*. Use *well* (adverb) instead of *good* (adjective).

3. **C** Error in comparative degree. Don't use *more* with an adjective in the comparative degree. Delete *more*.

4. **C** Pronoun-antecedent agreement. The antecedent *woman* is singular; the pronoun *they* is plural. Use *she*.

5. **A** Pronoun shift. The sentence is cast in second person. Use *you work* instead of *one works*.

6. **C** Verb form. The past tense of *rise* is *rose*.

7. **E** No error.

8. **D** Comma splice. Two independent clauses should be separated by a semicolon or a period.

9. **B** Diction error. *Effect* is usually a noun. Use *affected*.

10. **E** No error.

11. **C** Faulty parallelism. Coordinate items in a series should be expressed in the same grammatical form. Use *finding*.

12. **B** Verb tense. The sentence is cast in the present tense. Use *meets* instead of *met*.

13. **D** Idiom error. The phrase *of it* is unnecessary. Delete it.

14. **C** Subject-verb agreement. *Attitude* is singular; *were* is plural. Use *was*.

15. **B** Subject-verb agreement. The subject *following* is singular; the verb *have* is plural. Use *has*.

16. **B** Idiom error. The standard usage is *prefer to*.

17. **D** Pronoun-antecedent agreement. The antecedent *cowboy* is singular; the pronoun *them* is plural. Use *one* in place of *them*.

18. **D** Idiom error. In standard usage the phrase is *disdain for*.

19. **A** Pronoun reference. The pronoun *it* does not refer to any specific noun or pronoun.

20. **A** Subject-verb agreement. The subject *neither* is singular; the verb *are* is plural. Use *is*.

21. **D** Faulty parallelism. The series of verbs should be in the past perfect tense. Use *begun* instead of *began*.

22. **A** Pronoun choice. A possessive pronoun precedes a gerund. Use *your*.

23. **B** Diction error. *Like* is a preposition and should not be used in place of a conjunction. Use *as*.

24. **B** Pronoun reference. The pronoun *he* refers to *brother* instead of to *grandfather*.

25. **D** Verb tense. Don't use *would have* in an *if* clause to express the earlier of two actions. Use the past perfect *had*.

26. **B** Verb tense. The sentence is cast in the past tense. Use *did* instead of *does*.

27. **B** Pronoun choice. Pronouns in the objective case are used to refer to persons who receive an action. In this sentence "action alarmed *her*."

28. **B** Idiom error. The phrase *end result* is redundant. Use *result*.

29. **E** No error.

30. **D** Pronoun-antecedent agreement. The antecedent *tribesman* is singular; the pronoun *their* is plural. Use *his* in place of *their*.

## Sentence Correction

**Note**: *Although many choices contain multiple errors, only one error is listed for each incorrect answer.*

31. **A** B. Subject-verb agreement. *Transportation* is singular; *are* is plural.
    C. Pronoun-antecedent agreement. *Those* is plural; *transportation* is singular.
    D. Faulty comparison. *Transportation* is being compared to *buses*, an illogical comparison.
    E. Incomplete comparison. What *transportation* is being compared to remains unclear.

32. **D**  A. Diction error. An adverb (*loudly*), not an adjective (*loud*), is needed to modify the verb *screech*.
    B. Dangling participle. The phrase that begins *While passing* should modify *I* (the speaker), not *siren*.
    C. Dangling participle. The phrase that begins *While passing* should modify *I* (the speaker), not *screech*.
    E. Clumsy construction. The clause *I heard . . . the siren scare me* is awkward.

33. **C**  A. Misplaced modifier. The phrase *every day except Thursday* modifies *buried* instead of *visit*.
    B. Clumsy construction. The grammatical subject *cemetery* is situated too far from the verb *is*.
    D. Misplaced modifier. The clause that begins *where famous composers* modifies *Thursday* instead of *cemetery*.
    E. Redundancy. *Famous and well-known* mean the same thing.

34. **C**  A. Idiom error. The standard idiom is *the kind of man*.
    B. Sentence fragment. The construction lacks an independent clause.
    D. Diction error. Avoid using *which* to refer to people. Use *who*.
    E. Idiom error. The standard phrase is *the sort of man*.

35. **B**  A. Pronoun choice. A possessive pronoun (*your*) should precede a gerund (*challenging*).
    C. Faulty verb form. *Brought*, not *brung*, is the past participle of the verb *to bring*.
    D. Sentence fragment. The verb *has brought* has no subject.
    E. Clumsy construction. The phrase that begins *by you* is awkward.

36. **C**  A. Faulty verb tense. The past progressive (*was needing*) does not accurately establish the time when the blood is needed.
    B. Faulty verb tense. Use the simple present tense to refer to a current situation.
    D. Sentence fragment. The clause that begins *that Casey* lacks a main verb. The *-ing* form of a verb (*having been* and *needing*) may not be used as the main verb without a helping verb, as in *is needing*.
    E. Wordy. The words *involved* and *he*, among others, are not needed.

37. **E**  A. Faulty parallelism. The phrase *keeping appointments* is not grammatically parallel to *how tax money was spent*.
    B. Clumsy construction. The phrase *the keeping of appointments* is awkward.
    C. Faulty parallelism. The phrase *for keeping appointments* is not grammatically parallel to *how tax money was spent*.
    D. Faulty parallelism. The phrase *nor keeping appointments* is not grammatically parallel to *about what happened*.

38. **E**  A. Dangling participle. The participial phrase that begins *encountering resistance* should modify *water* instead of *variations*.
    B. Clumsy construction. The phrase *varies in its flowing distance* is awkward.
    C. Dangling participle. The participial phrase that begins *encountering resistance* should modify *water* instead of *speed*.
    D. Faulty verb form. The verb *has flown* is a form of *to fly*, not *to flow*.

39. **A**  B. Subject-verb agreement. *Products* is plural; *is* is singular.
    C. Diction error. *Makes* is not a synonym for *is*.
    D. Subject-verb agreement. *Products* is plural; *is* is singular.
    E. Mixed construction. The construction that begins *as wood chips* has no grammatical or logical relation with the rest of the sentence.

40. **E**  A. Subject-verb agreement. *Melody* is singular; *are* is plural.
    B. Comma splice. A comma may not be used to separate two independent clauses.
    C. Faulty coordination. The clause that begins *but it is what* is not logically related to the earlier part of the sentence. The conjunction *but* is not appropriate.

D. Sentence fragment. The construction lacks a main verb. The *-ing* form of a verb (*being*) may not be used as the main verb without a helping verb, as in *is being*.

41. **D** A. Misplaced modifier. The clause that begins *which weakens the reader* modifies *heroine* instead of *subplots*.
B. Subject-verb agreement. *Subplots* is plural; *weakens* is singular.
C. Diction error. *Who's* is a contraction meaning *who is*. Use *whose*.
E. Faulty parallelism. The *not only . . . but also* construction implies a succession of grammatically parallel ideas. The phrase *irresistible heroine* is not grammatically parallel to *weaken the story*.

42. **D** A. Pronoun-antecedent agreement. *Anyone* is singular; *their* is plural.
B. Idiom error. In standard usage, nouns are defined by other nouns, not by clauses. Because *meditation* is a noun, *is when* is nonstandard.
C. Subject-verb agreement. *Someone* is singular; *relax* is plural.
E. Shift in pronoun person. Pronouns shift from third person (*anyone*) to second person (*you*).

43. **E** A. Faulty pronoun reference. The pronoun *it* lacks a specific referent.
B. Double negative. The phrase *doesn't guarantee neither* contains two negatives. Use *doesn't guarantee either* or *guarantees neither*.
C. Pronoun-antecedent agreement. *Its* is singular; *homes* is plural.
D. Subject-verb agreement. *Guarantees* is plural; *there's [there is]* is singular.

44. **E** A. Clumsy construction. Without a pronoun referring to *governors*, the construction is awkward.
B. Clumsy construction. See A.
C. Clumsy construction. See A.
D. Pronoun reference. The pronoun *it* does not refer to any specific noun or pronoun.

45. **D** A. Comma splice. A comma (between *food* and *while*) may not be used to separate two independent clauses.
B. Pronoun-antecedent agreement. *Women* is plural; *her* is singular.
C. Diction error. *Theirselves* is nonstandard. Use *themselves*.
E. Sentence fragment. The clause *while carrying their babies with them* lacks a main verb.

46. **B** A. Pronoun reference. The pronoun *it* lacks a specific referent.
C. Redundancy. The phrase *his own personal gain* is redundant. One's personal gain, by definition, must be for oneself. Omit *own*.
D. Pronoun-antecedent agreement. *Their* is plural; *anyone* is singular.
E. Pronoun-antecedent agreement. *Their* is plural; *anyone* is singular.

47. **E** A. Faulty comparison. Use *than* instead of *compared to* in comparisons.
B. Double negative. The phrase *hardly no* is nonstandard. Use *hardly any*.
C. Subject-verb agreement. *Data* is plural; *exists* is singular.
D. Faulty comparison. To complete the comparison use *than* instead of *in comparison to*.

48. **A** B. Shift in pronoun person. Because the sentence is cast in third person (*one*), the second person pronoun *you* should not be used.
C. Shift in pronoun person. Because the sentence is cast in third person (*one*), the second person pronoun *you* should be used.
D. Idiom error. The standard idiom is *in the event*.
E. Clumsy construction. The phrase *necessary for anyone to write* is awkward.

### *Revision-in-Context*

49. **C**  Choice A is a sentence fragment.

    Choice B violates standard English idiom. The phrase *for example* should be followed by a noun, not by a prepositional phrase.

    Choice C is a complete sentence and serves as an appropriate topic sentence for the second paragraph. It is the best answer.

    Choice D serves neither as a good transition from the first to the second paragraph, nor as an effective topic sentence for the second paragraph.

    Choice E is a sentence fragment; also the phrases *for instance* and *for example* are redundant.

50. **C**  Choice A contains an error in subject-verb agreement. The plural subject *rights* should have a plural verb, *were*.

    Choice B shifts verb tenses from present perfect (*have seized*) to past perfect (*had repressed*). Confusion ensues.

    Choice C succinctly and accurately revises the original sentence. It is the best answer.

    Choice D is a confusion of verb tenses, which renders the sentence almost incomprehensible.

    Choice E has a severe pronoun reference problem. It is unclear to whom the pronouns *they, their,* and *them* refer.

51. **A**  Choice A clearly and succinctly explains the fate of the kulaks. It is the best answer.

    Choice B is wordy and awkwardly expressed.

    Choice C is wordy and contains a usage error. Because *forcing* is a gerund, *Stalin* should be a possessive (*Stalin's*).

    Choice D contains a dangling participle. It says that Stalin lost his right to own private property, an idea contrary to what the writer intended.

    Choice E is not accurately expressed and contains an error in subject-verb agreement. The compound subject *loss and collectivization* requires a plural verb.

52. **C**  Choice A is wordy and repetitious. It also contains an error in idiom. The word *by* should be *in*.

    Choice B unnecessarily repeats the phrase *political opponents*.

    Choice C is succinctly and accurately expressed. It is the best answer.

    Choice D is awkward and, like B, repetitious.

    Choice E is in the passive voice and is awkwardly expressed.

53. **E**  Choices A, B, and C are trite and abrupt transitions. They should be avoided.

    Choice D is not a good answer because the essay does not discuss international agreements on human rights.

    Choice E accurately and smoothly provides a link between the content of the essay and the concluding paragraph. It is the best answer.

54. **A**  Only choice A accurately describes the function of the last paragraph. The conclusion—that people will eventually claim their rights—grows out of the discussion in paragraphs 1, 2, and 3. Therefore, choice A is the best answer.

55. **B**  Choice A contains the nonstandard usage *is because*.

    Choice B is correctly worded and concise. It is the best answer.

    Choices C, D, and E are wordy, awkward, or both.

56. **C**  Choice A subordinates the important information about Bonita (her job and earnings), and emphasizes the fact that Bonita is seventeen.

    Choice B lacks parallelism and is awkwardly worded.

    Choice C accurately and economically combines the sentences. It is the best answer.

Choice D fails to subordinate the less important information about Bonita.  It also unnecessarily repeats Bonita's full name.

Choice E lacks a main verb; therefore, it is a sentence fragment.

57. **E** Choice A contains too little information. Exactly who paid the bills remains unclear.

Choice B contains a verb in the past perfect tense, which is inconsistent with the rest of the essay.

Choice C is awkwardly written in passive voice.

Choice D contains a redundancy: *punctually* and *on time*.

Choice E is clear and accurate. It is the best answer.

58. **C** Only choice C is correct. The paragraph gives a specific example of a teenager with a credit card.

59. **B** Choice A is a reasonable transition except that the phrase *this plan* does not have a specific referent.

Choice B effectively links the two paragraphs by alluding specifically to material in previous paragraphs. It is the best answer.

Choice C is almost incomprehensible.

Choice D is inappropriate in the context.

Choice E fails to include an appropriate transitional word or phrase.

60. **A** Choice A is consistent in style, tone, and content with the previous sentence. It is the best choice.

Choice B is awkwardly expressed, and by using *should*, changes the passage from the indicative to the imperative mood.

Choice C is a sentence fragment.

Choice D is awkwardly worded. The imperative *must* is inconsistent with the rest of the paragraph.

Choice E is wordy and, like B and D, changes the mood of the passage from indicative to imperative.

# SELF-SCORING GUIDE FOR THE SAT II ESSAY

## PRACTICE TEST C

**Using this guide.** Rate yourself in each of the six categories on the left. Circle the item that most accurately describes your performance. Enter the numbers on the rating guide below. Then calculate the average of the six ratings to determine your total score. On the SAT II itself, two readers will rate your essay on a scale of 6 (high) to 1 (low). The score will be reported to you as the sum of the two ratings, from 12 (best) to 2 (worst).

Note that on the SAT II, essays are judged in relation to other essays written on the same topic. Therefore, this Self-Scoring Guide may not yield a totally accurate prediction of the score you can expect to earn on the actual exam. Because it is difficult to achieve objectivity when assessing your own writing, you may improve the validity of your score by having a trusted friend or teacher read your essay and rate it using this scoring guide.

Remove scoring guide by cutting on dotted line

| | 6 | 5 | 4 | 3 | 2 | 1 |
|---|---|---|---|---|---|---|
| **PURPOSE OF THE ESSAY** | Very clear and insightful; fresh and engaging | Quite clear and insightful; interesting | Fairly clear and with some insight; marginally interesting | Somewhat clear but some confusion, too; fairly dull | Largely unclear and confusing | Extremely confusing |
| **ORGANIZATION AND DEVELOPMENT** | Meticulously organized and thoroughly developed; coherent and unified | Well organized and sufficiently developed; basically coherent and unified | Reasonably organized and developed; mostly coherent and unified | Somewhat organized and developed; some incoherence and lack of unity | Little organization and meager development; mostly incoherent and void of unity | No apparent organization or development; incoherent and lacking unity |
| **USE OF SENTENCES** | Effectively varied and engaging; essentially error-free | Varied and interesting; one or two minor errors | Adequately varied and interesting; some errors | Somewhat varied and marginally interesting; one or more major errors | Little variation and basically dull; some major errors | Uniformly repetitious and dull; numerous major errors |
| **CHOICE OF WORDS** | Interesting, sensitive, and effective; basically error-free | Generally interesting, clear and effective; one or two inaccuracies | Occasionally interesting and effective; one or two errors in diction or idiom | Somewhat dull and ordinary; some errors in diction or idiom | mostly dull and conventional; several errors | Dull, immature; numerous errors in diction and idiom |
| **GRAMMAR AND USAGE** | Error-free | Occasional minor errors | Several minor errors | Some major errors | Frequent major errors | Severely flawed |
| **OVERALL IMPRESSION** | Demonstrates excellent skills and writing competence | Demonstrates good skills and competence | Demonstrates adequate skills and competence | Suggests fair skills and competence | Demonstrates poor skills and competence | Demonstrates lack of skill and competence |

For rating yourself

***Rating Guide***
Each category is rated 1 (low) to 6 (high)

Purpose of the Essay     _____
Organization and Development     _____
Use of Sentences     _____
Choice of Words     _____
Grammar and Usage     _____
Overall Impression     _____
TOTAL     _____
    Divide total by 6 to get final score: ☐

For a second opinion

***Rating Guide***
Each category is rated 1 (low) to 6 (high)

Purpose of the Essay     _____
Organization and Development     _____
Use of Sentences     _____
Choice of Words     _____
Grammar and Usage     _____
Overall Impression     _____
TOTAL     _____
    Divide total by 6 to get final score: ☐

# ANSWER SHEET FOR
# PRACTICE TEST D

## Usage

1. Ⓐ Ⓑ Ⓒ Ⓓ Ⓔ
2. Ⓐ Ⓑ Ⓒ Ⓓ Ⓔ
3. Ⓐ Ⓑ Ⓒ Ⓓ Ⓔ
4. Ⓐ Ⓑ Ⓒ Ⓓ Ⓔ
5. Ⓐ Ⓑ Ⓒ Ⓓ Ⓔ
6. Ⓐ Ⓑ Ⓒ Ⓓ Ⓔ
7. Ⓐ Ⓑ Ⓒ Ⓓ Ⓔ
8. Ⓐ Ⓑ Ⓒ Ⓓ Ⓔ
9. Ⓐ Ⓑ Ⓒ Ⓓ Ⓔ
10. Ⓐ Ⓑ Ⓒ Ⓓ Ⓔ
11. Ⓐ Ⓑ Ⓒ Ⓓ Ⓔ
12. Ⓐ Ⓑ Ⓒ Ⓓ Ⓔ
13. Ⓐ Ⓑ Ⓒ Ⓓ Ⓔ
14. Ⓐ Ⓑ Ⓒ Ⓓ Ⓔ
15. Ⓐ Ⓑ Ⓒ Ⓓ Ⓔ
16. Ⓐ Ⓑ Ⓒ Ⓓ Ⓔ
17. Ⓐ Ⓑ Ⓒ Ⓓ Ⓔ
18. Ⓐ Ⓑ Ⓒ Ⓓ Ⓔ
19. Ⓐ Ⓑ Ⓒ Ⓓ Ⓔ
20. Ⓐ Ⓑ Ⓒ Ⓓ Ⓔ
21. Ⓐ Ⓑ Ⓒ Ⓓ Ⓔ
22. Ⓐ Ⓑ Ⓒ Ⓓ Ⓔ
23. Ⓐ Ⓑ Ⓒ Ⓓ Ⓔ
24. Ⓐ Ⓑ Ⓒ Ⓓ Ⓔ
25. Ⓐ Ⓑ Ⓒ Ⓓ Ⓔ
26. Ⓐ Ⓑ Ⓒ Ⓓ Ⓔ
27. Ⓐ Ⓑ Ⓒ Ⓓ Ⓔ
28. Ⓐ Ⓑ Ⓒ Ⓓ Ⓔ
29. Ⓐ Ⓑ Ⓒ Ⓓ Ⓔ
30. Ⓐ Ⓑ Ⓒ Ⓓ Ⓔ

## Sentence Correction

31. Ⓐ Ⓑ Ⓒ Ⓓ Ⓔ
32. Ⓐ Ⓑ Ⓒ Ⓓ Ⓔ
33. Ⓐ Ⓑ Ⓒ Ⓓ Ⓔ
34. Ⓐ Ⓑ Ⓒ Ⓓ Ⓔ
35. Ⓐ Ⓑ Ⓒ Ⓓ Ⓔ
36. Ⓐ Ⓑ Ⓒ Ⓓ Ⓔ
37. Ⓐ Ⓑ Ⓒ Ⓓ Ⓔ
38. Ⓐ Ⓑ Ⓒ Ⓓ Ⓔ
39. Ⓐ Ⓑ Ⓒ Ⓓ Ⓔ
40. Ⓐ Ⓑ Ⓒ Ⓓ Ⓔ
41. Ⓐ Ⓑ Ⓒ Ⓓ Ⓔ
42. Ⓐ Ⓑ Ⓒ Ⓓ Ⓔ
43. Ⓐ Ⓑ Ⓒ Ⓓ Ⓔ
44. Ⓐ Ⓑ Ⓒ Ⓓ Ⓔ
45. Ⓐ Ⓑ Ⓒ Ⓓ Ⓔ
46. Ⓐ Ⓑ Ⓒ Ⓓ Ⓔ
47. Ⓐ Ⓑ Ⓒ Ⓓ Ⓔ
48. Ⓐ Ⓑ Ⓒ Ⓓ Ⓔ

## Revision-In-Context

49. Ⓐ Ⓑ Ⓒ Ⓓ Ⓔ
50. Ⓐ Ⓑ Ⓒ Ⓓ Ⓔ
51. Ⓐ Ⓑ Ⓒ Ⓓ Ⓔ
52. Ⓐ Ⓑ Ⓒ Ⓓ Ⓔ
53. Ⓐ Ⓑ Ⓒ Ⓓ Ⓔ
54. Ⓐ Ⓑ Ⓒ Ⓓ Ⓔ
55. Ⓐ Ⓑ Ⓒ Ⓓ Ⓔ
56. Ⓐ Ⓑ Ⓒ Ⓓ Ⓔ
57. Ⓐ Ⓑ Ⓒ Ⓓ Ⓔ
58. Ⓐ Ⓑ Ⓒ Ⓓ Ⓔ
59. Ⓐ Ⓑ Ⓒ Ⓓ Ⓔ
60. Ⓐ Ⓑ Ⓒ Ⓓ Ⓔ

# PRACTICE TEST D

## USAGE

INSTRUCTIONS: The underlined and lettered parts of each sentence below may contain an error in grammar, usage, word choice (diction), or expression (idiom). Read each sentence carefully, and identify the item that contains the error. Indicate your choice by filling in the corresponding space on your answer sheet. Only the underlined parts contain errors. Assume that the rest of each sentence is correct. No sentence contains more than one error. Some sentences may contain no error, in which case the correct choice is (E) (No error).

SAMPLE QUESTIONS

1. Jill ran speedily to the crest of the hill in
          (A)                (B)
   a more faster time than her teammate, Jack.
      (C)              (D)
   No error.
      (E)

2. Neither promise have been kept, regardless
      (A)            (B)                (C)
   of numerous opportunities to do so.
                                (D)
   No error.
      (E)

SAMPLE ANSWERS

1.  Ⓐ  Ⓑ  ●  Ⓓ  Ⓔ

2.  Ⓐ  ●  Ⓒ  Ⓓ  Ⓔ

---

1.  The achievements as well as the failures of the

    space program, has been  a matter of contention
                     (A)          (B)
    for many years, as interest groups of many kinds
                                            (C)
    compete  for a share of the federal budget.
             (D)
    No error.
      (E)

2.  Experts in marine life say that there is a closer
                                      (A)
    relationship between barracudas with man-
                                    (B)
    eating sharks than had been thought to exist
                         (C)          (D)
    before. No error.
            (E)

3.  The policeman would not have went into the
                                  (A)
    building had he known that he was going to be
             (B)                    (C)
    ambushed by Mugsy, Frankie, and him. No error.
                                    (D)      (E)

4.  Because Hannah was very close to her family,

    it was inconceivable to her, as she read about
    (A)                    (B)
    the Holocaust, to imagine what it must be like
                    (C)                  (D)
    for children to be severed forcibly from their

    parents. No error.
             (E)

5. As Kathy opened the refrigerator, she
   (A)
   immediately noticed that a huge chunk of

   chocolate icing had been bit off the birthday
                            (B) (C)
   cake and instantly suspected that Mark was
                                          (D)
   responsible. No error.
                (E)

6. Edith Wharton's novel *Ethan Frome* was made
                                          (A)
   into a movie that failed to capture the
                 (B)
   mood and meaning of her story. No error.
        (C)          (D)        (E)

7. One evening when Diana arrived at the center,

   Michelle told her that she had been astonished
                 (A)          (B)
   to learn from the secretary in the office that
    (C)
   she had been fired. No error.
   (D)              (E)

8. The book's main point is that a number of
                            (A)
   executive jobs are now thought to be unsuitable
                  (B)
   for women, or at least incompatible with her
                                          (C)
   other duties as mother or homemaker. No error.
              (D)                        (E)

9. Unfortunately, the old city of Mostar was
      (A)
   severely effected by the war that altered the
            (B)                (C)
   political and economic landscape of the former

   Yugoslavia for decades to come. No error.
                        (D)        (E)

10. The reasons for the Vietnam defeat included

    weak support on the home front, the

    unfamiliarity of American soldiers of guerilla
         (A)                          (B)
    warfare, and the problems of jungle fighting and

    not knowing who was friend and who was foe.
        (C)                      (D)
    No error.
       (E)

11. When they walked in the museum they took a
                       (A)
    sharp right, and went down the corridor until

    they found the door to the office that belongs
                                      (B)    (C)
    to Michael and him. No error.
        (D)            (E)

12. An incident that further embittered the colonists
                      (A)
    occurred in a Boston street when British troops

    fired on a mob of citizens, killing five and
     (B)                       (C)
    wounding six of them. No error.
                 (D)         (E)

13. On the Dallas Cowboys they have three players
                          (A)
    who grew up in Altoona, Pennsylvania, and

    graduated from its high school, although not at
        (B)       (C)    (D)
    the same time. No error.
                    (E)

14. The confrontation that took place between he
                                              (A)
    and his family during the dinner scene caused

    Tom to run away, but as his final speech
                        (B)
    suggests, he never was able to forget his
    (C)                  (D)
    mother and sister. No error.
                        (E)

15. How, one may ask, does one judge the morality

    of another's behavior if you don't even know
       (A)              (B)  (C)
    how to define or explain one's own, in spite of
                                        (D)
    ample opportunity to think about it. No error.
                                        (E)

16. The philosophy of communism is thought to    B
    have been born              (A)
    be born in Marx's writings and to have
    (B)
    resulted in one of the most widespread
    (C)
    economic and political upheavals that the world

    has seen. No error.
    (D)      (E)

17. Reflecting on the magnitude of the national
    (A)
    debt, one might well ask themselves
                  (B)      (C)
    how the most powerful nation on earth, the

    United States, could have gotten itself into such
                                (D)
    an impossible position. No error.
                            (E)   no pronoun
                                  reference

18. If you read the sports section of the paper, they
                    (A)                          (B)
    say that the Oakland A's, the team that has won
                            (C)
    the division title for four of the last five years,
                        (D)
    are likely to win again. No error.
                                (E)

19. The assignment included forming into groups of
                      (A)              (B)
    four, discussing the questions about the book,
                                    (C)
    choosing a format, and a presentation in front
                            (D)
    of the class. No error.
                    (E)

20. Of the hundreds of actors (and actresses!) who
    (A)
    have played Hamlet since Shakespeare wrote
                                          (B)
    the play, not one of them, I am sure, have done
                                          (C)
    as masterful a job as Mel Gibson. No error.
              (D)                    (E)

21. The earliest pirates in this hemisphere,

    who lived on West Indies islands, stole cattle,
    (A)
    smoked the meat and sold it to passing ships,
                            (B)
    attacked and burned colonial settlements, and

    were stealing gold and jewels from Spanish
    (C)                            (D)
    galleons. No error.
            (E)

22. Nechema's beauty and kindness, in addition to
                                  (A)
    her bravery during the two-year occupation of
                        (B)
    her town by an enemy battalion, is what appeal
                                  (C)
    to most readers about the young girl. No error.
    (D)                                  (E)

23. They had busy schedules, so finally they met
                              (A)
    after work and drove together to a meeting at

    the school, where Philip gave his talk on the use
    (B)                        (C)
    of computers in biomedical research. No error.
                  (D)                    (E)

24. Either rice or oats is the grain used as the
    (A)            (B)          (C)
    foundation of most natural breakfast cereals,

    although neither wheat nor bran lag far behind
                                        (D)
    in popularity. No error.
                   (E)

25. If the driver of the dump truck would have
                                   (A)
    checked his brakes before descending the steep

    hill, the vehicle might never have swerved from
                    (B)                          (C)
    the road, and the driver would not be lying in

    the hospital, as he is, with a cast on his leg.
                  (D)
    No error.
    (E)

26. The tickets that allowed three people free
               (A)
    admission to the concert were waiting at the

    box office half an hour prior to the start, just

    like Sarah had said they would be. No error.
    (B)         (C)        (D)       (E)

27. Beethoven's music, now loved throughout the
                         (A)
    world, aroused considerable controversy when

    it was first played, however, its power and
                    (B)
    nobility came to be widely accepted and even
             (C)
    praised before its composer died. No error.
                   (D)                  (E)

28. Regardless of her credentials, which were
    (A)
    indeed impressive and which included three

    years' experience as a cook, her skills in the
    (B)
    kitchen were fewer than a beginner. No error.
                  (C)          (D)        (E)

29. Interest in the marching band, in the orchestra,

    and in learning to play instruments, have
        (A)                                (B)
    doubled within the last half year. No error.
            (C)        (D)              (E)

30. Being lost in the mountains of Colorado for
    (A)
    two days as a boy, Dave was careful always
                            (B)
    to take a detailed map with him when he set out
    (C)                                (D)
    for a backpacking adventure in the wilderness.

    No error.
    (E)

**DON'T STOP.   PLEASE CONTINUE WITH THE NEXT QUESTIONS.**

# SENTENCE CORRECTION

INSTRUCTIONS: The underlined sections of the sentences below may contain errors in standard English, including awkward or ambiguous expression, poor word choice (diction), incorrect sentence structure, or faulty grammar, usage, and punctuation. In some items, the entire sentence may be underlined. Read each sentence carefully and identify which of the five alternative versions most effectively and correctly expresses the meaning of the original. Indicate your choice by filling in the corresponding space on your answer sheet. Choice (A) always repeats the original. Choose (A) if none of the other choices improves the original sentence.

SAMPLE QUESTION

My old Aunt Gertie loves to
 sew,  and cooking also.

SAMPLE ANSWER

(A)  sew, and cooking also
(B)  sew and to cook
(C)  sew, and to cook also
(D)  sew and cook besides.
(E)  sew and, in addition, cook.

31.  In this article it characterizes Mrs. Strauss as being brilliant, ruthless, and likely to resign soon.

(A) In this article it characterizes Mrs. Strauss as being brilliant, ruthless, and likely to resign soon.
(B) Mrs. Strauss, characterized in this article as being brilliant, ruthless, and likely to resign soon.
(C) In this article Mrs. Strauss is characterized as brilliant, ruthless, and she is likely to resign soon.
(D) This article, in which Mrs. Strauss is characterized as being brilliant, ruthless and likely to resign soon.
(E) This article characterizes Mrs. Strauss, who is likely to resign soon, as being brilliant and ruthless.

32.  The President said softly but with firmness that all citizens must contribute their fair share to the reduction of the national debt.

(A) softly but with firmness that all citizens must contribute their fair share
(B) softly but firmly that all citizens must contribute their fair share

(C) softly but firmly that all citizens must contribute his fair share
(D) softly but with firmness that all citizens must contribute his fair share
(E) softly but with firmness that all citizens must contribute a fair share

33. During February the amount of students absent from school with colds were incredibly high.

(A) the amount of students absent from school with colds were
(B) the amounts of students absent from school with colds were
(C) the number of students absent from school with colds was
(D) colds that kept the amount of students absent from school were
(E) absenteeism of students from colds was

34. It said on the news that they discovered the remains of a four-thousand-year-old man in the Alps.

(A) It said on the news that they discovered the remains of a four-thousand-year-old man in the Alps.
(B) They said on the news in the Alps that they

discovered the remains of a four-thousand-year-old man

(C) On the news it said that in the Alps they
discovered the remains of a four-thou-
sand-year old-man.

(D) During the news it said that the remains of
a four-thousand-year-old man was
discovered in the Alps.

(E) The news said that the remains of a
four-thousand-year-old man were
discovered in the Alps.

35. Mr. Winters claimed that it was the job of <u>us
peer counselors to be certain that everyone
who is a freshman were included</u> in the survey.

(A) us peer counselors to be certain that everyone who is a freshman were included

(B) us peer counselors, to assure that everyone
who is a freshman were included

(C) we peer counselors to ascertain that everyone who is a freshman were included

(D) us peer counselors to see that everyone
who is a freshman was included

(E) we peer counselors to be sure that no
freshmen were left out

36. <u>Addressing themselves to the improvement of
the arts program, the committee spent the first
two months of its tenure.</u>

(A) Addressing themselves to the improvement
of the arts program, the committee spent
the first two months of its tenure.

(B) Addressing itself to the improvement of
the arts program in the school, the
committee spent the first two months
of its tenure.

(C) The committee spent the first two months
of its tenure addressing the improvement of the arts program.

(D) During the first two months of their tenure,
improving the arts program was
discussed by the committee.

(E) The improvement of the arts program during the first two months of their tenure
was discussed by the committee.

37. Standing on the bridge of the ship, <u>there blew
the most strong winds</u> that I had seen for at
least a decade at sea.

(A) there blew the most strong winds

(B) there were the strongest winds

(C) the strongest winds were blowing

(D) I experienced the most strong winds

(E) I observed the strongest winds

38. <u>The bureau not only is charged with the responsibility of administering public lands, but</u>
inherited a monumental problem.

(A) The bureau not only is charged with the
responsibility of administering public
lands, but

(B) The bureau is not only charged with the
responsibility to administer public lands,
but also have

(C) The bureau is charged both with the
responsibility of administering public
lands, while it

(D) The bureau, both charged with the responsibility of administering public lands and

(E) The bureau, which is charged with the
responsibility of administering public
lands, has

39. <u>It saves the taxpayers billions of dollars since
there has been</u> no moon flights since the 1970s.

(A) It saves the taxpayers billions of dollars
since there has been

(B) To save taxpayers billions of dollars, there
have been

(C) Saving the taxpayers billions of dollars,
there has been

(D) The savings to taxpayers billions of dollars
there have been

(E) By saving the taxpayers billions of dollars,
there have been

40. It was in Istanbul that an Englishwoman, Florence Nightingale by name, set up headquarters <u>from which to conduct one of the most heroic and most brave</u> campaigns in the history of medicine.

   (A) from which to conduct one of the most heroic and most brave
   (B) in which to conduct one of the most heroic and bravest
   (C) where to conduct one of the bravest
   (D) where she would conduct one of the bravest
   (E) from which she would be conducting among the most heroic and brave

41. The story's underlying theme is <u>about seeking revenge after</u> the death of the king.

   (A) about seeking revenge after
   (B) about the seeking of revenge of
   (C) searching a revenge for
   (D) seeking vengeance over
   (E) the search for revenge after

42. <u>What helps soccer give my life meaning is</u> kicking the ball over the goalkeeper's hands for a score, hearing praise from the coach, and applause from the crowd.

   (A) What helps soccer give my life meaning is
   (B) What makes soccer give my life meaning by
   (C) Helping soccer give meaning to my life by
   (D) Being that soccer gives meaning to my life by my
   (E) Since soccer gives meaning to my life

43. When caffeine is added to food, as it often is to sodas and colas, <u>it has the exact same effect in</u> the human body as the caffeine found naturally in coffee and tea.

   (A) it has the exact same effect in
   (B) it has the same effect on
   (C) its effectiveness is the same to
   (D) the exact same effects take place in
   (E) it effects

44. The ferryboat had been a vessel of considerable <u>beauty, full of good woods and brass for most of her career it has carried passengers</u> between Brett Island and the mainland.

   (A) beauty, full of good woods and brass for most of her career it has carried passengers
   (B) beauty, full of good woods and brass. For most of its career it carried passengers
   (C) beauty, full of good woods and brass, for most of her career she carried passengers
   (D) beauty, full of good woods and brass; for most of its career it has carried passengers
   (E) beauty. Full of good woods and brass for most of its career; it carried passengers

45. At one time the city fathers had envisioned building a nuclear desalinization plant, <u>and financial woes make that an impossible dream</u>.

   (A) and financial woes make that an impossible dream
   (B) and that dream becomes impossible due to financial woes
   (C) but that dream had been made impossible by financial woes
   (D) but financial woes made that an impossible dream
   (E) however, the financial woes made the dream an impossible one

46. For instance, <u>the author, showing us the modern city of Astoria in the opening paragraphs by cleverly combining</u> the history of the Flavel family with the folklore of the Columbia River.

   (A) the author, showing us the modern city of Astoria in the opening paragraphs by cleverly combining
   (B) we are shown the modern city of Astoria in the opening paragraphs, and the author cleverly combines
   (C) the author shows us the modern city of Astoria in the opening paragraphs by cleverly combining

(D) the author, who shows us the modern city of Astoria in the opening paragraphs, and cleverly combines

(E) we are shown the modern city of Astoria in the opening paragraphs by the author, cleverly combined

47. One event in Richard's life story that moved me greatly was <u>when he was separated from his family</u>.

(A) when he was separated from his family
(B) when he and his family were separated
(C) his separation from his family
(D) the separating from his family
(E) the separation between he and his family

48. The White House Chief of Staff, in addition to the President's children and spouse, <u>are in a position to influence policy despite that they were not elected</u>.

(A) are in a position to influence policies despite that they were not elected
(B) hold a position to influence policy despite being unelected
(C) is in a position to influence policy, yet being unelected
(D) although not elected, may hold positions that influence policy
(E) although not elected, may influence policy

E

**DON'T STOP.   PLEASE CONTINUE WITH THE NEXT QUESTIONS.**

# REVISION-IN-CONTEXT

INSTRUCTIONS: The passages below are the unedited draft of two students' essays. Some of each essay needs to be rewritten to make the meaning clearer and more precise. Read the essays carefully.

Each essay is followed by six questions about changes that might improve all or part of its organization, development, sentence structure, use of language, appropriateness to the audience, or its use of standard written English. Choose the answer that most clearly and effectively expresses the student's intended meaning. Indicate your choice by filling in the corresponding space on the answer sheet.

## ESSAY A

*[1] It is difficult to deny that the world of music has changed greatly in the past thirty years. [2] The style, sound, technology, and lyrics of music have been altered greatly. [3] In the last three decades, several new categories of music have come into being.*

*[4] One reason why music has changed so greatly is that artists use music as a tool to publicize certain social messages. [5] Although many artists of the 1970s used this method as well, their issues were not as severe that banning their album was possible. [6] For example, one rap-singer, Ice-T, used his album to promote "cop-killing." [7] The idea was so offensive that many believed the album should be banned. [8] The controversy caused by Ice-T made the Arista record company refuse to continue production of the album.*

*[9] Another way in which music has changed is lyrics. [10] When you listen to certain heavy metal or rap groups, one may notice foul and obscene language used. [11] Some of the references to sex are shocking. [12] In past eras, such language in recorded music was unheard of.*

*[13] Technological changes in music have occurred. [14] With the advent of highly advanced musical devices and many digital effects, the sounds of music have been completely altered. [15] Rock and roll was invented in the early 1950s. [16] When you listen to heavy metal, you hear more distorted guitar sounds than in music of the 60s and 70s. [17] In the era of electronic instruments, the variety of possible sounds is incredible. [18] Present day sounds could never have been achieved in previous years because the technology was not at hand. [19] New music utilizes electronically produced sounds never heard before. [20] Computers generate everything from the human voice under water to the sound of whales. [21] There are no limits to what the music of the future will sound like.*

49. Which of the following is the best revision of the underlined segment of sentence 5 below?

    *Although many artists of the 1970s used this method as well, their issues were not as severe that banning their album was possible.*

    (A) the issues were less severe than those which caused banning their album to be possible
    (B) their issues were not as severe that their albums were in danger of being banned
    (C) they never raised issues that could have caused their albums to be banned
    (D) the issues they raised were not serious enough that banning their album was a possibility
    (E) they raised less serious issues and banning their albums was not likely

50. Taking into account the sentences which precede and follow sentence 10, which is the most effective revision of sentence 10?

    (A) Listening to certain heavy metal or rap groups, lyrics containing obscenities are often heard.
    (B) Obscene language is common in the songs of heavy metal and rap groups.
    (C) Certain heavy metal and rap groups use foul and obscene language.
    (D) Obscenities are often heard when one listens to the lyrics of certain heavy metal or rap groups.
    (E) Listening to obscene language and listening to the lyrics of certain heavy metal and rap groups.

51. In the context of the entire essay, which revision of sentence 13 provides the most effective transition between paragraphs 3 and 4?

    (A) Technological changes in music also have occurred.

    (B) Also, technology has changed musical sounds.

    (C) Noticeable changes in music's sounds have come about through technological changes.

    (D) Changes in musical technology has changed musical sound, too.

    (E) But the most noticeable change in music has been its sound.

52. In a revision of the entire essay, which of the following sentences most needs further development?

    (A) Sentence 3
    (B) Sentence 7
    (C) Sentence 8
    (D) Sentence 19
    (E) Sentence 20

53. Which of the following sentences should be deleted to improve the unity and coherence of paragraph 4?

    (A) Sentence 14
    (B) Sentence 15
    (C) Sentence 16
    (D) Sentence 17
    (E) Sentence 18

54. Taking into account the organization of the entire essay, which is the best revision of sentence 2 in the introductory paragraph?

    (A) In the past thirty years, not only the style, sound, and technology has changed, but the lyrics have, too.

    (B) Having undergone a change in the style, sound, technology, musical lyrics have altered also.

    (C) Changes in musical sound have occurred, while the technology and lyrics have tremendously altered the style of music.

    (D) Musicians have changed the purpose and the lyrics of music, and technology has changed its sound.

    (E) Along with changes in sound and technology, the lyrics of music have changed, too.

## ESSAY B

*[1] From the colonial times until today, the appeal of the underdog has retained a hold on Americans. [2] It is a familiar sight today to see someone rooting for the underdog while watching a sports event on television. [3] Though that only happens if they don't already have a favorite team. [4] Variations of the David and Goliath story are popular in both fact and fiction. [5] Horatio Alger stories, wondrous tales of conquering the West, and the way that people have turned rags-to-riches stories such as Vanderbilt into national myths are three examples of America's fascination with the underdog.*

*[6] This appeal has been spurred by American tradition as well as an understandably selfish desire to feel good about oneself and life. [7] Part of the aura America has held since its creation is that the humblest and poorest person can make it here in America. [8] That dream is ingrained in the history of America. [9] America is made up of immigrants. [10] Most were poor when they came here. [11] They thought of America as the land of opportunity, where any little guy could succeed. [12] All it took was the desire to lift oneself up and some good honest work. [13] Millions succeeded on account of the American belief to honor and support the underdog in all its efforts.*

*[14] The underdog goes against all odds and defeats the stronger opponent with hope. [15] It makes people feel that maybe one day they too will triumph against the odds. [16] It changes their view of life's struggles because they trust that in the end all their hardships will amount to something. [17] Despair has no place in a society where everyone knows that they can succeed. [18] It's no wonder that the underdog has always had a tight hold upon American hopes and minds.*

55. Which of the following is the best revision of the underlined sections of sentences 1 and 2 (below), so that the two sentences are combined into one?

    *From the colonial times until today, the appeal of the underdog has retained a hold on Americans. It is a familiar sight today to see someone rooting for the underdog while watching a sports event on television.*

    (A) the appeal of the underdog has retained a hold on Americans, and it is a familiar

sight today to see underdogs being the
one rooted for

(B) the appeal of the underdog has retained a
hold on Americans, but it is a familiar
sight today to see someone rooting for
the underdog

(C) the underdog has retained a hold on Americans, who commonly root for the underdog, for example,

(D) the underdog has retained a hold on Americans, commonly rooting for the underdog

(E) the underdog's appeal has retained a hold
on Americans, for example, they commonly root for the underdog

56. To improve the coherence of paragraph 1, which
of the following sentences should be deleted?

(A) Sentence 1
(B) Sentence 2
(C) Sentence 3
(D) Sentence 4
(E) Sentence 5

57. Considering the content of paragraph 2, which
of the following is the best revision of the paragraph's topic sentence, sentence 6 ?

(A) This appeal got spurred by American tradition as well as by an understandably selfish desire to feel good about oneself and
one's life.

(B) The appeal of the underdog has been
spurred by American tradition.

(C) The appeal has been spurred by Americans'
traditional and selfish desire to feel
good about themselves and life.

(D) American tradition as well as Americans' desire to feel good about oneself and their
life has spurred the appeal of underdogs.

(E) American traditions include an understandably selfish desire to feel good about themselves and the appeal of the underdog.

58. In the context of paragraph 2, which of the following is the best way to combine sentences 8,
9, 10, and 11?

(A) That dream is ingrained in the experience
of America, a country made up of poor
immigrants who believed that in this

land of opportunity any little guy had a
chance to succeed.

(B) That dream was ingrained in our history, a
country made up of immigrants, poor and
hopeful that any little guy is able to succeed in America, the land of opportunity.

(C) That dream has been ingrained America's history that poor immigrants look on America as a land of opportunity, which any little guy had been able to succeed in.

(D) The American experience has ingrained in it
the dream that by immigrants coming to
this country poorly could succeed because
America is the land of opportunity.

(E) Ingrained in the American experience is the
dream of poor immigrants that they
could succeed here, after all, this is the
land of opportunity.

59. Taking into account the sentences that precede
and follow sentence 13, which of the following
is the most effective revision of sentence 13?

(A) Americans believe that the underdog
should be honored and supported, which
led to their success.

(B) Because America believed in honoring and
supporting the underdog, they succeed.

(C) And succeed they did because of America's
commitment to honor and support the
underdog.

(D) Honoring and supporting underdogs is a
firmly held value in America, and it led
to the success of underdogs.

(E) They succeeded with their efforts to be supported and honored by America.

60. Which of the following revisions of sentence 14 is
the best transition between paragraphs 3 and 4?

(A) Underdogs, in addition, went against all odds
and with hope defeat stronger opponents.

(B) The underdog, feeling hopeful, going
against all odds, and defeating stronger
opponents.

(C) It is the hope of the underdog who goes
against the odds and defeats the stronger
opponent.

(D) The triumph of the underdog over a strong
opponent inspires hope.

(E) The underdog triumphs against all odds and
defeats the stronger opponents.

**PLEASE STOP WORK.   USE WHATEVER TIME IS LEFT BEFORE THE 40-MINUTE
TEST PERIOD EXPIRES TO CHECK YOUR ANSWERS.**

# ESSAY

## Time allowed: 20 minutes

INSTRUCTIONS: Plan and write an essay in response to the assigned topic. During the 20 minutes allowed, you should develop your thoughts clearly and effectively. A plain, natural style is probably best. Try to include specific evidence or examples to support your views.

The number of words is up to you, but quantity is far less important than quality. In general, however, a single paragraph may not give you the chance to develop your ideas sufficiently. You must limit your essay to the answer sheet. Please be advised, therefore, to write on every line, keep narrow margins, and write compactly enough to fit your essay in the space allowed. Try to write as legibly as you can.

BE SURE TO WRITE ONLY ON THE ASSIGNED TOPIC. AN ESSAY WRITTEN ON ANOTHER TOPIC WILL RECEIVE NO CREDIT.

---

*We thought that he was everything*
*To make us wish that we were in his place.*

These words from Edwin Arlington Robinson's famous poem ''Richard Cory'' describe what people often feel when they see others who apparently lead happier, richer, more content lives than they do.
The kind of envy to which Robinson refers may serve as a strong motivating force for some people to improve their condition and place in life. On the other hand, envy may also be a self-defeating and ultimately frustrating emotion because it may lead people to strive in vain for unattainable goals. In your view, is envy generally a positive or a negative force in people's lives? Please use evidence from your studies, your reading and your personal observation to support your opinion.

This space reserved for your personal bar code.

**SAT II: WRITING**
**ESSAY**
**Time allowed: 20 minutes**

FOR OFFICE USE

First reader _____

Second reader_____

Third reader (if needed) _____

Topic:  **ENVY**

The space below is for your essay. Please restrict your writing to the designated area.

_____

_____

_____

_____

_____

_____

_____

_____

_____

_____

_____

_____

_____

_____

_____

_____

_____

Please continue your essay on the next page if you need more room.

# ANSWERS

| | | | | | |
|---|---|---|---|---|---|
| 1. A | 11. A | 21. C | 31. E | 41. E | 51. E |
| 2. B | 12. E | 22. C | 32. B | 42. A | 52. A |
| 3. A | 13. A | 23. E | 33. C | 43. B | 53. B |
| 4. D | 14. A | 24. D | 34. E | 44. B | 54. D |
| 5. B | 15. C | 25. A | 35. D | 45. D | 55. C |
| 6. D | 16. B | 26. B | 36. C | 46. C | 56. C |
| 7. D | 17. C | 27. B | 37. E | 47. C | 57. B |
| 8. C | 18. B | 28. D | 38. E | 48. E | 58. A |
| 9. B | 19. D | 29. B | 39. B | 49. C | 59. C |
| 10. B | 20. C | 30. A | 40. D | 50. B | 60. D |

# PERFORMANCE EVALUATION CHART

## I. Self-rating Chart

Usage, Questions 1–30                                  Number correct _____
Sentence Correction, Questions 31–48          Number correct _____
Revision-in-Context, Questions 49–60          Number correct _____
                                                                              Subtotal _____

*Penalty.* Subtract 1/4 point (.25) for each incorrect answer. _____
(No penalty for unanswered questions)
TOTAL SCORE _____

## II. Key to Self-rating

| | Usage | Sentence Correction | Revision-in-Context | Total |
|---|---|---|---|---|
| Excellent | 27–30 | 17–18 | 11–12 | 55–60 |
| Very good | 23–26 | 14–16 | 9–10 | 46–54 |
| Good | 19–22 | 11–13 | 7–8 | 37–45 |
| Fair | 15–18 | 9–10 | 5–6 | 29–36 |
| Poor | 10–14 | 6–8 | 3–4 | 19–28 |
| Very poor | 0–9 | 0–5 | 0–2 | 0–18 |

# Answers Explained

## Usage

1.  **A** Subject-verb agreement. The subject *achievements* is plural; the verb *has* is singular. Use *have*.
2.  **B** Idiom error. Use *and* instead of *with*.
3.  **A** Verb form. The present perfect form of *to go* is *have gone*.
4.  **D** Verb tense.  Verbs in the present perfect refer to actions which occurred at no specific moment in the past and which may still be in progress. Use *have been*.
5.  **B** Verb form. The past perfect form of *to bite* is *bitten*. Use *had been bitten*.
6.  **D** Pronoun reference. The pronoun *her* may not refer to a possessive noun.
7.  **D** Pronoun reference. The pronoun *she* may refer to *Diana*, *Michelle*, or to the *secretary*. Use a specific noun in place of a pronoun.
8.  **C** Pronoun-antecedent agreement. The antecedent *women* is plural; the pronoun *her* is singular. Use *their*.
9.  **B** Diction error. Use *affected* in place of *effected*.
10. **B** Idiom error. The phrase *unfamiliarity . . . of* is nonstandard. Use *with guerilla warfare*.
11. **A** Diction error. *In* means ''within''; *into* refers to movement from outside to inside. Use *into*.
12. **E** No error.
13. **A** Pronoun reference. The pronoun *they* doesn't refer to any specific noun or pronoun.
14. **A** Pronoun choice. Pronouns in the objective case are used after prepositions. Use *him*.
15. **C** Pronoun shift. The sentence is cast in third person. Use *one doesn't* in place of *you don't*.
16. **B** Verb tense. Present perfect verbs refer to action occurring at no specific past time. Use *have been born*.
17. **C** Pronoun-antecedent agreement. The antecedent *one* is singular; the pronoun *themselves* is plural. Use *oneself*.
18. **B** Pronoun reference. The pronoun *they* does not refer to any specific noun or pronoun.
19. **D** Faulty parallelism. The phrase is not parallel in grammatical form to the other phrases in the series. Use *making a presentation*.
20. **C** Subject-verb agreement. The subject *one* is singular; the verb *have* is plural. Use *has*.
21. **C** Faulty parallelism.  Items in a series should be in grammatically parallel form.  Use *stole* in place of *were stealing*.
22. **C** Subject-verb agreement. Compound subjects need plural verbs. Use *are*.
23. **E** No error.
24. **D** Subject-verb agreement.  A compound subject consisting of singular nouns joined by *or* or *nor* gets a singular verb. Use *lags*.
25. **A** Verb form.  In an *if* clause, don't use *would have* to express the earlier of two actions.  Use the past perfect *had*.
26. **B** Diction error. *Like* is a preposition and is not an acceptable substitute for the conjunction *as*, to introduce subordinate clauses.
27. **B** Comma splice. Two independent clauses may not be joined by a comma. Use a semicolon or a period between *played* and *however*.
28. **D** Faulty comparison. It is illogical to compare *skills* and a *beginner*. Use *beginner's skills*.
29. **B** Subject-verb agreement. The subject *interest* is singular; the verb *have* is plural. Use *has*.
30. **A** Verb tense.  The participle *being* describes an action that occurs at the same time as the action in the main verb. Use *having been*.

## Sentence Correction

**Note**: *Although many choices contain multiple errors, only one error is listed for each incorrect answer.*

31. **E**  A. Faulty pronoun reference. The pronoun *it* has no specific referent.

    B.  Sentence fragment. The construction lacks a main verb.

    C.  Faulty coordination. The two coordinate clauses state seemingly unrelated information and contain ideas of unequal importance.

    D.  Sentence fragment. The construction lacks an independent clause.

32. **B** A.  Faulty parallelism. *Softly* is not parallel in form to *with firmness*. Use *firmly*.

       C.  Pronoun-antecedent agreement. *All* is plural; *his* is singular.

       D.  Faulty parallelism. *Softly* is not parallel in form to *with firmness*. Use *firmly*.

       E.  Faulty parallelism. *Softly* is not parallel in form to *with firmness*. Use *firmly*.

33. **C** A.  Subject-verb agreement. *Amount* is singular; *were* is plural.

       B.  Diction error.  Use *amount* for mass quantities and *number* for quantities that can be individually counted.

       D.  Clumsy construction.

       E.  Idiom error. The proper idiom is *students with colds*.

34. **E** A.  Faulty pronoun reference. The pronoun *they* lacks a specific referent.

       B.  Misplaced modifier. The phrase *in the Alps* modifies *news* instead of *discovered*.

       C.  Faulty pronoun reference. The pronouns *it* and *they* lack specific referents.

       D.  Subject-verb agreement. *Remains* is plural; *was* is singular.

35. **D** A.  Subject-verb agreement. *Everyone* is singular; *were* is plural.

       B.  Subject-verb agreement. *Everyone* is singular; *were* is plural.

       C.  Pronoun choice. Pronouns in the objective case follow prepositions. Use *us*, not *we*.

       E.  Pronoun choice. Pronouns in the objective case follow prepositions. Use *us*, not *we*.

36. **C** A.  Shift in pronoun number. *Themselves* is plural, *its* is singular.

       B.  Sentence fragment. The construction is incomplete.

       D.  Pronoun-antecedent agreement. *Their* is plural; *committee* is singular.

       E.  Misplaced modifier. The phrase *during the first two months* modifies *program* instead of *committee*.

37. **E** A.  Faulty comparison. The superlative form of *strong* is *strongest*.

       B.  Dangling participle. The phrase *standing on the bridge of the ship* should modify *I*.

       C.  Dangling participle. The participial phrase should modify *I* instead of *winds*.

       D.  Faulty comparison. The superlative form of *strong* is *strongest*.

38. **E** A.  Faulty parallelism. The phrase *not only is charged* lacks a grammatical parallel.

       B.  Subject-verb agreement. *Bureau* is singular; *have* is plural.

       C.  Mixed construction. The word *both* suggests two, but only one responsibility is given.

       D.  Faulty parallelism. The phrase *charged with the responsibility* lacks a grammatical parallel later in the sentence.

39. **B** A.  Subject-verb agreement. *Flights* is plural; *has been* is singular.

       C.  Dangling participle.  The phrase *saving the taxpayers billions of dollars* lacks a specific noun or pronoun to modify.

       D.  Mixed construction. The first part of the sentence is unrelated to the latter part.

       E.  Diction error. The sentence is illogical.

40. **D** A.  Redundancy. The phrases *most heroic* and *most brave* are redundant.

       B.  Redundancy. *Most heroic* and *bravest* are redundant.

       C.  Clumsy construction.

       E.  Wordy. The phrase *from which she would be conducting* may be trimmed to *where she would conduct*.

41. **E**  A.  Mixed construction.  Stories may be *about* revenge, but themes cannot.  The subject and verb, *theme is*, should be followed by a predicate noun, not by a prepositional phrase.
   B.  Idiom error. See A.
   C.  Idiom error. The correct idiom is *searching for revenge.*
   D.  Diction error. The correct idiom is *seeking vengeance for.*

42. **A**  B.  Sentence fragment. The construction lacks a main verb. The *-ing* form of a verb (*helping*) may not be used as the main verb without a helping verb, as in *was helping.*
   C.  Same as B.
   D.  Diction error. *Being that* is a nonstandard usage and is not the equivalent of *because, since,* or any other subordinating conjunction.
   E.  Sentence fragment. The construction lacks a main clause.

43. **B**  A.  Redundancy. The phrase *exact same* contains a redundancy.
   C.  Idiom error. The standard idiom is *its effectiveness is the same on.*
   D.  Wordy. The phrase *exact same* is redundant; *take place* could be trimmed to *occur.*
   E.  Diction error. *Affects* is a verb, *effects*, a noun (usually).

44. **B**  A.  Run-on sentence. Punctuation is needed between *brass* and *for* to separate the independent clauses.
   C.  Comma splice. A comma may not be used to separate two independent clauses.
   D.  Shift in verb tense. The sentence is cast in the past perfect tense. The verb *has carried* is in the present perfect.
   E.  Sentence fragment. The construction *Full . . .career* lacks a verb.

45. **D**  A.  Faulty coordination.  The conjunction *and* fails to convey a precise relationship between the two clauses.
   B.  Shift in verb tense. The sentence, cast in the past tense, shifts to the present.
   C.  Passive construction.
   E.  Comma splice.  A comma (between *plant* and *however*) may not be used to separate two independent clauses.

46. **C**  A.  Sentence fragment.  The construction lacks a main verb.  The *-ing* form of a verb (*showing, combining*) may not be used as the main verb without a helping verb, as in *was showing and were combining.*
   B.  Shift in grammatical subject. The subject shifts from *we* to *author*. Insofar as possible, the subject in clauses of a compound sentence should be maintained.
   D.  Sentence fragment. The construction lacks a main clause.
   E.  Misplaced modifier. The phrase *by the author* modifies *paragraphs* instead of *shown.*

47. **C**  A.  Idiom error.  *Event* is a noun that must be defined by another noun in a predicate nominative, not by a subordinate clause.
   B.  Idiom error. See A.
   D.  Clumsy construction.
   E.  Pronoun choice. *Between* is a preposition. Objective case pronouns follow prepositions. Use *him.*

48. **E**  A.  Clumsy construction. The phrase *the fact* should be inserted between *despite* and *that.*
   B.  Subject-verb agreement. *Chief of Staff* is singular; *hold* is plural. The intervening phrase beginning with *in addition to* does not change the number of the subject.
   C.  Faulty verb form. *Being* is not the equivalent verb of *is* or *are.*
   D.  Mixed construction. The use of *positions* (plural) suggests that the subject of the sentence is something other than *Chief of Staff* (singular).

*Revision-in-Context*

49. **C**  Choice A contains an awkwardly expressed clause that begins *which caused.*
Choice B contains a faulty comparison: *not as severe that.*
Choice C accurately revises the sentence. It is the best answer.
Choice D contains an awkwardly expressed clause that begins *that banning.*
Choice E contains faulty diction. The conjunction *and* is not an effective connecting word in the context.

50. **B**  Choice A contains a dangling participle and a weak passive construction.
Choice B accurately continues the thought begun in sentence 9. It is the best answer.
Choice C contains redundant language; *foul* and *obscene* are redundant.
Choice D contains a weak passive construction (*Obscenities are heard*) and is wordy.
Choice E lacks a main verb; therefore, it is a sentence fragment.

51. **E**  Choices A and B are adequate, but dull, transitional statements.
Choice C is a wordier version of A and B.
Choice D contains an error in subject-verb agreement;  the subject *changes* is plural, but the verb *has* is singular.
Choice E serves as a good transitional statement that highlights the most important change in music discussed in the essay. It is the best answer.

52. **A**  Only choice A requires development, since no mention is made in the essay of "new categories" of music. All the others choices are factual statements that require no further elaboration.

53. **B**  All choices except B contribute to the discussion of changes in musical sounds brought about by technology. Choice B, however, wanders from the topic.

54. **D**  Choice A unnecessarily repeats the phrase *in the past thirty years* and fails to list the changes in music in the order they are discussed in the essay.
Choice B is awkwardly expressed and confusing.
Choice C fails to list the changes in music in the proper order. Also, *technology and lyrics* appear to be a single item.
Choice D succinctly and accurately states the main idea of the essay. It is the best answer.
Choice E, by subordinating the initial clause, gives lyrics in music undeserved importance.

55. **C**  Choice A contains the extremely awkward phrase *to see underdogs being the one rooted for.*
Choice B uses the coordinating conjunction *but*, which makes no sense in the context.
Choice C clearly and concisely combines the thoughts contained in the two sentences.  It is the best answer.
Choice D contains a clause and a phrase that have no grammatical relationship.
Choice E contains a comma splice between *Americans* and *for example.*

56. **C**  All sentences except 3 contribute to the discussion of the underdog. Sentence 3 is an unnecessary digression. Therefore, it is the best answer.

57. **B**  Choice A is grammatically correct, but it refers to Americans' desire to feel good, a topic not discussed in paragraph 2.
Choice B accurately introduces the topic of the paragraph. It is the best answer.
Choices C and D are similar to A.
Choice E is awkwardly expressed and contains the pronoun *themselves*, which refers grammatically to *traditions* instead of to *Americans.*

58. **A**  Choice A clearly and accurately combines the sentences. It is the best answer.
Choice B is awkward and cumbersome.
Choice C contains an awkward shift in verb tense from present (*look*) to past perfect (*had been*).
Choice D contains the adverb *poorly*, which should be an adjective and should modify *immigrants* instead of *coming*.
Choice E contains a comma splice between *here* and *after all*.

59. **C**  Choice A is not an effective revision. It changes the focus of the discussion and contains a pronoun *their*, which refers grammatically to *Americans* instead of to *underdog*.
Choice B contains an awkward shift in verb tense from past (*believed*) to present (*succeed*).
Choice C follows naturally from the preceding sentence and is accurately expressed. It is the best answer.
Choice D is grammatical, but it shifts the focus of the discussion.
Choice E is confusing and contains the pronouns *they* and *their*, which lack a specific referent.

60. **D**  Choice A contains some transitional material but shifts verb tenses from past (*went*) to present (*defeat*).
Choice B, which lacks a main verb, is a sentence fragment.
Choice C, although grammatically correct, seems incomplete because the pronoun *it* lacks a specific referent.
Choice D provides a smooth transition between paragraphs and introduces the topic of paragraph 3. It is the best answer.
Choice E lacks any meaningful transitional material.

# SELF-SCORING GUIDE FOR THE SAT II ESSAY

## PRACTICE TEST D

**Using this guide.** Rate yourself in each of the six categories on the left. Circle the item that most accurately describes your performance. Enter the numbers on the rating guide below. Then calculate the average of the six ratings to determine your total score. On the SAT II itself, two readers will rate your essay on a scale of 6 (high) to 1 (low). The score will be reported to you as the sum of the two ratings, from 12 (best) to 2 (worst).

Note that on the SAT II, essays are judged in relation to other essays written on the same topic. Therefore, this Self-Scoring Guide may not yield a totally accurate prediction of the score you can expect to earn on the actual exam. Because it is difficult to achieve objectivity when assessing your own writing, you may improve the validity of your score by having a trusted friend or teacher read your essay and rate it using this scoring guide.

*Remove scoring guide by cutting on dotted line*

| | 6 | 5 | 4 | 3 | 2 | 1 |
|---|---|---|---|---|---|---|
| **PURPOSE OF THE ESSAY** | Very clear and insightful; fresh and engaging | Quite clear and insightful; interesting | Fairly clear and with some insight; marginally interesting | Somewhat clear but some confusion, too; fairly dull | Largely unclear and confusing | Extremely confusing |
| **ORGANIZATION AND DEVELOPMENT** | Meticulously organized and thoroughly developed; coherent and unified | Well organized and sufficiently developed; basically coherent and unified | Reasonably organized and developed; mostly coherent and unified | Somewhat organized and developed; some incoherence and lack of unity | Little organization and meager development; mostly incoherent and void of unity | No apparent organization or development; incoherent and lacking unity |
| **USE OF SENTENCES** | Effectively varied and engaging; essentially error-free | Varied and interesting; one or two minor errors | Adequately varied and interesting; some errors | Somewhat varied and marginally interesting; one or more major errors | Little variation and basically dull; some major errors | Uniformly repetitious and dull; numerous major errors |
| **CHOICE OF WORDS** | Interesting, sensitive, and effective; basically error-free | Generally interesting, clear and effective; one or two inaccuracies | Occasionally interesting and effective; one or two errors in diction or idiom | Somewhat dull and ordinary; some errors in diction or idiom | Mostly dull and conventional; several errors | Dull, immature; numerous errors in diction and idiom |
| **GRAMMAR AND USAGE** | Error-free | Occasional minor errors | Several minor errors | Some major errors | Frequent major errors | Severely flawed |
| **OVERALL IMPRESSION** | Demonstrates excellent skills and writing competence | Demonstrates good skills and competence | Demonstrates adequate skills and competence | Suggests fair skills and competence | Demonstrates poor skills and competence | Demonstrates lack of skill and competence |

For rating yourself

**Rating Guide**
Each category is rated 1 (low) to 6 (high)

Purpose of the Essay _____
Organization and Development _____
Use of Sentences _____
Choice of Words _____
Grammar and Usage _____
Overall Impression _____
TOTAL _____
    Divide total by 6 to get final score: ☐

For a second opinion

**Rating Guide**
Each category is rated 1 (low) to 6 (high)

Purpose of the Essay _____
Organization and Development _____
Use of Sentences _____
Choice of Words _____
Grammar and Usage _____
Overall Impression _____
TOTAL _____
    Divide total by 6 to get final score: ☐

# ANSWER SHEET FOR
# PRACTICE TEST E

## Usage

1. Ⓐ Ⓑ Ⓒ Ⓓ Ⓔ
2. Ⓐ Ⓑ Ⓒ Ⓓ Ⓔ
3. Ⓐ Ⓑ Ⓒ Ⓓ Ⓔ
4. Ⓐ Ⓑ Ⓒ Ⓓ Ⓔ
5. Ⓐ Ⓑ Ⓒ Ⓓ Ⓔ
6. Ⓐ Ⓑ Ⓒ Ⓓ Ⓔ
7. Ⓐ Ⓑ Ⓒ Ⓓ Ⓔ
8. Ⓐ Ⓑ Ⓒ Ⓓ Ⓔ
9. Ⓐ Ⓑ Ⓒ Ⓓ Ⓔ
10. Ⓐ Ⓑ Ⓒ Ⓓ Ⓔ
11. Ⓐ Ⓑ Ⓒ Ⓓ Ⓔ
12. Ⓐ Ⓑ Ⓒ Ⓓ Ⓔ
13. Ⓐ Ⓑ Ⓒ Ⓓ Ⓔ
14. Ⓐ Ⓑ Ⓒ Ⓓ Ⓔ
15. Ⓐ Ⓑ Ⓒ Ⓓ Ⓔ
16. Ⓐ Ⓑ Ⓒ Ⓓ Ⓔ
17. Ⓐ Ⓑ Ⓒ Ⓓ Ⓔ
18. Ⓐ Ⓑ Ⓒ Ⓓ Ⓔ
19. Ⓐ Ⓑ Ⓒ Ⓓ Ⓔ
20. Ⓐ Ⓑ Ⓒ Ⓓ Ⓔ
21. Ⓐ Ⓑ Ⓒ Ⓓ Ⓔ
22. Ⓐ Ⓑ Ⓒ Ⓓ Ⓔ
23. Ⓐ Ⓑ Ⓒ Ⓓ Ⓔ
24. Ⓐ Ⓑ Ⓒ Ⓓ Ⓔ
25. Ⓐ Ⓑ Ⓒ Ⓓ Ⓔ
26. Ⓐ Ⓑ Ⓒ Ⓓ Ⓔ
27. Ⓐ Ⓑ Ⓒ Ⓓ Ⓔ
28. Ⓐ Ⓑ Ⓒ Ⓓ Ⓔ
29. Ⓐ Ⓑ Ⓒ Ⓓ Ⓔ
30. Ⓐ Ⓑ Ⓒ Ⓓ Ⓔ

## Sentence Correction

31. Ⓐ Ⓑ Ⓒ Ⓓ Ⓔ
32. Ⓐ Ⓑ Ⓒ Ⓓ Ⓔ
33. Ⓐ Ⓑ Ⓒ Ⓓ Ⓔ
34. Ⓐ Ⓑ Ⓒ Ⓓ Ⓔ
35. Ⓐ Ⓑ Ⓒ Ⓓ Ⓔ
36. Ⓐ Ⓑ Ⓒ Ⓓ Ⓔ
37. Ⓐ Ⓑ Ⓒ Ⓓ Ⓔ
38. Ⓐ Ⓑ Ⓒ Ⓓ Ⓔ
39. Ⓐ Ⓑ Ⓒ Ⓓ Ⓔ
40. Ⓐ Ⓑ Ⓒ Ⓓ Ⓔ
41. Ⓐ Ⓑ Ⓒ Ⓓ Ⓔ
42. Ⓐ Ⓑ Ⓒ Ⓓ Ⓔ
43. Ⓐ Ⓑ Ⓒ Ⓓ Ⓔ
44. Ⓐ Ⓑ Ⓒ Ⓓ Ⓔ
45. Ⓐ Ⓑ Ⓒ Ⓓ Ⓔ
46. Ⓐ Ⓑ Ⓒ Ⓓ Ⓔ
47. Ⓐ Ⓑ Ⓒ Ⓓ Ⓔ
48. Ⓐ Ⓑ Ⓒ Ⓓ Ⓔ

## Revision-In-Context

49. Ⓐ Ⓑ Ⓒ Ⓓ Ⓔ
50. Ⓐ Ⓑ Ⓒ Ⓓ Ⓔ
51. Ⓐ Ⓑ Ⓒ Ⓓ Ⓔ
52. Ⓐ Ⓑ Ⓒ Ⓓ Ⓔ
53. Ⓐ Ⓑ Ⓒ Ⓓ Ⓔ
54. Ⓐ Ⓑ Ⓒ Ⓓ Ⓔ
55. Ⓐ Ⓑ Ⓒ Ⓓ Ⓔ
56. Ⓐ Ⓑ Ⓒ Ⓓ Ⓔ
57. Ⓐ Ⓑ Ⓒ Ⓓ Ⓔ
58. Ⓐ Ⓑ Ⓒ Ⓓ Ⓔ
59. Ⓐ Ⓑ Ⓒ Ⓓ Ⓔ
60. Ⓐ Ⓑ Ⓒ Ⓓ Ⓔ

# PRACTICE TEST E

## USAGE

INSTRUCTIONS: The underlined and lettered parts of each sentence below may contain an error in grammar, usage, word choice (diction), or expression (idiom). Read each sentence carefully, and identify the item that contains the error. Indicate your choice by filling in the corresponding space on your answer sheet. Only the underlined parts contain errors. Assume that the rest of each sentence is correct. No sentence contains more than one error. If a sentence contains no error, the correct choice will always be (E) (No error).

SAMPLE QUESTIONS

1. The committee <u>chairman</u> asked <u>he</u>
            (A)                    (B)
and the <u>other</u> photographers <u>not</u> to take flash
            (C)                    (D)
pictures during the hearings. <u>No error</u>.
                                  (E)

SAMPLE ANSWERS

1.  Ⓐ  ●  Ⓒ  Ⓓ  Ⓔ

2. The hurricane <u>in</u> September was <u>far</u>
                    (A)                  (B)
<u>more worser</u> than the one we <u>experienced</u>
      (C)                              (D)
in July. <u>No error</u>.
            (E)

2.  Ⓐ  Ⓑ  ●  Ⓓ  Ⓔ

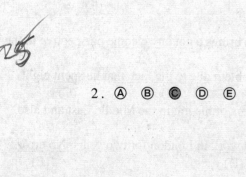

---

1.  <u>As young children</u>, my parents instilled their
            (A)
    moral values in my sister and <u>me</u>, so that by the
                                    (B)
    time we <u>had</u> reached our teens, we knew right
              (C)
    from wrong and were able, <u>for the most part</u>, to
                                      (D)
    stay out of trouble. <u>No error</u>.
                            (E)

2.  The FBI agents chose <u>not</u> to arrest Sutton at the
                            (A)
    bank that afternoon, but they <u>do</u> arrest him at
                                      (B)
    the airport <u>when</u> he was <u>about</u> to board a flight to
                  (C)              (D)
    Atlanta. <u>No error</u>.
                (E)

3.  <u>There's</u> no doubt that the AIDS awareness
            (A)
    program, which is scheduled to begin on April
    19th, <u>would have been</u> put off for another
                  (B)
    month because <u>of the lack of time</u> to plan it
                          (C)
    <u>well</u>. <u>No error</u>.
     (D)      (E)

4.  I agree with Peters and <u>him</u> that experience
                                (A)
    <u>has shown</u> repeatedly that social problems of
          (B)
    this kind <u>are</u> amenable <u>only</u> to slow and costly
                  (C)              (D)
    solutions. <u>No error</u>.
                    (E)

5.  Because the competition for passengers is fierce

    and airlines routinely accept more reservations

    than they can accommodate, one can't find
         (A)                          (B)

    hardly any flights that are not overbooked.
    (C)                          (D)

    No error.
    (E)

6.  If a child did something wrong, as their
       (A)

    counselor, you could take away their privileges
               (B)

    and explain that they have betrayed the trust that
                         (C)                  (D)

    had been placed in them. No error.
                            (E)

7.  He brings a not unwelcome perspective to the
                  (A)

    problem due to the fact that he spent eight
            (B)              (C)

    years of his life in the Middle East and also

    his work in London for two years. No error.
    (D)                              (E)

8.  True, the policy provides for a rapid rate of
    (A)

    return, but doesn't their views have a
                      (B)   (C)

    remarkable similarity to a philosophy that

    has long been rejected by the party leaders?
    (D)

    No error.
    (E)

9.  Mirsky observed that in all of Pushkin's tales
            (A)

    he glorified the little man, the insignificant
    (B)

    underling who overcomes the odds and wins
             (C)    (D)

    justice in a repressive and corrupt state. No error.
                                               (E)

10. Returning to his apartment late that night, Don
                                     (A)

    noticed the same newspaper lying at his
                               (B) (C)

    neighbor's door that he saw in the morning
                          (D)

    when he left. No error.
                  (E)

11. By means of modern lighting techniques,
    (A)

    foodstores cleverly enhance the color of the

    produce on their shelves to attract customers,
              (B)

    entice impulse buying, and most important,
                   (C)

    it creates the appearance of freshness and
    (D)

    wholesomeness. No error.
                   (E)

12. Helene spoke to the social worker about her

    dislike of the abuse she had endured from her
    (A)             (B)              (C)

    father and about the lengthy church services she

    had been forced to attend with him. No error.
    (D)                                (E)

13. Greta Garbo, the sensational and talented

    Hollywood star of the 1930s, became a recluse
                        (A)

    for most of her adult life and remained isolated
                                  (B)

    but looking beautifully until the day she died.
        (C)      (D)

    No error.
    (E)

14. In her retirement, my grandmother is as active
       (A)

    as she was when working for the government,
           (B)   (C)

    but now, instead of holding a full-time job, she

    does volunteer activities and sports. No error.
    (D)                                   (E)

15. When analyzing the stories of modern short
         (A)
    story writers like Carver and Leavitt,
                 (B)
    the underlying purpose of the stories is
              (C)
    sometimes hard to discern. No error.
              (D)            (E)

16. His soliloquy, spoken soon after the battle

    had ended, was full of passionate intensity,
    (A)
    especially when he vowed that he would
                 (B)
    make his mother love him more than his sister.
    (C)                      (D)
    No error.
    (E)

17. The fact that Naomi, the book's main character,
                          (A)
    and some would say its hero, is a mere child
                     (B)        (C)
    during the Revolution, makes the story even

    more appealing to young readers. No error.
    (D)                               (E)

18.  Cold and forbidding on its surface, the expanse
         (A)                (B)
    of water looked as though it would hold no life;

    however, in the depths of the Caspian, the
    (C)
    greatest of all inland seas, aquatic life is

    more than abundant. No error.
    (D)                  (E)

19. Larry told a long-winded story about two men

    riding on a train who had an argument about
                     (A)
    them arriving too late for an appointment with a
    (B)
    lawyer, or perhaps with a judge or some sort of
            (C)        (D)
    official. No error.
            (E)

20. When another task is piled on already
                               (A)
    overburdened workers, you can be sure that,

    instead of having them done well, no one will
           (B)        (C)
    perform up to par. No error.
            (D)        (E)

21. The soldiers' attitude toward women is impolite
        (A)          (B)
    and disrespectful; they believe that women exist
                      (C)
    simply for the enjoyment of men. No error.
          (D)                     (E)

22. Shortly after he won the lottery, Victor told the
    (A)        (B)
    press that for years he had been planning a trip

    to the West and that the first place he intended
         (C)
    to go was to California. No error.
            (D)              (E)

23. The booby is one of the most unique birds in the
                          (A)
    world because it will land on ships at sea and
          (B)
    allow itself to be caught, but why anybody
          (C)
    would want to catch one remains a mystery.
                      (D)
    No error.
    (E)

24. Ray Bradbury and Isaac Asimov stand

    side by side as two of America's greatest
    (A)
    writers of science fiction, but the latter, having
                                        (B)
    written more than 500 books, is by far the the
            (C)
    most prolific. No error.
    (D)          (E)

25. When distinct lines separate one class from

    another, it is understood that, if you are of a
                             (A)            (B)
    higher rank than another person, you have the
                                       (C)
    authority to rule over them. No error.
                             (D)      (E)

26. While looking around the infirmary, I observed

    many other patients which happened to be
         (A)           (B)
    suffering from the same upper respiratory
             (C)
    infection as I. No error.
                 (D)   (E)

27.  As dusk fell and the clock chimed six, the
         (A)                    (B)
    old woman's eyes grew vacant,

    her moaning was heard, her skin paled, and
             (C)
    her breathing soon ceased, to the regret

    of almost no one, since she had been a lifelong
       (D)
    shrew. No error.
           (E)

28. The whole class has known from the outset that,
                              (A)
    if they fail to turn their work in on time,  you
    (B)                                          (C)
    lose a grade on papers and on homework
                              (D)
    assignments. No error.
                  (E)

29. Behind almost all successful candidates for

    public office stands a staff, a team of volunteers,
                   (A)
    a group of fundraisers, and, of course, a
                                 (B)
    platform that  must have convinced voters to
                        (C)
    cast their ballots for them. No error.
                        (D)      (E)

30. The program that Jason has planned for himself
                   (A)                       (B)
    during his freshman year is  filled up with
                                    (C)
    difficult courses in French, English, and

    psychology. No error.
       (D)       (E)

**DON'T STOP.  PLEASE CONTINUE WITH THE NEXT QUESTIONS.**

## SENTENCE CORRECTION

INSTRUCTIONS:  The underlined sections of the sentences below may contain errors in standard English, including awkward or ambiguous expression, poor word choice (diction), incorrect sentence structure, or faulty grammar, usage, and punctuation. In some items, the entire sentence may be underlined. Read each sentence carefully and identify which of the five alternative versions most effectively and correctly expresses the meaning of the original. Indicate your choice by filling in the corresponding space on your answer sheet. Choice (A) always repeats the original. Choose (A) if none of the other choices improves the original sentence.

SAMPLE QUESTION

It did not matter to Victor <u>as to whether</u> the girl's family was rich or poor.

(A) as to whether
(B) about
(C) whether
(D) weather
(E) as to whether or not

SAMPLE ANSWER

Ⓐ  Ⓑ  ●  Ⓓ  Ⓔ

31. The present senior class <u>has a greater amount of scholarship winners than last year</u>.

(A) has a greater amount of scholarship winners than last year
(B) have a greater amount of scholarship winners than last years
(C) include a greater number of scholarship winners than last year's
(D) have more scholarship winner's than last year's
(E) has more scholarship winners than last year's

32. <u>A more easier and direct route exist</u> between Mt. Kisco and Pleasantville than the one we took.

(A) A more easier and direct route exist
(B) An easier and direct route exist
(C) An easier and more direct route exists
(D) Easier and direct routes exist
(E) A both more easy and a more direct route exists

33. <u>I plan to major in biochemistry and my interviewer at Colgate was a biochemist and I felt more confident.</u>

(A) I plan to major in biochemistry and my interviewer at Colgate was a biochemist and I felt more confident.
(B) Because my interviewer at Colgate was a biochemist and I plan to major in it, I felt more confident.
(C) Because my interviewer at Colgate was a biochemist, and I plan to major in biochemistry, which gave me more confidence.
(D) My interviewer at Colgate was a biochemist, because I plan to major biochemistry, I felt confident during the interview.
(E) Since I plan to major in biochemistry, and my interviewer at Colgate was a biochemist, I felt confident during the interview.

34. <u>When one is visiting a foreign country, you can</u> almost always find someone who speaks English.

(A) When one is visiting a foreign country, you can
(B) When visiting in a foreign country, you can
(C) When you visit a foreign country, one might
(D) While one is on a visit to a foreign country, you can
(E) During one's visit to a foreign country, you may

35. At five years old, my father took me to go to get a haircut for the very first time.

   (A) At five years old, my father took me to go to get a haircut for the very first time.
   (B) At five years old, my father took me to get my first haircut.
   (C) My father took me at five years old to go to get a haircut for the very first time.
   (D) When I was five, my father took me for my first haircut.
   (E) At five I was taken by my father to get my first haircut, something I had never had before.

36. Both speakers succeeded in reaching their audience because both talked in a down-to-earth manner and because their opinions came across strong.

   (A) their opinions came across strong
   (B) both opinions that they expressed were strong
   (C) they strongly expressed their opinions
   (D) their expression of opinions was strong
   (E) strongly their opinions were expressed

37. The real estate agent said that if we agreed to purchase the house today, we would have saved $2000.

   (A) that if we agreed to purchase the house today
   (B) that had we agreed to purchase the house today
   (C) that if we would of agreed to purchase the house today
   (D) that if today the purchasing of the house was agreeable
   (E) that if we agree to purchase the house today

38. We needed no more time; months of planning had prepared us for the bicycle trip from Seattle to San Francisco.

   (A) We needed no more time; months of planning had prepared us
   (B) We needed no more time, months of planning had prepared us
   (C) No more time was needed for our months of planning had prepared us

   (D) No more time was necessary; months of planning which had prepared us
   (E) Needing no more time, our months of planning had prepared us

39. I was told by no uncertain terms that my teammates had no confidence for me being the goalie.

   (A) I was told by no uncertain terms that my teammates had no confidence for me
   (B) I was told by no uncertain terms that my teammates had no confidence in my
   (C) I was told in no uncertain terms that my teammates had no confidence in my
   (D) In no uncertain terms, I am told by my teammates had no confidence for me
   (E) Told in no uncertain terms, my teammates had no confidence in my

40. The Holocaust is the time in history that will always be remembered by me.

   (A) The Holocaust is the time in history that will always be remembered by me.
   (B) Of all the times in history, the Holocaust will always be remembered by me.
   (C) Of all historical times, the time I will always remember will be the Holocaust.
   (D) The Holocaust is the time in history that I will always remember.
   (E) I will always remember the Holocaust of all the time of history.

41. They not only spoke enthusiastically about the new fertilizer but also praising the farmers who tried it.

   (A) They not only spoke enthusiastically about the new fertilizer but also praising
   (B) They not only spoke enthusiastically about the new fertilizer but also to praise
   (C) They spoke enthusiastically not only on the new fertilizer but also praising
   (D) They not only spoke enthusiastically about the new fertilizer but also praised
   (E) They spoke both enthusiastically about the new fertilizer, but they also praised

42. <u>Frederick Henry is not a warrior at all, he is an ambulance driver who disapproves of the war and wants it to end</u>.

   (A) Frederick Henry is not a warrior at all, he is an ambulance driver who disapproves of the war and wants it to end.
   (B) No warrior is Frederick Henry; he is, instead, an ambulance driver who, wanting the war to end, disapproves of it.
   (C) Frederick Henry, an ambulance driver and not a warrior, disapproving of the war and wanting to see it end.
   (D) An ambulance driver and not a warrior, who wants to see the war end because he disapproves of it, is Frederick Henry.
   (E) Ambulance driver Frederick Henry is no warrior; he disapproves of the war and wants to see it end.

43. <u>No one but her and me know</u> where the key to the house is hidden.

   (A) No one but her and me know
   (B) No one but her and me knows
   (C) Nobody but she and me knows
   (D) Nobody but she and I knows
   (E) No one but her and I know

44. This book <u>not only</u> shows its readers what might happen if they try to deal with the problem by themselves <u>but it's all right to seek help</u>.

   (A) but it's all right to seek help
   (B) but explains help is all right to seek.
   (C) explaining that it's all right to seek help
   (D) and also explains that it's all right to seek help
   (E) but also explains that it's all right to seek help

45. <u>He acknowledged that he had made a mistake, which</u> surprised me very much

   (A) He acknowledged that he had made a mistake, which
   (B) His acknowledgement that he had made a mistake
   (C) He acknowledged that a mistake had been made by him
   (D) Acknowledging that he had made a mistake, this
   (E) He acknowledged that he had made a mistake; which

46. Some of the trees looked as though they were about to die, or <u>as though they already had died</u>.

   (A) as though they already had died
   (B) if they had already
   (C) as they did already
   (D) as if they're dying
   (E) whether they already had died

47. Thinking it over, <u>the solution to our problems are</u> more announcements and publicity.

   (A) the solution to our problems are
   (B) our problems can be solved by
   (C) our problems are to be solved by
   (D) I believe that the solution to our problems is
   (E) I think that the solution to our problems are

48. In order to understand the importance of yearbooks to high school seniors, <u>we studied their sources of popularity</u>.

   (A) we studied their sources of popularity
   (B) we studied the sources of their popularity
   (C) we studied its sources of popularity
   (D) it's source of popularity was studied
   (E) their sources of popularity were studied by us

**DON'T STOP. PLEASE CONTINUE WITH THE NEXT QUESTIONS.**

# REVISION-IN-CONTEXT

INSTRUCTIONS:  The passages below are the unedited draft of two students' essays. Some of each essay needs to be rewritten to make the meaning clearer and more precise. Read the essays carefully.

Each essay is followed by six questions about changes that might improve all or part of its organization, development, sentence structure, use of language, appropriateness to the audience, or its use of standard written English. Choose the answer that most clearly and effectively expresses the student's intended meaning. Indicate your choice by filling in the corresponding space on the answer sheet.

## ESSAY A

*[1] When you turn on the radio or pop in a tape while the house is quiet or going to work or school in your car, you have several choices of music to listen to. [2] Although, in recent years, CDs have become the medium of choice over records and even tapes. [3] On the radio you have your rap on one station, your classical on another, your New Wave music on another, and then you have your Country. [4] Some young people feel that country is for fat old people, but it isn't. [5] It is music for all ages, fat or thin.*

*[6] Country music is "fun" music. [7] It has an unmistakeable beat and sound that gets you up and ready to move. [8] You can really get into country, even if it is just the clapping of the hands or the stamping of the feet. [9] You can't help feeling cheerful watching the country performers, who all seem so happy to be entertaining their close "friends," although there may be 10,000 of them in the stadium or concert hall. [10] The musicians love it, and audience flips out with delight. [11] The interpersonal factors in evidence cause a sudden psychological bond to develop into a temporary, but nevertheless tightly knit, family unit. [12] For example, you can imagine June Carter Cash as your favorite aunt and Randy Travis as your long lost cousin.*

*[13] Some people spurn country music. [14] Why, they ask, would anyone want to listen to singers whine about their broken marriages or their favorite pet that was run over by an 18-wheeler? [15] They claim that Willie Nelson, one of today's country legends, can't even keep his income taxes straight. [16] Another "dynamic" performer is*

*Dolly Parton, whose most famous feature is definitely not her voice. [17] How talented could she be if her body is more famous than her singing?*

*[18] Lorretta Lynn is the greatest. [19] Anyone's negative feelings towards country music would change after hearing Loretta's strong, emotional, and haunting voice. [20] Look, it can't hurt to give a listen. [21] You never know, you might even like it so much that you will go out, pick up a secondhand guitar and learn to strum a few chords.*

*[22] Well, maybe that's pushing it.*

49. Which is the best revision of the underlined segment of sentence 1 below?

    *When you turn on the radio or pop in a tape <u>while the house is quiet or going to work or school in your car</u>, you have several choices of music to listen to.*

    (A) while the house is quiet or in your car going to work or school
    (B) driving to work or school while the house is quiet
    (C) while the house is quiet or you are driving to work or school.
    (D) while driving to work or school in your car, and the house is quiet
    (E) while there's quiet in the house or you go to work or school in your car

50. To improve the coherence of paragraph 1 which of following sentences should be deleted?

    (A) Sentence 1
    (B) Sentence 2

(C) Sentence 3

(D) Sentence 4

(E) Sentence 5

51. Taking into account the sentences that precede and follow sentence 8, which of the following is the best revision of sentence 8?

(A) Clap your hands and stamp your feet is what to do to easily get into country.

(B) You're really into country, even if it is just clapping of the hands or stamping of the feet.

(C) You can easily get into country just by clapping your hands or stamping your feet.

(D) One can get into country music rather easily; one must merely clap one's hands or stamp one's feet.

(E) Getting into country is easy, just clap your hands and stamp your feet.

52. With regard to the writing style and tone of the essay, which is the best revision of sentence 11?

(A) The interpersonal relationship that develops suddenly creates a temporary, but nevertheless a closely knit, family unit.

(B) A family-like relationship develops quickly and rapidly.

(C) A close family-type relation is suddenly very much in evidence between the performer and his or her audience.

(D) All of a sudden you feel like a member of a huge, but tight, family.

(E) A sudden bond develops between the entertainer and the audience that might most suitably be described as a ''family,'' in the best sense of the term.

53. Considering the essay as a whole, which of the following best describes the function of paragraph 3?

(A) To present some objective data in support of another viewpoint

(B) To offer a more balanced view of the essay's subject matter

(C) To ridicule those readers who don't agree with the writer

(D) To lend further support to the essay's main idea

(E) To divert the reader's attention from the main idea of the essay

54. Which of the following revisions of sentence 18 provides the smoothest transition between paragraphs 3 and 4?

(A) Loretta Lynn is one of the great singers of country music.

(B) Loretta Lynn, however, is the greatest country singer yet.

(C) But you can bet they've never heard Loretta Lynn.

(D) The sounds of Loretta Lynn tells a different story, however.

(E) Loretta Lynn, on the other hand, is superb.

## ESSAY B

*[1] Throughout history, people have speculated about the future. [2] Will it be a utopia? they wondered. [3] Will injustice and poverty be eliminated? [4] Will people accept ethnic diversity, learning to live in peace? [5] Will the world be clean and unpolluted? [6] Or will technology aid us in creating a trap for ourselves we cannot escape, for example such as the world in 1984? [7] With the turn of the millenium just around the corner, these questions are in the back of our minds.*

*[8] Science fiction often portrays the future as a technological Garden of Eden. [9] With interactive computers, TVs and robots at our command, we barely need to lift a finger to go to school, to work, to go shopping, and education is also easy and convenient. [10] Yet, the problems of the real twentieth century seem to point in another direction. [11] The environment, far from improving, keeps deteriorating. [12] Wars and other civil conflicts break out regularly. [13] The world's population is growing out of control. [14] The majority of people on earth live in poverty. [15] Many of them are starving. [16] Illiteracy is a problem in most poor countries. [17] Diseases and malnourishment is very common. [18] Rich countries like the U.S.A. don't have the resources to help the ''have-not'' countries.*

*[19] Instead, think instead of all the silly inventions such as tablets you put in your toilet tank to*

*make the water blue, or electric toothbrushes. [20] More money is spent on space and defense than on education and health care. [21] Advancements in agriculture can produce enough food to feed the whole country, yet people in the U.S. are starving.*

*[22] Although the USSR is gone, the nuclear threat continues from small countries like Iraq. [23] Until the world puts its priorities straight, we can't look for a bright future in the twenty-first century, despite the rosy picture painted for us by the science fiction writers.*

55. Considering the context of paragraph 1, which of the following is the best revision of sentence 6?

    (A) Or will technology create a trap for ourselves from which we cannot escape, for example the world in *1984*?
    (B) Or will technology aid people in creating a trap for themselves that they cannot escape; for example, the world in *1984*?
    (C) Or will technology create a trap from which there is no escape, as it did in the world in *1984*?
    (D) Or will technology trap us in an inescapable world, for example, it did so in the world of *1984*?
    (E) Perhaps technology will aid people in creating a trap for themselves from which they cannot escape, just as they did it in the world of *1984*.

56. With regard to the essay as a whole, which of the following best describes the writer's intention in paragraph 1?

    (A) To announce the purpose of the essay
    (B) To compare two ideas discussed later in the essay
    (C) To take a position on the essay's main issue
    (D) To reveal the organization of the essay
    (E) To raise questions that will be answered in the essay

57. Which of the following is the best revision of the underlined segment of sentence 9 below?

    *[9] With interactive computers, TVs and robots at our command, we will barely need to lift a*

*finger to go to school, to work, to go shopping, and education is also easy and convenient.*

    (A) and to go shopping, while education is also easy and convenient
    (B) to go shopping, and getting an education is also easy and convenient
    (C) to go shopping as well as educating ourselves are all easy and convenient
    (D) to shop, and an easy and convenient education
    (E) to shop, and to get an easy and convenient education

58. Which of the following is the most effective way to combine sentences 14, 15, 16, and 17?

    (A) The majority of people on earth are living in poverty and are starving, with illiteracy, and disease and being malnourished are also a common problems.
    (B) Common problems for the the majority of people on earth are poverty, illiteracy, diseases, malnourishment, and many are illiterate.
    (C) The majority of people on earth are poor, starving, sick, malnourished and illiterate.
    (D) Common among the poor majority on earth is poverty, starvation, disease, malnourishment, and illiteracy.
    (E) The majority of the earth's people living in poverty with starvation, disease, malnourishment and illiteracy a constant threat.

59. Considering the sentences that precede and follow sentence 19, which of the following is the most effective revision of sentence 19 ?

    (A) Instead they are devoting resources on silly inventions such as tablets to make toilet tank water blue or electric toothbrushes.
    (B) Instead, they waste their resources on producing silly inventions like electric toothbrushes and tablets for bluing toilet tank water.
    (C) Think of all the silly inventions: tablets you put in your toilet tank to make the water blue and electric toothbrushes.

(D) Instead, tablets you put in your toilet tank to make the water blue or electric toothbrushes are examples of useless products on the market today.

(E) Instead of spending on useful things, think of all the silly inventions such as tablets you put in your toilet tank to make the water blue or electric toothbrushes.

60. Which of the following revisions would most improve the overall coherence of the essay?

(A) Move sentence 7 to paragraph 2
(B) Move sentence 10 to paragraph 1
(C) Move sentence 22 to paragraph 2
(D) Delete sentence 8
(E) Delete sentence 23

**PLEASE STOP WORK.  USE WHATEVER TIME IS LEFT BEFORE THE 40-MINUTE TEST PERIOD EXPIRES TO CHECK YOUR ANSWERS.**

# ESSAY

## Time allowed: 20 minutes

INSTRUCTIONS:  Plan and write an essay in response to the assigned topic. During the 20 minutes allowed, you should develop your thoughts clearly and effectively. A plain, natural style is probably best. Try to include specific evidence or examples to support your views.

The number of words is up to you, but quantity is far less important than quality. In general, however, a single paragraph may not give you the chance to develop your ideas sufficiently. You must limit your essay to the answer sheet. Please be advised, therefore, to write on every line and write compactly enough to fit your essay in the space allowed. Try to write as legibly as you can.

BE SURE TO WRITE ONLY ON THE ASSIGNED TOPIC. AN ESSAY WRITTEN ON ANOTHER TOPIC WILL RECEIVE NO CREDIT.

> Conflict between generations is the theme of countless stories, dramas, and books, as well as a source of friction in the general society. Although such conflict is often hurtful and sometimes even fatal, it is not only inevitable but also necessary because it leads to productive change.
> Do you agree with the assertion that in the long run, conflict between the generations is a positive, rather than a negative, force for change? In an essay, explain your reasons, using evidence drawn from your studies, your reading, or your observation.

This space reserved for your personal bar code

**SAT II: WRITING**
**ESSAY**
**Time allowed: 20 minutes**

FOR OFFICE USE

Topic: **CONFLICT**

First reader _____
Second reader _____
Third reader (if needed) _____

The space below is for your essay. Please restrict your writing to the designated area.

_____

_____

_____

_____

_____

_____

_____

_____

_____

_____

_____

_____

_____

_____

_____

_____

_____

Please continue your essay on the next page if you need more room.

## ANSWERS

| | | | | | |
|---|---|---|---|---|---|
| 1. A | 11. D | 21. C | 31. E | 41. D | 51. C |
| 2. B | 12. E | 22. D | 32. C | 42. E | 52. D |
| 3. B | 13. D | 23. A | 33. E | 43. B | 53. B |
| 4. E | 14. D | 24. D | 34. B | 44. E | 54. C |
| 5. C | 15. A | 25. D | 35. D | 45. B | 55. C |
| 6. A | 16. D | 26. B | 36. C | 46. A | 56. E |
| 7. D | 17. E | 27. C | 37. B | 47. D | 57. E |
| 8. C | 18. A | 28. C | 38. A | 48. B | 58. C |
| 9. B | 19. B | 29. A | 39. C | 49. C | 59. B |
| 10. D | 20. C | 30. C | 40. D | 50. B | 60. C |

## PERFORMANCE EVALUATION CHART

### I.  Self-rating Chart

Usage, Questions 1–30                                   Number correct _____
Sentence Correction, Questions 31–48          Number correct _____
Revision-in-Context, Questions 49–60          Number correct _____
                                                                        Subtotal _____

*Penalty.* Subtract 1/4 point (.25) for each incorrect answer.  _____
(No penalty for unanswered questions)
TOTAL SCORE _____

### II. Key to Self-rating

| | Usage | Sentence Correction | Revision-in-Context | Total |
|---|---|---|---|---|
| Excellent | 27–30 | 17–18 | 11–12 | 55–60 |
| Very good | 23–26 | 14–16 | 9–10 | 46–54 |
| Good | 19–22 | 11–13 | 7–8 | 37–45 |
| Fair | 15–18 | 9–10 | 5–6 | 29–36 |
| Poor | 10–14 | 6–8 | 3–4 | 19–28 |
| Very poor | 0–9 | 0–5 | 0–2 | 0–18 |

# ANSWERS EXPLAINED

## Usage

1. **A** Misplaced modifier. *As young children* modifies parents; it should modify *sister and me*.
2. **B** Tense shift. The sentence is cast in the past tense. Use *did*.
3. **B** Verb tense error. The future tense is used to indicate events taking place in the future. Use *will be*.
4. **E** No error.
5. **C** Double negative. Both *can't* and *hardly* are negative words. Delete *hardly*.
6. **A** Pronoun-antecedent agreement. The pronoun *they* is plural; the antecedent *child* is singular. Use *children*.
7. **D** Faulty parallelism. Coordinate parts of a sentence should be in the same grammatical form. Use *worked*.
8. **C** Subject-verb agreement. The subject *views* is plural; the verb *doesn't* is singular. Use *view*.
9. **B** Pronoun reference. The pronoun *he* cannot be used to refer to a possessive noun.
10. **D** Verb tense. The past perfect tense is used to refer to action completed prior to a specific time in the past. Use *had seen*.
11. **D** Faulty parallelism. The phrase *it creates* is not parallel to the other verbs in the series. Use *to create*.
12. **E** No error.
13. **D** Diction error. Adjectives are used with linking verbs to modify verbs. Use *beautiful*.
14. **D** Idiom error. The phrase *does activities and sports* is nonstandard usage. Use *participates in activities and sports*, or some other standard phrase.
15. **A** Dangling participle. The phrase beginning *when analyzing* has no noun or pronoun to modify.
16. **D** Incomplete comparison. Use *more than she loved his* instead of *more than*.
17. **E** No error.
18. **E** No error.
19. **B** Pronoun choice. A possessive pronoun is needed before a gerund. Use *their*.
20. **C** Pronoun-antecedent agreement. The antecedent *task* is singular; the pronoun *them* is plural. Use *it*.
21. **C** Pronoun reference. The pronoun *they* may not refer to a possessive noun.
22. **D** Idiom error. The word *to* is redundant. Delete it.
23. **A** Diction error. *Unique* means "one of a kind." Therefore, *most unique* is illogical. Use *unusual* instead of *unique*.
24. **D** Comparative degree. The comparative degree is used for comparing two objects, the superlative for comparing three or more. Use *more* instead of *most*.
25. **D** Pronoun-antecedent agreement. The antecedent *person* is singular; the pronoun *them* is plural. Use *him*.
26. **B** Diction error. Use *who* instead of *which* when referring to people.
27. **C** Faulty parallelism. Each item in a series should be in the same grammatical form. Use *she began to moan*.
28. **C** Pronoun shift. The sentence is cast in third person. Use *they* instead of *you*.
29. **A** Subject-verb agreement. A compound subject requires a plural verb. Use *stand*.
30. **C** Idiom error. The word *up* is unnecessary. Delete it.

## Sentence Correction

**Note**: *Although many choices contain multiple errors, only one error is listed for each incorrect answer.*

31. **E** A. Faulty comparison. *Winners* is being compared to *year*, an illogical comparison.
    B. Diction error. Use *number* for quantities that can be counted; use *amount* for mass quantities.

    C.  Subject-verb agreement. *Class* is singular; *include* is plural.

    D.  Punctuation error. *Winners* is neither a possessive nor a contraction. Therefore, no apostrophe is needed.

32. **C** A.  Subject-verb agreement. *Route* is singular; *exist* is plural.

    B.  Faulty parallel. Unlike *easier*, *direct* is an adjective not in the comparative degree.

    D.  Faulty parallel. Same as B.

    E.  Wordy. *Both* and the repetition of *more* are unnecessary.

33. **E** A.  Faulty coordination. The relationship among the three independent clauses is obscure.

    B.  Faulty pronoun reference. *It* does not refer to any specific noun or pronoun.

    C.  Sentence fragment. The construction is made up of three dependent clauses.

    D.  Comma splice. A comma (between *biochemist* and *because)* may not be used to separate two independent clauses.

34. **B** A.  Shift in pronoun person. The sentence shifts from third person, *one*, to second person, *you*.

    C.  Shift in pronoun person. The sentence shifts from second person, *you*, to third person, *one*.

    D.  Shift in pronoun person. The sentence shifts from third person, *one*, to second person, *you*.

    E.  Shift in pronoun person. The sentence shifts from third person, *one*, to second person *you*.

35. **D** A.  Wordy. Several words may be trimmed without loss of meaning. Use *for my first haircut*, for example.

    B.  Misplaced modifier. *At five years old* should modify *I* (the speaker), not *father*.

    C.  Wordy. Omitting needless words improves any sentence.

    E.  Redundancy. *First* and *never had before* are redundant.

36. **C** A.  Diction error. An adverb (*strongly*) is needed to modify *across*.

    B.  Shift in grammatical subject. *Speakers* is the grammatical subject of the sentence. Shifting the subject to *opinions* in the last clause is a stylistic, but not a grammatical, flaw.

    D.  Shift in grammatical subject. Shifting the subject to *expression* is a stylistic flaw.

    E.  Clumsy construction.

37. **B** A.  Shift in verb tense. The past perfect tense, *had agreed*, is needed.

    C.  Diction error. *Would of* is a nonstandard usage. Use *would have*.

    D.  Clumsy construction. Incomprehensible.

    E.  Faulty verb tense. A verb in the present tense is not suitable here.

38. **A** B.  Comma splice. A comma may not be used to separate two independent clauses.

    C.  Punctuation error. A comma between *needed* and *for* is needed for clarity.

    D.  Semicolon error. A semicolon is used to separate two independent clauses.

    E.  Dangling participle. *Needing no more time* should modify *we* instead of *months*.

39. **C** A.  Idiom error. The standard idioms are *in no uncertain terms* and *no confidence in*.

    B.  Idiom error. In standard idiom is *in no uncertain terms*.

    D.  Mixed construction. The phrase *had no confidence for me* is grammatically unrelated to the rest of the sentence.

    E.  Dangling modifier. The phrase *Told in no uncertain terms* modifies *teammates* instead of *I*.

40. **D** A.  Passive construction. The subject of the sentence should be the performer of the action.

    B.  Passive construction. *I* should be the grammatical subject.

    C.  Needless repetition of times/time, will/will, all/always.

    E.  Idiom error. The last segment hardly resembles English.

41. **D** A.  Faulty parallelism. The verb *spoke* is not parallel in form to *praising*.

B. Faulty parallelism. The verb *spoke* is not parallel in form to the infinitive *to praise*.

C. Faulty parallelism. The phrase *on the new fertilizer* is not parallel to the verb *praising*.

E. Incomplete construction. The use of *both* suggests the need for a second adverb to follow *enthusiastically*.

42. **E**  A. Comma splice. A comma (between *all* and *he*) may not be used to separate two independent clauses.

B. Clumsy construction. Although grammatically correct, much of the sentence is awkwardly worded.

C. Sentence fragment. The construction lacks a main verb. The *-ing* form of a verb (*disapproving, wanting*) may not be used as the main verb without a helping verb, as in *was disapproving* and *is wanting*.

D. Clumsy construction. The inverted construction is awkward, and the subject and verb are too far apart.

43. **B**  A. Subject-verb agreement. *No one* is singular; *know* is plural.

C. Pronoun choice. A pronoun from the nominative case (*she*) may not be paired with a pronoun in the objective case (*me*).

D. Pronoun choice. An object of the preposition *but* (*but* is a preposition when it means "except") needs an objective case pronoun.

E. Subject-verb agreement. *No one* is singular; *know* is plural.

44. **E**  A. Faulty parallelism. The verb *shows* lacks a grammatical parallel, a verb in the same form.

B. Clumsy construction.

C. Faulty parallelism. The verb *explaining* is not parallel in form to *shows*.

D. Faulty parallelism. Parallel ideas introduced by *not only* must be completed with *but also*.

45. **B**  A. Ambiguous pronoun reference. *Which* may refer either to *mistake* or to the acknowledgement.

C. Passive construction.

D. Dangling participle. The phrase *acknowledging that he had made a mistake* modifies *this*, but it should modify *he*.

E. Semicolon error. Use a semicolon to separate two independent clauses.

46. **A**  B. Incomplete construction. The word *died* is missing.

C. Idiom error. The words make no sense.

D. Redundancy. The phrase reiterates the information in *as though they were about to die*.

E. Idiom error. *Whether* makes no sense in the context.

47. **D**  A. Subject-verb agreement. *Solution* is singular; *are* is plural.

B. Dangling participle. *Thinking it over* lacks an acceptable noun or pronoun to modify.

C. Dangling participle. *Thinking it over* lacks an acceptable noun or pronoun to modify.

E. Subject-verb agreement. *Solution* is singular; *are* is plural.

48. **B**  A. Misplaced modifier. *Their* should modify *popularity*, not *sources*.

C. Pronoun-antecedent agreement. *Its* is singular; *yearbooks* is plural.

D. Diction error. *It's* is a contraction meaning *it is*.

E. Passive construction.

## Revision-in-Context

49. **C**  Choice A says that the house is *in your car*, an unlikely place for it to be.

Choice B contains an idea that the writer could not have intended.

Choice C accurately states the intended idea. It is the best answer.

Choice D, like B, contains an idea which is quite absurd.

Choice E is wordy and awkwardly expressed.

50. **B**   All the sentences except sentence 2 contribute to the development of the essay's topic. Therefore, choice B is the best answer.

51. **C**   Choice A is awkwardly expressed.
Choice B is awkward and contains the pronoun *it*, which has no specific referent.
Choice C is accurately expressed and is consistent with the sentences that precede and follow sentence 8. It is the best answer.
Choice D is written in a style that is different from the rest of the essay.
Choice E would be a good choice, but it contains a comma splice. A comma may not be used to join two independent clauses.

52. **D**   Choice A is quite formal and is not in keeping with the style and tone of the essay.
Choice B is close to the style and tone of the essay, but it contains the redundancy, *quickly and rapidly*.
Choice C has a formal tone inconsistent with the rest of the essay.
Choice D uses the second person pronoun and is consistent with the folksy, conversational style of the essay. It is the best answer.
Choice E uses an objective tone far different from the writing in the rest of the essay.

53. **B**   Choice A is only partly true. While the paragraph gives another viewpoint, the data it contains are hardly objective.
Choice B accurately states the writer's intention. It is the best answer.
Choice C, D, and E in no way describe the function of paragraph 3.

54. **C**   Choice A provides no particular link to the previous paragraph.
Choice B provides a rather weak transition between paragraphs.
Choice C creates a strong bond between paragraphs by alluding to material in paragraph 3 and introducing the topic of paragraph 4. It is the best answer.
Choice D could be a good transition were it not for the error in subject-verb agreement. The subject *sounds* is plural; the verb *tells* is singular.
Choice E provides a weak transition and its writing style is not consistent with the rest of the essay.

55. **C**   Choice A is awkward and shifts the pronoun usage in the paragraph from third to first person.
Choice B is awkward and contains a semicolon error. A semicolon is used to separate two independent clauses. The material after the semicolon is a sentence fragment.
Choice C is succinctly and accurately expressed. It is the best answer.
Choice D contains a comma splice between *world* and *for*. A comma may not be used to join two independent clauses.
Choice E is awkwardly expressed and contains the pronoun *it*, which lacks a clear referent.

56. **E**   Choice A indirectly describes the purpose of paragraph 1 but does not identify the writer's main intention.
Choices B, C, and D fail to describe the writer's main intention.
Choice E accurately describes the writer's main intention. It is the best answer.

57. **E**   Choice A is grammatically correct but cumbersome.
Choice B contains an error in parallel construction. The clause that begins *and getting* is not grammatically parallel to the previous items on the list.
Choice C contains a mixed construction. The first and last parts of the sentence are grammatically unrelated.
Choice D contains faulty parallel structure.
Choice E is correct and accurately expressed. It is the best answer.

58. **C**  Choice A is wordy and awkwardly expressed.
Choice B contains an error in parallel structure. The clause *and many are illiterate* is not grammatically parallel to the previous items on the list of problems.
Choice C is concise and accurately expressed. It is the best answer.
Choice D is concise, but it contains an error in subject-verb agreement. The subject is *poverty, starvation . . .etc.*, which requires a plural verb; the verb *is* is singular.
Choice E is a sentence fragment; it has no main verb.

59. **B**  Choice A contains an error in idiom. The standard phrase is *devoting to*, not *devoting on*.
Choice B ties sentence 19 to the previous sentence and is accurately expressed. It is the best answer.
Choice C fails to improve the coherence of the paragraph.
Choice D is unrelated to the context of the paragraph.
Choice E is insufficiently related to the context of the paragraph.

60. **C**  Choice A should stay put because it provides a transition between the questions in paragraph 1 and the beginning of paragraph 2.
Choice B is a pivotal sentence in paragraph 2 and should not be moved.
Choice C fits the topic of paragraph 2. Therefore, sentence 22 should be moved to paragraph 2.
Choice C is the best answer.
Choice D is needed as an introductory sentence in paragraph 2. It should not be deleted.
Choice E provides the essay with a meaningful conclusion and should not be deleted.

# SELF-SCORING GUIDE FOR THE SAT II ESSAY

## PRACTICE TEST E

**Using this guide.** Rate yourself in each of the six categories on the left. Circle the item that most accurately describes your performance. Enter the numbers on the rating guide below. Then calculate the average of the six ratings to determine your total score. On the SAT II itself, two readers will rate your essay on a scale of 6 (high) to 1 (low). The score will be reported to you as the sum of the two ratings, from 12 (best) to 2 (worst).

Note that on the SAT II, essays are judged in relation to other essays written on the same topic. Therefore, this Self-Scoring Guide may not yield a totally accurate prediction of the score you can expect to earn on the actual exam. Because it is difficult to achieve objectivity when assessing your own writing, you may improve the validity of your score by having a trusted friend or teacher read your essay and rate it using this scoring guide.

| | 6 | 5 | 4 | 3 | 2 | 1 |
|---|---|---|---|---|---|---|
| **PURPOSE OF THE ESSAY** | Very clear and insightful; fresh and engaging | Quite clear and insightful; interesting | Fairly clear and with some insight; marginally interesting | Somewhat clear but some confusion, too; fairly dull | Largely unclear and confusing | Extremely confusing |
| **ORGANIZATION AND DEVELOPMENT** | Meticulously organized and thoroughly developed; coherent and unified | Well organized and sufficiently developed; basically coherent and unified | Reasonably organized and developed; mostly coherent and unified | Somewhat organized and developed; some incoherence and lack of unity | Little organization and meager development; mostly incoherent and void of unity | No apparent organization or development; incoherent and lacking unity |
| **USE OF SENTENCES** | Effectively varied and engaging; essentially error-free | Varied and interesting; one or two minor errors | Adequately varied and interesting; some errors | Somewhat varied and marginally interesting; one or more major errors | Little variation and basically dull; some major errors | Uniformly repetitious and dull; numerous major errors |
| **CHOICE OF WORDS** | Interesting, sensitive, and effective; basically error-free | Generally interesting, clear and effective; one or two inaccuracies | Occasionally interesting and effective; one or two errors in diction or idiom | Somewhat dull and ordinary; some errors in diction or idiom | mostly dull and conventional; several errors | Dull, immature; numerous errors in diction and idiom |
| **GRAMMAR AND USAGE** | Error-free | Occasional minor errors | Several minor errors | Some major errors | Frequent major errors | Severely flawed |
| **OVERALL IMPRESSION** | Demonstrates excellent skills and writing competence | Demonstrates good skills and competence | Demonstrates adequate skills and competence | Suggests fair skills and competence | Demonstrates poor skills and competence | Demonstrates lack of skill and competence |

| For rating yourself | | For a second opinion | |
|---|---|---|---|
| *Rating Guide* Each category is rated 1 (low) to 6 (high) | | *Rating Guide* Each category is rated 1 (low) to 6 (high) | |
| Purpose of the Essay | _____ | Purpose of the Essay | _____ |
| Organization and Development | _____ | Organization and Development | _____ |
| Use of Sentences | _____ | Use of Sentences | _____ |
| Choice of Words | _____ | Choice of Words | _____ |
| Grammar and Usage | _____ | Grammar and Usage | _____ |
| Overall Impression | _____ | Overall Impression | _____ |
| TOTAL | _____ | TOTAL | _____ |
| Divide total by 6 to get final score: | ☐ | Divide total by 6 to get final score: | ☐ |

Remove scoring guide by cutting on dotted line

# INDEX